LONDON

The London architect Horace Jones was responsible for several important projects in London, including Smithfield meat market and Leadenhall market, but his most memorable design was for a 'bascule' bridge near the Tower of London, the furthest downstream of London's bridges. Jones died in 1887, however, and the relatively plain brick façades he had planned were modified by George D. Stevenson to include the elaborate Victorian Gothic embellishments that make the bridge such a magnet for the lenses of tourists' cameras today. In 1894 *The Builder* magazine condemned this 'façadism' as 'the most monstrous and preposterous architectural sham we have ever known'. In his novel *Tono-Bungay* (1909), meanwhile, H.G. Wells found the fake archaism of Tower Bridge indicative of a cultural failure to celebrate industrial function. And, in an influential book on bridge engineering in 1916, H.H. Statham said that 'it represents the vice of tawdriness and pretentiousness, and of falsification of the actual facts of the structure'. The construction of Tower Bridge divided the ancient Pool of London into the Upper and the Lower Pool, and the lifting roadway still allows tall-masted ships to sail up towards London Bridge. The ironwork was originally a muddy brown colour matching the river water below, but it was brightened up for the Elizabeth II's Silver Jubilee in 1977.

PHOTOGRAPH: CARNEGIE, 2009

LONDON

A history

by

Jeremy Black

CARNEGIE

For Paul Webley

London: a history

Copyright © Jeremy Black, 2009

First published in 2009 by
Carnegie Publishing Ltd
Chatsworth Road,
Lancaster LA1 4SL
www.carnegiepublishing.com

British Library Cataloguing-in-Publication data
A catalogue record for this book is available from the British Library

ISBN 978-1-85936-172-6   *hardback*

Designed, typeset and originated by Carnegie Publishing
Printed and bound in Malta by Gutenberg Press

CONTENTS

ACKNOWLEDGEMENTS

I AM MOST GRATEFUL to Bill Gibson for his comments on an earlier draft, to Ian Archer, Lee Beier, John Blair, Roger Burt, Stephen Clarke, Elizabeth Gemmill, Paul Harvey, Malcolm King, Robert Peberdy, Charles Pender, Michael Prestwich, Nigel Saul, Henry Summerson, Richard Toye, and Mike Young for their comments on particular chapters, and to Bruce Coleman and Mark Stoyle for answering specific questions. Alistair Hodge has proved an exemplary publisher. None is responsible for any errors that remain. I would also like to record my debt to those who have written earlier on the subject. I benefited greatly from an opportunity provided by an invitation to speak to an Oxford conference in May 2009 on 'Capital Cities and Provinces', which helped to develop some of the themes taken up in this book.

HALF-TITLE PAGE PHOTOGRAPH

The statue popularly known as Eros, in Piccadilly Circus. Viewers of BBC television's *QI* might recall Alan Davies' disbelief at quizmaster Stephen Fry's assertion that this bronze statue of Eros is actually an aluminium statue of Anteros, the god of selfless love. The statue surmounts the Shaftesbury Memorial, the Greek god supposedly symbolising the altruistic love of the poor that was held to be a great virtue of Anthony Ashley-Cooper, 7th Earl of Shaftesbury (1801–85). From 1892 the memorial stood at the centre of the Circus, but was later moved to one side to aid traffic movement, while Piccadilly Circus itself had lost its circular shape with the construction of Shaftesbury Avenue as a new north–south arterial route in the 1880s. As in other improvement schemes, a great number of homes of the poor were demolished to allow the construction of the street.
PHOTOGRAPH: CARNEGIE, 2009

PREFACE

LONDON UNMASKED: or The New Town Spy. Exhibiting a striking picture of the world as it goes. In a ramble through the regions of novelty, whim, fashion and taste, as found in the cities of London and Westminster, their purlieus and vicinities ... particularly fortune-hunters, matrimonial brokers, modern Messelinas, dissipated fops, demireps, sycophants, loungers or time-killers, military fribbles, French, Italian and other foreign leaches, duellists, rapacious quackers, griping usurers, black legs, body snatchers etc ... By the Man in the Moon. What changes? This anonymous writer of 1784 certainly captured the vitality and variety that is London.

My book seeks to add both the dynamism of development and a focus on London's wider importance, to both the country and the world. This importance was refracted through other concerns, especially those of state, empire and trading systems, which together help explain why, of all Britain's cities, the history of London is uniquely difficult and yet fundamental. London's role at the cutting-edge in the moulding and expression of popular opinion in Britain and the Western world was captured by Elizabeth Montagu in 1762. Commenting on the extent of critical sentiment in London, she claimed

all mankind are philosophers and pride themselves in having a contempt for rank and order and imagine, they show themselves wise in ridiculing whatever gives distinction and dignity to Kings and other magistrates, not considering that the chains of opinion are less galling than those of law, and that the great beast the multitude must be bound by something. Alexander the Great was treated with contempt by a certain philosopher in a tub, but, in this enlightened age, the man who made the tub would use him with the same scorn.[1]

Authors habitually claim links with their subjects and, indeed, I was born and grew up in London, my wife is a Londoner, and so on. Yet, the nature of the subject is that London's importance is glimpsed as much, if not more so, in Newcastle as in Shoreditch, in Boston as in Ealing. The history of London is part of the world. At the same time, thinking about this book, I could not help returning to my past and that of my family. Yet again, as with my work on maps, I am particularly grateful to have had the chance to study geography to A-level at a leading school department. I heard the echoes of my individual project work on land-use along the A5 and A41 axes in Outer London and on the development of the Tube system.

I also take the opportunity to recall with great affection Roy Porter with whom I co-operated over many years on a number of projects, including several books. He encouraged me to write such a history, saying that it would be different to his. Rereading his *London: A Social History*, I am reminded that the loss to the profession caused by his early death matches the personal loss felt by his many friends.

I would like to thank Alistair Hodge for asking me to write this book, and to hope that he and it will have more success than John Tisdal, a Belfast printer, who in 1782 published *Flora's Banquet*, which declared 'It does not follow, that works of merit can only *originate* in the metropolis of England; and that, unless a new book is distinguished by a *London* title page … it is beneath the notice of the curious'. Alas, the promised second volume of this worthwhile collection of Irish poetry did not appear.

It is a great pleasure to dedicate this work to Paul Webley, a wise friend, an engaging companion, and a former colleague who has moved on to head a distinguished London institution.

INTRODUCTION

'London ... is the mart of many nations resorting to it by sea and land.'

BEDE, *C.*AD 731

EVERYONE THINKS THEY KNOW LONDON. Its landmarks have been used in a hundred films; its skyline is instantly recognisable; and the winding course of its river is familiar, in great detail, from the satellite imagery used to begin the BBC's *Eastenders*. For London is at the centre of the nation's attention, and has been, on and off, for two thousand years.

Yet familiarity does not necessarily bring enlightenment. The very size of the city has the power to obscure as well as to mesmerise; the unparalleled tangle of experience over such a long period of time becomes impossible to unravel, at least in one telling or from one perspective.

What, then, was London? The answer depends on who you ask, and when. London was a capital city, a port, an economic powerhouse, a magnet for talent and ambition. Are trade and wealth-creation really the abiding, defining characteristics of the city, as Bede implied? Or does London's history make more sense if you look at it more as a cultural entity than as one based merely on money and finance?

Two hundred and fifty years ago London was the first modern city, with the world's highest wages and best standard of living, at least for those in settled employment.

Yet it could just as easily be portrayed (and often was) as a sink of depravity, a slum of despair with some of the worst death rates in the world, in which urban expansion and population explosion outstripped the city's capacity to provide even the basic means of life to ordinary citizens. Was London, as the radical pamphleteer and champion of the virtues of rural England William Cobbett said disparagingly in the 1820s, the 'Great Wen' – a pathological swelling on the face of the nation? To those from the furthest corners of the land it could appear from afar to be a seething snakepit of avarice, prostitution, corruption

1

and vice … yet one that could be seductively attractive, full of opportunity for fortune or salvation.

To political commentators, or scheming courtiers, London was the heart of the nation state and of empire; to economists and financiers it was where you had to be to do real business; to lawyers there was nowhere else like it; to lightermen, sailors and watermen who worked the river or sailed the world it was their home port, the city on the most important artery of world trade; to socialites it was the tiny, febrile centre of their universe; to social reformers it was, and seems destined always to be, the den of iniquity, inequality, inequity.

The image of London held by the rest of Britain might include scenes of royal pageantry, or of heroism or defiance in the face of German bombs; it will usually include a red RT or Routemaster bus crossing Tower Bridge; perhaps now a gherkin-shaped office building which has arisen from an IRA bombsite. Their knowledge of famous London railway stations and streets might have been gleaned in childhood from playing the UK version of 'Monopoly', a board game based on property speculation, rents and cards of 'Chance' or 'Community Chest' (including the shrewd City investor's favourite, which invites the player to 'receive interest on 7% preference shares').

To the rest of the world the image might encompass cheery Cockneys and chatty Hackney-carriage drivers; Big Ben and the Tower ravens whose wings are clipped, just in

The three key components of Tudor 'London', as shown by William Smith in *A Particular Description of England* (1588), are seen here. In the foreground is Southwark; to the left is Westminster, which already more or less adjoins the ancient City of London to the right. Everything is here: all the important features of the early modern conurbation before the Great Fire of 1666. The Tower of London still dominates the view to the right, while old St Paul's (even without the spire it had lost to lightning in 1561) sits proud on top of Ludgate Hill. This was the London described by its first historian, John Stow, but nearly all of this London has disappeared, either by fire or by redevelopment.

LONDON.

case they should fly away and the kingdom should fall; the bells of St Mary-le-Bow (more likely now to be heard on a BBC English-language broadcast than for real above the Cheapside din); the Changing of the Guard and London Bridge (although possibly now the one that was dismantled and transshipped to Arizona in the 1960s to become the centrepiece of a themepark in the desert).

Importantly, in the past, what others got to find out about London emanated mainly from London itself, was written by Londoners (either born and bred or new-minted by migration), and reflected *their* perspectives. For virtually all national news was reported from or published in London ... and it still is. True, regional and local newspapers developed in the nineteenth century, but they got most of their information from the nationals, and *The Times* topped the lot, by being international and still focused on London.

Some things are beyond dispute. London was populous: for over ten centuries Britain's largest urban centre, for half that time the largest in Europe, and for a couple of hundred years the largest in the world. (Residents of the City itself, though, were at their most numerous around 300 years ago. Since then the number living within the ancient boundary has declined by over 95 per cent. Most of the residential population of the City left long ago to make way for business, commerce and 300,000 daily commuters.)

In most periods, too, London was prosperous, its merchants bankrolling the monarchy, and its economic dynamism sucking in the resources, people and energy of the land and the near Continent. London was central, also, in the sense that it was founded in the midst of the richest and most accessible part of the island, its communications to places that matter always relatively good, particularly by sea.

Bede was right. Trade has always been the engine of wealth, growth and development in London: wool and cloth exports led the way, and the economic lifeblood flowed through Britain's largest and most important port – in truth, Liverpool never really came close to matching London's volume and range of traded goods, particularly of the luxury kind. Not even the thousand trades of Birmingham could make that great city anything more than the 'second' city of the realm. That is a title that Manchester people, too, might claim or covet: the point is there was never any dispute over which city was number one.

London has always been the most cosmopolitan place in Britain, a true melting pot,

The interior of St Mary-le-Bow, not in Bow but right in the heart of the City in Cheapside. By tradition, those born within earshot of its bells may lay claim to the title Cockney. Like most City churches it was destroyed in the Great Fire of 1666, and the present church was designed by Wren.

PHOTOGRAPH: CARNEGIE, 2009

This photograph shows the scene in London Stock Exchange on 18 October 1984 after shares had plunged 14.4 points to 824.3. The pound sterling also tumbled to a new all-time low against the dollar, dropping 1.61 cents to $1.1844. The fall was blamed on the drop in oil prices, and the coal miners' strike, then in its eighth month. Almost exactly two years later the Conservative government of Margaret Thatcher moved decisively to deregulate the financial markets of the City, a 'Big Bang' that ushered in two decades of massive expansion in the financial sector. This more than anything now defines what the City of London's role is in the world.
© CORBIS

right from Roman times. Later, the city's environment was so deleterious to longevity that constant, year-in year-out, in-migration was needed to maintain the population and to provide workers to stoke the fires of economic development. Merchants of the Hanse, French and German Protestants, Dutch merchants, Jews, Scots (particularly after 1707), Irish (particularly after the Potato Famine of the late 1840s), Earls Court Australians and other colonials, Russians, Poles, and a huge range of other groupings have continued to come to London.

What is indisputable, also, is that London is forever changing, sometimes tragically by bomb or by fire, but more often by gradual and inexorable rebuilding, reinvention, road-widening, property speculation and economic change. From the Tower Bridge walkway more than 50 mighty construction cranes were visible even in the midst of credit-crunch Britain. Less than an average lifetime will separate the Olympics hosted by London in 1948 from that of 2012, but how could one begin to describe the change – in function as much as in physical appearance – witnessed by the East End and Docklands over that time?

London's economic force made it the place where all sorts of 'firsts' were invented, developed or implemented, and the world was able to marvel at reports (often in the *Illustrated London News*) of tunnels under rivers, of the world's greatest steamship being built on a Millwall riverbank by the world's greatest engineer, of steam trains travelling underground, of Barker's 'panorama' of the city viewed from the top of the Albion Mill on the south bank, itself a world first in terms of steam power harnessed to grind flour.

London has always been self-absorbed, self-promoting, inward-looking. When young, enterprising provincials made their way to London, as they did in their thousands, they knew that they would find everything they needed there – financial institutions, the law and all its multifarious (or nefarious) practitioners, a huge potential market, contacts, networks, the court – all in one place, along with coffee-houses, fine restaurants and gentlemen's clubs, salacious entertainments, fashionable assemblies and a cult of celebrity. London has always attracted or courted attention, from artists to novelists, from poets to film-makers. In which other city of the 1860s would you have found the French artist Doré being paid the huge sum of £10,000 a year (part-time) to draw scenes of city life for commercial publication?

People did get spat out of the vortex. Many who migrated to London became disillusioned, and some went home again. Some who made fortunes chose to retire to a quieter, landed seclusion, but many more, not just in the East End – the 'people of the abyss' in Jack London's memorable phrase of 1903 – would have left if only they been able to. But they couldn't. They came; they saw; and they were conquered. The filth, the squalor, the misery, and the poverty mapped so carefully by Charles Booth: these were as much the real London as the elegant squares of Belgravia and the fine villas of Kensington. The stews of Southwark, the opium dens of Limehouse, the child prostitution of Stepney … a walk and a world away from the heaths of Hampstead and the shops of Regent Street.

Ask anyone in the street of a provincial town, and they might answer that London is important because it is England's capital city, or Britain's (at least for part of the time); or that it was once the centre of empire, with a royal family firmly ensconced in its midst. But is that really true? Does a city ever become great because of such a status? In the case of London it seems unlikely. Certainly, kings and queens have had a castle here, as well as

Today Richard Whittington is perhaps history's most famous Londoner. Like tens of thousands of others, of course, he was a migrant worker. A younger son, he was sent from Gloucestershire to London to work in the City as a mercer. Becoming rich through trade, as Lord Mayor he championed London's cause in one of many spats between City and monarchy, and bequeathed huge sums of money to the city for charitable purposes and civic improvements, including at the Guildhall. His statue is rather tucked away, high up on the eastern side of the Royal Exchange. Whittington's fame today rests principally upon a rather fanciful early seventeenth-century tale of poor Dick being bound to a London merchant, having to sell his prized cat, turning away from London, only to return after hearing the bells of St Mary-le-Bow and discovering that his cat had rid a Moorish kingdom of rats and thereby gained him a fortune. In truth Whittington was never poor and there appears to be no direct evidence that he ever owned a cat.

PHOTOGRAPH: CARNEGIE, 2009

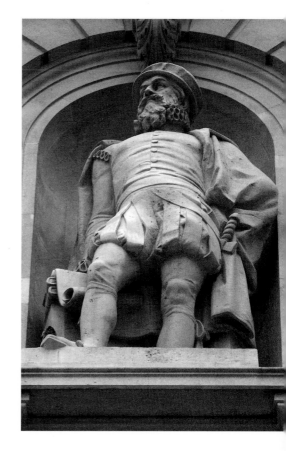

This is one representation of London's most famous cat, sitting on Whittington's lap, although the cat might have been a later addition to the engraving. Historians now doubt the existence of the cat, but in 1949 while attempting to locate Whittington's grave in the church of St Michael Paternoster Royal where he was buried in 1423, the excavators are said to have found, intriguingly, the mummified corpse of a domestic cat.

DETAIL FROM A CONTEMPORARY WOODCUT

palaces aplenty, and have usually lived within a narrow radius of the City, though rarely within it. Kings and queens are crowned right across the road, in Westminster Abbey, from where they subsequently lie in state, in Westminster Hall. And the pull of the court did help to support the luxury trades and a phalanx of lawyers, artists, courtiers, craftsmen, courtesans and hangers-on.

But the City authorities, and even most Londoners, have never been notably royalist in outlook. True, in 1381, a Lord Mayor of London famously plunged his dagger into the neck of Wat Tyler to protect his king, but he possibly did so more in the interest of preserving the City from the mob of murderous peasants, who had already stormed the Tower and ransacked the Savoy Palace, rather than to save his sovereign. When London opinion took against a king – and it did so quite often, from John or Henry VI to Charles I or James II – the City nearly always won. Both Matilda (against Stephen) and the Jacobite Bonnie Prince Charlie (against George II) saw their causes falter because of London's opposition. The Mayor of London, who by the early thirteenth century was emphatically not a royal appointee, but elected, was the only commoner to sign Magna Carta. And most commentators point out that the stout new defences at the Tower built by Edward I, 'Longshanks', were as much to safeguard the monarchy from the city as from foreign enemies. The truth of the matter is that the monarchy always did need the city – or at the very minimum its money – much more than the city needed the monarchy.

Can one perhaps help define London by what was missing? Unlike some European cities of comparable history and antiquity, there was relatively little civil strife among the population. Similarly the number of episodes of sustained violence is small; over-arching nobles did not wage war between each other on the city's streets. Famines and bread riots were not unknown in Paris and elsewhere, but London's food supply was well enough organised most of the time to avoid such problems. And civic government – perhaps a microcosm of the peculiar confusion that is the British constitution, with its checks, balances and modest but circumscribed democracy – seems to have muddled along fairly well. Instances of serious fraud, or of corruption in high office, have not been recurring or major features of the City authorities in London.

In fact, of course, we cannot really talk of one London at all. Properly speaking, the City – the ancient walled city rather than the financiers' Square Mile of today – is

For centuries London has been cursed by the twin destroyers of all things ancient: disaster and prosperity. In the former category there was the complete destruction of the first Roman town in AD 60 by Boudicca; then there was the Blitz that flattened swathes of the city. And in between there were innumerable conflagrations, of which the Great Fire of 1666 was simply the worst. Prosperity, meanwhile, was a more benign but just as ruthless destroyer: the power of the London economy, and access to ready finance, has in most periods led to constant rebuilding and redevelopment. In this view Edward I's river defences to the Tower of London are the oldest fabric to be seen. The next oldest is the white central tower of the former Port of London Authority building on Trinity Square, which dates from 1915. Norman Foster's 'Gherkin' at 30 St Mary Axe, which dominates the view, makes the point well: an IRA bomb blast destroyed the old, yet gave the opportunity to build anew.

PHOTOGRAPH: CARNEGIE, 2009

the true London, with its City wards, beadle, sheriffs and lord mayor (with his official home at Mansion House), ancient Guildhall, Customs House, city walls and royal castle. But when we think of London now, we casually and understandably include much else besides, including the separate City of Westminster and the no less ancient 'Borough' of Southwark.

Even by Tudor times many other places had become part of what was conceived of as 'London', already well beyond the ancient City limits: Holborn and Cripplegate to the north-west; the Minories and the beginnings of the East End; and in the west prime greenfield sites along Fleet Street and the Strand to Charing Cross and Westminster that were quickly being developed as a new focus of wealth and power. And now, at the beginning of the twenty-first century, any definition of London must surely include all those vast and sprawling suburbs – Pooter's Holloway, Betjeman's Metroland – and the airports, reservoirs, motorways, edge-of-conurbation shopping malls and the refuse dumps and sewage works on the south Essex marshes. For the generally easy, flat topography of the London region has always enabled and encouraged gentle, inexorable sprawl.

'Why, Sir, you find no man, at all intellectual, who is willing to leave London. No, Sir, when a man is tired of London, he is tired of life; for there is in London all that life can afford.'

SAMUEL JOHNSON

What we have, then, is a complex, bedevilling place whose history has been enacted upon so many different fields of play that it is hard to encompass in a single survey. The city contains many academic institutions of great international renown, but even if all the economic, social, urban, political and cultural historians who have been researching London over the last half-century agreed to collaborate on a project to write the single definitive history of the city, it would still end up incomplete and partial (in both senses). Instead, one can savour a multitude of insights from a myriad books by many different authors. Fortunately, local history flourishes and prospers in London, this city of a hundred villages, with dozens of local case studies and detailed works, as well as archaeological reports, appearing each year. Every one of them adds to the sum of knowledge, allowing future historians of London to see with new perspectives and gain new knowledge on time-honoured themes.

This book is no more than a general overview. It attempts to distil, from an immense mountain of information, historical memory and experience, an account which tries to explain why London developed in the particular, fascinating way that it did.

Perhaps uniquely, the idea for this particular London history was not conceived in the capital, but in another ancient Roman town far to the south-west close to the fastnesses of Dartmoor. Nor has it been published in London. It forms part of a series of books on British cities, published in another Roman town far away to the north. Does a view from the provinces give any unique insight? Perhaps not, but the distance, hopefully at least, can provide some valuable perspective.

Recently one true Cockney – a long-time docker turned cab driver whose Knowledge otherwise was exemplary, and who confessed to an interest in history – related how he had been at a total loss when his fare, an elderly vicar, had asked to be taken to Cripplegate. Cripplegate is one of the ancient city gates, one of the wards of the City … where the Roman fort had been built around AD 110. One of the most ancient of London places.

'Where's that, then?' the cabbie had implored.

For it has all gone, even the name (except for in the church of St Giles). Cripplegate was bombed out of existence in the Blitz and redeveloped (as the Barbican), with enormous, concrete residential towers overshadowing some tiny remains of those ancient city walls.

Everyone thinks that they know London. But can anyone, truly?

London as seething metropolis: a mid-Victorian aerial view showing recently built railways, canals, docks and bridges as well as little steamboats on the river and the Thames Tunnel. Also shown are the ancient Tower (*centre*), the Monument to the Great Fire, the Mansion House, the Royal Exchange and London Bridge railway station. Nearby countryside is also notable. The Pool of London, downstream from London Bridge, is cluttered with sailing vessels.

PHOTOGRAPH: CARNEGIE, WITH KIND PERMISSION OF IRONBRIDGE GORGE MUSEUM

CHAPTER
1

THE ROMANS were by no means the first people to settle in the London area, although they were definitely first to create an urban settlement here. In what is now the Greater London area, there was extensive pre-Roman human activity, in the Palaeolithic, Mesolithic, Neolithic, Bronze and Iron Ages. This activity reflected the size of the region, the role of the Thames valley as a communication route, and the fertility of much of the area, including the riverside water meadows. The woodlands of the Thames valley provided shelter for animals, such as deer, which, in turn, attracted hunters. Sites in which human remains of early hominids and finds of tool assembly have been discovered include Stoke Newington. Pollen and sediment studies suggest that the shift from nomadism to settlement and farming occurred in the Bronze Age, around 2000 BC. This shift probably led to the widespread clearing of woodland in the second millennium BC, although woodland remained a major resource.

By the Iron Age, southern England was an area of tribal states, with chieftain patterns of tribal control, proto-towns, and a developed economy that involved the use of coins. Much of the woodland had been cleared, especially in areas of light soil, and agriculture was both varied and extensive. It supported a growing population, a settled society and an aristocratic élite. Yet these states did not amount to a sophisticated governmental system. In contrast, the proto-towns, known to the Romans as *oppida*, were as developed as urban structures as early Roman cities in the West. Over the century following Julius Caesar's invasion of Britain, *oppida* rose to a new level.

London was not a centre in the world of Iron Age tribal polities, nor an area of particularly marked settlement. Instead, the state of the Trinovantes, with its capital at Colchester, was more prominent. Their territory covered a large area north of the Thames, including Essex and parts of Suffolk, although the boundary of their state should not be understood in modern terms of clear frontiers. It is doubtful that Middlesex was part of its sphere of control, as the Catuvellauni were dominant north of the Thames to the west of the Trinovantes, and their influence also extended into Essex. To the south, the Thames

ROMAN CAPITAL

London as it might have appeared towards the end of the period of Roman occupation, C.AD 375. This reconstruction drawing by Peter Froste shows the Roman city within its buttressed walls, along with the first London Bridge spanning the river Thames, which was wider than today in part because of the unreclaimed marshes and creeks on the Southwark bank. The square fort at Cripplegate (top) was no longer used for defence, and the amphitheatre beside had probably also fallen into disuse. By this date, too, the Roman forum had been demolished, leaving the rectangular open space directly inland from the bridge. London was the capital of Roman Britain, its location and easy communications making it an ideal centre from which a European imperial government could administer the whole of Britannia.

MUSEUM OF LONDON

was probably not an important boundary, but the concept of firm boundaries in this period is not a helpful one, and there was a contrast with the more distinct boundaries of the Anglo-Saxon period. In the Iron Age, the Atrebates and Cantiaci were dominant to the south of the Thames.

Although London was not a centre, there were Iron Age settlements in the London area, for example at Stratford, as well as at Westminster, where there have also been finds of Neolithic remains. Archaeological excavations throw up new discoveries, such as Iron Age ditches at Bermondsey. There have also been rich finds of Iron Age coins and objects from the Thames foreshore at Putney and Barnes. The impact of more knowledge about, and interest in, the early history of the London region can be seen in 'London Before London', the most recent gallery in the excellent Museum of London.

It is unclear what would have happened to south-east England but for the Roman conquest. The areas of Germany and Scotland that were not conquered by Rome were essentially to develop into a number of small kingdoms that focused on farming but also took part in trade, as did Ireland. Urban development was limited, although it could be argued that the later histories of Glasgow and Hamburg scarcely suggest that Roman conquest was necessary for subsequent prominence. Equally, London's role in Britain

The empire around AD 395, towards the end of Roman rule in Britain. The province of Britannia lay at one extremity of the Roman sphere of control. Londinium was always the most important city in the province, not only for administrative purposes but also for maritime trade with the rest of the empire.

CARNEGIE COLLECTION

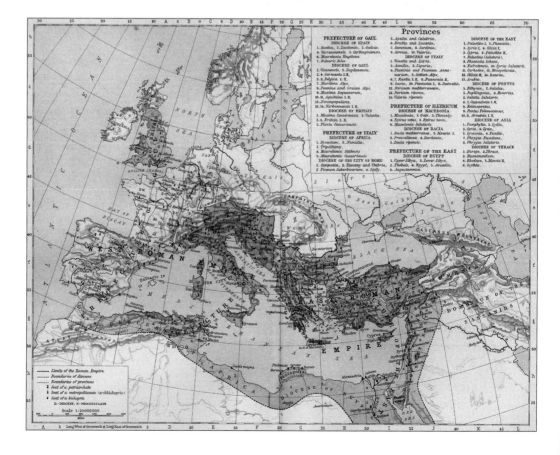

This statue of a British hunter-god was found under Southwark Cathedral. Dating from the Roman period, between AD 150 and 250, this limestone statue measures 73.5 cm. Too little is known about this particular statue to be definite about who or what it represents: it shares striking similarities with an altar relief of Diana, goddess of the hunt, from Goldsmiths' Hall, but there are other influences. The style is classical, but not directly Roman. We know that even before the Roman invasion there had been cultural and economic links between the south of England and the Roman world, and this statue is perhaps best seen as a concoction of various religious and mythological elements from different cultures.

PHOTOGRAPH COPYRIGHT GARY BLACK. CUMMING MUSEUM, ON LOAN FROM SOUTHWARK CATHEDRAL

reflected Rome's character as a wide-ranging empire dependent on communications, and, crucially, in the case of Britain, on maritime links.

Prior to the Roman conquest, southern Britain was already linked by trade with nearby areas of the Continent: northern Gaul (France) and the Low Countries. This was the world in which Rome now intervened more directly. After Julius Caesar had rapidly conquered Gaul, he turned his attention to Britain, in part because he argued, with some reason, that support from Britain was responsible for continued resistance in Gaul and in part for personal reasons: to acquire glory and to keep the army under his control active. Caesar's expeditions of 55 and 54 BC, however, were abandoned as a result of unexpectedly strong resistance as well as storms, but during the latter expedition the London area experienced conflict. In 54 BC Caesar crossed the river Thames and seized the capital, possibly in the area of Wheathampstead, of the regional tribal leader, Cassivellaunus.

Under Caesar's successors, trade links developed between the Roman empire and Britain, while there is literary evidence for diplomatic contacts between Rome and Britain in the Augustan period. However, despite plans by the Emperor Caligula in the late AD 30s, there was no military action until AD 43 when the Emperor Claudius launched a new invasion, both in order to gain a military reputation judged necessary to strengthen his position and because Rome's protégés in southern Britain had lost control. In the invasion the crossing of the Thames was contested, but the Romans, assisted by German auxiliaries who swam the river, were victorious, and, certain of triumph, Claudius then arrived to take command. Possibly benefiting from a newly constructed bridge across the Thames, he advanced to receive the surrender of Colchester. The Romans then rapidly conquered lowland England, simultaneously advancing along a number of axes, although there was considerable resistance, for example in Dorset.

The idea that London was the site of a trading base prior to the Roman invasion in AD 43 has been advanced, but the balance of archaeological evidence, the vast majority

As foundation legends, Rome might have her Romulus and Remus, but London has her Gog (*right*) and Magog (with the Phoenix on his shield, *left*), two legendary giants who act as guardians of the city. All sorts of pre-Roman Celtic, ancient Greek and Roman mythological references and traditions were jumbled up to produce these figures, almost certainly derived ultimately from folk tales which transformed real historical warriors incrementally into larger and more supernaturally powerful beings. The full details of the story were given in detail by Geoffrey of Monmouth in the 1130s. From the later medieval period, wicker representations of Gog and Magog have been carried ahead of the Lord Mayor's procession. These two fearsome figures still stand on the gallery of the Guildhall, looking down upon the assembled Corporation below. Unfortunately, the original flimsy figures gradually disintegrated long ago, while the ravages of vermin and rot, and then the Blitz of 1940, destroyed the next set of wooden statues; these new, limewood, representations date from the 1950s.

PHOTOGRAPH: CARNEGIE, 2009, WITH THANKS TO THE CITY OF LONDON

of which dates from after the Roman conquest, suggests otherwise. Instead, a settlement was probably established in London in about AD 50. This was in an area under direct Roman control, unlike those areas where client rulers were left in place: Surrey, Sussex and Hampshire under the Atrebates tribe and, initially, East Anglia under the Iceni. The name 'London' is of Celtic origin, adapted for Roman use as Londinium, and it clearly gives the name to all later successors.

The subsequent fame of London was to encourage mythological accounts of the city's* origins. Geoffrey of Monmouth, in his *Historia Regum Britanniae* [*History of the Kings of Britain*], finished in the mid-1130s, had Aeneas of Troy's grandson, Brutus, found

---

*   In this book the word 'city' in reference to London is given a capital letter only when referring specifically to the ancient heart of London – the Square Mile, the area governed by the Corporation of London – in order to distinguish this from the much wider area often referred to collectively and loosely as London, including Westminster and Southwark and an expanding patchwork of later suburbs. More recently additional confusion has arisen as 'the City' is often taken to mean the financial heart, even if this includes areas such as Docklands, well beyond the strict boundaries of the 'City of London'.

Britain and London, a significant linkage of the two. This claim tells us more about proto-nationalist ambitions in the twelfth century than about the true origins of London. Geoffrey, indeed, had Brutus call London 'New Troy'. This account of a Trojan origin was repeated by William fitz Stephen in about 1173 and by Matthew Paris in about 1252.

London was established at a strategic location on the north bank of the river Thames, which was then much wider than today. Not only was the southern bank then characterised by marshy tidal inlets, but on the northern shore land has since been reclaimed over the centuries, and the riverbank has moved progressively out into the river, in part to allow the construction of successive lines of river defences and new wharves. The waterfront the Romans found lay along the line of modern Upper and Lower Thames Street.

The local topography and the wider context ensured that London had the potential to be a valuable communications node, and the Romans developed it accordingly. The Thames provided a crucial and convenient communications route to the rest of the Roman Empire; then as now London's geographical location in relation to Europe was of immense and continuing importance. Today the river is tidal as far west as Teddington, but in Roman

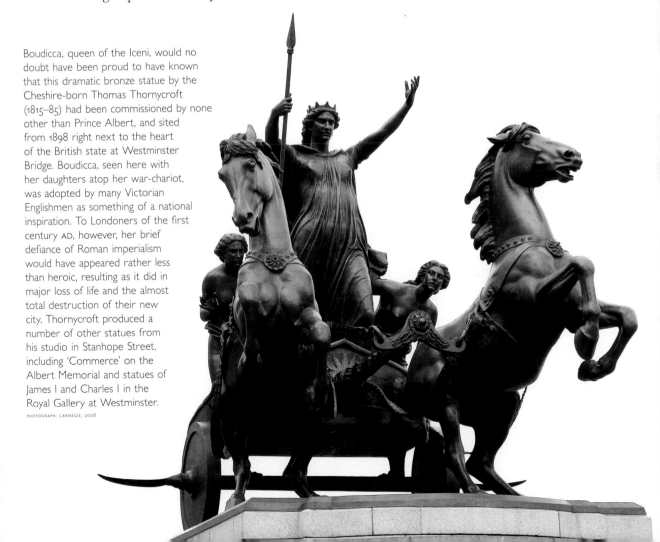

Boudicca, queen of the Iceni, would no doubt have been proud to have known that this dramatic bronze statue by the Cheshire-born Thomas Thornycroft (1815–85) had been commissioned by none other than Prince Albert, and sited from 1898 right next to the heart of the British state at Westminster Bridge. Boudicca, seen here with her daughters atop her war-chariot, was adopted by many Victorian Englishmen as something of a national inspiration. To Londoners of the first century AD, however, her brief defiance of Roman imperialism would have appeared rather less than heroic, resulting as it did in major loss of life and the almost total destruction of their new city. Thornycroft produced a number of other statues from his studio in Stanhope Street, including 'Commerce' on the Albert Memorial and statues of James I and Charles I in the Royal Gallery at Westminster.

PHOTOGRAPH: CARNEGIE, 2008

times possibly not much further upstream than the low gravel banks on the northern side that provided a good site for the Romans to build the first bridge. The two low hills of Ludgate and Cornhill were also attractive factors in the initial Roman choice of site.

The initial balance between military and civilian uses for bridge, harbour and, finally, city, is likely to have favoured the military uses, as lowland Britain was conquered, but this balance rapidly changed. Indeed, the development of communication node into city was an aspect of this shift away from military uses. Ermine Street, the route to the north, points to the modern City of London and this was likely the site of the original Roman base. Furthermore, it is in the city that finds of early Roman pottery are concentrated.

London's history as a Roman settlement, however, was almost cut short after barely a decade when, in AD 60, a major rising was staged by the Iceni under their female leader Boudicca (Boadicea is a later corruption of the name). The Iceni were enraged by callous

London was barely defensible and ill-prepared for Boudicca's vicious attack when it came. Two tributaries of the Thames can be seen in this reconstruction: the Fleet (*bottom right*) and the Walbrook (*centre*). The latter marked something of a boundary between the more Romanised east of the city and the western settlement which contained more modest, native dwellings. The new city had only been in existence for a few years when it was destroyed by Boudicca and her followers.
MUSEUM OF LONDON

Roman treatment, including the flogging of Boudicca, the widow of the king. In the rising, the major Roman settlements in Britain, which were then Colchester, St Albans and London, were destroyed and their inhabitants were slaughtered. The Roman governor, Gaius Suetonius Paulinus, advanced to defend London, but lacked enough troops to do so and, instead, decided to abandon the city, preferring to campaign at a distance.

The Roman historian Tacitus recorded of London:

Nor did the tears and weeping of the people, as they implored his aid, deter him from giving the signal of departure and receiving into his army all who would go with him. Those who were chained to the spot by the weaknesses of their sex, or their infirmity of age, or the attractions of the place, were cut off by the enemy … it was not on making prisoners and selling them, or on any of the barter of war, that the enemy was bent, but on slaughter, on the gibbet, the fire and the cross, like men about to pay the penalty, and meanwhile snatching at instant vengeance.

As a testimony to the totality of the devastation, a layer of burnt debris remains in the archaeological record, almost everywhere in the built-up area to the east of the Walbrook. In the event, Boudicca was defeated by Suetonius, at an unknown site, possibly in the Midlands. The Victorians were to celebrate the rising with Thomas Thornycroft's 1850 bold statue of Boudicca, now on the Victoria Embankment, a good example of the use of new London vistas to display national history.

This is a scenario of war, but the subsequent history of Roman London was largely pacific, and, in that, contrasted with large periods of its later fortunes, especially in the Anglo-Saxon and medieval centuries, but also subsequently. Roman London was speedily re-built and repopulated, a testimony to the dynamism of Roman Britain and to the economic possibilities of London, which quickly attracted not only foreign settlers but also the indigenous population. Indeed, Roman urbanisation brought out the possibilities for economic specialisation offered by developing networks of exchange in Britain. These networks were seen in particular in the Greater London area, with the role of the rural hinterland as supplier of food and other resources to London, supplies organised by the towns of the region such as Staines, Brentford and Ewell. The focus on the region was on the north bank of the Thames. Nevertheless, Southwark on the south bank was a large and important part of Londinium. Roman troops were in Southwark, as their tombstones attest.

Roman London was not a legionary base. Instead, it developed as a major city, at once a centre of government and, by the mid-second century, the key port linking Britain to the Continent and thus to the rest of the Roman world, which by then stretched as far as Mesopotamia (modern Iraq). As such, London's fortune was linked directly to that of

This is a Victorian representation of the large, elaborate Roman mosaic floor which was found near the heart of Roman London at Bucklersbury, near Poultry in the City. The exact date of the floor is unknown.
MUSEUM OF LONDON

Roman Britain and of the Roman world as a whole. The city had regional, national and international roles. It was, as the lowest bridging point on the Thames, a key point in the internal transport system as well as (eventually) the provincial capital, and the key link to the outside. London was therefore more suitable as a centre than the original official capital, Colchester, a situation that in some respects prefigured the relationship between London and Winchester in the eleventh century.

The role of London as a leading port made it different to other Roman major centres such as York, Lincoln, Chester and Gloucester, although each was also a river-port. At the same time, London did not approximate in importance to the leading centres outside Rome and Byzantium (the capital of the Eastern Roman Empire), for example Alexandria, Lyons and Trier, the last of which eventually became the centre of government for the western part of the empire when its governance was decentralised. In part, this relative lack of importance was because London was distinctly tangential to the crucial Rhine frontier, the vital defensive border for the western empire, which could be readily overseen from Trier; Britain's economic and demographic weight, meanwhile, were less than that of either Gaul or Spain.

Nevertheless, London became a city of considerable scale, a large, lively and dynamic city, and a very cosmopolitan community. London was also beautified by the range of large buildings associated with such cities, asserting its status within both Britain and the empire. The visit by Hadrian in AD 122, the first visit to London by an emperor, led to a pressing ahead with major projects, especially a large second forum and a very large basilica; and it has been suggested that, by the early years of the second century, London was in effect the provincial capital.[1] A substantial stone fort was built at Cripplegate in this period, which has been regarded as a mark of the status required for a provincial capital, notably the support and ceremonial troops required for the provincial governor and his staff, although this garrison seems to have been redeployed elsewhere in the same century. A big bronze statue of Hadrian was apparently erected as a part of the plan for the basilica. A large-scale fire between AD 125 and 130 cleared the way for new construction. The range of the fire, which appears to have affected at least sixty-five acres, indicates the scale of the city at that date.

The combination of the scale of the city, these buildings and the harbour, led to a differentiation within London by function and area that has been a lasting characteristic of

This third-century relief sculpture of Mithras was found in 1954 as part of a major excavation of an early religious site on the eastern bank of the Walbrook stream. The ceremonial sacrifice of a bull was a central part of the cult's belief system. In the corners of this 50 cm relief are the celestial gods of Light and Darkness as well as the wind gods Boreas and Zephyros. The cult of Mithras was particularly associated with urban centres and the high-ranking officials and army officers found there. The Mithraeum of Londinium was a rectangular building of around 18 m × 8 m with an apse at its western end.

MUSEUM OF LONDON

the city. The standard rectilinear grid street-plan, centred on forum and basilica, was an attempt to give shape to a more complex reality in which there were variations in land-use by function and fashion, commerce and manufacturing.

Trading opportunities were created by transport links and facilities, which included roads to Colchester, Canterbury and Richborough (for cross-Channel trade), and others to Chichester, Silchester (and on to Dorchester), St Albans and York. Some of these roads were to be the basis of later routes converging on London. That to St Albans, Watling Street, which went on to Towcester and Chester, was to be the basis of the A5. Ermine Street

Property values in London have always been high enough to prompt continuing speculative redevelopment, and most of the city walls were dismantled for building materials or to release land soon after they fell into disuse. In some places, such as here by Tower Hill Underground station, parts of the walls were saved by being incorporated into later buildings, in this case among the buildings between Great and Little Tower Hill. Visible through the lower half of the wall are bonding courses made from red Roman bricks. The wall above the highest of these brick courses dates from the medieval period, built atop what remained of the Roman work. In the third century AD the walls would have been around 20 feet high. (See also pages 51 and 74.)

PHOTOGRAPH: CARNEGIE, 2009

went to York, Stane Street to Chichester, and Portway to Silchester. Key road alignments in modern London derive directly from Roman predecessors, providing a geographical framework still identifiable to most Londoners. Edgware Road, arrow-straight from Hyde Park Corner through north-west London is ancient Watling Street; while Kennington Park Road/Clapham Road/Balham High Road is Stane Street. Reflecting the quality of Roman engineering, these roads were built to a high standard, with stone foundations and gravel surfaces. As goods and money were moved regularly across greater distances, inter-regional contact increased within Britain, and London was the central point in this system. Proximity to the English Channel ensured this position for a city that was far from geographically central within Britain.

The port was also a key opportunity for London, but one that had to respond to changes in the level of the Thames. The latter fell until the mid-third century as the sea-level lowered, and the total reach of the river was reduced, ensuring that the wharves along the river had to be altered and moved forward. Indeed, the port appears to have declined markedly in the third century. The low level of the river also affected the city wall built along the riverside in the late third century, although the river level did rise once more in the fourth century.

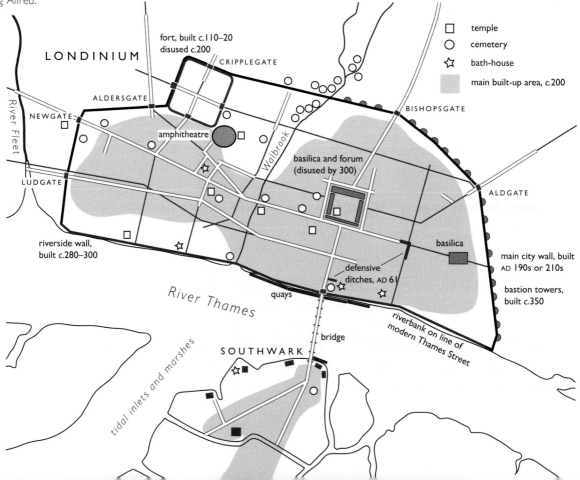

Trade to Britain was different to most Roman maritime trade, as the Atlantic and Channel tides were higher than those in the Mediterranean and Black Sea. Yet, the Romans developed an impressive sea-going capability. By the late Roman period, vessels up to 200 tons were common. Prime exports from Britain included grain, woollen goods and hunting dogs, while imports included consumer goods, notably wine, glass, pottery, marble, olive oil, and the preserved fish sauce called garum that was important to the Roman diet. The nature of trade contrasted with London's later position as the centre of the British empire. In many respects, Roman London, instead, was the key point for the imperial coloniser, Rome, and trade and governance were organised accordingly.

A development looking toward the future was the arrival and spread of Christianity, which continued the pattern of cultural and institutional links with the Continent seen with earlier religions, notably the Olympian cults and that of Mithras. The urban nature of religious activity was an important characteristic of the Roman period. Archaeological work has revealed a Mithraeum on the east bank of the Walbrook. This might have been sacked in the fourth century, possibly by Christians, although it did subsequently continue in use. A bishop of London, Restitutus, attended the Council of Arles in AD 314. Where the city's early Christians worshipped is as yet unknown. We do know that there was a large fourth-century public building or basilica on Tower Hill, but it is unlikely that this was used for religious purposes, for basilicas were the headquarters of Roman secular government, and only later did the word come to be used for Christian churches. During the Roman period there might have been a Christian church on the site of the later St Paul's, but we do not know.

A stone wall enclosing the landward part of the city was built at the close of the second century AD, a formidable undertaking that reflected the organisational skill of Roman Britain and the importance of Britain within the empire. At just over two miles long and about five metres high, the wall may have required considerably more than one million cubic feet of ragstone, much of it presumably moved by boat from the quarries near Maidstone. The wall may have been built in 193–7 as Clodius Albinus, the Governor, prepared to launch a bid to be Emperor, but later dates have also been suggested, including the reign of Caracalla (211–17). Albeit repaired and strengthened by bastions or towns, the wall was to be a key feature in the history of London for the majority of its subsequent history, and, as such, was an important, enduring physical legacy from the Roman period.

Albinus was defeated for imperial mastery by Septimus Severus (Emperor 193–211), who restored central control of Britain, establishing his residence for a while at York and dividing Britain in two. Under Severus, London was probably capital of Upper Britain and York of Lower, which constituted a diminution of London's status. The fort in the north-west corner of the city, at Cripplegate, was abandoned in about 200, perhaps when Britain was divided. London, moreover, was presumably hit by civil wars within the empire and

also by 'barbarian' attacks, with a serious impact on its trade. A fortified watch tower at Shadwell appears to date from the mid-third century. Rebellions, for example in 259–73 and 286 or 287 to 296, which divided Britain and other provinces from the remainder of the empire, posed particular problems for overseas trade. Indeed, there are signs of the deterioration of the coinage, although that was a general problem and not one confined to Britain.

In turn, the reconquest of Britain from a rebel general in 296 brought order to a London plundered by the defeated troops of the rebels. A gold medallion acclaiming the triumph of Constantius Chlorus (the nephew of Claudius II Gothicus and the father of Constantine the Great) in reconquering Britain provides the earliest known view of London, although the gate with twin towers was probably a conventional motif. The government of Britain was subsequently reorganised. York was the military centre, but London was the headquarters of the *vicarius* who directed Britain, which was now termed a diocese. London was also renamed Augusta, a sign of imperial favour, which suggests that the city rose to the rank of *colonia*. London also had in the early fourth century, the only mint within Britain, a product of the city's governmental and commercial roles and capabilities. The location of mints was determined by the need to service both military and official roles.

Documentary sources for late-Roman London are scanty. The archaeological record becomes more sketchy after the late second or early third century when there is evidence of large-scale demolition of buildings, both private and public. Moreover, for the later fourth century coinage finds are lower than would be anticipated on the basis of earlier finds, again suggesting decline. The distribution of late-Roman finds in London suggests that much of the western half of the walled city was more or less abandoned, with the main focus of continued settlement being to the east of the Walbrook stream, between the northern end of the bridge and the site of the forum, which had also been abandoned around AD 300. Roman London would have been affected by the growing crisis of the Roman empire in the fourth century as it came under pressure from 'barbarian' invaders, notably in 342–3, 360 and 367–8.

In southern Britain these attacks came from the Saxons of north-west Germany; the attacks led, in the third century, to the construction of a series of coastal forts on what was known as the Saxon Shore. London was not part of this system, but was in part defended by it. In 367–8, it is possible that London had to rely on its walls to resist a Saxon siege, while the devastation of the surrounding countryside by the Saxons hit the local economy hard, a situation that was, more definitely, to be reprised under the Vikings in attacks from the ninth to the eleventh centuries. The crisis apparently finished when a force under Theodosius sent from France crossed to Richborough and relieved London.

The defences of the city were certainly strengthened with the construction of bastions in support of the city wall, but it is not clear when these were built. Some of these semi-circular bastions were probably designed to carry catapults. Moreover, part of the riverside wall was rebuilt at the end of the fourth century, a period when the general Stilicho possibly came to Britain to strengthen its defences.

In the end, there was no dramatic single attack, but, rather, an overcoming of Roman Britain as a result of internal dissension within the empire as much as external attack. The precious metal hoard from Hoxhen in Suffolk extends to 413 and perhaps beyond, but Britain was adrift by then, politically, although not culturally. In 406, when Gaul was invaded from across the Rhine, Britain, threatened with being cut off from the rest of the Roman empire, created its own emperor, Constantine III. He, however, took a significant part of the island's military forces to Gaul to counter the 'barbarian' threat. These troops did not return. The disillusioned Romano-Britons, in turn, expelled his administration and appealed to the true emperor in Rome, Honorius (r. 393–423), for the restoration of legitimate rule. Hard-pressed in Italy by Alaric, the Visigothic leader, who captured Rome itself in 410, Honorius could do no more than tell them, from his capital in Ravenna, to look to their own defence.

Formal links with the Roman empire had come to an end.

Gold medallion showing London welcoming Constantius Chlorus.
THE GRANGER COLLECTION

This statue of a Roman soldier was found near Bishopsgate. Depicted with writing tablets as well as a sword, this figure has been interpreted as perhaps a civil servant in the Roman government.
MUSEUM OF LONDON

2

T HE LENGTHY PERIOD from the departure of Roman troops to the arrival of those of William the Conqueror in 1066 saw London experience radical changes in form and function, location and fortunes. Over these six centuries it declined from capital city to minor place; the Roman city was abandoned, and a new port town – Lundenwic – became established to the west; 250 years later Danish incursions prompted a move back within the old city walls, now repaired, and a combination of growing wealth, geography and politics helped propel London back to centre-stage, to become an emergent capital city.

The first century of this period was particularly traumatic, as London has never experienced a decline comparable to that in the fifth century AD. The collapse of Roman patterns of government and trade hit hard at town life in Britain, especially after mid-century. St Germanus, Bishop of Auxerre, who visited Britain in 429 to combat the Pelagian heresy, which denied the doctrine of original sin, noted the survival of cities, but that their defence was in local hands rather than those of Roman troops. The sole place he is known to have visited was St Albans, not London. According to Germanus, Christianity appears to have been flourishing, although whether that was the case throughout society remains controversial.

From mid-century, however, the situation appears to have deteriorated as a result of 'barbarian' invasion, and indeed in about 446 an unsuccessful appeal for help was sent to Rome, which, however, was in no position to send assistance. The *Anglo-Saxon Chronicle* relates that, slightly later, in 457, Hengist, the semi-legendary founder of the kingdom of Kent, '... fought with the Britons on the spot that is called Crecganford [possibly Crayford], and there slew four thousand men. The Britons then forsook the land of Kent, and in great consternation fled to London.' However, as this was recounted much later, in the late ninth century, it was perhaps no more than a legend.

Already prior to the attacks of the mid-fifth century, the collapse of the superstructure of Roman administration had greatly affected commerce in and with Britain. In part, this collapse reflected the extent to which Britain remained a society largely true to its agrarian

ANGLO-SAXON CENTURIES, 410–1066

roots and less Romanised than other provinces such as France and Spain. Outside the towns, indeed, the British influence on Roman Britain was considerable. The collapse of the Roman order was followed by a return to a subsistence economy, the abandonment of most towns and the end of the minting of coins. Whether this amounted to complete collapse is now questioned to some extent, notably in Kent, where urban forms of lifestyle probably did survive in Canterbury.

Little is known of London in the fifth or sixth centuries, and the old walled town was probably a vacant site, as also was Southwark. There are contradictions between different sources of evidence, because the early Germanic invaders were illiterate, and later written sources provide a different account from that of the archaeological evidence, while the latter has been affected by later building work and the destruction of material in centuries of cellaring, as well as the difficulty of excavating ephemeral timber structures before such methods were developed in the 1930s. It is therefore difficult to distinguish between the consequences of the end to imperial Roman rule and that of the Anglo-Saxon/Jute invaders, who brought Germanisation.

It is likely that the British population fell dramatically, not least because of plague. In the conquered areas, which from the late fifth century included London, it has been argued that the Romano-Britons largely fled, or survived as slaves and peasants. There is also the contrary argument that there were few Anglo-Saxon/Jute[1] settlers, and that the great majority of the population remained British, but acculturated to a militarily dominant invading élite. At any rate, the Roman city seems to have been substantially deserted, with the remaining population focusing on agricultural activity rather than urban functions. Despite this, the buildings, walls and streets, even if abandoned and grass-grown, did survive as a framework for urban growth when it resumed.

London was of scant importance to the Anglo-Saxon settlers. They not only concentrated on agriculture, but also were largely self-sufficient. Trade was of limited importance to their economy, and certainly far less than for the economy of Roman Britain. London thus lost the advantages of location which had propelled it to significance, and then to predominance, under the Romans. Instead, the location parameters of settlement under the Anglo-Saxons initially reverted to those of the pre-Roman centuries. Links with the Continent were greatly frayed. Moreover, Anglo-Saxon rulers initially did not live within the Roman city walls, and had little interest in defensive enclosures.

Yet, alongside claims of abandonment and desertion, advances in archaeology, especially following the large-scale funding from 1973 of rescue archaeology in London, are filling in some of the gaps in the record and suggesting that there was actually more activity in London than hitherto believed. Indeed, during the early Saxon period, the centre of settlement shifted to the west of the abandoned Roman city, along the banks of the Thames and inland towards the later Strand and Covent Garden. Excavations in Covent Garden in the 2000s produced finds from the early Saxon period of the late sixth or seventh centuries. The cremation urns discovered in 2005 have been dated to 550–650, while a grave dated

John Morris, historian of Londinium, felt certain that 'London must ... be classed with Trier, Mainz and other administrative centres ... that contained in the third century a substantial Christian community, large enough and rich enough to afford a church building'. Such a church might have been located on Ludgate Hill, but we do not yet know for sure. This photograph shows St Martin-in-the-Fields, one of London's most famous and most visited churches, located prominently on the tourist routes at Trafalgar Square and famous for its open-door policy to the public. Documentary records of a church on this site date back only to the early thirteenth century. That church was rebuilt under Henry VIII and survived the Great Fire, but was rebuilt in the 1720s in James Gibbs' neo-classical style we see today. However, in 2006, during restoration work, archaeologists discovered a massive late-Roman sarcophagus, complete with human skeleton, 5 ft 6 ins in height, which appears to have been buried according to Christian practice. Nearby were also found tell-tale remains of a Roman tile kiln of the fifth century AD, as well as Anglo Saxon burials of the seventh century. The main significance of the sarcophagus is that it lay so far away from Londinium and the known cemetery to the north-west of the city walls. It is also quite late in date, and the tile kiln is one of the latest Roman finds in or around the city. Might the burial possibly betoken a very early Christian site? Speculation of a connection with St Martin of Tours, who was canonised in AD 397 – around the same time as the Roman burial – pushes the available evidence rather too far, but St Martin-in-the-Fields does lie within what was to become post-Roman Lundenwic, and could be on a site of very early religious as well as secular importance.

PHOTOGRAPH: CARNEGIE, 2009

This gilded silver brooch was made in southern England around AD 500 and was found in 1908 in Mitcham associated with the burial remains of an obviously wealthy woman of the time. Other early Saxon sites have been found around London, including Croydon and Twickenham. But was London itself inhabited in the two centuries after the Roman departure? The historical record is empty and, as yet, archaeology has failed to answer this intriguing question.
MUSEUM OF LONDON

to 650–700 contains an early Saxon brooch. As Covent Garden was outside the old city walls, these finds do not indicate continued occupation of Londinium itself; they do, however, provide evidence for development to the west of the Roman city. This is confirmed by the distribution of other Saxon finds in the area, including those in association with the churches of St Martin-in-the-Fields and St Bride's, Fleet Street. At this time, too, we know that the lower Thames valley and the Thames estuary remained areas of settlement, with new villages also founded by the Anglo-Saxons. Thus, settlement on Canvey Island was quite widespread from the fifth–sixth centuries.

The revival of both Christianity and the volume of trade brought an increase in activity in what was now London, both the old Roman centre and the town of Lundenwic. This increase, in part, drew on the energy and wealth of the East Anglian and Kentish royal dynasties and on the developing importance of links with the Continent. Christianity also meant a spread of education and literacy, and the beginnings of written law, and, partly as a result, society grew to become somewhat institutionalised, certainly in comparison with the fifth and sixth centuries.

At the beginning of the seventh century, a church, dedicated to St Paul, was established in London. Like many other early Saxon churches, the first St Paul's was sited within the former Roman city, in this instance on top of Ludgate Hill. Small and built of timber, we know that it burned down in 675 before being rebuilt, again in timber. Of these earliest structures no fabric remains, although during the rebuilding after the Great Fire of 1666 Sir Christopher Wren said that in the foundations of his new church could be seen, 'Quantities of Urns, broken Vessels and Potteryware ... Graves of several Ages and Fashions in Strata, or Layers of Earth, one above another ... [showing] great Antiquity from the British and Roman Times.' Whether Wren was right in thinking that there might have been a Roman religious site on Ludgate Hill is unknown. St Paul's was the seat of the bishop for the East Saxons, the people who dominated Essex, Middlesex and part, possibly all, of Hertfordshire. All or part of Surrey was at one time part of the kingdom of the East Saxons, but it was not central to this kingdom.

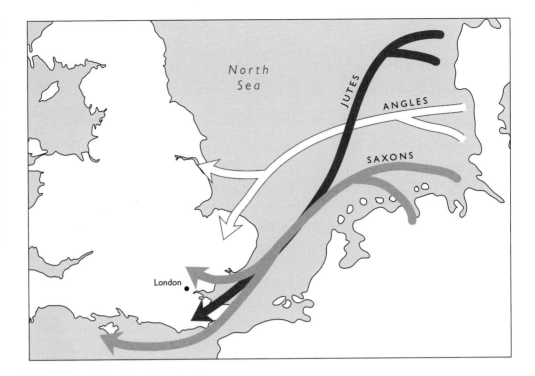

Nor was the kingdom a prominent one matching those of East Anglia or Kent, the Bretwalda (over-king). Whatever its role in the East Saxon kingdom, let alone the possibility of a separate identity for the Middle Saxons (the basis of the name Middlesex), London was not a key political centre: Anglo-Saxon England developed into a number of major kingdoms, but none of them centred on London. Initially Kent and East Anglia were the most important kingdoms.[2]

Interestingly, Pope Gregory the Great regarded London as the obvious primatial see for the southern English, with York as its northern counterpart, but Augustine, who was sent by Gregory in 596–97 to convert the English, understood the political realities of the time. Augustine remained at Canterbury, then capital of Kent and the key early site of Christian conversion, and, as a result, Canterbury rather than London become the primatial see. Indeed, London's conversion owed much to the dominance of Kent, because King Saeberht of Essex, the ruler of the London area, was the nephew of the powerful King Ethelbert of Kent. Thus, the establishment of a bishopric in London was a sign of the influence of Kent. London lay in the new diocese but on its boundary, which reflected its position within the kingdom of the East Saxons. The influence of Kent may have played a role in the location of the episcopal centre, but so also probably did London's prestige as a former capital.

This prestige had a growing significance as the process of conquest and settlement was replaced by one of stabilisation and a search for hierarchy and dominance among the

Anglo-Saxon polities. At the end of the sixth century, there was a heightened interest in ancient monuments. The relevance of the survival of the Roman walls to London's position is unclear, but Pope Gregory was presumably affected by a determination to draw on the prestige of London's position during the Roman period; it has been suggested that there was a document in Rome listing the cities in Britain, with London very prominent on the list. York was another Roman site that became a see. Mellitus, who was sent by Gregory in 601 and who became bishop of London in 604, had to retire to Canterbury, however, because Saeberht, who died in about 616, was succeeded by heathen sons. It is possible that a partition of his kingdom led to a separate kingdom for Middlesex.

Bede claimed that the East Saxons stayed pagan until King Sigerberht was converted in 653. In 666, Wulfhere, ruler of the Midland kingdom of Mercia (658–75), who was overlord of Essex and Sussex, sold the see of London. However, in the 670s, Theodore of Tarsus, Archbishop of Canterbury, supported the restoration of the cathedral of St Paul and of the diocese. This restoration also led to the establishment of ecclesiastical centres in the London region, including a monastery at Chertsey and a nunnery at Barking. Surrey, was detached from the diocese and transferred to Winchester in the late 700s. A continuation of the influence of Kent was shown by the laws of King Hlothere (r. 673–85), who had in London a wic-reeve, an official who was to witness the transactions of Kentish merchants at the king's hall.

Lundenwic and Lundenburh. The 'old town' of Lundenwic lay around the site of the later Covent Garden, Trafalgar Square and the Strand, well to the west of the old walled city. Only in the late ninth century did King Alfred re-occupy the former Roman city. From this date the Saxon settlement was probably abandoned in favour of the defensible city, now known as Lundenburh.

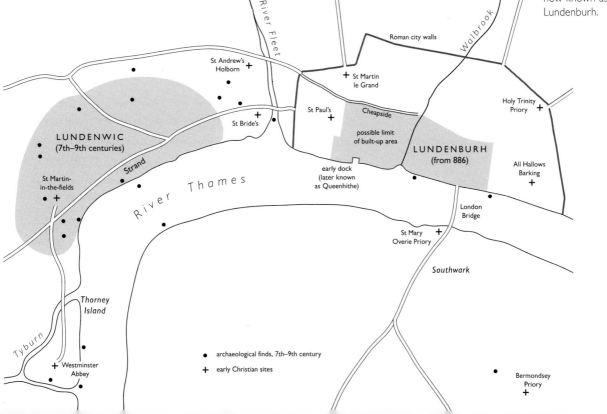

As the centre of a bishopric, London was one of a number of towns, but, in relative terms, it was more important within Britain as a port known as Lundenwic. This port developed in the seventh and eighth centuries, as did ports at Ipswich, Sandwich and Southampton. It was centred not on the area of the old Roman city but, instead, to the west of the river Fleet, around the Strand. Near Charing Cross, there was a reinforced embankment upon which ships were beached so that they could be unloaded. Writing in the 730s, Bede described the city as 'a mart of many peoples', while already, in the 670s, London had been referred to in a charter as a place 'where ships land'. From at least partial abandonment in the fifth century, London had become a thriving and important centre by the later seventh, with a bishopric, a port and a king's hall; and this activity represented a reassertion of the city's primacy within south-east England. The honours were shared with Canterbury, but the political position of the latter was to be affected by the decline of the Kentish kingdom, which ceased to have any real significance.

London's fortunes lay in commerce. The growth of trade meant an increased use of coinage as well as opportunities for taxation. Thanks to extensive metal-detector finds in recent years, far more information on coinage is available than it was in the 1980s. It is now clear that the volume of coinage in the early eighth century was very high in eastern and southern England, and indeed possibly more so than at any time before the arrival in the twelfth century of silver from deposits in the Harz mountains in Germany. This wealth reflected the scale and importance of English wool exports; this trade was centred on London, providing a crucial theme in its economic fortunes that was to last for centuries; in the form of woollen cloth, indeed, it was still important in the eighteenth century. In the Anglo-Saxon period a key movement of wool was from the Cotswolds via the Thames water-system.

Archaeological research since the 1980s has thrown increasing light on this trading city, although centuries of subsequent building have left only so much to uncover. There is evidence for urban development in what had been Roman London as well as in the port city to the west. Within the old Roman walls, there was a cathedral, with the high status of an ecclesiastical precinct, and possibly a royal palace, but not the functions apparently discharged by Lundenwic. The place-name -wic, also seen in Ipswich and Sandwich, indicated a centre of trade. It is unclear what was traded, although imported pottery has been found in the site of Lundenwic, and wool or woollen cloth was probably exported. Moreover, silver coins minted in London were sent abroad.

The revival of commerce appears to have owed much to the improvement of the economy of Merovingian Gaul, with which there was considerable trade via the port of Quentovic near Boulogne. There was also trade to the Low Countries. As so often in its history, London's fortunes are part of a much wider sphere, the stability and prosperity of which was linked directly to the fortunes of the city. Whereas, in the eighth century, ships were moored and there were no wharves, by the mid-ninth century the first wharves in the city were constructed. Excavations at Bull Wharf indicate this process, which was also part of what became a more general reclamation of the waterfront that continued from the late Anglo-Saxon period, not least as rubbish was dumped into the Thames.

London's position also reflected the nature of communications within England. Water-routes were the most important. Initially the two major water systems had centred on the Wash/Humber and Severn/Avon respectively, but the latter had declined from the late sixth century as the related trade from the Mediterranean via Atlantic Spain and France to Cornwall had declined. Instead, the Thames system centred on London had grown in significance, a system that also benefited from tributaries such as the Lea.

The London Stone is a curious little lump of limestone now preserved behind a grille at 111 Cannon Street. Before St Swithins was demolished in 1962, the stone had been built into that church's walls; before that the stone, then apparently much larger, had stood at the centre of Cannon Street, the symbolic centre of London and – allegedly – of Roman Britain. Its true origin, purpose and significance are lost to history.

PHOTOGRAPH: CARNEGIE, 2009

An emphasis on water-routes has displaced an earlier stress on ridge-routes, but, as far as the latter are concerned, it is notable that valleys were prone to flooding, while their soil was often heavy and difficult to traverse, as well as to work. The Thames provided a serious instance of these problems. As a result of such difficulties, most land routes sought to follow ridges, where drainage was better and the soil drier. Bridging and ferry points that could be reached by such land routes were the central points in the communication system, linking in with the key water-routes, as London exemplified. Thus, the advantages of Roman London were rediscovered. The greater role of bridges is suggested by the extent to which, from the 740s, labour service for bridge-building and repair became an important provision in charters.

The crucial beneficiaries of warfare and political change from the seventh century were to be the kingdoms further west and on the frontier of settlement. The key kingdoms in England were to be those of Northumbria, Mercia and Wessex, in the North, Midlands and South respectively. The last centred on Winchester. In addition to these major kingdoms, there were a number of subsidiary ones, several of which survived in semi-autonomous form within the larger kingdoms. Kent and East Anglia were leading examples. Neither kingdom, however, left a place for London. Instead, in political terms, it was a quasi-frontier town between Anglo-Saxon states; and this remained London's position until the expansion of Wessex in the early tenth century. Whatever the political consequences, London's role as a frontier town on the borders of several kingdoms and sub-kingdoms was possibly a benefit because it represented an opportunity for inter-state trade. Moreover, in the absence of a garrison, the frontier role helped ensure a relative freedom from close royal control. This factor is intangible, but possibly important; and London's position was not unlike some other key towns and cities, such as Tamworth, York and Lincoln, all of which were on or close to administrative boundaries, with a centrality yet also a liminality.

Prior to the advance of Wessex, London had been affected by changes in political control. Thus, under the powerful King Offa of Mercia (r. 757–96), London, alongside Essex and Kent, was brought under Mercian control. Indeed, Offa may well have been the founder of the first monastery in Westminster. The claim that he was the founder of the church of St Alban in Wood Street, which has sometimes been seen as the chapel of a royal palace in London, attracts little credit. Charters from the kings of Mercia for the 730s–770s granted remission of tolls at the port of London to various ecclesiastical institutions, including the bishop of Worcester and the minster of Thanet, which had its own small fleet. Wool, hides and slaves were exported; indeed Bede referred to an individual sold as a slave to Frisian merchants at London. London may have been an emporium over which control was shared between Mercia and Kent, with facilities for which they could obtain tolls, such as keeping ships safe, offered by both; or there may have a Mercian monopoly over London's trade. The role of London probably affected the dynamics of Mercia. Its heartland in the north-west Midlands was not monetarised, but access to London provided control over a wealthy area with much money, and this situation, in turn, enhanced the importance of London within Mercia.

Mercian control had a profound influence in another way, as the speech/dialect of the London area, like those of Oxford and the South Midlands, derives from Mercian forms of English, rather than from Wessex or eastern English forms. This derivation ultimately helped to shape the linguistic structures and etymology of modern English.

Offa's spreading authority diminished the role of the Thames as a boundary, a development that benefited London. Indeed, Cenwulf of Mercia (r. 796–821) proposed that London become the archepiscopal see for southern England, replacing both Canterbury and the see Offa had established at Lichfield. Cenwulf, who had harshly suppressed a rebellion in Kent in 798, had a long-standing dispute with Archbishop Wulfred of Canterbury, whom he suspended between 817 and 821. The Pope, however, rejected the proposal. In 2001 a gold coin of Cenwulf, issued in London, was found in Bedfordshire. The coin suggests an increase in London's prominence, as does the fact that several of Cenwulf's charters were issued from there: the city may have been a royal residence for a while. In 825, following victory at Ellandun over the Mercians, Egbert, king of Wessex conquered south-east England, so that the Thames again was not a boundary. In turn, Mercian influence over London was re-established in the 830s.

London was also affected by the Danish advances in southern England that proved the high point of the Viking attacks. Serious and deadly attacks on London were mounted in 842 and 851. In response, there was probably a move from Lundenwic into the relative security of the old walled city even before King Alfred established a burh there in 886. Danish invaders took up winter quarters nearby: in Thanet in 850 and Sheppey in 854, and London may well have become an important Danish base, because of its nodal location and walls. Indeed, London probably had a Danish garrison from 871, when the Danes under Ivar 'the Boneless' wintered in the city: coins were minted there. London seemed to be securely in the Danish ambit of influence, as York and Dublin were to be, although in 872 the Danes moved north and wintered at Torksey, near Lincoln. Five years later, the Vikings conquered Mercia, although western Mercia was left under a client king, Ceolwulf II, and London would probably have been in his portion; nevertheless, the Danes might have retained control.

King Alfred's successful defeat of the Danish attack in 878, notably his victory at Edington in Wiltshire, however, led to a change of status for London. This change was not immediate, but arose because Wessex's successful defiance of the Danes opened up the possibility that Alfred would be able to campaign into the South East and to challenge the Danish position in London. Indeed, he had already done so in the early 870s. This pressure became more intense, aided by the departure of the Danish Great Army for the Continent in 879. A Danish raid in 884 led to a battle at the Kent hamlet of Plucks Gutter, where the rivers Stour meet, in which Alfred prevailed. In the aftermath of these events, Alfred retook London. The *Anglo-Saxon Chronicle* recorded that in 886, 'Alfred occupied London, and all the English people that were not under subjection to the Danes submitted to him. And he then entrusted the burh [fortified proto-town] to the control of Ealdorman Æthelred [ruler of Mercia],' The Welsh monk Asser wrote, 'In the same year [886], Alfred, King of the Anglo-Saxons … honourably rebuilt the city of London, and made it again habitable.' Already, in 883, an English army had been deployed near London, and it probably besieged the city and may well have pushed the Danes back.

London was re-occupied primarily for defensive purposes. This is almost certainly what precipitated the shift away from Lundenwic, which had no defensive wall. By 888–89, certainly, the main settlement was now back in London, or Lundenburh as it was now known. This shift was probably eased by the extent to which Lundenwic had been devastated by the fighting. At any rate, the latter settlement was discarded. The only major '-wic' settlement that continued was Ipswich, which had its own hinterland, was not simply dependent on trade, and was within the Viking world. Other trading settlements, such as London, Southampton and York, were all reconstructed on different sites. The legacy of Lundenwic included a number of churches, as well as the place-name Aldwych, the 'old wic', or town. However, the ease with which wooden and wattle and daub constructions rotted helped to ensure that the site of the former Lundenwic reverted to open land.

The residents of the new burh at London did not simply rely on the old Roman walls they found. The defences were strengthened by some rebuilding and maintenance, and enhanced with another burh at Southwark, which was intended to help prevent Danish expeditions up-river, as well as to protect the crucial river-crossing. The Roman bridge had possibly been rebuilt in mid-century, as part of the river defences, and maintenance enforced through the obligation of bridgework. Such a pattern was also seen on the Continent; under Charles the Bald of France (r. *c*.843–77), fortified bridges were constructed to obstruct Viking passage up-river, as at Paris in 885.

The process by which burhs became proper towns is far from clear, but, within the burh defences of London, there was certainly a process of urban regeneration, which proved a marked contrast to the Roman ruins still in the city. Alfred allocated blocks of land to the Archbishop of Canterbury and the Bishop of Worcester. New streets were established between the Thames and Cheapside west of Walbrook and also near Cannon Street. Yet the role of the wall and its gates helped to ensure that the new road pattern was shaped by the alignments of the Roman city.

London now was part of Wessex's sphere of control and, thereafter, the city developed within the English, later British, state. This fact was highly significant, as a more peripheral city would have faced more significant problems. For example, York had major advantages as a centre of government and was also a river port of some significance. Moreover, urban development occurred earlier in north-eastern England than in the South. This was because the Danelaw was integrated into the Danish commercial empire, which helped to lead to urban development in York, Lincoln, Stamford and Nottingham; growth in London and Oxford came later.

From a northern perspective, such as Northumbria in the late seventh century, London might appear geographically peripheral, tucked away as it is in the south-east corner of England. Yet York in the tenth century could scarcely be a centre of government as it was marginal to a state now centred in southern England. Moreover, York was not under firm control from Wessex until the 950s when the Danes were driven out. London's growing significance, in part, derived from the transformation of Wessex into the Old English monarchy, a transformation aided by the earlier destruction of the other Anglo-Saxon ruling houses by the Danes, and by Alfred's care in handling the Mercians. Thus, London, which had become a frontier city anew when Alfred and the Danish leader Guthrum chose a frontier along the Thames and the Lea, ceased to be in a frontier-zone between English polities. Æthelred's position in London may reflect both his own role in capturing the city and the importance of the historical link with Mercia, but, when he died in 911, control over London passed to Alfred's eldest son, Edward the Elder.

This leather, copper alloy and bronze Viking sword belt was found in 1878 in Temple, just off Fleet Street. We know that Cnut's besieging Viking army surrounded the city, so it is not inconceivable that this item belonged to one of his men.
MUSEUM OF LONDON

This is a grave slab that might commemorate a follower of Cnut, Viking invader and king of England 1016–35. There is an inscription which reads ':[k]ina: let: lekia: st | in: þensi: auk: tuki:, Old Norse for 'Ginna and Toki had this stone laid'. The illustration on the slab shows a lion battling a snake.
MUSEUM OF LONDON

In turn, the Danes were driven from close to London: Edward the Elder (r. 899–924), Athelstan (r. 924–39), and Edmund (r. 939–46) conquered East Anglia, eastern Mercia and Danish Northumberland, while English Mercia was absorbed by Wessex. The eroding of the distinction between Mercia and Wessex was very important to London's changed status. As a sign of London's importance, it was allocated eight moneyers under Athelstan, a number matched only by Canterbury and Winchester, while most towns only had one moneyer. This was a time in which re-coinages were a key demonstration of national authority and power, and the coinage proved a way to assert the role of the Crown as the expression of a new Englishness.

Yet London was not yet a centre of government, nor a capital city, not least as royal councils met in other cities. Winchester was an important symbolic centre for some reigns, especially those of Edward the Elder, Eadwig (955–59) and Edgar (959–75), but less so for that of Athelstan.[3] London, in contrast, had more commercial pulling-power.

Despite the paucity of documentary references, we do know that the second half of the century was an important period in London's development, benefiting from a prolonged period in which no attacks took place. A significant part of London's medieval street system dates from this period, and the population rose. Trade increased and facilities for trade improved markedly; quays were built on the Thames, including at Queenhithe and New Fresh Wharf, just downstream of London Bridge. A wharf also existed at Billingsgate by 1015, while London Bridge, which is sometimes dated to the reign of Æthelred the Unready, was probably instead repaired then (remains of wooden piles of that date have been found in the river bed). The role of markets was also illustrated by street-names. *Ceap*, the Anglo-Saxon word for market, was the basis for Westcheap and Eastcheap.

Yet, towards the close of the tenth century, Danish pressure resumed, and London was again exposed to attack. This period is obscure, and we do not know what effect the pressure had on London's commerce. In 982, there was a serious fire, possibly as a result of Danish attack. In 994, however, another attack was repelled: the *Anglo-Saxon Chronicle* recorded an attack by a Norwegian and Danish force of 94 ships, but added that the attackers 'suffered more harm and injury than they ever thought any garrison would do to

Queenhithe is London's most important early quay or 'river dock'. There is some evidence for Roman use, but more secure evidence comes from the ninth century AD, when the western half of the old Roman city around Ludgate Hill was repopulated under King Alfred. New streets ran south to the river from Cheapside, and a wharf or little harbour known as *Aedereshyd* (later Queenhithe, after Matilda) was created; we know of two separate grants of land were made here by Alfred in 889 and 898–9. In simple terms both Queenhithe and Billingsgate were small artificial inlets of the river, as seen here. They were still tidal, not being enclosed, but did provide an area of relative calm out of the main stream. For the next 500 years, Queenhithe remained one of London's busiest wharves, and continued in use by the fur trade among other businesses until the twentieth century. Today Queenhithe can be a sorry sight, plastic bottles floating in on the tide. There is little sign of the quay's former importance to the history of London's trade.

PHOTOGRAPH: CARNEGIE, 2009

them'. The city did not fall, and it was able to repel another attack in 1009. Indeed, London remained outside Danish control until 1013, and was a centre of resistance, but it did contribute to the *Danegeld* given to buy off Danish attacks. London's symbolic importance was shown by the burial in St Paul's of Archbishop Ælfseah of Canterbury, who had been killed by the Danes, and whose body was taken by the citizens into London.

Although London was exposed to Danish attacks, the key centres of Wessex, in Hampshire, especially Winchester, were less well suited functionally to a state that encompassed most of modern England. The development of London as a walled city reflected its importance. Moreover, there was an important psychological shift away from the traditional centres of Wessex when, from 1016 to 1042, the Wessex dynasty was displaced by the Danes, under Cnut and his sons. Cnut's father, Sweyn Forkbeard, had failed to capture London in 1013 (whereas he took Oxford and Winchester), and the city only submitted to him later that year after the rest of England had submitted. After Sweyn's death in 1014, the city was recaptured by Æthelred the Unready, and it was subsequently central to his position and operations as he resisted Cnut.

Æthelred held London until his death in 1016, and, as a sign of the city's importance, he was buried at St Paul's. London then supported his son, Edmund Ironside, the *Anglo-Saxon Chronicle* recording 'all the councillors who were in London, and the citizens, chose Edmund as king'. However, Cnut's Danish fleet then appeared in the Thames. As its passage upstream was blocked by the troops on London Bridge, Cnut reportedly dug a channel or short canal around the southern end of the bridge in Southwark and dragged his ships along it in order to encircle the city fully. London was then besieged, but the city resisted, Edmund raised the siege, and Cnut moved off. Following a decisive defeat to the Danish forces, however, Edmund then decided that he needed to come to terms. Late in 1016, therefore, he and Cnut partitioned the kingdom, Edmund receiving Wessex, and Cnut taking control of Mercia, including London. Cnut and his army then took up winter quarters in London. Edmund died in November of the same year, and under the terms of the earlier peace accord Cnut was able to take over the entire kingdom. London had to raise the large sum of £10,500 to pay off part of Cnut's army in 1018.

Cnut and his sons presented themselves as the heirs to the Old English monarchy, but, in fact, there were major differences. These included the extent to which England was now part of a state spanning the North Sea. Cnut also ruled Denmark and Norway, and thus a capital on the east coast of England was more suitable than Winchester. Without his predecessors' cultural, religious and historical ties to Winchester and what it represented, Cnut made London his military and governmental centre in England and, when he died, his *litsmen*, or personal guard, were in London. His successors continued this situation. It was in Westminster that Cnut's son, Harold Harefoot, was buried in 1039, whereas Cnut, like the Old English kings, was buried in Winchester. Harold Harefoot's half-brother,

Harthacnut (who had Harold's body exhumed and thrown into the river), died in 1042 at the wedding feast of a prominent thegn held in Lambeth.

With the end of Cnut's dynasty in 1042, that of Wessex returned. Edward the Confessor was chosen king by popular acclamation in London in 1042 and ruled until 1066. The expression of the view of the citizens in the royal succession, already seen after the deaths of Cnut and Harold Harefoot, showed that a citizen body existed, as had not been the case in the tenth century.

Meanwhile, London benefited from the commercial growth of England, a growth that offered important opportunities to the Crown as towns were more clearly under royal government than rural areas. London was the most important town, its development reflecting the strength of the economy. From the ninth century, English cloth exports were earning large amounts of Continental silver, which helped to make England particularly wealthy. This wealth proved the basis of an effective silver currency which, in turn, assisted the process of governance.

Cnut was the son of a Danish king, Sweyn Forkbeard, who invaded England with around 10,000 Vikings from all around Scandinavia in 1015. For over a year, Cnut's Vikings fought a series of engagements against Edmund Ironside, who was declared king of England after the death of Æthelred the Unready in April 1016. This later illustration, now in the Bibliothèque Nationale in Paris, shows Cnut's unsuccessful siege of 1016, with the Thames in the foreground and the towers of the city walls. Edmund raised extra troops in Wessex, returning to London to end the siege and defeat Cnut at Brentford. The English success was short-lived, however, and following a decisive victory Cnut gained Mercia, including London. His astute political manoeuvrings then brought him the undisputed throne of England after the death of Edmund Ironside in November 1016.

BIBLIOTHÈQUE NATIONALE DE FRANCE

As a settlement Westminster is not as ancient as London itself, but for the last thousand years has been central to the history of the city and of the nation. The first 'west minster' was founded in AD 960 upon a small river island formed where the river Tyburn entered the Thames (see map on page 29). This 'ait' or 'eyot' of Thorns gave its name to Thorney Island, upon which the abbey was built. In this modern aerial photograph, we see the great nineteenth-century Houses of Parliament, with the medieval Westminster Hall prominent in the centre of this view. The present Westminster Abbey was begun in the mid-thirteenth century, although Hawksmoor's great west front was not added until 1745. Just to the right of the abbey can be seen the Jewel Tower and the trees of the College Garden, reputedly England's oldest garden in constant cultivation.

The strength of the English monetary economy helped give London a particular advantage as a commercial city, at the same time as the wealth encouraged invasion. Trade between the east coast and the Low Countries and the Rhineland were especially important. London was well placed to serve and foster links with the Low Countries and Germany. Indeed, there was a post-Viking 'assimilation ... of the Rhineland, the Low Countries, and south-east England into a single trading region based upon the profitable route between London, Bruges and Cologne'.[4] Millstones and pottery were imported from the Rhineland. Long-distance trade with Italy and Spain also grew, with the export of wool and probably slaves in return for spices and wax. This trade was organised by pepperers based around St Antonin's in Cordwainer and Soper Lane.

Part of the city's wealth was spent on the Church. Apart from expenditure on parish churches, there was the construction of monasteries, nunneries and hospitals. These were located on the edge of the built-up area or at a greater distance, and thus helped define what were in effect early suburbs. The wealth of the region also led to the growth of London, probably from about 950, so that by 1100 the city had a population of between 10,000 and 20,000. In part, this growth was a matter of the transference of the plan of the burh, a network of streets, into the reality of a developed community, a transfer not always made with the other burhs established by Alfred. This process involved both infilling and the

Edward the Confessor, from the Bayeux Tapestry. Edward's death in January 1066 prompted the invasion of William, Duke of Normandy that was to change the trajectory of London's and England's history fundamentally. Edward's reign saw growing prosperity alongside political instability.

development of new streets lined with timber houses, although late Old English urban street patterns were less regular than the Roman ones, and much of the land within the walls remained unoccupied in this period. The late tenth and early eleventh centuries was a crucial period in which property boundaries became demarcated. In effect the city became more fixed, and subsequently the major buildings and plots were to achieve a degree of consistency not seen over the previous four centuries.

There is very little evidence of the first parish churches prior to 1000, but, thereafter, the situation changed and many churches, for example those of St Alphage, near Cripplegate, and St Mildred, Bread Street, were founded during the reign of Edward the Confessor. The role of the river in London's development in the later Anglo-Saxon period was indicated by the reconstruction of the bridge, as well as of new quays. From the mid-eleventh century, timber waterfronts were regularly replaced.

London's significance was demonstrated by its role when, in 1051–52, the leading figure in the realm after the king, Earl Godwine, sought to seize power; and also by Edward's establishment of Westminster as the key devotional centre for the dynasty. In 1051 Godwine, summoned before the *Witan*, or council, in London to answer accusations, in turn, established himself in force at Southwark, only to find that the key power-brokers, as well as London, backed the king. In 1052, control over London was still crucial when the crisis came to a new head, with Godwine again arraying his strength at Southwark. In this case, supported by a larger fleet and backed by a section of London opinion, Godwine was able to force Edward to give way.

This denouement probably encouraged Edward to focus on Westminster, where he both rebuilt the monastery as a larger structure and also constructed the first royal palace on the site, whose great hall was a massive timber building. The monastery with its abbey church became part of a large palace complex. In contrast, there is no contemporary evidence for claims that there was a royal palace in the city, possibly close to Aldersgate, and the source, Matthew Paris, was considerably later. At any rate, Edward had a greater opportunity to direct affairs in Westminster than in London.

Westminster was close to London but also on a protected island site in the marshland where the river Tyburn entered the Thames. Thorney or Thorn Island was the location both of the new palace and of St Peter's Monastery or the west minster. The early history of the monastery is unclear in large part because of the subsequent fabrication of documents there. Thorney Island was occupied before the mid-tenth century and there are claims of an early foundation, including by Offa, but the key figure was Dunstan, bishop of London from 959 to 961, who was prominent in the monastic revival of the period. Westminster was refounded or re-formed and re-endowed, acquiring a large estate in about 959.

In the 1050s Edward employed Norman architects for the new church of Westminster Abbey. The first large Romanesque building in England, it was dedicated in December

1065 and Edward was buried there in January 1066. His body was later ceremoniously translated within the abbey in 1163. We should not read Edward's focus on Westminster as a down-playing of London – a replacement of a centre within the walls by one outside the walls – but rather as the replacement of Winchester by London. The extra-mural site of Westminster may have recalled the French royal mausoleum at St Denis outside Paris.

London was not to be a key site of battle in 1066, a year of three kings, but it was a centre of strategic control and the base of Harold's fleet. In deciding how best to respond to threats from Normandy (William the Conqueror) and Norway (Harald Hardrada), Edward's successor (and Godwine's eldest son), Harold, who had been crowned at Westminster, focused on retaining control of south-east England. He was concerned to block the route to London from the Channel. The challenge from Norway appeared secondary, and Harold only marched north, to contest Harald Hardrada's landing near York, when he was convinced that William would not invade from Normandy. In the event, William's subsequent landing in Sussex challenged Harold's position in the South East, which encouraged Harold to fight.

After his victory at Hastings on 14 October 1066, William quickly focused on London. At Southwark an English force attempted to halt the advancing Norman army.

The coffin of England's only saint-king still lies in a cavity near the top of the marble shrine prepared for it shortly after the king was canonised by Pope Alexander III in 1161, almost a century after the Confessor's death. The Benedictine monastery at Westminster was dissolved in 1540, and the shrine was damaged, but it was repaired under Mary Tudor. In terms of national history Edward the Confessor's chastity and inept dynastic politicking, including hinting to William Duke of Normandy that he favoured him as his successor, brought about the crisis that led to the Norman invasion of 1066. Of greater significance for the London area was Edward the Confessor's piety, which prompted him to embark upon rebuilding the Saxon church at Westminster and to commission the great Romanesque abbey which was completed just weeks before Edward's death. The great Gothic abbey we see today (minus the western towers which were added much later, in the eighteenth century) dates from another rebuilding by Henry III (r. 1216–72).

BY COURTESY OF WESTMINSTER ABBEY

The English force was defeated, and Southwark suffered William's considerable wrath. The defences on London Bridge held out, however, and William was forced to seek a crossing point of the Thames further upstream. As William's forces approached the capital towards Ludgate from the north-west, realistic prospects of a successful military defence evaporated, and morale among London's defenders crumbled. Based at Westminster, William prepared for a siege, but this did not prove necessary. At Berkhamsted the leading figures of the regime submitted to William, and on Christmas Day he was crowned in Westminster Abbey. A high level of tension was indicated when the acclamation of William as king by the English in the church led Norman troops outside to fear opposition, and they reacted by setting fire to several buildings and killing some of the bystanders.

The previous unification of England by the house of Wessex ensured that the kingdom fell rapidly, unlike the more lengthy processes by which the Iron Age and Romano-British kingdoms had fallen to Rome and the Anglo-Saxons respectively. Unlike earlier invaders, Cnut and William seized a kingdom and a throne, and, in effect, London served as its capital. Indeed, William issued a charter to London promising to maintain its laws and customs as in Edward the Confessor's reign.

At heart, however, this was a seizure of power. Perhaps it was Londoners' self-interest and sense of physical and financial self-preservation that helped them decide to stand aloof from the several episodes of serious resistance to Norman conquest during the following years, including in Kent and Shropshire, the Welsh marches and Northumbria. But, equally, it might well have been awe and fear of the Norman military presence now firmly established in their midst. For archaeologists have found evidence that William set to work almost immediately fortifying parts of London, including the south-east corner of the city walls, the site of the Tower of London: 'several strongholds were made ready in the City to safeguard against … the huge and fierce population'. Work on the massive stone keep we now know as the White Tower probably began somewhat later, in the late 1070s, and in the fabric of the Tower there is evidence of a pause in building in the 1080s, perhaps coinciding with a great fire in 1087. But the Norman presence in London was certainly powerful from the very beginning. The keep was an affirmation of military control over a conquered city, one made more necessary because the majority of the population remained English.

Somehow this tiny medieval remnant has survived. It is a small part of a fourteenth-century Augustinian priory that stood near the site of the earlier parish church of St Alphage, itself demolished at the end of the sixteenth century. London Wall, the street, does not in fact follow the alignment of the city walls, which lie to the north.

PHOTOGRAPH: CARNEGIE, 2009

L ONDON'S IMPORTANCE grew greatly in the medieval period, as it benefited enormously from two directions: the development of the city's economy, and of the organs of government at Westminster. As a result, the history of the city and that of state and country came to be linked ever more closely. Yet we should beware of seeking too eagerly early signs of later greatness, for the nature of London's medieval experience was not so very different from that of other, smaller urban centres in the rest of England. London was certainly a significant trading centre, relatively well connected and cosmopolitan, but it could be remarkably provincial and inward-looking too. In the preface to his *Eneydos* (1490), William Caxton, the founder of printing in London and thus in England, recounted a tale of London boatmen who stopped in Kent and could not make themselves understood because the Kentish dialect was so strong. One farmer's wife, indeed, thought they were French because their language was so strange.

Under William the Conqueror, there were two large fortified enclosures within London, at opposite ends of the City. William's construction, at the south-east end, of the White Tower in what was to become known as the Tower of London – now a UNESCO World Heritage Site – testified to the importance attached to London within a regional and indeed national context, and perhaps also to its military strength: William very nearly had to fight to enter it in 1066. At the opposite end of the City, south-west of St Paul's and guarding the route from Westminster near the important City entrance at Ludgate were two further military structures. These were both much smaller than the Tower of London, were not (initially at least) royal castles, and might well have been of relatively slight military effectiveness.

London's great medieval castle, with London Bridge and the city beyond, depicted c.1480. By this date, the Tower of London had evolved and grown, with circuit walls, moat and riverside defences, but the original Tower of William I still dominates the scene. High-quality dressed Norman stone from Caen was used for the corners and windows of the Tower, with reddish Kentish ragstone for the remainder. The name White Tower appears to have been used after 1240, when Henry III had the Tower painted with whitewash.

COPYRIGHT BRITISH LIBRARY, MS ROYAL 16 F.II, FOL. 73, THE POEMS OF CHARLES, DUKE OF ORLEANS

MEDIEVAL DEVELOPMENTS, 1066–1485

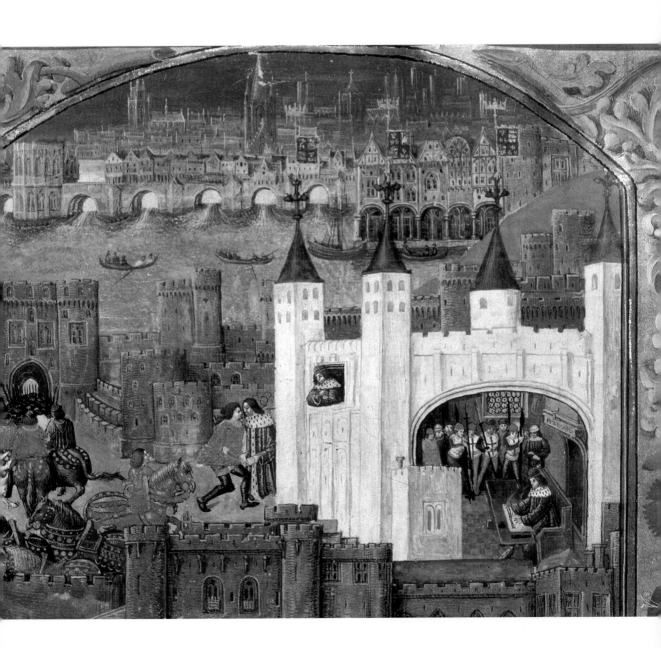

The first was Montfichet's Tower, which had been built near Ludgate by one of William's supporters around 1070: 'Gilbert de Montfichet … a kinsman of the Conqueror, fought stoutly at this battle [Hastings]'; the Tower was demolished in 1213 by King John, who had confiscated the possessions of its then owner. Of greater importance, size and longevity was Baynard's Castle. This was also built shortly after the Conquest, on a site – where the city walls abutted the Thames river bank – that corresponded to that of the Tower of London in the east. Whether London's first historian, John Stow, was correct in believing that 'Edward the 4 tooke on him the crowne in Baynards castell', we do know that the castle buildings survived in at least some form until the Great Fire of 1666.

Combined with the city walls, these castles indicated considerable investment into London's defence as well as into the maintenance of royal and Norman control over the city. William the Conquerer did not seek to work alongside the Anglo-Saxon state, but to overcome and replace it entirely. But in the case of London he felt obliged to nurture support and minimise opposition. Soon after his coronation, therefore, William issued a charter confirming London's laws and customs. In the words of London historian John Northouck (1773), he 'granted a charter to the citizens in their own language; a great favour at a time when the French tongue began to be the prevailing language. This charter consists of four lines and a quarter, beautifully written in the Saxon character, on a slip of parchment of the length of six inches, and breadth of one, which is preserved in the city archives as a great curiosity.'

London was a key point, but not the only one in William's new kingdom. The order for the land survey known as Domesday Book (1086) was not decided by William, the previous year, at Westminster, but at a court held at Gloucester, where William was staying as part of the cycle of Crown-wearings that took him to Winchester, Windsor and Gloucester. Domesday, indeed, omitted both London and Winchester from its coverage. Moreover, in 1086, it was at Salisbury that William held a great assembly in which vassels

renewed their oaths of allegiance. Far from being fixed, early medieval government was mobile, the king and his court eating everything available at one base before moving on to the next. Furthermore, when William's heir, William II, unexpectedly died in the New Forest in 1100, very probably as the result of a hunting accident, the first step of his younger brother, Henry, was to rush to take control of the Treasury at Winchester, as a key step to his seizure of power as Henry I.

At this stage, Westminster was not the formal capital of England, and indeed such a concept was not properly developed and is somewhat anachronistic. Moreover,

Not many wooden effigies survive from the Middle Ages. The most significant of these is perhaps the fifteenth-century wooden tomb effigy of Henry V that survives in Westminster Abbey. Further north there is also a good, unrestored example, probably depicting a monk, near to Bess of Hardwick's tomb in Derby Cathedral. This photograph is of the restored effigy of a knight in Southwark Cathedral which is thought to date from the final decades of the thirteenth century. The cathedral authorities have speculated that the figure might represent a member of the Warenne family, who were major benefactors to the Augustinian priory in Southwark. The Saxon minster at Southwark had become an Augustinian priory in 1106.

PHOTOGRAPH: CARNEGIE, 2009

Winchester, the ancient capital of Wessex, remained important as a royal ceremonial centre. Yet William II had rebuilt in stone the great hall of Edward the Confessor's palace, which is the basis of the Westminster Hall that survives today, thereby underlining Westminster's separate status as a royal residence, independent of London.

Over the subsequent century, London became more important, with the population growing to possibly 10,000 or 15,000 or even 20,000 by 1110 and to over 30,000 a century later, a figure far greater than that for any other city in the British Isles. In this expansion trade was key, and as in later centuries migration to the city was a major factor in growth. Although most incomers arrived from elsewhere in the South East and East Anglia, part of the expanding population came from abroad, including from Normandy. Thus, for example, London provided opportunities for merchants from Rouen.

The gradual strengthening of central government in England, and its particular character, also helped London. The focus of the kings on protecting their ancestral inheritance of Normandy and on their ambitions to secure other territories in France, notably Maine, greatly affected the government of England: the people of England had to pay much of the bill and, also, deal with the consequences of an absent monarch. As a result, while royal powers were put into commission to cope with the absence of successive kings, the administrative development of the Old English state was resumed, and, in particular, government remained 'public' to a far greater extent than in France. While France was little more than a confederacy of princely courts, with that of the king the first among equals, England had not fragmented, and this ensured both need and opportunity for a capital for the state.

Moreover, the business of government was increasingly concentrated in Westminster, both as a result of the movement of functions from Winchester and as a consequence of the lessening of peripatetic kingship. Government in the twelfth century was a dynamic process. The expansion of royal judicial activity under Henry I (r. 1100–35) – focused on Westminster – was matched by the growth of the Exchequer, likewise a court, which provided a regular and methodical collection of royal revenues and control of expenditure. Written records became more common, which was important to the development and consistency of government, and to its need for a permanent base.

These processes continued under Henry's grandson, Henry II (r. 1154–89), with government becoming less dependent on the personal action of the monarch. While government existed to do what the king wanted, its practices ceased to be dictated by him, as it developed its own routines. Westminster was therefore of increasing importance, although it should not be confused or conflated with London itself. For example, to refer to London as where Parliament developed in the thirteenth and fourteenth centuries is unhelpful, as London was exactly where Parliament did not develop: rather, it was a product of the royal, judicial and governmental centre at Westminster. Nevertheless the growth in government activity in Westminster did create a major market for the artisans and merchants of the city, especially for high-value products. And there was constant interaction between London and Westminster, even though the two retained separate identities. Indeed, medieval London should be seen as one of three very different elements in what amounted to a single conurbation: London, Westminster and Southwark.

A turning point came in the 1190s when Hubert Walter, Archbishop of Canterbury, and the effective head of the government from 1193 to 1198 (part of the period in which Richard I, the Lionheart, campaigned abroad), both developed governmental practices and institutions that had a semi-permanent headquarters in Westminster and purchased from the monks of Rochester a section of Lambeth where he created an archepiscopal palace. Under John (r. 1199–1216) the Exchequer and the courts of Common Pleas and the King's Bench were moved to Westminster.

Meanwhile, the centrality of economic factors was suggested by the decision to demolish the Roman river-wall in order to improve opportunities for trade. It is possible that the demolition actually began under Cnut, but more likely in the late eleventh or early twelfth century, at which time a possible further motive was a wish to reduce the City's capacity to resist the Crown.[1] Documentary evidence for the removal of the river-wall is not good, but it can be re-created from the archaeological record;[2] its removal was to be of long-term importance to the history of the city.

Moreover, London's role as a centre of communications, in this case across the Thames, was demonstrated by the replacement of London Bridge, hitherto built from timber, by a stone-arched bridge, designed by Peter of Colechurch, a process that began in 1176 and was completed in about 1209. With its nineteen arches, high gateways, and superstructure accommodating chapel, shops and houses, the bridge impressed contemporaries, and also reflected the administrative sophistication of the City authorities, not only in construction but also in repair, not least from the pressure of the tides, as well as in keeping the bridge clean.[3] Rent from the houses and shops provided the income for these tasks.

The landward city walls were maintained during the medieval period, essentially on the same lines, although with periodical rebuilding in order to keep them in good repair. These walls, part of which can still be seen in St Alphage's Gardens, were built on Roman foundations, a demonstration of the value of the latter. The walls figured prominently in Matthew Paris's illustration of London from his itinerary from London to Jerusalem, which prefaces his *Chronica Majora* of *c*.1252. The Tower, Westminster Abbey and St Paul's were all shown, as were lesser buildings, but the castellated walls were the key feature. The use of Caen stone from Normandy for most of the White Tower, which was intended as palace as well as fortress, reflected the lack of good building stone in the London region. Stone was seen as particularly useful, its use strongly encouraged because of the frequency and destructiveness of fire; long before the Great Fire of the seventeenth century there were several other serious conflagrations, including that of 1212 in which many Londoners

At the dissolution of the monasteries most of the monastic buildings and extensive landholdings of St Bartholomew's Priory in Smithfield, just to the north-west of the city walls, were redeveloped into private houses. Only the eastern half of the main church – the great Romanesque presbytery or choir – survived; seen here, it now serves as the parish church of St Bartholomew the Great, just off Cloth Fair. Bartholomew Fair was held in the grounds of the priory for several days each year (at first from 24 August and from 1753, under the Gregorian calendar, from 3 September) from 1133 until it was suppressed in 1855. The fair was the setting for Ben Jonson's play of that name, first performed in 1614.

PHOTOGRAPH: CARNEGIE, 2009

were trapped on London Bridge as the fire took hold of the timber building on the bridge, destroying them all just three years after Peter of Colechurch's new stone bridge had been completed. The relative paucity of buildings that survive from the medieval period is in part due to continued medieval use of timber.

The impact of Norman building was increased by the pressures of time on the existing urban fabric, as buildings decayed or were destroyed. Thus, the cathedral church of St Paul was devastated by fire in 1087. Its replacement provided an opportunity to create a Romanesque successor to the Anglo-Saxon style, and a work that was as expressive of the new Norman order in religion as was the White Tower in military might. The new church was built by the Normans on a truly colossal scale, comparable almost with Winchester. The choir was begun in about 1090 and the nave some twenty years later. It is not known how long the building process lasted, but there was yet another fire in the 1130s, which slowed progress. The fabric of the Romanesque nave appears to have been mid-twelfth century, and work may not have been completed until the later twelfth century, creating a Romanesque cathedral, with a Gothic rib vault over the nave dated to c.1175–1200, and the west front dated to the 1180s or 1190s at the earliest.[4] The eastern arm of the church was rebuilt and lengthened to twelve bays from 1251 to 1312 in the Gothic style, giving a dramatic vista to the east end with its rose window immortalised in an engraving by Hollar.

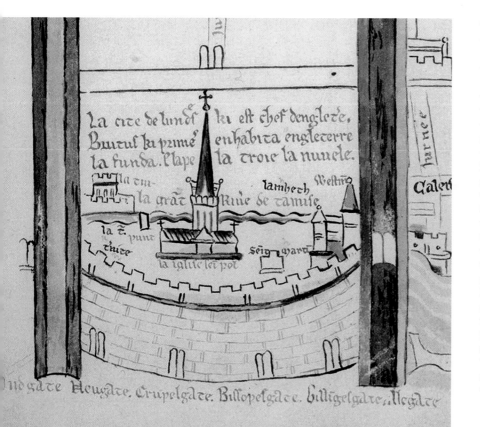

This depiction of London by the St Albans monk Matthew Paris dates from around 1250. It was drawn as part of what has become known as a 'road map' for pilgrims to Jerusalem, although few will actually have carried it with them on the journey, often using it instead as a devotional tool for pious contemplation at home. Significantly, however, the journey starts from London: pilgrims could visit the shrine of Edward the Confessor (Westminster is shown to the right of this drawing), and more pragmatically could get their money exchanged, perhaps to Venetian ducats, in one of the money-houses of Lombard Street. In the drawing St Paul's is in the centre, one of the earliest views of the great medieval cathedral and its tall spire. Some of the city gates are listed along the bottom; the Tower is at the left, and Lambeth dutifully gets a mention too.

The tallest and longest section of surviving city walls stands in Cripplegate, between London Wall and the Barbican estate. Above Roman and early medieval stonework sits a castellated section of very early London brickwork. We can date this work to 1477, when Lord Mayor Sir Ralph Jocelyn 'caused part of the wall about the City of London to be repaired … betwixt Aldgate and Aldersgate. He also caused Moorfield to be searched for clay, and brick thereof to be made and burnt.' Just six years earlier, in 1471, these very walls had seen military action (see page 57), and were clearly still seen to be of considerable defensive value. The use of local London clay for brick-making was a pragmatic development and would develop into a considerable industry in time. Here the brickwork is decorated with a regular diaper pattern of darker bricks, in much the same style as that of the near-contemporary gatehouse of Lambeth Palace (see page 79).

PHOTOGRAPH: CARNEGIE, 2009

At its total extent of 644 feet, Old St Paul's was the longest cathedral in England, with Winchester the second longest at 554 feet. The spire, admittedly only timber, reached 520 feet, much higher than that at Salisbury, which is 404 feet. St Paul's medieval spire was possibly the tallest in Europe, and a building only surpassed in London by the Post Office Tower of 1964. The enormously tall spire figured prominently in all views of the city, which suggests that the citizens took pride in it. Until destroyed by lightning in 1561, the spire of St Paul's was an important part of London's visual identity. The spire was not rebuilt, but the medieval cathedral church itself survived until the Great Fire of 1666.

The political importance of London was an aspect of its role in government, not least as a key source of finance, through taxation and, particularly, from the fourteenth century, as a source of loans; but the role of the city was not restricted to this activity. Instead, London played an important part at key moments in national history and of crisis, as a reprise of the part it had frequently played in the eleventh century. Moreover, this role was not simply a matter of the use by others of London as a venue for action but, rather, of activity by Londoners themselves, which took forward the situation already seen in the eleventh century. In 1135, for example, the city's support for Stephen of Blois, William I's grandson through the female line, was a major step in his progress towards the throne. The contemporary *Gesta Stephani*, which called London 'the capital, the queen of the whole kingdom', recorded that the citizens claimed that 'it was their own right and particular privilege that if their king died from any cause a successor should immediately be appointed by their own choice'. The citizens certainly exaggerated, but it is interesting that they should have seen themselves in such a light.

The citizens were as loyal to Stephen thereafter as circumstances permitted during the lengthy civil war with Henry I's daughter Matilda, who also claimed the throne. Matilda appeared in the ascendant after her capture of Stephen at the battle of Lincoln in 1141, but crucially she alienated London. The 'commune'[5] of 1141, in which citizens and barons joined, asked Matilda for permission to live under the laws of Edward the Confessor, rather than those of Henry I, which were harsher, but she refused, which consolidated London support for Stephen. The war was finally ended in 1153, by which date London's own system of government was well established, with wards and parishes providing the necessary structures. The pressure of the war probably speeded this process of consolidation. Thus, government was a key theme, with the growth of civic consciousness, the move towards the commune, and the emergence of municipal institutions and organisations. The City was the first in Britain to develop institutions of this type, and while the City government became a major political and financial force by the fourteenth century, there were already important developments in the twelfth century. Thus, London shared in the powerful wave of civic self-determination and the emergence of institutions of popular government that had began in Pisa in 1063 and spread northwards and westwards across Europe.

London was again to play a major role in the crisis of King John's reign (1199–1216). The barons opposed to John were able to march straight into the City through gates left open for them, although a royal force held onto the Tower and resisted them, until the Tower was transferred to the keeping of the Archbishop of Canterbury. The Mayor of London was one of the twenty-five men responsible for enforcing Magna Carta, and constitutionally the whole baronial movement might have been influenced by recent developments in the structure of government of the City.[6] London was the target for so much military action because it had become the most important place, politically and economically. It was not only shaping developments, but also vulnerable to external threats.

A key theme in London's history in the Middle Ages was that of relations with the Crown, and there was a determination to entrench the City's situation by preserving the privileges that could be claimed. In a society that was referential to the past and reverential of it, this process was based heavily upon precedent and perceptions of history. Thus, in the twelfth century, there was a desire to preserve the laws associated with Edward the Confessor, a process aided by the progressive enhancement of his reputation. Edward had issued a writ confirming the laws and jurisdiction of the London guild of *cnihtas*, and this writ was placed on the altar of the London priory of Holy Trinity, Aldgate, in 1125 as confirmation of the guild's gift of land and rights. A link can be drawn thence to the 1191 commune, which advanced claims for the City's interests, and, in turn, brought together Londoners of both English and Norman ancestry.[7] The latter was important because a particular point of the city's identity was that it took precedence over differences in ancestry and lineage and, instead, brought otherwise distinct groups into a commonality of shared identity and interest. This process was successful so that, by 1191, the distinction between Anglo-Saxons and post-1066 settlers was more or less obsolete.

There was also the development of a sense of identity expressed in specific laws and customs, most prominently a collection, known as the London Collection, that was assembled in the early thirteenth century during the period of opposition to King John. Pride in London's history played a role in this assertiveness, a pride also seen in William fitz Stephen's account of the City written in about 1173 and put at the start of his life of Thomas Becket, the London-born Archbishop of Canterbury. Aside from repeating Geoffrey of Monmouth's account of a Trojan origin for the city, fitz Stephen claimed that London matched Rome in its governmental system. Discussion in Stephen's reign also included reference to London as the capital and its citizens, as a result, as in effect barons.[8]

In a parallel process, various craft and mercantile guilds emerged, defined their roles, and asserted their economic and political interests, controlling local production and trade in a process involving regulation, lobbying, litigation and violence. These guilds, which were to become the City Livery Companies of a later age, facilitated the spatial and social differentiation of the city. Thus, the major craft centres focused on the West Cheap while, for example, Old Fish Street and Bread Street were both names with meaning. The guilds were also linked to the dense and varied texture of ecclesiastical foundations and activity.

The first Mayor of London, Henry Fitz-Ailwin de Londonestone, served from 1189 until his death in 1212. London profited well from the political turbulence of the twelfth century, as the City managed to secure incremental enhancements to its ability to govern its own affairs. In 1141, under King Stephen, London's right to choose its own sheriffs was confirmed; then in 1189 Richard I's desire to raise money by way of taxes and loans from rich London merchants resulted in the establishment of the post of an elected Mayor (as opposed to a royal appointment), in a similar manner to those of Liege and Rouen. Further concessions were granted by William Longchamp, Chief Justiciar and key figure in Richard I's absence on crusade, and by King John, all of which left London in a powerful position of autonomy and a possible thorn in the side of the monarchy. This modest statue of 'Fitz-Eylwin' can be found high up upon Holborn Viaduct, which was built to cross Farringdon Street in the 1860s.

PHOTOGRAPH: CARNEGIE, 2009

Tax records from the lay subsidy of 1332 reveal the patterns of work and wealth in the medieval City. Organised by ward, these records highlight the importance of internal as well as international trade: a line of wards with wealthy taxpayers, from the Tower to the Vintry, shows the importance of trade via the river Thames. Many people were engaged in fishmongering from Bridge and Billingsgate to Queenhithe, but of much greater wealth were those associated with the wool trade, whose merchants paid large sums in tax from wards such as Tower and Dowgate, where the Steelyard was located. In another tax assessment of 1319, for instance, most of Dowgate's wealthier taxpayers were associated with wool, including the drapers Stephen, son of Richard de Abbendon and Henry Nasard, both of whom were assessed for 100s. in tax. The 1332 tax rolls show John de Oxenford, a wealthy wine merchant of the Vintry, the pepperer Benedict de Fulsham, cordwainers and saddlers in Farringdon Within, and the goldsmiths of Cheapside including John Makeheved in Bread Street.

London's importance ensured that public pressure on the political system focused there, as in its crucial role in the overthrow of Edward II in 1326. London's earlier support for

Four three or four hundred years before their dissolution by Henry VIII, monastic establishments abounded around the perimeter of London. None was founded right in the commercial or residential heart of the City, although the Crutched Friars (1249) had a site near Tower Hill, and both the Blackfriars and Greyfriars had sites within the western run of the city walls. One of the earliest and most influential foundations was the Augustinian priory of Holy Trinity, Aldgate, which enjoyed royal patronage as well as attracting bequests from London citizens. At one time the priory's business affairs extended to no fewer than 87 of the City's parishes, showing how intertwined religious concerns were with commercial and land-holding interests. In the early fifteenth century, it was decided to bring together the priory's valuable business documents into one volume, which survives as the Aldgate Cartulary. Mostly in Latin, and containing around 1,000 documents brought together in 205 folios, the cartulary was the brainchild of Thomas de Axbridge between 1425 and 1427: For 'the world,' bemoaned the monk, 'has progressed to such evil and contradicts ancient facts unless copies of charters are everywhere produced in evidence.' On this folio we see some well-executed floral patterns and a representation of a mitred cleric (bottom right), who might or might not be associated with the priory.

These late fourteenth- or early fifteenth-century funeral effigies were originally in the City church of St Martin Outwich near Bishopsgate, but were transferred to St Helen's when the former church was demolished in 1874. They depict John de Oteswich and his wife.

PHOTOGRAPH: CARNEGIE, WITH PERMISSION

Edward's political opponents had led the king to launch an eyre in 1321 in order to enforce royal justice and to challenge and forfeit London's rights. In 1326, amid the mounting political crisis, order in the city collapsed and the Treasurer, Walter de Stapeldon, Bishop of Exeter, who had been left in charge when Edward fled London, was killed in Cheapside, precipitating the fall of Edward's government.

Public pressure was most dramatically seen with the Peasants' Revolt in 1381, when, with the help of dissatisfied Londoners, the rebels, from rural areas in south-east England, occupied the city. The Tower of London was seized; John of Gaunt's Savoy Palace on Strand – considered the grandest and richest aristocratic house in the country – was destroyed and ransacked; and prominent figures were murdered, including Simon of Sudbury, Archbishop of Canterbury and Chancellor, who was responsible for the unpopular poll tax. Seeking the abolition of serfdom and also targeting foreigners, the rebels did not wish to create a new governmental system, but, rather, to pressurise the young king, Richard II, into changes of policy that would demonstrate their concept of good kingship. On 15 June 1381, as the crisis continued, Richard met the main body of the rebels under Wat Tyler at Smithfield. During the meeting, William Walworth, Mayor of London, believing that Tyler was threatening Richard, lunged forward and stabbed him in the neck, whereupon one of the king's knights despatched him with a sword through the stomach. Astutely, Richard averted further violence by promising to be the rebels' leader, but, as soon as the rebels returned home, Richard revoked his promises and punished the leaders.

London continued as a volatile part of the political world. In 1426, competition for control of the realm during the minority of Henry VI between Humphrey, Duke of

Gloucester, the young king's uncle, and Cardinal Henry Beaufort, led to Parliament's being held at Leicester, rather than London, where Gloucester's popularity had given rise to fears of violence. A generation later, in 1450, London was overrun by rebels as it had been in 1381. Cade's Rebellion in Kent reflected anger about extortion by manorial officials, as well as widespread hostility to the government. Having defeated a royal army at Sevenoaks, the rebels seized London and killed unpopular officials, including James Fiennes, Lord Saye and Sele, who had recently been Treasurer, before, having withdrawn to Southwark for the night, being prevented by the citizens from recrossing into the City. The drawbridge at the centre of London Bridge proved a key point of conflict. As in 1381, a royal pardon destroyed the cohesion of the rebels, and Cade was subsequently captured in Sussex. While in London, he had initially benefited from a measure of local support that in part reflected divisions within the City government. Henry VI's response to the rising was distinctly unimpressive: he ran away, despite attempts by the Mayor to persuade him to stay, even offering to pay his household expenses for six months if he would do so. This cravenness helped inspire subsequent Yorkist sympathies in the city.

London also took an autonomous role in the Wars of the Roses, the civil wars that began in the mid-1450s, finally ending with the victories of Henry VII in 1485–87 and the establishment of the Tudor dynasty. London's role was not simply confined to being the location for political murder – of the deposed Henry VI in 1471; of Edward IV's brother, George, Duke of Clarence, allegedly drowned in a butt of malmsey wine, in 1478; and of Edward V and his brother Richard, Duke of York, the young Princes in the Tower, in 1483 – all of which happened in the Tower. Richard III's usurpation of the throne in 1483 was London-based, launched as it was by a sermon at Paul's Cross and a speech in the Guildhall. Richard appreciated the importance of London's support, or at any rate its tolerance.

In addition, the city took a political role, in particular successfully defying the Lancastrians under Queen Margaret of Anjou, wife of Henry VI, in 1461 after their victory at St Albans, a battle in which many Londoners had fought for the unsuccessful Yorkists. It was thus the Londoners, rather than Richard, Earl of Warwick (who, indeed, had been defeated at St Albans), who acted as the true 'kingmaker' in that year, and, without London's backing, there would have been no Yorkist dynasty. There was continuity with the Londoners' role in the civil war of Stephen's reign, when Matilda, victorious over Stephen at Lincoln in 1041, had been defied. These battles confirmed the sense that, whoever held London, held England. Yet, there were also contrasts: Matilda was admitted to London until she made herself so objectionable that the citizens threw her out, whereas Margaret was not once allowed inside the walls.

The political engagement of the citizens was shown once again in 1460 when Thomas Bourchier, Lord Scales, was murdered by boatmen while on his way to seek sanctuary at Westminster. He had commanded the Tower for the Lancastrians, firing guns into the City, until forced, by lack of food, to surrender. Eleven years later, Thomas Neville, the Bastard of Fauconberg, a Lancastrian commander, was repulsed by the citizens in hard fighting, as well as by the garrison under Anthony Woodville, Lord Scales, when he tried to fight his way in via Aldgate. In revenge, he burned down the eastern suburbs, which were not protected by the walls. Fauconberg was offered a pardon if he surrendered, but the promised was broken, and he was hanged, drawn and quartered, 'hys hedd … sett uppon London Brydge, lokyng into Kent warde …' as a deterrent to other would-be attackers. In contrast with Henry VI and Margaret, Edward IV (r. 1461–70, 1471–83) worked very hard to win the loyalty of London and its leading citizens, on one occasion inviting the Mayor and Aldermen to join him on a hunting party in Waltham Forest.

The crises of the Wars of the Roses revealed, as earlier crises had done, that London opinion was divided. These divisions reflected the complex and varied alignment of London identities and interests, but, in addition, there was a systemic tension between the politically prominent citizens of the City, who generally sought good relations with the Crown, and other elements that were willing at times to take a more oppositional stance. This tension was seen in 1461, when the willingness of the City authorities to supply the Lancastrians was thwarted by the populace, who shut the gates.

Serious factionalism within the city had been seen a century earlier, in the 1370s. Sir

Richard Whittington's is not the only tale of a young provincial man of relatively modest means being attracted by the glistening opportunities afforded by London. William Walworth, seen here in a niche above Holborn Viaduct, arrived in London from Durham to serve an apprenticeship with the Company of Fishmongers. He rose to be alderman of Bridge Ward Within and eventually to be Lord Mayor twice, in 1374 and, famously, in 1380. For William earned his knighthood for helping Richard II in his hour of need during the Peasants' Revolt. Not only did Lord Mayor Walworth raise the guard in the king's cause; he also sprang forward to wound the rebel leader Wat Tyler when it appeared that the king's life might be in danger (a dagger kept in Fishmongers' Hall was thought to be that used in this famous deed, but now appears to be much later in date). In the 1590s London-born romance writer Richard Johnson (1573–1659) compiled a book entitled *Nine Worthies of London*, highlighting the careers of men of humble origin who went on to thrive, prosper or achieve fame in London. Alongside Walworth, the others chosen by Johnson were: Sir Henry Pritchard, a hugely wealthy vintner; Sir William Sevenoke, a grocer, philanthropist and Lord Mayor who built almshouses and a school; Sir Thomas White, a merchant tailor from a poor family who founded St John's College, Oxford, and went on to become Lord Mayor of London; Sir John Bonham, a mercer who made a fortune overseas; Christopher Croker, another vintner; Sir John Hawkwood, son of a tanner from Essex; Sir Hugh Calverley, a silk weaver; and the crusading Sir Henry Maleverer, a grocer of Cornhill.

PHOTOGRAPH: CARNEGIE, 2009

A medieval roof boss from the cathedral at Southwark.

The tiny church St Ethelburga-the-Virgin within Bishopsgate had an equally tiny parish, of just 3 acres. The building survived the Great Fire but was devastated by an IRA bomb in 1993.

Nicholas Brembre, who became Mayor in 1377, was close to Richard II, raising an armed force to back him during the Peasants' Revolt. Brembre was supported by the Grocers' and Fishmongers' companies; the former was the dominant company in the city, which helped in the manipulation of mayoral elections. One of Brembre's principal rivals, John of Northampton, a draper elected Mayor in 1381, was the head of a faction linked to John of Gaunt, Duke of Lancaster, Richard II's uncle, and this faction was linked to the interests of the smaller companies and the populace as opposed to the greater companies, especially the Grocers and the Fishmongers, and their dominance of the city. In turn, Brembre's election in 1381 led to the Fishmongers recovering their position, and in 1384 Brembre had John arrested. Tried before Richard II, John was imprisoned, but, in turn, released with the rise of the opposition to Richard that led to Brembre's fall: in 1388, Brembre was one of the advisors of Richard impeached by the Merciless Parliament and executed.

Yet, as a reminder of the difficulty of analysing politics, a discussion in terms of the clash of rival interest groups centring on the victuallers and the non-victuallers (Grocers and Drapers) can seem too schematic, just as tricky as attempting to discern a fault-line of 'natives versus foreigners'. In practice politics operated more flexibly, with fluid interest groups that might come together in different ways at different times, often under the leadership of particularly charismatic civic leaders, such as John of Northampton. He can be seen as the 'Red Ken' of his day, stirring up opposition to the establishment, at least in part to advance his own interests.

London's position as a key site of contention continued after the Wars of the Roses. In 1497, the Cornish rising focused on London, upon which the Cornish rebels marched, but Henry VII gathered an army at London and defeated the Cornishmen at Blackheath. The political centrality reflected in these episodes was an expression of London's role as the site of legitimation and, as such, London's place reflected and encouraged a growing geographical fixity in the state. The modern concept of a specific capital is not one that would have been recognised in the twelfth century, hence the slow erosion in the status of Winchester and the rise of London, while York retained an important *de facto* role as a northern capital as late as the seventeenth century.

Round churches are rare in England. Like the church of the Holy Sepulchre in Cambridge (c.1130), the round nave of Temple Church (1185), seen here, was inspired by that of Holy Sepulchre in Jerusalem.

The rectangular chancel, which extends to the right of this view, was added half a century after the nave was consecrated. The modern statue atop the column shows two knights sharing one horse, a reference to the Templars' poverty, somewhat ironic since with papal blessing (and tax concessions), they had grown enormously wealthy in the twelfth century, benefiting from charitable donations towards their crusading work. In London the order came to own a significant parcel of land to the west of the City, between Fleet Street and the river. In 1307 the Papacy brutally suppressed the Templars, and their London property passed to Edward II, who in turn rented the land to lawyers, an association which remains to this day in the form of Inner and Middle Temple, whose church the Temple Church remains.

PHOTOGRAPH: CARNEGIE, 2009

Within the Temple Church are several effigies of knights, including (*far left*) those of Geoffrey de Mandeville (d. 1144), Keeper of the Tower, first Earl of Essex, and a key figure in the civil war of Stephen's reign, and William Marshal, first Earl of Pembroke (1146–1219) (*right*), considered by the Archbishop of Canterbury to be 'the greatest knight that ever lived'.

PHOTOGRAPHS: CARNEGIE, 2009, WITH THANKS TO THE CHURCH AUTHORITIES

A key change was that the centre of government ceased to be peripatetic, both within England and in the Anglo-French dynastic polity as a whole. Thus, in part, London's political rise was a product of the decline of what had begun in 1066 as an Anglo-Norman or Anglo-French polity. The relative importance of the 'French' dominions was declining by the early thirteenth century, when John lost Normandy (1204), Maine, Brittany and Anjou to Philip Augustus of France; although Edward III not only succeeded in holding on to what he had left, but also sought to reverse the decline in the mid-fourteenth century, launching the Hundred Years' War and laying claim to the French throne. Moreover, Edward I, Edward II, Edward III and Richard II at times all moved the centre of government to York when war with Scotland made this convenient. Indeed, Edward I kept the courts and exchequer there from 1298 to 1304. Such movements could not, however, prevent a change in the focus of the monarchy towards London, which was linked to the development not only of the court as a place of royal residence, but also of more fixed governmental offices. As officials and records congregated in what became the centre of government, so the logic of treating it as the centre of politics also grew. London's role in Magna Carta played a part in this, while the pageantry associated with the monarchy at coronations and joyeuses entrées was also significant.

This process of treating London as the centre of politics could also be seen with Parliament. Initially, quasi-parliamentary bodies, and indeed Parliament, did not meet only in Westminster. The Provisions of Oxford (1258), by which the barons sought to take power out of the hands of Henry III, were not issued in London, although a subsequent set of Provisions was published at Westminster in 1259. In 1301 the future Edward II was created Prince of Wales at a Parliament held in Lincoln, and in 1330 Parliament met in Nottingham, providing the occasion for Edward III's seizure of power from his mother Isabella and her lover, Roger Mortimer. Just as the composition of Parliament was fairly fluid for many years, so the same was true of its organisation. However, the practice that Parliament met in Westminster grew steadily. Parliament was still meeting outside Westminster on occasions in the first fifty or sixty years of the fifteenth century: at Leicester in 1414 and 1426, Bury St Edmunds in 1447, Reading in 1453, and Winchester, Coventry and Leicester in the successive sessions of the Parliament of 1449–50. The reasons for meeting outside Westminster were broadly twofold. Sometimes kings and their councillors felt the need to impress royal authority on a particular part of the country for a particular reason. In 1414, for example, the heresy of Lollardy stood high on the government's agenda and Leicester was a centre of Lollardy. Equally, there might be occasions when the government was fearful of trouble in Westminster and wanted to retreat to its political heartland. This was the case in 1459 when, in the dying years of Lancastrian kingship as the Wars of the Roses gathered pace, Queen Margaret, wife of Henry VI, moved the political centre of the regime back to the Lancastrian heartlands of Leicester and Coventry.

Nevertheless, the general settling down of Parliament in Westminster gathered pace in the second half of the fifteenth century, in the Yorkist period. Although parliamentary sessions were adjourned to York in 1464 and to Reading in 1467, parliaments were not generally held outside Westminster in the Yorkist years: London was safe as it was a generally Yorkist city. There was a parallel trend in the same period for parliaments to become longer, in the sense of being stretched over several sessions. The MPs always preferred meetings in London because hotel accommodation was more easily available: MPs principally stayed in the cheap accommodation provided by inns, but those who were magnate retainers might well have stayed in the great town houses of their employers. Bishops and peers purchased London houses for this purpose.

Increasingly law courts also met in London. Prefiguring the impact of the Reformation in the sixteenth century and the dissolution of the monasteries in the late 1530s, the lawyers benefited from an earlier dissolution of a religious institution, as well as from the increased governmental role of London. From 1161, the Knights Templar had owned the New Temple, an important area to the south of Fleet Street as well as their first and largest house. After the dissolution of the order, which was accused of heresy, Edward II gave the Temple to the Earl of Pembroke; subsequently it came into the hands of the younger Hugh Despenser, following whose execution in 1326 as part of the overthrow of Edward II, it reverted to the Crown. Then the Pope decreed that all Templar property should be transferred to the Knights to the Hospital of St John. In turn, the Hospitallers around 1340 leased the Temple to lawyers, who held it thereafter. This area became the site for societies of lawyers which, by 1388, had adopted the names of the Inner and the Middle Temple. These societies were the centre of the legal profession; as there was no university in London, so legal education developed outside a university context.

The royal law courts had already settled in Westminster, with King's Bench and Common Pleas normally meeting there from the thirteenth century. In Westminster Hall, these courts were separated from one another, and from the throng of humanity, by wooden partitions. Then, in 1268, the Council of London, under the guidance of Cardinal Ottobono, the papal legate, enacted important new regulations for the English Church. Here, as in so many fields of activity, London could be seen to be of great national significance, right at the heart of affairs.

Meanwhile, London's governmental system developed apace. The City was divided into twenty-four wards by 1127, each with its own alderman. Farringdon ward was split in two in 1394, while the modern complement of twenty-six wards finally came into being in 1550 with the creation of Bridge Ward Without, the only ward south of the Thames. This development was a matter of internal differentiation, and partly a product of negotiations with the Crown. Although Anglo-Saxon urbanism owed much to royal direction, there was significant autonomy in London prior to the Norman Conquest, with the City having its own courts as well as distinctive customs and laws. The quest for autonomy was driven forward subsequently, for both practical and symbolic reasons, and this quest gathered pace in the twelfth century. As early as the reign of Henry I, London gained from the Crown the right to appoint its sheriff and justiciar and to collect royal revenues in the City, the latter in return for an annual payment that, in effect, lessened the scope of royal officials. However, twelfth-century kings were extremely guarded in their response to bids for civic independence, Henry II particularly so. It was only Richard I's desperate need for cash to finance his participation in the Third Crusade, and then to pay his ransom, that led to his breaking with his father's policy. In 1191, Richard, who was then raising funds by selling privileges, recognised the 'commune' of London, a term borrowed from French usage. This entity, which was a reprise of the situation achieved under different circumstances during Stephen's reign, was confirmed by King John in Magna Carta (1215). Richard also gave the City the ability to negotiate directly with the Crown. The Angevin kings were also forthcoming with charters and privileges to other towns.

The independence displayed by London posed a problem for John and his successor, Henry III (r. 1216–72). Henry's very prickly relationship with London helps account for his advancing the position of Westminster, for example by building the Abbey. As a consequence, it was not surprising that the Londoners were staunch supporters of Simon de Montfort in his opposition to Henry in 1258–65. In 1264 a large contingent of Londoners served in

This bronze statue of Richard I (r. 1189–99), by the Italian sculptor Baron Carlo (Charles) Marochetti was placed outside the House of Lords in 1860, and captures the Lionheart well as noble warrior king and pious crusader against Saladin. In fact, Richard spoke practically no English and spent hardly any time as king in England. His main significance for London was that he was captured after returning from the Third Crusade; the Holy Roman Emperor demanded a ransom of 150,000 marks, which had to be raised by a harsh tax assessment of a quarter of the value of all religious and secular property. Before the Crusade Henry II had already imposed a huge 'Saladin Tax', and for some hard-pressed citizens this new tax was too much to bear. Even the wool crop of the Cistercian and Gilbertine houses was seized. In London in 1196 opposition to the tax was led by one William Fitz Osbert, a crusader in Portugal who returned to London and put himself at the head of the city's poor, making rousing and dangerous speeches outside St Paul's against the tax and also the City authorities. Richard I's Justiciar, Hubert Walter, felt he had to act against this demagogue and besieged Fitz Osbert in the sanctuary of St Mary-le-Bow on Cheapside, reportedly burning down the church in order to capture him. He and nine followers were hanged, although the poor of London continued to venerate Fitz Osbert for some time afterwards.

This is the exact view that would have greeted the rebel leader and Guardian of Scotland, William Wallace, at his trial for treason against Edward I of England in 1305 (he was found guilty and executed brutally at Smithfield). No building in Scotland could compare with this, for Westminster Hall has by far the largest wooden hammerbeam roof in Britain. Given the frequency with which London's medieval wooden fabric succumbed to fire, this is a hugely important early survival from the Middle Ages. In 1305, at the time of Wallace's trial, the roof was probably supported by tall pillars to give three separate aisles. By the time that a second treason trial – of Charles I of England and Scotland – took place here in 1649, the pillars had been removed to leave this vast, open space at the heart of the palace of Westminster. Both defendants, Wallace and Charles sat, separated by 350 years, on the steps from where this photograph was taken. Also held here were coronation banquets (the last for George IV in 1821) and royal lyings-in-state (the last being for the Queen Elizabeth, the Queen Mother, in 2002).

PHOTOGRAPH: CARNEGIE, 2009

de Montfort's army when he defeated and captured Henry at Lewes.

The sole English city to have tried to develop some independence in the twelfth and thirteenth centuries was the very city which at the same time was becoming the centre of settled royal presence and national government. Thus, London's short-lived ambitions represented on-the-spot tension with the Crown. In other circumstances, we might have imagined that regional distance from royal government could have led to urban ambition, but it did not. Provincial towns supported the Crown.

London's opposition to Henry III underlay much in the poor relations of his son, Edward I, with the City, as Edward had been a firm opponent of de Montfort, defeating him at Evesham in 1265 and restoring his father to power. As king, Edward I (r. 1272–1307) revoked the City's liberties and installed a government under his own officers from 1285 to 1299. Edward's reign thus saw a major reaffirmation of royal power in London, not least also with the building of an important extension of the royal castle. The White Tower was encircled not only by a strongly defensive, towered curtain wall but also by substantial river defences and a broad moat. This development was important to the extent to which, from then on, London was increasingly the royal capital,⁹ and not a town following an independent political course. The exceptional power and authority of the Crown in England and its strong centralising tendencies were key factors in London's development. The Crown granted a wide range of privileges but, as with the nobility, was less and less prepared to see alternative power bases emerge. As a result, London was very different from some of the major European cities of the later Middle Ages which, in effect, operated like urban republics, especially in Italy, Germany, the Low Countries and the Baltic, for example Ghent. London's fundamental role in the overthrow of Edward II in 1326 reflected its continuing capacity for pursuing its own course, but it did so as a central part of the kingdom and not in opposition to it.

The complex relationship between Crown and City was intertwined with that between London and Westminster, which had a distinct juridical and administrative identity, with the Abbot of Westminster as its lord. While the monarch had the Tower as military

The great White Tower constructed during the first forty years of Norman rule was later surrounded by a succession of walls and defensive towers. On the far left here is Beauchamp Tower, part of the first major thirteenth-century curtain wall. The imposing gatehouse in the centre of this photograph is Byward Tower, part of the next set of encircling defences that were built by Edward I, probably England's greatest castle-building monarch. This was the main entrance to the whole complex, and visitors would already have had to negotiate a barbican, an outer gatehouse (the now vanished 'Lion Tower' associated with the royal menagerie), and another large gatehouse (the surviving Middle Tower). The shallow arch on the walkway crossed the moat, which was drained in 1830. In 2007 there was talk of refilling the moat in time for the 2012 Olympics.

PHOTOGRAPH: CARNEGIE, 2009

fortress, Westminster (and Whitehall) were the principal royal palaces. The two centres were physically very close and could hardly manage without one another, especially after the loss of Normandy in 1204, which meant that the monarch was generally no longer overseas for years at a time; but they were also always rubbing against one another. The City made bids for independence, which the king slapped down as far as he could, as he could not afford to lose control of a community whose size, wealth and volatility made it potentially very dangerous politically, as several kings discovered. Crucially the king also needed the City's money, not least from the fourteenth century, when Italian loans were no longer forthcoming.

Tension between Crown and City slackened under Edward III (r. 1327–77), a conciliatory ruler as far as domestic issues (not the French) were concerned. His promotion of Windsor meant that he was often at a distance from London, but he spent much more time in the South East than his predecessors did, and was probably nearer to London more of the time than Edward I. In his later years, in particular, Edward III spent his time largely in palaces close to London, at Sheen and King's Langley in particular. Tension between Crown and London, nevertheless, lasted intermittently at least until the Civil War (1642–46), in which London's support for Parliament was arguably decisive, before tension revived under the later Stuarts, especially in the 1680s.

The achievement of autonomy by the Londoners under a mayor elected from among the aldermen rested on the strength of the local government offered by the ward system. Although each ward was headed by an alderman, a prominent figure who represented the oligarchic tendencies in the City, the ward also had a wardmote or local forum. The council or court of aldermen lent coherence to the City's government, while the self-regard of the leading citizens was indicated by their calling themselves barons. This designation suggested equality with the landed élite and was a sign of rivalry and distance, also seen for example in the extent to which London's merchants held back from involvement in tournaments and heraldic display until the 1470s.[10]

Local governmental structures and a political culture focused on cohesion did help to limit social division within London, but many tensions remained within the City, with status providing a key issue. Citizenship became an earned right, given in return for membership of a guild, itself secured either by apprenticeship or by purchase, and by payment through civic taxation; this citizenship was marked by taking the civic oath. In return, economic privileges and legal rights were granted, notably the rights to buy and sell property, to trade and to enjoy the protection of the courts. Importantly, from 1319, would-be citizens had to gain the approval of those already practising that trade, and citizenship was dependent upon support from existing trade associations. Those excluded were called 'foreigners', irrespective of their place of birth, and most were confined to poorly paid occupations. Those who were literally foreign made recurrent bids for citizenship.

When this impressive water gate – St Thomas's Tower – was built in the 1270s, it stood right on the river bank. Access to the tower could only be gained by boat via the gated archway in the centre. The wharf in the foreground was begun around a hundred years later, and a short waterway was constructed to give continued access from the river: just visible in this photograph is the blocked-up archway on the wharf, above which are the words 'Entry to the Traitors' Gate'.

PHOTOGRAPH (FROM TOWER BRIDGE): CARNEGIE, 2009

The original water gate of St Thomas's Tower, seen from the wharf. This major entrance to the Tower complex became known as Traitors' Gate in the seventeenth century, after several famous victims passed this way to execution on Tower Green.

PHOTOGRAPH: CARNEGIE, 2009

In the economy several complementary developments during the high Middle Ages were of importance to London. Nationally trade and commerce became more intense in England in the twelfth century, with the development of markets and ports, and, in the thirteenth, the increasingly market-orientated nature of part of the English agrarian economy produced more wealth for taxation; about 30–40 per cent of all grain grown was marketed, while there was also a significant rise in wool exports from the twelfth century. The agrarian economy helped provide for a growing urban sector, while the increase in commerce fostered urban development.

The substantial yields of royal revenues were visible in the rebuilding of Westminster Abbey by Henry III, who also promoted the cult of Edward the Confessor as part of a tradition of a divinely appointed kingship and as an intensely personal devotion. He identified himself very closely with St Edward, a ruler who was devout, wise and peaceful, qualities he could see in himself. The loss of Anjou deprived the dynasty of its burial site at Fontevrault, while Westminster was also developed in rivalry with St Denis, where the French royal mausoleum was enhanced by Louis IX, Saint Louis. More generally, royal favour helped lead to an increase in Westminster's income. Henry's contributions included enlarging the palace at Westminster, as well as beginning the royal menagerie at the Tower of London, which included an elephant house. Henry III was buried at Westminster in 1272, as was Edward I in 1307 in the royal mausoleum established by his father.

Edward, however, had been unfavourably influenced against the abbey when the treasure he had deposited in the crypt was stolen in 1303, a robbery helped by some of the monks, which led to ten of them being sent to the Tower, while six others were executed.[11] Subsequently, there was a lengthy break in Westminster's expansion because Edward II took little interest while Edward III rebuilt Windsor Castle as a centre of chivalry and royal residence. Thereafter, the expansion of Westminster continued, with

Parts of the Guildhall, including the walls, date back to a major rebuilding in the early fifteenth century, and there is archaeological evidence for a much earlier civic building on this site, perhaps making use of Roman alignments and even fabric (part of this is the site of the Roman amphitheatre). Several important trials took place here, as well as meetings of the Corporation. It is without doubt one of the most remarkable early civic buildings in Britain.

PHOTOGRAPH: CARNEGIE, 2009, WITH THANKS TO THE CITY OF LONDON

A detail of the 'Copperplate' map showing central London, c.1559. This is a real jumble of late-medieval wooden buildings, cramped streets and courtyards. The river Thames is at the bottom, with London Bridge just visible below the church of St Magnus the Martyr. Along the riverbank are the important Hanseatic warehouses and wharf of the 'Stilliards'. On Cannon Street the 'London Stone' still sits in the centre of the street. Part of St Mary-le-Bow is visible off the left-hand side of this section of the map, and in the centre of Cheapside, just to the right of the church, can be seen the Great Conduit that brought at least some fresh water into the city centre.

Richard II rebuilding Westminster Hall and also financing work on the abbey church and making generous gifts to the monks. Richard, like Henry III, was devoted to Edward the Confessor. However, the palace's role was affected by royal absences abroad, notably by Edward III and Henry V during their wars in France.

From 1066 there was also increasing subdivision of plots within the existing structure of London's property boundaries. At the same time, the city's physical fabric became more fixed, in part possibly due to the increased use of stone for building. Other English towns also achieved a remarkable degree of stability in boundaries between parishes and properties at this time, a stability that extended well beyond the Middle Ages.

This fixity also became one of image, notably with the City's common seal, the 'Seal of the Barons of London', produced in about 1220. The impact of religion was seen with the depiction of St Paul and St Thomas Becket on the respective sides of the seal, but there was also a panorama of London: one side of the seal shows St Paul standing in the middle of the City, directly behind one of its gates, holding an upright sword in one hand and the banner of England in the other, with the circuit of walls round his feet, along with London's two castles, the Tower and Baynard's Castle, at each end, and not only St Paul's right in front of him but several other churches as well, suggesting a rather spectacular skyline.

London's population growth, by natural increase and immigration, was especially rapid in the late thirteenth century, rising possibly to about 80,000 in the early fourteenth century, so that it was the only British city to fall into a 'European' category of serious size. The city went on expanding north and east throughout the thirteenth century. Economic growth also prompted the development of the urban infrastructure. The provision of an effective water supply was especially important, and supported the population in a relatively healthy fashion.[12] Springs near Bond Street produced water that was piped via the 'Great Conduit' to Cheapside along a lead pipe installed in the mid-thirteenth century, a system that continued in use until the Great Fire of 1666. Another scheme, for clearing out of the City Ditch – necessary in light of the health hazards posed by fetid water – was promoted by Sir John Philipot, Lord Mayor for 1378–79, and was made funded by the levying of a household rate.

Regulations were also introduced to ensure safety, including the banning of thatch in the twelfth century, a step taken against the risk of fire, and confining dangerous crafts to single areas. Noxious crafts were also a recurring issue. Leather tanning, in particular, was a disgusting

A wax replica of the Seal of the Barons of London showing the figure of St Paul, patron saint of London's cathedral. He is shown holding his sword, and a banner with the three lions representing England. At his feet is a panorama of city buildings and churches, with the city wall and river in front.

MUSEUM OF LONDON

industry, and every town tried to keep it outside the walls, mainly for reasons of hygiene. The Walbrook stream at the heart of the City had long been used for this and other semi-industrial activities, such as butchering, and was little better than an open sewer and dumping ground. In 1288 it had to be 'made free from dung and other nuisances' and a century later, it was said to be 'stopped up by divers filth and dung thrown in by persons who have houses along the said [water]course'.

The southern counties of England were the wealthiest as well as the most populous part of the realm, all of which benefited London greatly. The new tax valuations required for the lay subsidy of 1334, for instance, indicate that the five wealthiest counties per square mile were, in order, Middlesex, Oxfordshire, Norfolk, Bedfordshire and Berkshire. For geographical and economic, as much as for political and governmental reasons, Winchester had by then long lost out to London, which was now obviously the most dynamic and important commercial centre in the country. There were cultural consequences. It was in London that Geoffrey Chaucer, the son of a vintner, was born in about 1343. He was to hold a position in the Customs and wrote the *Canterbury Tales* in about 1387, a key work in the development of English-language literature, as opposed to works in French or Latin. Several of the pilgrims in the *Canterbury Tales* reflect figures from London life. Gower, Langland and Thomas Usk were also all London poets in this period: Usk was a native Londoner, but Gower came from Kent and Langland from the Midlands.

London's social structure shared the inegalitarian and hierarchical nature of the rest of society, though without rigid stratification. The smallest group in London were the wealthy and prominent, their power expressed in, and deriving from, their ability to organise others economically and politically. For the wealthy were employers and landowners, and they enjoyed political power as a result of social status and the oligarchical nature of the City's government. Deriving particular wealth from

This is a painting on vellum of Geoffrey Chaucer (c.1343–1400) reading his poems to the court of Richard II. Chaucer was born in London to a family of vintners and undertook a wide range of employment before becoming Comptroller of the Customs for the port of London in 1374 and Clerk of the King's Works fifteen years later, in which role he oversaw several royal building programmes including the wharf at the Tower of London. Along with near-contemporary poets such as Gower and John Barbour in Scotland, Chaucer is recognised as a major figure in bringing vernacular language into the realm of respected literature.

BRIDGEMAN ART LIBRARY

For a pillow the effigy of John Gower (c.1328–1408) in the nave of Southwark Cathedral (*left*) uses three of the poet's more important books. For a time the literary achievement of Gower was ranked alongside that of his contemporary and friend, Geoffrey Chaucer, and only more recently has his reputation been overshadowed. Born in Kent, Gower later lived in Southwark, where he was a benefactor to what was then the Augustinian priory church of St Mary Overie, just to the north of St Saviour's church, now the cathedral. He funded a chantry chapel and was buried there. Gower has been described as the first poet to write in English, although his books were also composed in French and Latin.

PHOTOGRAPH: CARNEGIE, 2009, WITH THANKS TO SOUTHWARK CATHEDRAL

dealing in wool and cloth, the strength of this group extended into the rural hinterland, where they enjoyed influence as a result of their roles as a key source of credit, as the controllers of rural industry, and, frequently, as owners of landed estates. This ownership was an expression of London's wealth as well as of the openness of English society to the purchase of status for cash. This enduring openness helped to further the integration of London with wider English society, and thus lessened any tendency that the city might act as an urban quasi-republic on the model of major towns in Italy, the Baltic and the Low Countries.

The most numerous urban group in London was, of course, the poor. Their poverty stemmed from the precarious nature of much employment and from the absence of any effective system of social welfare. Most lacked the skills that commanded a wage able to provide basic support, and many enjoyed only seasonal or episodic employment. Day-labourers, servants and paupers were economically vulnerable and often socially isolated; a large number were immigrants from the countryside, for, like other medieval towns, London could only maintain and expand its population by constant immigration. As a result of poverty, the poor were very exposed to changes in the price of food and generally lived in inadequate housing. As they could not afford much fuel, the poor were often cold and wet in the winter, and the circumstances of their lives made them prone to disease, although disease and its consequences could also be great social levellers.

Between rich and poor, though not separated rigidly from them in economic terms, there was a third group enjoying a more settled income than the poor. Many were artisans,

Decorative roundels adorn the London Leather, Hide and Wool Exchange building (1878–1912) on Leathermarket Street, Southwark. In order to produce stable, hard-wearing leather, hides are being soaked (probably in human or animal urine) to soften them (*left*), before tanners use knives to scrape off remaining hair fibres (*right*). In the tanning process itself the particular enzymes found in dog faeces were found to be very effective, but animal brains could also be used. The foulness of this ancient process led to recurring attempts to banish its practice beyond urban limits. In London's case, Southwark and particularly Bermondsey enjoyed the economic benefits, but endured the hideous smells, of this noxious business.

PHOTOGRAPH: CARNEGIE, 2009

their economic interests and social cohesion frequently expressed through fraternities of workmen. The status and wealth of women continued to be derived from their husbands and fathers, and thus defined by them. Arranged marriages were the norm, and wives were not normally allowed to make wills, because in law they could not own property separately from their husbands. Although different standards were applied to men and women, pre-marital and extra-marital sex were mortal sins for both. That these points were scarcely unique to London does not make them less important as a description of life in the city.

An account of London society in terms of constant groups can suggest a structural rigidity, but, in practice, there was a dynamism arising from change. In particular, London was affected by the multiple strains of the fourteenth century. The most striking was the Black Death, an epidemic of bubonic plague, which hit between 1348 and 1351, killing between a third and a half of London's population. Mortality in towns was probably much higher than elsewhere, and burial grounds expanded in size and number to meet the unwelcome demand. The fourteenth-century plague burial site at East Smithfield has been excavated, with heart-rending but neatly laid-out rows of corpses (one pit was over 400 feet long). To the north-west, meanwhile, there was a patch of land belonging to the king at the time of Domesday (1087), beyond the city walls north of Aldersgate, by the name of 'nanes maneslande': during the Black Death, this 'No Man's Land' was, according to Stow in 1598, purchased by Ralph Stratford, bishop of London 'which he inclosed with a brick wall, and dedicated to the burial of the dead'. Adjoining this, Sir Walter de Manny, a Hainaut soldier of fortune and founder of Charterhouse, bought Spittle-Croft, the property of St Bartholomew's Hospital 'for the same use of burying the dead … and was long remembered by an inscription fixed on a stone cross upon the premises', according to Northouck. Stow had seen this cross, which bore a Latin inscription claiming that over 50,000 dead had been buried there during the Black Death.

Later plague attacks followed in 1361, 1369 and 1375, as well as subsequently. In fact, the Black Death was only part of a wider crisis affecting the English population. Aside from epidemic disease, there were problems arising from an inability to sustain earlier economic expansion and from a downturn in the climate moving toward the Little Ice Age of the seventeenth century, which reduced the length of the growing season. The resulting pressure on the agrarian economy greatly affected the towns. A smaller rural population meant less demand for goods produced in towns or traded from them.

The city became much less densely settled. The aftermath of the Great Plague of 1665, for which information is more plentiful, highlights the difficulty of assessing movement of people into and out of the city during and after the plague attack, and the situation is far more problematic for the Black Death two hundred years earlier. But what is clear is that the overall population of London (including Southwark and Westminster) might have been halved, to about 40,000, by the 1370s. The great loss of life from the plague did create opportunities in the late fourteenth century in the countryside for employment, and not least for a less restrictive labour regime than hitherto. Moreover, the fall in the rural population also created opportunities offered by less expensive land and higher wages.

Partly as a result of this late-medieval decline in its population, London's bounds – its territorial limits – in 1550 were essentially still those of the 1170s, while, over the same period, the names of streets and areas were clarified. The long-standing reclamation of the waterfront continued, in large part as wharves were built into the Thames, and in order to provide docking for bigger ships. The late thirteenth and early fourteenth centuries were particularly important for this piecemeal reclamation, but there were plenty of wharves by 1300, and the reclamation continued until 1500. Noted areas of reclamation included Blackfriars, the precinct of the House of the Dominican Friars, and, on the other side of the river Fleet, the precinct of the Priory of the Carmelites of Whitefriars. The merchant capitalists of London emerge as active and successful property developers.[13] The river itself remained the major route for travel between the City and Westminster, although they were linked on land by the Strand.

The fall in the rural population and the new agrarian economy probably both hit migration to London, a migration that, given the high death-rate, was crucial to the city's population stability, let alone growth. Partly as a result of falling numbers in London, however, rents fell, while vacant lots became more common. With fewer people, houses became a less satisfactory investment, and the maintenance of much of the housing stock probably declined. In turn, lower rents might have improved living standards for much of London's population, who would also have benefited from labour shortages and the resulting higher wages. Thus London did remain attractive to immigrants. By 1400, moreover, the plague was largely urban in its impact, which accentuated the sink effect of the city, in turn creating and maintaining opportunities for new migrants. Judging by surviving names, many immigrants to London were of East Anglian origin. The East Midlands were also a major source, contributing to the development in London of the particular form of standard English. Immigrants, however, came from all over southern England, as well as from further afield. Richard Whittington (d. 1423), who was already established in London as a mercer in 1379, was the youngest son of a Gloucestershire landowner. Whittington went on to be Mayor in 1397–98, 1406–7 and 1419–20. The story of early poverty and a valuable rat-catching cat, now presented in Christmas pantomimes, did not emerge until the 1600s, centuries after Whittington's death, and a large part of his fame rests upon the charitable benefactions he made rather than any special political importance during his time in office. In *Piers Plowman* William Langland wrote of clerks going to London to sing masses, criticising them for deserting their role in local communities in favour of the opportunities for money offered by the capital.

At the same time, the process of spatial differentiation within London was confirmed by new flows of immigrants, although other factors also played a role. In part, this was a matter of regulation. For example, in 1361, an attempt was made to ban slaughtering within the City – one of many such attempts – and this encouraged butchers to locate in St Clement Danes, to the west of Temple Bar and the City boundary. London's economic role also led to a process of spatial differentiation in the South East, especially in the Greater London area. The massive importance of London, Southwark and Westminster, increasingly to be seen as triple nuclei, overshadowed other towns in the area and stunted their economic and commercial development. Market charters and the success

Part of the mainly medieval curtain wall near London Wall. In the distance the wall bends to the right to join another surviving section in St Alphage Gardens (see page 51).

or failure of market towns were a measure of this. For example, Kingston, Croydon, Brentford, Staines and Uxbridge were successful market towns because they were at a sufficient distance from the city itself, but many would-be markets failed completely, including Acton, Enfield, Harrow, Isleworth and Pinner. For this reason, Middlesex had probably the lowest ratio of market towns to population of any English county in the early sixteenth century, a significant consequence of London's 'shadow' effect.

Amid serious economic difficulties, however, there was much prosperity in both England and London in the late fourteenth and fifteenth centuries. The rising cost of labour encouraged a relative shift in the agrarian economy from cereal production to the keeping of sheep for wool, an activity that required less manpower. The export of wool had been fundamental to the national economy for centuries, but now domestic clothiers were increasingly turning that wool into cloth for sale at home and abroad. Cloth exports, in large part through London to the Low Countries, a major centre of consumption and manufacturing, especially in Bruges and Ghent, brought much prosperity, particularly to East Anglia and London, although they hit cloth production in the Low Countries.

London, where the cloth finishing industry developed apace, also benefited from the new-found activity and sophistication of the South East's economy, and, in turn, contributed to

One of the great treasures of Westminster Abbey: the great 'Cosmati' pavement in front of the high altar which was laid down by Italian workmen in 1268. It is made of onyx, purple porphyry, green serpentine, yellow limestone and glass.

In Southwerk at the Tabard as I lay
Redy to wend[en] on my pilgrymage
To Caunterbury with ful devout corage,
At nyght was come into that hostelrye
Wel nyne and twenty in a compaignye
Of sondry folk, by aventure yfalle
In felaweshipe, and pilgrimes were they alle,
That toward Caunterbury wolden ryde.
The chambres and the stables weren wyde,
And wel we weren esed atte beste …

Geoffrey Chaucer made famous the medieval Tabard Inn in lines 20–28 of his Prologue to the *Canterbury Tales*. For, as these lines show, this is where he set out on his pilgrimage to Canterbury. The ancient inn was just behind Borough High Street in Southwark, and was just one of many such buildings, as John Stow described at the end of the Tudor century: '… towards London bridge on the same side, be many fayre Innes, for receipt of trauellers, by these signes, the Spurre, Christopher, Bull, Queenes head, Tabarde, George, Hart, Kinges Head, &c. Amongst the which, the most auncient is the Tabard, so called of the signe, which as we now tearme it, is of a Iacquit, or sleeuelesse coat …' The Tabard burned down in 1669, but was rebuilt. This print of the Tabard is dated to 1875, just before the building was demolished. Its site was close to the George Inn, which does still survive (see page 174).
CARNEGIE COLLECTION

them. Tax revenue per acre in 1332 was higher from wards near the river, such as Vintry, Dowgate and Bridge, or in the centre, than further away. One reason was that these were the wards where rich people lived, providing access to the shops and markets along and near Cheapside, and also to the quays and wharves along the river. The poor, in contrast, lived in the north and east. Imports to London from abroad included groceries, skins, glass, wine, furs, fruit, salt, building materials and, by the 1480s, books.[14] William Caxton established the first English printing press, at Westminster, in 1476.

As a powerful aid to economic growth, regional and national communication systems both improved, which in turn helped internal and foreign trade and travel. The pilgrims of Geoffrey Chaucer's *Canterbury Tales* (*c*.1387) have the Tabard inn in Southwark as their meeting-place. From the fifteenth century, Kendal in distant Cumbria, was served by regular packhorse trains moving goods as far as London. Every significant centre had such ties, and the network of regular carriers' routes was instrumental in creating the national transport system. A significant number of these routes led to London and to its port. Across England from the very late twelfth century, fords at major crossing points were replaced by bridges which increasingly rested on stone arches and were able to accommodate carts. This stronger emphasis on land routes did not put London at a disadvantage, instead supplementing its position as England's most important major port. Despite these late medieval developments, to much of England London still seemed a very distant, if not menacing, place: it was common for Cornishmen to make a will before they set off on a trip to the capital.

Markets and fairs provided key intermediary points in the integration of London with the national economy. Faversham and Henley were key centres for the grain trade to London. For 2,000 years communications and systems of marketing and exchange of goods and services have been fundamental to London's relative position within England and Europe, key strands linking ancient Rome's roads to the current development of internet and related information, communication and commercial systems.

The important role of the Low Countries in London's trade did not preclude economic links elsewhere, especially with the leading Italian commercial cities, Genoa, Venice and Florence, as well as with France and the Hanseatic League of German Baltic cities, notably Lübeck. From the High Middle Ages the powerful merchants of the League had developed a depot and trading house at the confluence of the Walbrook stream and the Thames. Known as the Stalhof – crudely translated to English as Stilliarde or Steelyard – this trading post was considered one of the largest and most important in medieval Britain, acting as a major conduit for the export of English cloth. A new walled depot at the Steelyard was built in the 1470s and its prosperity continued through much of the Tudor century. The Steelyard buildings were lost in the Great Fire, though remnants have been discovered on the site, now under Cannon Street station.

The Italians were important in London from the late thirteenth century, when they started to sail to England directly through the Straits of Gibraltar, although the number of ships coming direct from the Mediterranean was limited. The Italians were primarily in England to buy wool to export to the Low Countries and northern France, but were engaged in a wide range of trading and financial activities. London's key economic links in the fifteenth century were with northern continental Europe, including Antwerp, Bruges and Ghent. London and its merchants played a major role in this trade, but the relationship was not equal, with that of London often subordinate to the Low Countries' interests. This subordination proved vexing to many Londoners, and encouraged the expression of xenophobic sentiments, notably in the Peasants' Revolt in 1381, the riots of 1456–57 and the Evil May Day in 1517.

As the relative wealth of the South East within England grew, London benefited directly, not least as a source of goods and services and as a significant market for the economy of most of the region, notably for food and raw materials. London drew grain supplies from all over the South East.[15] Suppliers to London's corn merchants could be found particularly in north Kent, the Thames valley, Hertfordshire and Essex, while London butchers also drew on north-west Essex and the Weald, and London's wood supply was primarily provided from Surrey, west Kent, east Berkshire, the Chilterns and Hertfordshire. Mercantile credit was crucial to this production system.

Foreign visitors commented upon the prosperity of London and England as a whole, although few gained direct experience of the North, a situation that remained the case until the nineteenth century. This relative prosperity helped underwrite late-medieval government and the political system, as well as London's major role in the Wars of the Roses. Prosperity and government were linked through entrepreneurial activity which also overlapped with personal and factional favouritism. Richard Whittington made much of his money by acting as Collector of Customs in London and Calais, in turn lending money to Richard II, Henry IV and Henry V. Within London, merchants dominated the Court of Aldermen.

The importance of trade was also indicated by the measures taken to combat piracy, including the squadron equipped and led by the prominent merchant John Philipot, which achieved a striking success against the Scots in 1378. After serving as Lord Mayor in 1378–79, Philipot paid part of the cost of two stone towers built below London Bridge, between which a chain was hung in order to provide protection against French attack. There was no attack, but there was a serious threat of French invasion in 1385 and 1386. Quarter of a mile downstream from the bridge, the Tower remained central to the City's defences and to royal power in the area. Already at the end of the thirteenth century Edward I had ordered the reclamation of part of the river Thames to create Water Lane and the Outer

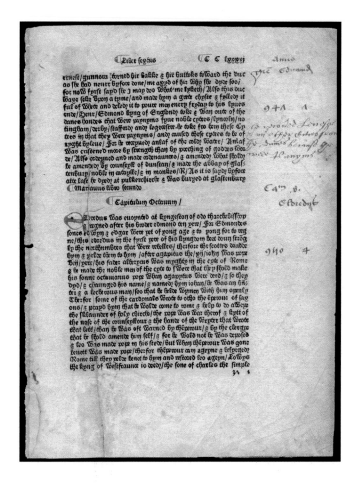

William Caxton was born in Kent and apprenticed to a London mercer as a teenager. He travelled widely on business and saw printing in progress in Germany. He set up a short-lived press in Bruges and by September 1476 we know that Caxton had taken a year's lease on a property, from the Sacrist of Westminster Abbey, in which he set up his printing press. The first book printed in England, *The Dictes or Sayengis of the Philosophres*, was completed on 18 November 1477. Caxton is known as Britain's first printer, but his role was actually larger than that, in some ways more akin to an entrepreneurial publisher than to a mere book printer. For Caxton selected the works to be translated or printed, in part on the basis of likely commercial results, and he also edited at least a quarter of the books that were printed under his name. As with some modern publishers, Caxton was not averse to accepting subventions to aid publication, or sponsorship from wealthy individuals. This page is from a popular history of the world, Ralph Higden's *Polychronicon* of 1482, printed at Westminster by Caxton. Some features of the old manuscript tradition were preserved: the main black text was printed, but the red capitals would have been added by hand. In the right margin is a note in late Tudor 'secretary' handwriting.

Ward. An enormous, new riverside curtain wall was built, at the centre of which was the new water gate of St Thomas's Tower, its popular name of Traitors' Gate reflecting the Tower's continuing role as national, royal prison. During the fourteenth century Edward III and Richard II extended the wharf, which was the last major military extension to the medieval castle, part of the work being supervised by none other than poet and sometime clerk of works Geoffrey Chaucer.

The cultural significance of London increased with the rise of the vernacular English language, which was moulded in the South East. The role of Latin and Anglo-Norman or Old French – the French spoken in England – declined. In the thirteenth century, the English language was increasingly identified with an English people and nation, and this theme became more important with the Hundred Years' War with France which continued for most of the period from 1337 to 1453. Indeed, in 1356, proceedings in the London Sheriffs' courts switched to English. The Guild of Brewers agreed to keep records in English in 1422.

The law also had a harsher impact in London. Sir John Oldcastle, who was responsible for an unsuccessful Lollard uprising in 1414, was captured near Welshpool three years later,

The imposing gatehouse of Lambeth Palace built by Archbishop John Morton in the first years of the Tudor dynasty. For London this is a very early use of brick. Dorset-born and educated in Oxford, Morton became a successful ecclesiastical lawyer in London before being made archbishop by Henry VII.

condemned by Parliament as an outlawed traitor and convicted heretic, and first hanged and then burned at the gallows at St Giles's Fields. Lollardy looked towards Protestant activity in London in the early sixteenth century, as it did in other parts of England where it flourished, such as Norfolk, Coventry and Kent. Earnest traditional devotion was also to provide a seedbed for Protestantism, as people who took their religion seriously could be turned towards evangelicalism.

The earlier rise of a national consciousness and its expression in London led to tension, if not hostility, toward those judged to be outsiders. A Jewish community, possibly immigrants from Rouen in Normandy, was in place by 1130. Based on Jews' Street (Old Jewry) and round St Lawrence, this community benefited from the favour of William I and, even more, William II and Henry I. The role of the Jews in helping to finance the Crown and other leading figures led, however, to growing criticism. In 1189, this resulted in a violent response, including the burning down of the London Jewry and the slaughter of thirty Jews. Thereafter, public hostility to Jews became more conspicuous. Anti-semitism, indeed, became a feature of English life, culminating in Edward I's expulsion of the Jews in 1290. They were not officially allowed to return until Oliver Cromwell granted permission in the 1650s.

There was hostility also towards Italians, Flemings and the French. For example, from the 1230s, there was opposition to what were judged foreign elements in the Church. Boniface of Savoy, Archbishop of Canterbury, made himself unpopular in London when he used Provençal troops to take goods under the royal right of purveyance. Despite their economic importance, Hanseatic merchants were not always welcomed in all quarters.

The favour that the Crown showed towards alien merchants, often as a result of the money and loans they provided, created resentment among their London rivals, and underlined the extent to which the proximity of city and court could present problems as well as opportunities for Londoners. The Crown failed to support the interests of London merchants, not least by selling the right for aliens to make direct exports, and thus circumvent the overseas staple under the control of London merchants that these exports often supported. Partly as a result, the City of London frequently turned to those opposed to the Crown, for example to Simon de Montfort in the 1260s, the Lord Appellants in the 1380s, and Richard, Duke of York in the 1450s.[16] This linkage re-emerged in the late sixteenth and early seventeenth centuries as

Built in the 1360s, this building was used to store part of the monarch's wealth and was known as the Jewel Tower. To the bottom left can be seen the now dry moat that used to be fed from the Thames. The building served to store parliamentary records until becoming offices for the Board of Trade in 1869.

PHOTOGRAPH: CARNEGIE, 2008

tension between monopolists linked to the court and other merchants opposed to their privileges.

London was the centre for overseas links within England, its importance increasing as its own merchants also became more prominent. London was also the forcing ground for an expression of nationhood that in part reflected a hostility to what was judged alien. London itself benefited from the lengthy conflict with France, for most of the period from 1337 to 1453, as it was the key centre in which the financing and supplying of the war effort were organised.

Late-medieval London was not all commercial bustle, trade and politics. Religion and ecclesiastical issues were as prominent here as elsewhere. In and around the city the role of religion bore a clear institutional imprint, notably with the thirteen conventual churches and 126 parish ones in London and its suburbs noted by William fitz Stephen in the 1170s. London's skyline boasted the largest church with the highest spire in the country – St Paul's – but other church buildings, precincts, graveyards and related street-patterns imposed a particular order on the city's topography. The great religious houses and hospitals were largely outside the walls, where there was room for them at the edge of urban settlement. This situation was also a testimony both to the extent of existing property rights within the walls, and to the readiness of Londoners to rely on parochial provision.

The guild church of St Lawrence Jewry, which acts as the church for the Corporation. The name comes from the medieval Jewish quarter in this district. There appears to have been a Jewish community here from Saxon times.
PHOTOGRAPH: CARNEGIE, 2009

Alongside the religious guilds, secular guilds and units of local government, the City's many parish churches – some pre-Conquest but many founded in the eleventh century – helped to ensure a detailed pattern of belonging, with the churches serving as the centres of identity for particular neighbourhoods. One distinctive feature of medieval and post-medieval London was the extraordinary number of tiny parishes. For ordinary Londoners, these tiny entities were probably at least as important as the big issues of state, and probably defined their loyalties and their allegiances. Certainly for the middling sort, they were central to the organisation of social and cultural activity and to political involvement.

This sense of local identity, ringing out with church bells, and maintained by frequent processions, linked the generations, with parish churches the venues for weddings, baptisms and burials. The memory represented by a sense of family coherence focused upon churches. The importance of this role helps to explain the disruption caused by the Protestant Reformation of the sixteenth century. Indeed, within London the pattern of distinctive local parishes and communities was an aspect of a marked continuity that linked the medieval centuries to what came later.

CHAPTER

4

THE SOCIETY of sixteenth-century London can be discerned more readily and more clearly than that of the previous century. Surviving records, both private and state, are more copious, partly thanks to the introduction of printing in England, by William Caxton in London, as well as a marked rise in both literacy and population, more extensive governmental activity, and the effective nationalisation of the Church. There are also more surviving buildings, especially secular buildings, and also more of the material culture, the world of things. As a result, Tudor London seems markedly closer to us.

The use of English in its standard form was a fourteenth- and fifteenth-century development that was pushed further under the Tudors, when it became both the language of authority and of a culture that still echoes today. That this culture does so is in large part thanks to the oft-seen and cited plays of William Shakespeare, who moved to London from Stratford-upon-Avon. The Lord Chamberlain's Men, a theatrical company in which Shakespeare had a stake, produced plays at the Theatre and the Globe. The Theatre, the first purpose-built public playhouse in England, was opened in Shoreditch by James Burbage, an actor and master carpenter, in 1576, and it was followed by the Curtain in 1577 and the Globe Theatre in Southwark in 1599. Burbage's lease had run out in 1597 and he dismantled the Theatre, using some of its timbers for the Globe. These theatres were all located outside the city walls due to measures by the City authorities, which had been encouraged by preaching against plays. A ban on public playing in the City was pressed for from the 1570s and was realised in the 1590s.

Published in 1572 but surveyed perhaps twenty years earlier, this map was included in a major German atlas, the *Civitas Orbis Terrarum*. The figures in the foreground provide the sense of a panorama, as do the three-dimensional boats and buildings, but this is essentially a plan. The basic shape of the walled Roman and medieval city is unchanged, with only relatively small extra-urban pockets of development to the east and to the north as far as Charterhouse. Southwark, too, is still modest in scale. Of much greater significance are the extensive tracts west of the river Fleet between the City and Westminster, along Holborn and particularly the Strand towards Charing Cross and Whitehall: the city has burst out of the walls. St Paul's is shown with its impressively slender spire, which dates the survey to before 1561.

MUSEUM OF LONDON

LONDON UNDER THE
TUDORS, 1485–1603

In addition to the depiction on stage, we can see Londoners as individuals, as we frequently cannot see their fifteenth-century predecessors, thanks to more lifelike and more numerous portraits, by painters such as Hans Holbein. Moreover, films and television dramas set in Tudor London (albeit filmed elsewhere, often at Lacock) make its world appear familiar, although the use of Victorian coaches in the BBC2 series *The Tudors* did affect the authenticity of it somewhat.

Yet, as so often with the past, a suggestion of common humanity should not blind us to difference. Both the facts and details of life, and, more obscurely, the attitudes of the period, were very different to those of today. As far as the attitudes of the period were concerned, London was not only an economic, political and cultural space, but also a world shadowed by another of spirits, good and bad; and these spirits were seen and believed to intervene frequently in the life of humans. This belief brought together both Christian notions, in particular providentialism, a conviction of God's direct intervention in the life of individuals, the intercessionary role of saints, sacraments, prayer and belief, and a belief in the existence of heaven, purgatory, hell and the devil, with, on the other hand, a related and overlapping group of ideas, beliefs and customs that were particularly Christianised, but that also testified to a mental world that was not explicable in terms of Christian theology.

A wooduct image of London, with rooftops, church spires and city wall from the Chronicle of England, originally published by William Caxton in 1480. This edition was printed by Caxton's successor, Wynkyn de Worde, eleven years later.
MUSEUM OF LONDON

This was a London of good and evil knowledge and magic, of fatalism, of the occult, and of astrology and alchemy, each of which could be reconciled with Christianity by committed contemporaries, but could also be seen as a very different source of values. This London was deeply challenged and partly transformed by the Protestant Reformation.

Yet, at the same time, the Reformation scarcely brought this London to an end. There was extensive belief in witchcraft, which was also acted out on the stage. In *The Witch of Edmonton* (*c.*1621) by William Rowley, Thomas Dekker and John Ford, Elizabeth Sawyer, a lonely and bullied old woman becomes a witch having made a pact with the devil. Moreover, the publication of astrological almanacs developed as part of London's world of print, and was still large-scale in the 1790s; the London earthquake of 1692 was seen as a warning of God's anger, an attitude still present in the 1750s; and, in 1762, there was great controversy about the veracity of a ghost which appeared in Cock-Lane. In fact, this ghost

This is the classic biscuit-tin view of the great medieval London Bridge, from Visscher's 'facsimile' of London, 1616. Replacing the Roman and several earlier timber bridges on this important site, the construction of Britain's first major stone arch bridge was begun by Peter of Colechurch, Warden of the Bridge, in 1176; it was completed in 1209. In all nineteen stone arches, plus another that accommodated a drawbridge, were built, varying in width from 15 feet to 30 feet. In this view one can clearly see the rubble-filled wooden 'starlings' that were built both upstream and downstream of the stone arches in order to protect them from the flow of river and tide. These starlings narrowed the stream even further so that the river positively raced through the arches when in full flow, a fact that Peter Morice used to good effect when he installed a waterwheel under the northernmost arch to drive a water pump (see page 90).

The buildings on the bridge quickly became a lucrative source of revenue, particularly after the foundation of the Bridge House Estates by royal charter in 1282, which administered the bridge and later became heavily involved in the funding and maintenance of several other London bridges, including Tower Bridge, Blackfriars and most recently the Millennium footbridge. In all, the medieval London Bridge was just over 300 yards long, but the buildings reduced the road carriageway to just 12 feet wide, producing great congestion. When Westminster Bridge was opened in 1750 it was decided to remove the buildings on London Bridge. Because of the difficulty of navigating upstream through the bridge, the majority of London's port trade took place downstream, in the Pool of London. Queenhithe and the other upstream wharves lost out to Billingsgate and the Legal Quays that were regulated from the mid-sixteenth century (on the far bank, to the right of this view). Prominent in the foreground are St Mary Overie (from 1905 Southwark Cathedral) and the city gate at the end of the bridge, with the felons' heads displayed upon spikes perhaps suggesting the aftermath of the Gunpowder Plot.

was the product of a commercial and litigious society, as it was dreamed up by one James Parsons in order to make a creditor who had sued him appear to be a murderer.

New developments did not necessarily equate with what would now be seen as scholarly. Thus, in *The London Dispensatory* (1653), Nicholas Culpepper discussed lapidary medicine: the use of precious stones in order to ensure health. Giuseppe Balsamo, 'Count Cagliostro', began his career as an alchemist seeking to transmute excrement, hair, herbs, minerals, urine and wood into gold in London in 1776–77. At the same time, the scientific inquiry that could lead to an interest in the occult, seen for example with the astrologer and mathematician John Dee (1527–1608), also produced what would subsequently be seen as more conventional scientific interests, ones that led towards the scientific revolution of the late seventeenth century, a movement that had a strong base in London with the foundation of the Royal Society. Already, under Elizabeth I, London, although it still lacked a university, was an intellectual powerhouse. Alongside the active development of the vernacular in a series of literary forms, there was a noted group of botanists and horticulturalists near Lime Street, as well as the publication of scientific books and advances in medical practice.[1]

Discovered a century ago under the floor of 30–32 Cheapside, this is the greatest hoard of Elizabethan and Jacobean jewellery ever found. It appears to be the working stock of one of the Cheapside goldsmiths who occupied the property. We do not know exactly when or why this valuable hoard was concealed.

MUSEUM OF LONDON

Diverse developments such as England's commercial expansion and financial development, the flowering of drama in the Elizabethan and Jacobean period, and, under the Stuarts, the defeat of the Crown in the Civil War of 1642–46, cannot be understood without reference to London's central role in the political, economic and cultural life of the country. This role was more prominent than it had been in the Middle Ages, in part because of the importance of the religious and ecclesiastical changes directed from the royal court. In spatial terms, the seizure by Henry VIII of the directing power over the Church represented an important shift of authority to Westminster from Rome and Canterbury. As a result, patterns of authority altered greatly. So did the assumption of London as a central place, for both good and ill. Notably, there was a greater centralisation of royal power in London, power that was derived from the rest of England.

Whatever the political and religious crises and changes, London retained and developed its position as the leading place in the English economy. Indeed, the Tudor age turned out to be the last period before the settlement of the Atlantic littoral of the Americas, and the resulting major development of the Atlantic economy, gave crucial opportunities to west-coast ports, especially Bristol and, later, Liverpool and Glasgow. As yet, however, London's position had not been challenged. Instead, it had become more significant in the fourteenth and fifteenth centuries, especially from 1470, so that, by 1500, 70 per cent of England's crucial export – woollen cloth – was passing through the city. And, not surprisingly, cloth figured hugely in London's trade figures, with the so-called 'new draperies' – a light worsted cloth of high quality, the market for which quickly expanded in world markets – accounting for up to three quarters of everything that was exported from the wharves of London. By the Tudor century virtually all of the trade in raw wool, and most of the trade in woollen cloth, was in the hands of English merchants, although the Hanse still accounted for around 30 per cent, and the Italians for perhaps 15 per cent of this crucial trade. A hugely important role was played by the Company of Merchant Adventurers of London, who developed the trade and then monopolised the export of woollen cloth until as late as 1689, and used the proceeds to fund a wide range of imports. Products such as linen, iron, hemp and wax were all imported in bulk, complemented by a dizzying range of light manufactured goods, particularly from the Low Countries, including iron pots, books, spectacles and cloth-making tools. Continental workshops found a ready market in London.

One of the glories of English Perpendicular architecture, the Henry VII Lady Chapel at the east end of Westminster Abbey was built during that king's reign and contains his tomb by the Florentine artist Pietro Torrigiano, one of the very first examples of Italian Renaissance design to be introduced into Britain.

PHOTOGRAPH: CARNEGIE, 2008

Growth from then until 1550 provided much prosperity, increasing the number of affluent citizens, and thus greatly influencing the nature of the local market. Furthermore, this wealth underwrote the credit monopoly enjoyed by London. The evidence for change concentrates on cloth exports, but there are other indicators that this period was a key one in the strengthening of London's position within the national economy.[2] This position also enabled London to play a larger role in public finances, notably contributing 24 per cent of the subsidies raised in 1541–42 compared to 9 per cent in 1515–16.

London benefited from being best placed to trade with Antwerp, the leading port in the Low Countries, and indeed in northern Europe, and the key site of northern and western Europe's trade and finance. Antwerp's fortunes, however, were to be affected greatly by the Wars of Religion which broke out in the mid-1560s, not least by the lengthy and ultimately successful Spanish siege of 1585. In the short term this favoured Amsterdam economically, also well located from London's point of view. London was a long-term beneficiary: its population, behind that of Antwerp in 1550, had overtaken it by 1600. Many of the foreign immigrants to London in Elizabeth's reign came from the French-speaking Walloon provinces of the Low Countries, their move a consequence of the disruption of the Dutch Revolt.

As far as foreign trade was concerned, London was also well located for trade to Iberia, the Mediterranean and the wider world. In addition, given the extent to which commerce involved transhipment, as goods were moved from one trade to another, with profit derived from this intermediary role, London also benefited from its ability to play a key part in serving both trades to the Low Countries and the north, and those to the south. Moreover, transhipment helped to increase the gap between London's position and that of other east-coast ports such as Newcastle, Hull, Boston and King's Lynn. London increased its dominance of England's international trade, and the London market became the key one for foreign imports, a position bringing great prosperity to the city.

The city's economy benefited greatly from the substantial growth in the English economy during the sixteenth century, a growth reflected in and sustained by the marked rise in the country's population after the stagnation of the previous century. This rise provided both more producers and more consumers for the economy. Each benefited London, but so also did the role of London as an organisational centre for economic activities. There were mutually beneficial relationships, with the opportunities that economic growth provided for mercantile enterprise making London important to the economy across England. In particular, the export of cloth focused on London, with about 88 per cent of cloth exports going through the city in the 1540s, and 40 per cent of the freemen members of guilds linked to cloth production or sale.

Jobs and customs revenues depended on this trade, and, partly as a consequence, London was already by 1553 a financial centre of European importance. The prominence of trade

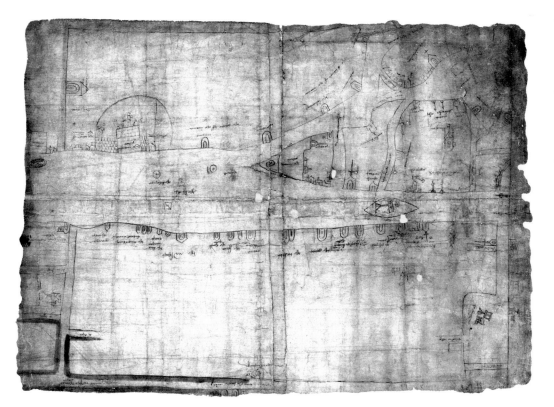

was marked by the Royal Exchange opened by Sir Thomas Gresham in 1571, in emulation of Antwerp's Bourse, a step applauded in Thomas Heywood's play *If You Know Not Me You Know Nobody* (1605). With its offices, colonnades, courtyards and shops, this Exchange became the centre of enterprise, and its success was to lead Sir Robert Cecil to open a competing New Exchange on the Strand.

The city's growth in part reflected organisational developments in London's commercial infrastructure, including the movement of anchorages from Queenhithe and Billingsgate downriver to Deptford, Wapping and Ratcliffe, a move that provided more space. London's first dry dock was built at Rotherhithe in 1599, followed by another, for the expanding East India Company, at Blackwall in 1614–17. In January 1661 the diarist Samuel Pepys took a barge to Blackwall and 'viewed the dock and the new Wet dock, which is newly made there, and a brave new merchantman which is to be launched shortly'. Ships could be repaired and fitted out here, but the docks were not yet used for loading; that would have to wait for a later succession of dock schemes from the end of the century. Nevertheless, these early schemes demonstrate a key form of organisation that was provided by the development of trading companies, such as the East India, Hudson's Bay and Levant Companies, which could raise investment and share risk from a wide range of participants.

Aside from commerce, London was a key centre for manufacturing. The prime market for this production was the large and growing population of the city, the largest market in Britain for clothes, shoes and other goods, but London-made goods also circulated into England and abroad. The marked growth in England's population and wealth expanded the market both for these goods and for imports handled via London. There was also a continual process of striving for new opportunities, a tendency that looks towards the present. In 1580, for instance, a Dutch engineer called Peter Morice so impressed the City authorities with the power and efficiency of his water pump (or 'forcier') that he was granted permission to install an under-shot waterwheel beneath one of the northern arches of London Bridge, which was used to pump fresh water to a conduit at Leadenhall. Further wheels were installed over the years, including one to grind corn. None of these facilities survived the Great Fire, but waterwheels continued in use under London Bridge until Rennie's new bridge was built in the 1820s.

Population figures are far from exact for this pre-census age, but London's population grew from about 1520. London was not one of the leading cities in population terms in 1500, when it had about 50–60,000 inhabitants. At that point, the leading city in Christian Europe was Paris, with about 225,000 followed by Naples (125,000), Milan (100,000), Venice (100,000), Granada (70,000), Prague (70,000), and Lisbon (65,000). Cities in the 50–60,000 band included Genoa, Bologna, Antwerp and Verona.[3] Nevertheless, London was soon on a marked upward trend. The rise in its population was probably

At one time all of the grand houses on the river had their own water gates to give easy access to the river for transport. This, the York House water gate, is a unique survivor. York House had been one of several bishops' palaces along the river between the City and Westminster. At the time the water gate was built in the 1620s, the house was owned by George Villiers, 1st Duke of Buckingham, James I's controversial favourite. The water gate now stands some way from the riverbank, landlocked behind the Victoria Embankment, which was built out into the river in the nineteenth century, narrowing the stream considerably at this point. Nothing else remains of York House itself.

PHOTOGRAPH: CARNEGIE, 2009

from approximately 50–60,000 in 1500, to about 200,000 in 1600, about 375,000–400,000 in 1650, and about 500,000–600,000 in 1700, which was then nearly 10 per cent of a substantially larger national population. In contrast, the second largest city in England in 1600 was Norwich, with about 15,000 inhabitants.

The rate of London's growth in the sixteenth century was far greater than over the last century, and if that was also true of Norwich, Exeter and Bristol and other major English cities, London's growth was proportionately far greater than that of the three named cities which was about 20–35 per cent. This growth was made more impressive after taking into account the high death-rate of London's population, especially among infants and children, as the densely packed City was particularly conducive for infection. The human toll was heavy. For example, after giving birth to a stillborn child, Ann, the wife of the poet John Donne (c.1572–1631), died in 1617 and her husband, who became Dean of St Paul's in 1621, long remained depressed. Suffering was a frequent theme in his poetry, and his last sermon was on the theme of 'Death's Duel'. The high death-rate was countered by migration to London, this migration playing a different demographic role to the situation today and over the last two centuries when immigration has essentially supplemented indigenous growth. Immigration meant that the majority of the city's population had been born elsewhere, and immigration also helped keep the average age of the population relatively low.

While expanding, the city did remain compact and densely built-up, so the growing throngs of people ensured that London seemed crowded. Thomas Platter, a Swiss visitor, observed in 1599, 'This city of London is not only brimful of curiosities, but so popular also that one simply cannot walk along the streets for the crowd.' The crowds were especially dense on London Bridge, which was at once thoroughfare, and, with its numerous buildings, a place of residence and centre of shopping. Despite the rise in the city's population and its geographical expansion, London Bridge remained the sole bridge across the Thames in the London area until the mid-eighteenth century.

This situation encouraged the large-scale use of ferries to cross the Thames. This use accentuated the crowded nature of the river, which owed much to the combination of sea and river traffic. The two depended on each other. Passenger traffic up and down the river added to the melée. Thames watermen – with their traditional clinker-built 'wherries'

Thames watermen helping some nervous passengers down the stairs on to their wherries, a cartoon by Thomas Rowlandson (1756–1827). In terms of function, watermen dealt with passengers, while lightermen dealt with the transportation of goods. Jointly they belonged to a City Company, but without livery.

– were licensed by the City to operate a river-borne taxi service. Fares were regulated by Act of Parliament in 1514, and apprenticeships were introduced to help improve safety and the standard of service in 1555. In the late seventeenth century Samuel Pepys used such boats to commute to work at the Admiralty, and in his day no fewer than 10,000 watermen were licensed to work the Thames, criss-crossing the river under oar. The protruding bows of the wherries allowed passengers easy access to and from the hundred or so sets of river steps that were used for the purpose, while all of the riverside mansions along the Strand had their own water gates giving access to this important form of transport. A particularly good trade for the watermen was said to be had taking theatre-goers to Southwark.

London's numbers put pressure on housing and employment, at the same time as they added to the vitality of the city. Migrants, from home and abroad, provided labour, unskilled and skilled, and the latter contributed to the development of new trades and products, for example in glass-making and brewing. The latter, which expanded greatly to supply the rising population, benefited from immigrants from the Rhineland; in the fifteenth century beer brewing had been introduced by the Dutch. The improvement in London map-making also owed much to foreign immigrants, notably, in the seventeenth

This is Fishmongers' (or Fish) Hall at the northern end of London Bridge. Fourth in order of precedence, and one of the twelve 'Grand' Livery Companies, the fishmongers have had a presence on this site since the latter half of the fourteenth century when three Lord Mayors of the period, John Lovekyn, Sir William Walworth and William Askham – fishmongers all – helped secure this important riverfront site and develop it. At the far side, the site fronts Thames Street (the ancient river front), and the site included the company's livery hall as well as warehouses, a counting house and a dwelling. John Stow tells of two companies 'of Stockfishmongers [for dried fish] and Saltfishmongers [for fresh fish], of old time [which] had their seuerall Hals, to wit, in Thames streete twaine, in newe Fishstreete twaine, and in olde Fishstreete twaine: in each place one for either companie, in all sixe seuerall [i.e. separate] halles …' By 1536 the companies had amalgamated and improved their hall. The Tudor hall was destroyed in the Great Fire of 1666; the rebuilt hall was then demolished in stages when the 1827 London Bridge was built upstream of the old bridge, right next to the livery hall. Completed in 1835, this hall was severely damaged in the Blitz on 9 September 1940 and was not restored until well after the war. This photograph was taken at low tide in early summer, with the water level low enough to show the hall's foundations and river stairs.

PHOTOGRAPH: CARNEGIE, 2009

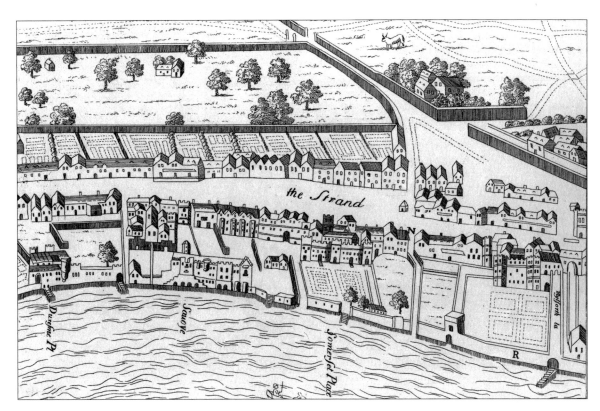

The Strand around 1572, based on the Agas map. At the top can be seen the former monastic garden that was to become Covent Garden, while along the Thames are the original Somerset House, used at this time as a royal palace, and the Savoy Hospital, built upon the site of the Savoy Palace destroyed in the Peasants' Revolt of 1381.

IMAGE COURTESY OF DAVID HALE, MAPCO

century, Wenceslaus Hollar, a Bohemian trained in Antwerp. Foreign immigrants were particularly active in the luxury trades, notably silk-weaving.[4]

Each migrant from abroad or, more commonly, from England represented an individual decision that life might be better in London. For many, this hope proved illusory, as, in practice, rural penury often translated into urban poverty. Moreover, urban degradation was more pernicious because of the absence of the social and community support that was more prevalent in rural parishes, although far from invariable there. However, as an important advantage for London, the social system was more fluid in towns: mobility was greater and social control laxer. Again, this contrast with rural and, often, small-town England, helped define part of London's lasting character. There was acute social differentiation in the city, and this can be seen as an instance of social control stemming from the sway of capital, but, at the same time, this was not a differentiation expressed in traditional terms of deference as that in rural England generally was. In practice, the sense of opportunity in London surpassed the reality, but it contributed, nevertheless, greatly to a feeling of flux that centred there.[5]

The new population led to a physical expansion of London, especially to the west, as well as into the properties seized from the Church. Twenty-three religious orders had

had estates in or abutting the City, and their seizure by Henry VIII in 1536–40 in the dissolution of the monasteries provided plentiful opportunities for expansion. In this way the Reformation brought significant alterations to the fabric of London and its suburbs beyond the city walls. There had been earlier instances of moves against ecclesiastical institutions, such as the suppression of the Knights Templar in 1312 and the seizure of the alien priories, but nothing on the scale of those stemming from the Reformation. Shrines were smashed, monasteries, nunneries and chantry chapels seized and destroyed, and fraternities brought to a close, such as that of St John the Baptist associated with the Merchant Taylors' Company.

As a result of the Dissolution, monastic buildings were used for different purposes or demolished to provide stone and other building materials. For example, the Priory of St Mary at Merton was demolished and used to build Henry VIII's magnificent new palace at Nonsuch. Important sites within the city were also freed for development. Thus, Austin Friars went to the Lord Treasurer, Sir William Paulet, and Blackfriars to the Master of the Revels, Sir Thomas Cawarden. Northumberland House at the west end of the Strand was to be built for the Earl of Northampton on the site of a convent. Some sites were levelled and not used for building. Thus, that of the Priory of St Mary Spital was turned into a setting for military practice.

London as a whole became an enormous building site, with status proving a key drive to the re-building. This concern with status owed much to the desire to display power and politesse, and to secure respect, on the part of the new (and newly promoted) nobility who had benefited from Henry VIII's largesse. Thus, Edward Seymour, the brother of Henry's third wife, Jane, who in 1547 became Protector (guardian) to his young heir Edward VI, swept away a site to the south of the Strand to build Somerset House, which, in turn, was demolished and replaced by the present buildings in 1776.

London provided an ideal site for display, helping to link Crown to élite, indicating yet again the very diverse nature of utilitarian activity and expenditure. This aspect of the pursuit of status should be seen as functional as well as wasteful, despite the fact that display, conspicuous consumption and social pretension were all castigated by moralists and mocked by some playwrights, for example in the characters of Sir Petronel Flash and his wife Gertrude in *Eastward Ho* (1605) by George Chapman, Ben Jonson and John Marston.

Southwark was a significant place in its own right in the Middle Ages, the largest town in the very wealthy bishopric of Winchester. These sad remains are of a gable wall with rose window, once part of the great hall of Winchester Palace, the bishop's residence. The hall was built in the twelfth century and the rose window was added later.
PHOTOGRAPH: CARNEGIE, 2009

The Strand proved a key area for rebuilding as there had been numerous town residences there for bishops and abbots. Buildings and land freed for development provided the space for aristocratic residences including Essex, Arundel and Salisbury Houses. In what was to be crucial to the future shape of the city, this rebuilding was not carried out in accordance with any overall plan. Nor was the opportunity taken to create grand prospects of the type decided by Sixtus V (r. 1585–90) for Rome. Indeed, at times, the result of the Dissolution proved singularly unfortunate not only for the general prospect of the city but also for specific neighbourhoods. For example, Whitefriars Monastery was granted to William Butte, the royal physician, but, instead of becoming an area of new-found grandeur, Alsatia as it became known was a centre of marginal and illegal activities. The inhabitants of this area had won exemption from the jurisdiction of the City authorities, and the legal 'sanctuary' thus created allowed this district between Fleet Street and the Thames to act as a notorious base for crime of all sorts, at least until the area's anomalous position was removed at the end of the seventeenth century.

The process of development was a continual one, recording shifts in individual and family fortune as well as entrepreneurial activity. Thus, after the site of Bermondsey Abbey, a Benedictine monastic foundation demolished in 1541, became Bermondsey House, which, from 1567 until 1583, was the seat of the Earl of Suffolk, the house, in turn, was redeveloped by the 1590s into rental properties. The extensive Winchester Palace, built on the south side of the Thames (near modern Clink Street) in 1109, became a prison for royalists during the Civil War. By the time of John Norden's map of 1593, the built-up area linked London with Westminster along Fleet Street and the Strand, an area that was comparatively affluent and focused on governmental, legal and gentry activities, rather than the commerce of the City or the industry, such as ship-building, to the east.

Increasingly Westminster became the West End. Henry VIII's development of Whitehall and St James's Park was followed by the aristocracy taking over the town-palaces of the bishops, while, as Parliament became a more central political element in government, so there were more reasons for the gentry to reside at least part of the year in the area, a process that was to be deplored by James I (r. 1603–25), although his attempts to get the

Elizabeth I in Parliament. Royal policies faced growing parliamentary criticism in Elizabeth's later years. The rise of Puritanism was an issue in the Parliament of 1587, while the sale of monopolies to manufacture or sell certain goods caused problems in those of 1597 and 1601.

S. James Parke

Charing crosse

York

The Courte Gate

The Courte

Preuy bridge

Kings streate

Chanoi row

Westmynster hall

A

Starre Chamber

The Quee nts bridge

The Lambeht

gentry to leave London failed. The rise in litigation, the centralisation of patronage, and the emergence of a London season, all contributed to these developments, which preceded the better-known town-building to the west in the century from the creation of Covent Garden in the 1620s.[6]

Westminster Abbey played a significant role in this process as the chapter were landlords of a large section of what became the West End, just one way in which the Reformation had a major but varied impact upon patterns of development in London. Westminster had a very different governmental structure to the City, with Westminster's parish vestries more powerful than the court of burgesses created for Westminster in 1585. These vestries were in large part under the control of gentry residents, which contrasted markedly with the commercial élite represented by the 26 Aldermen of the City.

Expansion also occurred to the south. In 1550 the City purchased the 'liberties of Southwark' from the Crown, so that this already very populous parish – known as the 'Borough' to distinguish it from the 'City' – came under the latter's jurisdiction, although it proved difficult to achieve control and Southwark, still part of Surrey, became something of a 'Wild South', with little law or regulation. Much of the area contained low-grade housing. This and the availability of land made Southwark attractive to entrepreneurs, and it became home first to rings for bull- and bear-baiting and then also to theatres. Southwark and Bedmondsey became major centres of the leather industry, which made use of the tidal tributaries of the Thames to wash away at least some of the foulness. Expansion downriver, meanwhile, included anchorages, ship-building yards and also the large palace at Greenwich built by Henry VII in about 1500. The failure of the Crown to implement an integrated approach to the suburbs ensured that the governance of both London and, more specifically, the suburbs was fragmented.[7]

London continued to expand, while buildings within the City were constantly being renewed. It was relatively ease to clear, alter or improve the medieval wooden and mud structures, and opportunities for redevelopment were frequent. Increasing prosperity provided one stimulus, while, as ever in London, fire contributed both need and opportunity for reconstruction. The overall urban structure of the City, with its property boundaries, city walls and Liberties, was retained through most of this redevelopment, and a contrast developed between the City and the suburbs, a contrast common elsewhere in Europe.

Since the Middle Ages there have always been at least two centres of power and authority within the metropolis. It might be argued that although ultimate authority might reside with the Crown and court at Whitehall and Westminster (and the Tower), the real power lay among the citizens, merchants and magistrates of the City of London. As Celia Fiennes remarked succinctly, 'London is ye Citty properly for trade, Westminster for ye Court'. For while the royal presence in the capital was intermittent and usually strapped for cash, especially to fund wars, the City interest over decades and centuries grew consistently stronger, richer and more self-confident. Between the two, literally and symbolically, sat the courtiers and nobility, who occupied the middle ground around the Strand and the growing West End. Two copies of the original Agas map of 1591 survive, one in the City collections at the Guildhall. The Eleanor Cross at Charing Cross is at the top, with royal palace of Whitehall below, its two arches over the public road (Kinges Street) giving access to the hunting grounds of St James's, as well as the cockpit and tiltyard. Westminster is at bottom left, and Lambeth bottom right.

The anonymous Copperplate Map of the 1550s makes this clear. Buildings outside the walls are shown, including the linear development north along Bishopsgate Street, but the general impression there is of a rapid shift to rural activities, with fields and animals. Other activities depicted outside the walls include the laying out of cloth to dry or bleach, and citizens practising their archery, part of a civic duty to protect country and city. Many of the dwellings outside the walls, however, were shacks, the 'mean cottages' criticised by John Stow; and these often temporary residences tended not to be depicted, appearing inconsequential and not worthy of inclusion. Maps can mislead as well as depict.

Further afield, there was a growing sense of London's social influence extending into the adjacent rural areas: London was becoming a centre, with other places in its orbit.

Moorfields, north of the city wall, in 1559. This is the copper printing plate (reversed here for ease of viewing) of one of the three surviving sections of the 'Copperplate Map', the first known printed map of London. Bishopsgate Street is prominent on this section, with two of London's medieval monastic hospitals: St Mary Bethlehem (Bedlam), and St Mary Spital. The medieval city walls, Moorgate, Bishopsgate, and the church of All Hallows-on-the-Wall can also be seen.

For example, the Tudor monarchs had a whole series of palaces in the hinterland such as Woking, Hatfield, and Oatlands, while courtiers quickly developed their own versions, such as Sutton House, Theobalds and Wimbledon. The last two were the houses of Elizabeth I's leading minister, William Cecil, Lord Burghley, while in 1607 James I persuaded Burghley's son, Robert, 1st Earl of Salisbury to exchange Theobalds for Hatfield, which Salisbury then improved. Sutton House was built in 1535, when Hackney was still a village outside London, for Ralph Sadleir, a royal official. The sole sixteenth-century window remaining in the house is known as the Armada Window, said to have been made from timbers from a ship that sailed in that campaign. Such houses were the beginning of the outward spread of the élite which led to the emergence of Richmond in the seventeenth century and to subsequent élite building in the Thames valley.

London's impact on its hinterland was characterised perhaps even more significantly by the need to provide for and support the city and its people. The perishable nature of fresh food combined with transport problems to ensure that market gardening focused close to London, for example at St Martin's Field. Pasture land was also located near to the city, to provide milk, but also to secure pasturage for animals that had been driven to London for

Father and daughter, two outdoor statues in London. Henry VIII, in classic pose, can be found above the Georgian entrance gate to Barts hospital, which he refounded in 1546. Elizabeth's statue of 1586 can now be seen from Fleet Street at St Dunstan-in-the-West, although until 1760 it had stood on the western side of Ludgate.

PHOTOGRAPHS: CARNEGIE, 2009

slaughter. The Piazza built at Covent Garden in the seventeenth century was constructed on the 'great pasture'. In the suburbs could also be found food processing, such as brewing and butchering, as well as industrial processes that were seen as polluting, for example brick-making and brewing, both of which led to much smoke.

Within the city, manufacturing included glasshouses and cannon foundries, both near the Tower. The visual impact of industry was present in the many windmills. The overlap of such activities with urban life led to complaints as there was no firm segregation, notably in Westminster. As settlement increased, there were particular complaints there about the butchering of animals and the keeping of livestock.

As the commercial entrepôt between England and the wider world London's trade and commerce have always been emphasised by its historians. Yet at the same time the city was also developing in other ways: it was becoming the prime site (and, as moralists and playwrights noted, sight) of consumption, and also a major centre of manufacturing and production. The growing prosperity of the country fed into that of London, not only through demand for goods produced there, but also through the desire for goods that could be imported via London. Nor should the economic effects of London's focal position as the national centre of government and the law be overlooked, as recourse to such institutions brought litigants, courtiers and their retinues to London and Westminster in ever-increasing numbers, as government in the Tudor period, from Henry VII onwards, became more organised, systematic and bureaucratic. The legal area to the west of the City around the Inns of Court was an important aspect of London's functional differentiation, and was linked to the gentility of the population to the west along the Strand.

London money also financed economic expansion elsewhere in England, by providing investment in industrial plant and credit for trade. London's financial role did not merely lead to more of the same, as there were also important qualitative changes to the economic activity that was financed. These included cutting-edge industrial activity, but, more significantly, London helped to mould a national economic market and, therefore, to dislocate traditional open marketing, where local producer-sellers met consumer-buyers. It is clear, however, that the specialisation for the London market that was crucial to this development was also accompanied by the persistence of more local economic patterns.

The London market was particularly important in the South East, with grain, for example, moved to London from Kent both overland and by sea from Sandwich. As a result, in the harsh harvests of the 1590s, serving the city led to food shortages elsewhere in the South East. Yet the difficulties of transportation across the Weald ensured that there was no comparable effect in Sussex. As London was the greatest market, provincial manufacturers and merchants were by 1600 typically opening London offices and engaging in regular trade with the capital. The network of regular carriers' routes focused on London was instrumental in creating the national transport system. London money moreover acted as a source of expenditure elsewhere, not least as cash was translated into aspiration and status. Thus, in 1552, William Clifton, a wealthy London merchant, purchased Barrington Court, a moated medieval house in Somerset, and commissioned a new house there on the Elizabethan E-plan.

Meanwhile, much of the drama of the English Reformation was played out in London. Those who opposed the royal will met summary punishment. The execution of the

A map of late Tudor London drawn in 1593 by Pieter Vanden Keere, and usually referred to by the name of its publisher, James Norden. The coats of arms around the map show the twelve great Livery Companies in their customary order of precedence, with Mercers at number 1 and Clothworkers at number 12. The Skinners and Merchant Taylors dispute their place in the order and have agreed to alternate each Easter, popularly but not implausibly giving rise to the phrase 'at sixes and sevens'.
MUSEUM OF LONDON

prominent, such as Sir Thomas More in 1535 in the Tower grounds, was matched by that of others who also fell foul of Henry VIII. The Treason Act of 1534 extended treason to cover words (not just deeds) and the denial of royal supremacy, and, the following year, Prior Houghton of the London Charterhouse and John Hale, vicar of Isleworth were among those punished with the full and brutal rigours of the law on treason for denying the royal supremacy over the Church that had been established by the Supremacy Act of 1534.

There was, in fact, a social pecking order to the place and manner of such executions. For at least 600 years up to the hanging of highwayman John Austin in 1783, Tyburn was where criminals and traitors of mean or common status, such as Cornish rebels in 1497 and the pretender Perkin Warbeck two years later, met their fate. Very often their heads were displayed on top of the south gate of London Bridge as a warning visible to all those entering the City. Robert Hubert, too, was hanged at Tyburn in 1666 after (falsely) confessing to having started the Great Fire; such was the despair and anger of Londoners in those desperate days that they 'tore [Hubert's] body to pieces as it was about to be handed to the beadle ...'

Tower Hill, literally in the shadow of royal might, by contrast, was generally reserved for the demise of more noble offenders, such as the Duke of Buckingham in 1521 and Sir Anthony Babington in 1586. The intimacy of Tower Green, meanwhile, usually witnessed the executions of those of the gentler sex, including three Tudor queens – Anne Boleyn, Catherine Howard and Lady Jane Grey – their noble status according them the relative dignity of beheading rather than hanging.

Of the eight Inns of Chancery that were in existence in the sixteenth century only Staple Inn in Holborn remains more or less intact, although this building, originally dated to the 1580s, was badly damaged by a German bomb and subsequently restored. Inns of Chancery were attached to the more senior Inns of Court (Staple Inn was attached to Gray's Inn), and provided elementary training for lawyers. The name of the building derives from the original purpose of the medieval building that stood on this site, the 'staple', where wool was weighed and sealed under the terms of the Statute of the Staple of 1353.

PHOTOGRAPH: CARNEGIE 2009

The Reformation did not simply involve London as a setting for the royal role. Instead, Londoners played a key part as a centre for early Protestantism, while the city's place within the country was in part a matter of cultural and religious activity. In particular, the city dominated printing, and this had a number of consequences. Aside from the networks through which Protestant printed material was distributed from London, the standardisation of language through London-based printing was related to the interlinked authority of print and capital. Trading contacts with northern Europe were important in the spread of Protestant thinking, and many Protestant refugees from the Continent moved to London. London and East Anglia became major sources of Protestant activity, while the key areas of violent opposition to the Reformation, such as Yorkshire in 1536 and Cornwall in 1549, were at a distance from the city.

London can thus be seen as the centre of change, although there were also many supporters of traditional Catholicism in and near the city. Moreover, in 1553, when the Protestant Duke of Northumberland sought to ensure the succession to the sickly Edward VI for Northumberland's daughter-in-law, the Protestant Lady Jane Grey, rather than for Edward's half-sister, the Catholic Mary Tudor, London joined the county élites and the Council in rallying to Mary, the legitimist candidate who gained power largely due to a large noble and gentry affinity in East Anglia. Thus, in a very different crisis, the city's response was different to that in 1381 and 1450 when London had not supported the more conservative position. Moreover, the subsequent rising, against Mary's decision to marry Philip II of Spain, and thus apparently ensure a Catholic succession, a rebellion in Kent,

The Fleet Street area, from the Fleet river in the east to Temple Bar in the west, has been associated with the worlds of printing and publishing for over 500 years. Near Stationers' Hall (part of which is seen here) Wynkyn de Worde set up Britain's first printing press with moveable type during the reign of Henry VII. Worde had already worked with William Caxton at the latter's Westminster shop until 1491, and in all he is thought to have been involved with the printing and publishing of over 800 different books. Worde was buried in the church of St Bride, Fleet Street, near where he worked. The Worshipful Company of Stationers and Newspaper Makers received its royal charter in 1557, although it had been formed as early as 1403.

PHOTOGRAPH: CARNEGIE, 2009

led by Sir Thomas Wyatt, found London resolute for the Crown. The rebels' advance was blocked at Southwark and the rising was then crushed.

Mary then pressed ahead with her plans for re-Catholicisation, plans reinforced by the punishment of those deemed heretics. On 4 February 1555 the first victim was burned at Smithfield. London, Kent and Sussex had a disproportionately high number of Protestant martyrs, being geographically nearest to Continental Protestantism, and also most exposed to royal power and attention. Indeed, the triangle of London, Canterbury and Windsor represented the focus of the politicisation of religion in the critical Reformation period of the 1530s to 1560s. In that area conformity was far easier to enforce and nonconformity far harder to conceal. This situation highlighted the extent to which it was not just London, but increasingly the London-centred hinterland as a whole that was influential. As a consequence, the balance of power, wealth and influence within England shifted steadily south-eastwards, and the relative dominance of the sub-region grew.

The image of London as the centre of Protestant martyrology was disseminated in *Acts and Monuments of the Church* (1563) by John Foxe, popularly known as the *Book of Martyrs*. By the 1600s, Wyatt was to emerge as a hero in the play *The Famous History of Sir Thomas Wyatt* by Thomas Dekker and John Webster.

Although London posed problems of political and religious management for the Crown, the Tudors did not face the breakdown of control there that was to confront Charles I in 1642. Instead, the relationship between Crown and city was one of essential co-operation. London provided the vital resources that enabled the Tudors to operate effectively, both in governing England and in acting as a European force. Indeed, without London, the Crown would have been significantly weaker, a situation that anticipated that of the eighteenth century. Many of the difficulties the Crown faced with London under the Tudors were, in turn, an aspect of the potential that it offered, as well as the extent to which its prominence ensured that London's influence was difficult to ignore. Thus, problems with religious dissidence and heterodoxy were, in part, a result of the role of London in the ecclesiastical and religious life of the country, a role that itself was linked with the Crown's ability to direct and arrange the religious situation. London, for example, was the centre of religious publishing, and thus of the dissemination of ideas, both governmental and independent.

It was not only the Crown that was challenged. In addition, the political and religious developments of the period (as well as the growth of population and the extent of poverty) also posed serious problems for the government of London, notably the City Corporation – the Lord Mayor, Court of Aldermen and Common Council, and, below this level, first the wards and then the parishes. Furthermore, the Livery Companies played important social and religious roles, and were part of a complex pattern of association in which institutions and formal structures interacted with the dynamics of individual and group identities and links.

The childless Mary Tudor was succeeded by her half-sister Elizabeth I (r. 1558–1603). Despite her caution in pursuing a relatively conservative Protestant church order, it became clear there would be no turning back to Catholicism. Over time Londoners who had lived in an unchallenged world of Catholicism died out, and an increasing percentage of the city's population came to be educated in a Protestant Christianity. This change was also true of London's clergy: in time, a better-educated and more committed Protestant parochial clergy developed, and the character of this clergy became important to the cultural dynamics of the city.

In many ways the Reformation in London, as elsewhere, represented a distinct breach in continuity. The religious roles of some buildings were maintained, but there were major changes reflecting the religious and political turmoil of these years. Westminster Abbey, a Benedictine monastic foundation, was the wealthiest religious community in England, with a net annual income of over £2,800 in 1535. Surrendered to Henry VIII in 1540 as part of the dissolution, the abbey was re-established as a cathedral for the new diocese of

First published in 1563, Foxe's *Book of Martyrs* was a hugely influential account of the persecution of Protestants, many in England. The deeds of the Catholic Bishop of London Edmund Bonner drew particular condemnation: 'This cannibal [Bonner] in three years space three hundred martyrs slew / They were his food, he loved so blood, he spared none he knew.' In this illustration from Part III, Bonner is seen punishing a heretic. Cheshire-born and Oxford-educated, Bonner (c.1500–69) became Bishop of London in 1539 under Henry VIII, but was deprived under Edward VI in 1549, only to be restored by the Catholic Mary in 1553. Bonner died in the Marshalsea prison under Elizabeth I and was buried in secrecy at St George's, Southwark, in 1569. Later scholars have revised down the number of Bonner's victims to around 120.
CARNEGIE COLLECTION

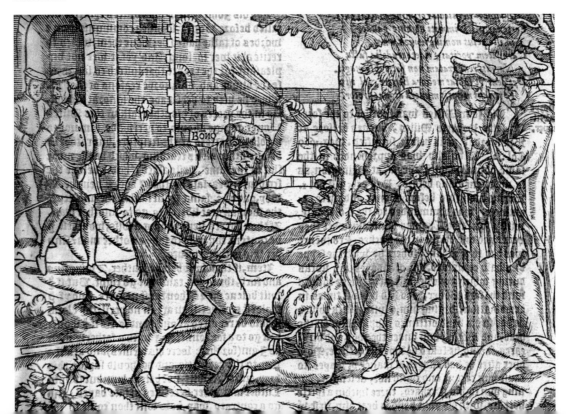

Westminster. Ten years later, when the diocese was abolished – the only one of the six new dioceses to be abolished – the abbey became a second cathedral for London, only for its monastic status to be restored under Queen Mary in 1556. In 1560, in turn, Elizabeth I refounded the abbey as a collegiate Protestant church enjoying exemption from episcopal control. The length and stability of her reign helped ensure that this arrangement was then maintained. Even when the ecclesiastical roles of buildings were continued, there were still major changes within churches, especially with the removal of fittings and vestments seen as idolatrous or superstitious, notably in 1549 and 1553, and again after Mary's reign.

A map of 1754 showing the Tower of London and the area around. The dotted line indicates the boundaries of the Tower Liberty. Before 1686 the liberties of the Tower consisted only of the area within its wall and land on Tower Hill immediately outside. Then in 1686 letters patent took the Liberty out of the City's jurisdiction and included within it other former monastic properties at Little Minories, the Old Artillery Ground and Well Close. The Liberty was divided into two precincts, Tower Within and Tower Without, which shared a courthouse and a prison. To the right of the map can be seen the Royal Hospital and Collegiate Church of St Katharine by the Tower, which had been founded as early as 1148. This whole area was demolished in 1825 to make way for St Katharine Docks (see page 239).

Under Elizabeth, London, and the South East as a whole, were centres of Puritanism, a tendency within the established Church calling for more radical church reform leading to a more severe, Calvinistic organisation and theology. The pattern of Puritan activity in London, as earlier that of Protestant enthusiasm, reflected not only individual and family convictions, but also commitment to the dynamics of particular communities, especially at the parochial level. In some parishes Catholicism maintained a degree of support, but elsewhere Protestant clerical and lay activism were more urgent.

Puritanism was linked with expressions of discontent toward not only the structure and forms of Church government, for example the role of bishops and the nature of clerical vestments, but also the political situation. In the last years of Elizabeth's reign, this tendency contributed to a more general sense of criticism, one that focused on London. Much of this criticism had a public resonance, as with opposition to the heavy taxation made necessary for the intractable war with Spain from 1585 to 1604, and also hostility to the granting of monopolistic commercial advantages to particular individuals. These advantages affected the freedom of economic activity within London, not least as monopolists sold permissions to produce and to trade. Thus, monopolies could act as another form of taxation, one that pressed especially hard on London. The City authorities also complained about the royal court's tolerance of aristocratic practices such as rowdiness, the violent assertion of honour and the patronage of brothels, theatres and gambling houses, as well as the reprieves given for convicted felons.

Despite serious differences over political, religious and economic issues, there was a widespread support for the government in its conflict with Spain and a more general economic interdependence of court and city, not least with the patronage of London tradesmen.[8] Moreover, London played a key role in the crisis of 1588 when the Spanish Armada neared England. The Council was convinced that London was the key target, and there was particular concern about the Spaniards landing on the Essex bank of the Thames and thus not needing to fight their way through Kent. Stratford and Gravesend were key points of concentration, but Tilbury subsequently served as a centre, not least for a visit by Elizabeth that provided an effective symbol of resistance. The crisis also ensured that a large number of men from south-eastern England had an opportunity to visit London or its environs.[9] The following year, London merchants put up much of the funding for the expedition against Lisbon, which was ruled by Philip II as Philip I of Portugal. They did so in order to gain commercial access to Lisbon, but the expedition failed.

London was the centre both of a more intense level of public politics and of a more

Sir Andrew Judde was Lord Mayor in 1550, and a member of the Skinners Company. This memorial, showing Judde and his family, is in the church of St Helen Bishopsgate.
PHOTOGRAPH: CARNEGIE, 2009, WITH PERMISSION

public culture. Public patronage and the exigencies and opportunities of the commercial marketplace were crucial to the development of culture, notably of the theatre. In turn, Shakespeare's plays expressed the aspirations and tensions of the emerging nation state, while their vocabulary and phrases came to occupy a major position in the language. The Reformation weakened patterns of control, providing new opportunities for the theatre. The numerous plays that were produced ranged widely in their subject matter, but the vitality of contemporary London was a frequent theme, as were the wealth and social pretension of groups in urban society. Londoners could see themselves depicted on the stage. This depiction was a matter not only of the presentation of London, but also of that of other cities. Thus, the social dynamics of cities such as Athens, Ephesus, Messina, Rome, Syracuse, Venice and Vienna, each of which was a setting for action in Shakespeare's plays, were the social dynamics of London, alongside the sense of difference that helped make them more interesting.

This identification with London was also true of other playwrights. Probably born in Westminster and educated at Westminster School, Ben Jonson (1572–1637) was made City Chronologer in 1628, succeeding Thomas Middleton. His play *Bartholomew Fair* (1614) depicted the outwitting of a country squire, as well as the attraction of the stall selling roast pork.

Although the plight of the poor could be depicted, the theatre and its morality were primarily located within a world of affluence, even if the audience was invited to mock the corrupt and lecherous wealthy, such as Sir Walter Whorehound in Thomas Middleton's comedy *A Chaste Maid in Cheapside* (1611). More generally, there were more clothes and furniture, more musical instruments and medicaments in Elizabethan London than there had been a century earlier, although such consumerism led to complaint from moralists, notably in sermons.

The poor were generally unable to share in this greater affluence, unless through crime, charity or as servants. Moreover, they were affected by the disruption to, if not dismantling of, traditional forms of social welfare as Church assets were reorganised or seized during the Reformation. Thus, some hospitals (the term hospital included buildings providing care for the destitute as well as for the sick), such as that attached to St Mary Spital, were dissolved, while others were re-established on more secular lines (see page 196).

Growing rapidly, London was a centre of social strain, as well as of demographic challenge, with plague hitting hard in 1518 and 1563. In the latter attack, about a quarter of the city's population died. Indeed, due to the high death-rate in London, it has been calculated that about 5,600 immigrants were needed annually by 1650 in order just to maintain London's population, compared to about 3,750 annually in the late sixteenth century. A significant aspect of such immigration was apprenticeship in London. This was a long-standing cause of labour flows,[10] and a process that created close social and cultural links with London from areas far distant, indeed helping to cement the emotional structure of the nation itself.

Migration to the city, as well as temporary periods of residence by others, meant that, by 1650, no fewer than one in six of the English population had lived in London for all or part of their lives. The growing population of England and London also led to price inflation, which was exacerbated by the debasement and increase in volume of the coinage. Due to the size of the population, food prices rose faster than wages, a contrast which hit poorer Londoners hard.

When the harvest was poor, it was not possible to alleviate the situation by imports or from large-scale food stores. Instead, the dearth of food led to a rapid rise in prices, contributing greatly to widespread malnutrition. This in turn weakened resistance to disease (as well as to the consequences of harsh weather), and death rates rose. This was particularly the case in the 1590s, with high rates of mortality in 1597. This situation contributed to a sense of crisis. Part of this process involved the traditional recourse of action against vagrants, as well as the allocation of stored grain, but there was also an attempt to improve the situation, notably by building up stores and organising the sale of subsidised grain.

There is controversy over the extent of poverty and the more general grimness of the social situation, with suggestions that poverty levels were in fact comparatively low and that the city was capable of absorbing people without great difficulty. Nevertheless, London seems to have shared in the national trend and its prominence and fears about the volatility of the city's population led to anxiety. At the national level, the number of paupers and vagrants grew, and concern led to a series of statutory national poor laws: in 1531, 1536, 1572, 1598 and 1601. Compulsory poor rates were introduced in 1572, but the situation was bleak, especially for able-bodied men unable to find work, in part because a distinction was drawn between migrants, who were welcome, and vagrants, who might become dependent on the parish. The latter were associated with begging and crime, although many were simply unsuccessful migrants. This was the group most likely both to suffer malnutrition and to be treated as in need of harsh control. The former royal palace of Bridewell was acquired by the City in 1553 as a house of correction, as an important component of an attempt to restructure the system of social welfare. Bridewell served as a model for institutions elsewhere; the able-bodied were made to work, with some also sent in chain-gangs to clean streets and ditches, and others, as indentured servants, to Virginia.[11]

As part of the attempt to clear the streets and to contain what was seen as disorder or immorality, criminals were arrested by parish constables and watchmen; measures were taken against bridal pregnancy and illegitimacy; and there were even attempts in some parishes to prevent the poor from marrying. Churchwardens presented people to higher church authorities for a wide variety of moral offences, including adultery and selling alcohol at the time of Church services. Parochial provision was central because, despite a number of efforts, it proved impossible to sustain a centralised system of poor relief in London.[12]

Unmarried mothers turned sometimes to abortion and infanticide, both treated as crimes, and the former hazardous to the health of the mother. This issue was not, of course, confined to London, but it was important to the character of life in the city. The women, often very young, who were punished as a result of these desperate acts suffered from the generally limited and primitive nature of contraceptive practices, as did those exhausted from frequent childbirth. Indeed, maternal mortality was a key aspect of the demographics of the period. That unwanted children were not only an economic liability, but also, when born to unmarried mothers, the reason for often severe social disadvantage, moral condemnation and legal penalties, made the situation particularly acute. In a society where women sought marriage as a source of precarious stability, the marital prospects of unmarried mothers were low, with the significant exception of widows, particularly if they

The story of St Paul's before the Great Fire is one of successive fire damage, rebuildings and restorations. The first cathedral was begun in AD 604. In the late seventh century there is some evidence that 'in the time of St Erkenwald, Bishop of London [AD 675–97], one part of St Paul's, formerly a heathen temple [perhaps a temple to Diana], had been pulled down for rebuilding', but the extent of this work is unclear. In 961 the *Anglo-Saxon Chronicle* records, 'This year … St Paul's minster was consumed with fire, and … was afterwards restored.' Another fire followed in 1087, and the Normans took this opportunity to build the great medieval church which, with enlargements in the 'New Work' between 1256 and 1314, survived until the Great Fire of 1666.

After the Reformation the great medieval church fell into disrepair, and in 1621 a local clerk, Henry Farley, took the then remarkable step of initiating a public campaign for its restoration. He composed a poem, *The Complaint of Paules*, and commissioned three oil paintings to illustrate his campaign, in a vain attempt to persuade James I to pay for the work 'to the reflourishing estate of the said church'. The third of these paintings is shown here, depicting the tower as Farley dreamed it might be improved, complete with several enormous gilded statues; a host of angels above clearly approve of the work.

SOCIETY OF ANTIQUARIES OF LONDON/BRIDGEMAN ART LIBRARY

possessed some property. Indeed, the particular status of widows played an important role in the dynamics of family structures and inheritance patterns.

As a result of the difficulties they faced, unmarried mothers frequently became prostitutes, or were treated as such. Rates of illegitimate birth, however, were far lower than today, although infanticide does probably affect such calculations. Moreover, many men and women never married, while marriages were generally late. At the end of the seventeenth century, English men married at about twenty-eight and women at about twenty-seven. Childbearing was thus generally postponed until an average of more than ten years past puberty, which, due to worse nutrition, itself occurred later than in modern Britain.

Domestic service was a common form of work for single people in London, both for those born here and for migrants to the city. As household tasks were arduous and manual, and the technological contribution minimal, such service was the life of many. Jobs such as the disposal of human excrement were unpleasant. Moreover, water-carrying could cause physical deformity, while cleaning and drying clothes involved considerable physical effort. Wages for servants were poor and pay largely in kind, which made life very hard for those who wished to marry and leave service, for married servants were relatively uncommon.

In addition, female servants were often sexually vulnerable to their masters. Although the following instances came from a later period, they are more generally instructive of gender relations. In 1729 the notorious Colonel Francis Charteris was convicted of raping Ann Bond, a servant, only to be pardoned by George II. The Chelsea bastardy examinations of claimants before a Justice of the Peace included

the voluntary examination of Sarah Powell, single woman ... who upon oath saith that she is pregnant of a bastard child or children which was or were unlawfully begotten on her body by one James Silvester of the parish of Chelsea ... with whom this examinant lived as a hired servant ... James Silvester in the month of June last, about two o'clock in the morning (being just after her mistress was gone to market) came to this examinant's bedside in his dwelling house and her waked out of her sleep, and did take the advantage of getting to her in bed.[13]

As a group the poor were not in a position to enjoy the growing comfort that characterised the wealthier sections of the community, with their finer, sometimes sumptuous, clothes, and their larger and healthier dwelling. It was a city of periodic food shortages for the many, but also of imported luxury goods and products for the few. Fiscal structures and financial developments exacerbated the situation, as the tax assessments of the better-off were unrealistically low, helping to sustain their consumption patterns. Moreover, the growing size of the population led to increased demand, especially for food, which exacerbated the sustained price inflation of the Tudor period that undermined the living standards of the poorer sections of society. At a time of inflation, only those with a surplus to sell could prosper. The urban poor were therefore hard-hit as they lacked access to the possibilities of cultivating waste land which much of the rural poor could seek.

At the same time, the enclosure of rural common land was a key aspect of an exclusion of the landless rural poor from the benefits of economic growth, an exclusion that, in turn, fed migration to London. There was relatively little political agitation in the London area as a result of these social and economic strains, but the potential for radicalism was shown when the disintegration of patterns of defence and hierarchy during and after the Civil War led to the Digger movement in Walton and Cobham in northern Surrey in 1649–50, as long-standing social problems were brought to a head in the establishment of a commune.[14]

The condition of the majority of London's population did not arouse the political and journalistic attention that it was to receive at the close of the nineteenth century, but it was a serious problem, the consequences of which included lower life expectancy and material deprivation. Furthermore, although there was some social mobility, most of the children of the poor were themselves poor. Education and literacy were not options for most of them, while the artisan community protected its livelihood by defending privileges as much against the poor in London as against artisans in other towns.

The social politics of London were the subject of humorous overturning in Francis Beaumont's play *The Knight of the Burning Pestle* (1607), in which an apprentice, Jasper, marries Luce, the daughter of his master, a merchant, against the latter's will, as he favours another suitor, only for Luce to be seized by her parents and locked up. Feigning death, Jasper is taken into the house in a coffin where he frightens the merchant by appearing as a ghost, and thus gains his consent. Thomas Dekker's comedy *The Shoemaker's Holiday* (1599) has a nobleman disguise himself as a shoemaker to pursue his love for another shoemaker's daughter. Reality was generally far bleaker, and tales in which plentiful food occurs as an element in the plot reflected the desire for a different world. In Philip Massinger's play *A New Way to Pay Old Debts* (c.1622), the greed of the villain Sir Giles Overreach is focused on the calculation of social advantage through family marriages, and failure leads to his becoming mad. The plight of young love, at the mercy of the power of parents or guardians, was a frequent theme in drama, as in Middleton and Dekker's *The Roaring Girl* (1610). Status and authority were both involved. Thus, in *The Witch of Edmonton*, Susan Carter is murdered by Frank Thorney, who has bigamously married her to secure his inheritance, as she is his father's choice and not his secret wife, the servant Winifred.

At the same time, rich and poor alike were exposed to infectious disease and to the polluted environment. In 1598 John Stow (1525–1605), the author of the *Survey of London*, noted the filthy state of the Fleet river, clogged with human waste. That was a challenge to all. The Walbrook, he noted, had been partly culverted: 'by common consent [the stream] was arched ouer with Bricke, and paued with stone, equall with the ground where through it passed, and is now in most places builded vpon, that no many may by the eye discerne it, and therefore the trace thereof is hardly knowne to the common people.' Stow's *Survey* was a milestone work in the recording and study of London's past, forming the basis of later histories, and a work that contributed greatly to the pride and self-identification of the city. For Stow's work was not one of mere antiquarianism; it offered insight into broader trends and aspects of the city and its place in the world:

> This Realme hath onely three principall Riuers, whereon a royall Cittie may well be scituated: Trent in the north, Seuerne, in the southwest, and Thames in the southeast: of the which, Thames both for the streight course in length reacheth furthest into the bellie of the land, and for the breadth and stilnesse of the water is most nauigable vp and downe the streame: by reason whereof London standing almost in the middle of that course, is more commodiously serued with prouision of necessaries, then any towne standing vpon the other two Riuers can be, and doth also more easily communicate to the rest of the Realme the commodities of her owne entercourse and trafficke.[15]

There was nothing uniquely harsh about the social politics of London, but the scale of the city was such that it represented a particularly bleak scenario, which in part was captured in Thomas Dekker's pamphlet *The Seven Deadly Sins of London* (1606), a recasting of the sins to take note of the energy of contemporary London. In a similar vein, he followed with *The Bellman of London* (1608). Yet, at the same time, the very attraction of London to migrants from elsewhere in England was a product of a sense of relative opportunity that qualifies this bleakness. Moreover, there was no equivalent migration flow from London to the countryside, nor to other towns.

London's reputation among those who did not live there was varied. It was at once a place of glamour, excitement and attraction, and also of filth, squalor, degradation and immorality – the stuff of ballads and folk songs. In the Middle Ages, many people in England could completely ignore London's existence, but the awareness of the city grew exponentially during the sixteenth century, so that by 1600 few were unaware of it, and many were directly influenced by it. Provoking dislike and suspicion, resentment of London's dominance was certainly not a rarity.

By the end of the Tudor period, London's grasp on the national imagination was far stronger than it had been in 1485. The combination of print and Protestantism was particularly important to this outcome, as London very much seemed both the source of the high rate of sweeping change across the country, and of the words, ideas and images through which change was defined, asserted and debated.

CHAPTER
5

'ALL THE WORLD'S A DESERT BEYOND HYDE PARK,' complained the ridiculous Sir Fopling Flutter in Sir George Etherege's sinuous comedy *The Man of Mode* (1676), a play designed for London audiences and where they could mock their fellow Londoners. Flutter's claim might easily be dismissed; but the grain of truth was that London did indeed remain central to English life and culture throughout this most turbulent of centuries; and this was a turbulence that Londoners could follow, in news-sheets and pamphlets, and that they also played a major role in shaping. Already, about 80 per cent of London craftsmen were literate by the 1600s, although literacy rates were lower both for the poor and women, groups that received less education and that, partly as a result, tended to be underrated in the sources that survive.

Whatever the political fate of London, its demographic strength was clear throughout the seventeenth century. By 1650, when London's population was about 375,000–400,000, its people accounted for about eight per cent of the population of England and Wales, and in western Europe London was now second only to Paris. In 1700, with its growth-rate greater than that of the population as a whole, London had more than half a million people, nearly one in ten of the English population, and also more than all the other English towns (settlements with more than about 2,000 people) put together. Indeed, only five of the latter – Norwich, Bristol, Newcastle, Exeter and York – had more than 10,000 inhabitants, and none of these could hope to compete with the capital. By 1750 London's population might have reached 750,000, having more or less doubled since the Civil Wars of the 1640s.

Sir John Reresby, MP for York, had claimed that London drained people from all over England, and 'was a nuisance to all the rest' of the country. He supported the imposition of a tax on London houses in order to help cover the costs of suppressing the Duke of Monmouth's rebellion of 1685 against James II. Nevertheless, the city's population made it a formidable resource in all sorts of ways, political, financial, economic and religious. During the French invasion scare of 1690, the city raised, besides its numerous militia, 7,400 auxiliary troops.

CONFRONTING THE STUARTS, 1603–1714

This beautiful panoramic view of Southwark, the Thames and London beyond is the first oil painting we have of London. It was executed in the mid-seventeenth century, just before the cityscape was to change dramatically because of the Great Fire of 1666. This is a bustling, vibrant and congested city, home and workplace to perhaps 400,000 people, whose ranks were supplemented by large numbers of migrants, temporary residents, visitors, merchants and traders from all over Europe and the world. What the artist chose not to depict was the smoke and foul air that John Evelyn and the Royal Society so complained of. On the far bank of the Thames one can see many wharves, water gates and stairs down to the river, while on the south bank the four flags are fluttering above the Southwark theatres, the Swan, the Hope, the Rose and the Globe, all of which were built about half a century before this view was painted.

MUSEUM OF LONDON

Physically London was transformed during the period, in part as an aspect of the spatial and social differentiation already noted for earlier periods. Indeed, in his *London and the Country carbonadoed and quartered into several characters* (1632), Donald Lupton referred to London as 'a great world' with 'so many worlds in her'. In terms of the shape of London, it was outward expansion that was more noticeable and arguably important. Much of London's new population lived in suburbs, where governance was far more loosely structured than in the City, and continued to be so. Already by 1640 Westminster had perhaps as many as 42,000 inhabitants, and the area between London and Westminster was progressively filled in with dwellings, although proposals in the 1660s for a second bridge across the Thames at Westminster were thwarted; such a bridge would have challenged the position of London Bridge, and thus of the City. The limited control of human society over the Thames was shown in 1663 when Whitehall was flooded.

At the dissolution of the monasteries, John, first Earl of Bedford had acquired the former garden of Westminster Abbey. The fourth earl, Francis Russell, developed this small but well-situated open area – the 'Convent's Garden' – into what came to be known as Covent Garden; this represented one key early stage in the city's expansion to the west. A large piazza was built in 1631 by Inigo Jones, the Surveyor to the King's Works and also architect of Whitehall's sumptuous Banqueting House. The surrounding houses were all in brick,

as were those at Covent Garden and at the new square at Lincoln's Inn Fields. In turn, there were further moves west. Thomas Wriothesley, fourth Earl of Southampton, laid out Southampton (now Bloomsbury) Square in the 1660s.

Moreover, the diarist Celia Fiennes recorded at the close of the century: 'There was formerly in the city several houses of noblemen with large gardens and out-houses, but of late they are pulled down and built into streets and squares and called by the names of the noblemen, and this is the practice by almost all.' For example, Clarendon House, Piccadilly, a spectacular palace built in 1664–67 for the Lord Chancellor, the 1st Earl of Clarendon, father-in-law of James, Duke of York, later James II (r. 1685–88), was sold after the earl's death in 1683 by the second Duke of Albemarle to 'certaine rich bankers and merchants' headed by Sir Thomas Bond. They demolished the house and developed the site, creating embryo streets including Albemarle, Bond, Dover and Strafford Streets.

Southampton or Bloomsbury Square c.1730. Along with Covent Garden half a mile to the south, this square was developed in the seventeenth century, among the first to be laid out. In February 1665, John Evelyn wrote: 'Dined at my Lord Treasurer's, the Earle of Southampton, in Blomesbury, where he was building a noble square or piazza, a little towne; his owne house stands too low … but good aire.' And in 1772 John Northouck wrote: 'The north side is entirely taken up with Bedford House, which is elegant … The square forms a magnificent area before it, and the grand street in front throws the prospect of it open to Holborn. Behind, it has the advantage of most agreeable gardens, commanding a full view of the rising hills of Hampstead and Highgate …'

MUSEUM OF LONDON

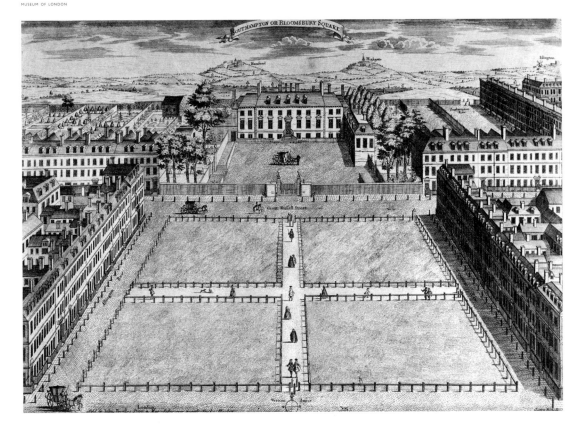

The fate of such a prominent house helped set an example for others. Bishops' palaces, such as Ely House, near Holborn, and Winchester House, were also pulled down, and their sites redeveloped.

Important as this expansion was in the late seventeenth century, it was even more apparent in the early eighteenth. The West End estates of landlords such as Sir Richard Grosvenor (whose family inherited Belgravia and Mayfair in 1677) and Lord Burlington were then developed as prime residential property. Their names are recorded in the urban fabric, most obviously with Grosvenor Square. The new development to the west had a marked impact on the already complex spatial differentiation and networks of London, and the social politics of the city.[1] As the nobility moved west from the Covent Garden area, Mayfair and St James's became the select side of town. Indeed, the streets there still bear the names of the politicians of the period, for example Harley Street, named after Robert Harley, Earl of Oxford, the leading Tory politician of the reign of Queen Anne (1702–14). Nevertheless, it is important to note that many poor also lived in the West End.

Building and gentrification helped make the area west of the City safer, and increased its appeal, as did a more general fashionability. Many of the newly laid-out streets in this area were paved (as opposed to cobbled), including Piccadilly in 1662, Holborn in 1664, and Drury Lane. Much of Piccadilly and Pall Mall drew its water from springs which provided cleaner water than that available in the City, where it was often contaminated by rubbish and sewage. Yet there was a constant sense of uncertainty in London, with the energy and imagination of entrepreneurs challenging any sense of order. At the close of Thomas Middleton's play *A Chaste Maid in Cheapside* (1611), the successful Allwits plan to establish a brothel in the Strand, while, in 1639, the Privy Council banned butchers' shops from the Strand to rid the area of the blood and gore that were associated with such premises.

Contributing to the development of the west, this was an age that put a cult on novelty at least in terms of buildings and residences. Thus, the Greenwich Observatory was regarded as an impressive new building. The first London squares were in evidence, including Lincoln's Inn Fields, Covent Garden Piazza and St James's Square. Housing took on similar values. Among the élite there was scant interest in living in old houses. New-build brick and stone structures seemed especially attractive, for both utilitarian and aesthetic reasons. In turn, the designs of London's new houses were given wider impact through publications such as Richard Neve's *The City and Country Purchaser and Builder's Dictionary*, which first appeared in 1703, with a second edition in 1726.

Moreover, moving west made it possible to escape some of the oppressive characteristics of London life, notably the noise and smell, although, in turn, it was necessary to confront the industrial activities already present there, such as brewing. In 1633 Charles I complained about the effect of brewing on the air at St James's Palace: the coal-smoke produced was held to be noxious. In his *Fumifugium: or the Inconvenience of the Air and*

Smoke of London Dissipated (1661), John Evelyn complained of 'the hellish and dismal cloud of sea-coal' (coal with a high sulphur content) which perpetually enveloped London, and he proposed to banish trades such as brewing, dyeing, soap- and salt-boiling, and lime-burning to a distance of several miles. In his passion to improve the city's environment, he found it remarkable that,

> this Glorious and Antient City, which from Wood might be rendred Brick, and (like another *Rome*) from Bricks made Stone and Marble … should wrap her stately head in Clowds of Smoake and Sulphur, so full of Stink and Darknesse, I deplore with just Indignation, That the *Buildings* should be compos'd of such a Congestion, mishapen and extravagant Houses; That the *Streets* should be so narrow and incommodious in the very Center, and busiest places of Intercourse: That there should be so ill and uneasie a form of *Paving* under foot, so troublesome and malicious a disposure of

These former weavers' houses in Fournier Street, Spitalfields, provide one surviving example of industry and 'busy-ness' being conducted within the city. From the 1550s French Protestant Huguenots had begun to settle just outside the City, and from the 1680s their numbers increased greatly – perhaps to as many as 20,000 – after their freedom to practise their faith was withdrawn in France. Many of those who came to London were highly skilled craftsmen in trades such as clock- and watch-making, metalworking and particularly silk-weaving. This terrace is one of the best surviving streets of town houses from the early Georgian period. They were built in the 1720s for senior Huguenot master silk-weavers and mercers. The single-fronted house at the centre of this photograph – no. 23 – is one of the best preserved. Industrial building experts more accustomed to identifying top-floor loomshops in the woollen districts of Yorkshire will immediately recognise the wide windows in the garrets which admitted plenty of light for the weavers.

PHOTOGRAPH: CARNEGIE, 2009

An engraving of Covent Garden, London, in 1647 by the Czech draughtsman and engraver Wenceslaus Hollar (1607–77). The church of St Paul, Covent Garden, which can be seen here in the centre, dates from the 1630s, an age of aristocratic and royal patronage before the turbulence and tragedy of civil war, plague and fire that hit London in mid-century. Inigo Jones was commissioned by Francis, 4th Earl of Bedford, to design a residential piazza at Covent Garden and was asked to add a modest church – a mere 'barn', it was said, would suffice – along the western end. Inigo Jones was baptised not far away, in the parish church of St Bartholomew the Less, although his cloth-working father had come to the capital from Wales. Inigo studied Italian architecture and was influential in London under James I and Charles I, during which time he designed elaborate masques for the court as well as several other buildings including the Queen's House at Greenwich (1616) and the Banqueting House in the palace of Whitehall. During the Civil War period, his property was sequestered by the parliamentarians and, for it to be restored, he had to pay a substantial fine in 1646.

the *Spouts* and *Gutters* overhead … because it is hereby rendred a Labyrinth in its principal passages, and a continual Wet-day after the Storm is over. Add to this the Deformity of so frequent *Wharfes* and Magazines of *Wood*, *Coale*, *Boards*, and other coarse Materials … when they might with far lesse Disgrace, be removed …

In 1662 a commission for highways and sewers was established, and Parliament sought to enforce a system of rubbish collection in response to a situation in which 'great quantities of sea-coal ashes, dust, dirt and other filth' were flung daily into the streets of London. This was not the sole source of smell and dirt. The habit of emptying rubbish into the Thames and its tributaries helped make them noxious, which was particularly apparent at low tide, when the Thames was especially smelly. *Fumifugium* itself was to enjoy lasting fame as an early example of environmental concern, and was reprinted in 1930 as part of the debate about the siting of Chelsea power station; five more editions were produced in the twentieth century. Also by way of moving undesirable activities away, the place of execution was moved, after a petition to Charles II from the residents in 1660, from Charing Cross to Tyburn, near the modern Marble Arch.

Aside from the development to the west, there was also a move from the City to the north, especially to Hackney. In Spitalfields, the Old Artillery Ground was sold for development and built over in the 1680s and 1690s, proving particularly attractive to Huguenots, who arrived in significant numbers in this period. There was also development to the east of the City, along both banks of the Thames. This latter development was closely linked to opportunities in maritime trade and ship-building, both of which employed large numbers, often in unskilled work, and these areas proved especially attractive for the poor.

Ships engaged in trade still anchored in the river during this period. As yet there were no proper wet docks where ships could unload safely at any state of the tide or river. Small vessels could still make their way upstream through London Bridge to berth at the many smaller wharves near Queenhithe and the Vintry, but, as ship size increased, the legally regulated quays below the bridge became more and more important. Around a quarter a mile of 'legal quays' on the north bank of the river between the London Bridge and the Tower, close to the Customs House, accommodated this growing number of ever-larger trading vessels. Ship-building, meanwhile, took place on shore and in inlets. The shoreline along the river to the east of the Tower was crowded with buildings, both residential and commercial. More generally, the suburbs to north and east of the City were largely fed by migration from rural England, including from the distant north, and were key sites of industrial expansion.

At the same time, topography and drainage still exerted a strong influence upon London's development. Marshland proved a particular problem due to the capillary action of water up wooden structures. Thus, there were few buildings in Pimlico or between Southwark and Lambeth. Instead, marshy areas, such as what became Waterloo, were largely devoted to agriculture, although drainage works served as a preliminary for development.

Seventeenth-century politics focused more clearly upon London than in the Tudor age, when provincial risings against the Crown had played a greater role. Now London drove and controlled national events, ensuring that the history of the two became inseparable. Violence was a theme at the outset of the seventeenth century, with Robert, 2nd Earl of Essex, a failed favourite, launching a coup attempt there in 1601, in a theatrical attempt that matched much seen on the stage. He wished to seize Queen Elizabeth and destroy his rival, the chief minister Sir Robert Cecil. Essex sought more power for the nobility and remarked, 'to serve as a servant and a slave I know not'. He was supported by six other peers, but not by the City of London, and he failed totally. Essex was beheaded.

Then, just four years later, a small group of Catholic conspirators managed to smuggle 800 kilograms of gunpowder into the cellars under Parliament, planning to blow it up when the new king, James I (James VI of Scotland), opened the session on 5 November

1605. The conspirators hoped that the destruction of the royal family and the Protestant élite would ignite rebellion and lead to the overthrow of the Protestant establishment. The plot was exposed, however, because of an attempt to warn a Catholic peer, William, 4th Baron Monteagle, to be absent. Captured in the cellars, Guy Fawkes was tortured to force him to reveal the names of his co-conspirators, and then executed.

James I wished to be remembered in London in a very different fashion. The Banqueting House in Whitehall was built by Inigo Jones, who introduced a classical architectural style to England where Renaissance influence had until then been fairly superficial. The Banqueting House was intended to be the nucleus of a massive new palace at Whitehall.

LEFT

Inigo Jones's Banqueting House.
PHOTOGRAPH: CARNEGIE

RIGHT

The sumptuous interior of the Banqueting House, centrepiece of the royal palace of Whitehall from its construction in 1619–22. The Flemish master Peter Paul Rubens was commissioned by Charles I to paint a series of canvases celebrating the life and reign of his father James. In 'The Apotheosis of James I', the corpulent king, with rosy cheeks and dressed in red velvet, can be seen at the bottom of the central oval canvas, being borne to heaven by Justice.
PHOTOGRAPH: CARNEGIE, 2009, WITH PERMISSION OF HISTORIC ROYAL PALACES

Fearful of assassination, James had disliked the colonnade in the previous hall on the site. The Banqueting House provided a venue for Londoners and others to see the king and royal family eat in public. Under James I and Charles I, tickets were issued for admission; William III was to be criticised for denying this spectacle to Londoners.

The Court as a setting for themes of royal power helped ensure that London offered a variety of political messages. The ceiling of the Banqueting House, commissioned by Charles I and painted in the early 1630s by Rubens, displayed the 'Apotheosis of James', seen being escorted to Heaven and depicted as the heir of King Arthur and the monarch of universal peace. Charles was presented by Rubens as God's representative on Earth.

At the other end of the spectrum, however, there was Puritanism, with its distinctively sober and pious lifestyle. This lifestyle could be satirised, as with the hypocritical zealot Zeal-of-the-Land Busy in Ben Jonson's play *Bartholomew Fair* (1614), and 'we of the separation' in his play *The Alchemist* (1610), but Puritanism proposed a set of values against which the royal Court seemed corrupt, and such values were popular in London. Living up to their caricature of prudishness, and concerned for public order, the Puritans succeeded in having the city's theatres closed down in 1642.

Nevertheless, James did not offend Puritan opinion to the extent that Charles I was to do. Instead, James's actions, such as the visit to St Paul's in March 1620, reflected the possibility of maintaining the nexus of Crown, Church and popularity in London. Yet the Crown's fiscal expedients and its sale of commercial privileges were unpopular in London. In John Donne's Elegy XIV, *A Tale of a Citizen and his Wife*, the citizen complains that

> Our onely City trades of hope now are
> Bawd, Tavern-keeper, Whore and Scrivener;

Wenceslaus Hollar's image of New Palace Yard, with the northern entrance to Westminster Hall on the left in 1647. For centuries Westminster Hall had been the venue for three great courts, the Court of Common Pleas, the King's Bench and the Court of Chancery. The three were amalgamated in 1875 and only moved to the new venue of the Royal Courts of Justice on the Strand seven years later.
© HISTORICAL PICTURE ARCHIVE/CORBIS

The much of Privileg'd kingsmen, and the store
Of fresh protections make the rest all poor.

There were also financial interests linked to the Crown, and they reached the height of power with Lionel Cranfield (1575–1645), a London apprentice who had risen through marriage to his master's daughter, becoming a prominent merchant and then customs official, who rose to be Treasurer and Earl of Middlesex, only to be impeached for maladministration and corruption in 1624.

Meanwhile, London was taking on a new function, one that was to be very important to its national significance, namely that of the centre of the English press. This function grew from London's continuous role, from Caxton onwards, as the nation's centre of printing, and also reflected the willingness to copy developments elsewhere, a key feature of entrepreneurship. An active world of newspapers had drawn closer in the Elizabethan period with the publication in London of news pamphlets, especially by the publisher John Wolfe. These and other pamphlets fostered a lower-cost marketplace of print, and encouraged entrepreneurs to seek profit in ephemeral publications. In 1620, the first English-language newspapers were imported from Amsterdam into London. These imports were a testimony to the interest there in foreign news, but also to the nature of a relationship between the two cities in which Amsterdam still took the leading role.

These imports encouraged the publication of 'corantos' (newsbooks or newspapers) in London from 1621. They were soon widely distributed across England using weekly postal services from London, and thus enhanced London's importance as a centre of news, both its disseminator and indeed its maker. Given that London's role and impact were in large part a consequence of its image, the development of its place in the world of printed news is a significant theme. Initially, this news did not centre on the capital. Instead, the 'corantos' focused on developments abroad, which reflected not only the importance of foreign trade to London, but also the political and religious interest in the Thirty Years' War (1618–48) on the Continent, as well as its links with political and religious tensions at home. The relationship between print and trade was also shown with the appearance of printed lists of London commodity prices. However, governmental unease led to a number of regulatory moves, culminating, as the consequence of a complaint from a Spanish agent, in the prohibition of 'coranto' printing in London by the Privy Council in 1632.

The circulation of news was related to the vigorous public politics of London, which included a vociferous response to public events. Thus, in 1623, Londoners applauded the return of Prince Charles from Madrid without the Spanish bride he sought. Such a bride would have been Catholic and was seen as a likely centre of Spanish influence. Both were unacceptable to the dominant strand in London influence.

In May 1640, moreover, as another instance of public politics, there were protests against

William Laud, Archbishop of Canterbury, including attacks on Lambeth Palace and on the prisons where detained protesters were held. As a consequence of the strength of Puritanism in London, the attempt to enforce the Arminian tendency within the Church of England was very controversial there. Associated with Laud, whom Charles I made archbishop in 1633, Arminianism rejected the Calvinist ideas of the Puritans, and Laud sought to enforce uniformity on a Church that for decades had been diverse in many respects.

This policy caused serious division in London where Laud was unwilling to permit Puritan clerics to comply with his regulations only occasionally. This authoritarianism compounded the offensive nature of Laudian ceremonial and doctrine, not least its stress on the sacraments and its favour for Church services that emphasised the cleric, not the congregation, an approach unwelcome to many Londoners. Arminianism was seen as crypto-Catholic, and thus conducive to tyranny, by its critics, who drew on a strong tradition of anti-Catholicism; and Charles I, who saw difference as subversive, could be harsh toward critics. At the same time, as a reminder of the degree to which London's politics, both secular and ecclesiastical, were (and still are) rarely a case of outside pressure versus the city, there was support for Arminianism and Laudianism in London. Indeed, Westminster Abbey has been seen as playing a key role in the development of the latter.

Charles I had pressed the City hard for loans and gifts in order to help him deal first with the parlous financial situation he inherited from James I, then with the unsuccessful

The Stuarts had a troubled relationship with London. The City's opposition during Charles I's Personal Rule gave crucial popular support to Parliament's cause, and, after his abortive attempt to seize the Five Members in January 1642, Charles I and his family were obliged to flee London. Yet after the Restoration Charles II sought to resurrect his father's reputation. Charles I ('The Martyr') is the only person since the Reformation to have been canonised by the Church of England, and in 1678 Charles II had this equestrian statue by the French sculptor Hubert Le Sueur re-erected on top of a plinth designed by Christopher Wren. The statue had actually been commissioned some 45 years earlier by Charles I's Lord Treasurer Weston, and had been duly erected at Weston's Roehampton home, although in the 1640s it spent some time in Covent Garden after Anthony Wither, a royalist, had paid for it to be moved there.

This statue is on the exact spot where in the 1290s Edward I had built the larger of London's two Eleanor Crosses (visible at the extreme left on the map on page 2), marking the route followed by the body of his dead queen from Lincoln to London. 'Charing Cross' was demolished by Parliament in 1647, although a tall replica stands nearby, outside Charing Cross station. London's other Eleanor Cross had stood in Cheapside; during the early months of the Civil War it had come under attack from Puritan iconoclasts, causing a minor riot when other Londoners rallied to the cross's defence. Parliament's Committee for the Demolition of Monuments of Superstition and Idolatry, however, ordered the demolition of the Cheapside cross in 1643, prompting the Duchess of Newcastle later to lament, in *An antient Cross* (1656), the 'rude Ignorance that's blinde, / That superstitiously beats down all things / Which smell but of Antiquity ...'

PHOTOGRAPH: CARNEGIE, 2009

In the febrile atmosphere of the early months of the Long Parliament crowds of ordinary Londoners, and particularly those from Southwark, played a significant part in raising the political temperature that would lead to the outbreak of the First Civil War in 1642. Charles I had badly misjudged the mood both of Parliament and of his capital, and he was forced to abandon his great minister Thomas Wentworth, first Earl of Strafford ('Black Tom the Tyrant' to his critics) to impeachment and execution in May 1641. Ironically the broad open space on Tower Hill, which had been kept open and protected from development by the Crown's Tower Liberty, now provided ample space for the estimated 200,000 spectators to witness this momentous act of theatre and political murder. In widely distributed prints, such as this one by Hollar, London was depicted unmistakeably as the location for major, historic events involving royalty, aristocracy and commoners alike.

wars with France and Spain in the late 1620s, and last with the cost, during the eleven years of his Personal Rule from 1629, of governing without the cash that only Parliament could grant. Mindful of the shared interests of Crown and London's oligarchical élite, the City authorities provided funds, including, in 1637, purchasing a new charter that confirmed established privileges. Moreover, London paid a large share of the extraordinary taxation justified as Ship Money. Yet, by 1639, this relationship was in serious difficulties, with most aldermen unwilling to help meet a demand for a loan made necessary by the cost of confrontation with Scotland. Moreover, there was accumulated anger about the extent to which royal pressure had created problems for the chartered companies, such as the East India and Levant Companies which, otherwise, could have been relied upon to support the Crown in return for their monopolistic privileges.

Charles I's failure to suppress opposition in Scotland in the Bishops' Wars of 1639–40 forced him to turn to Parliament, which he had dispensed with since 1629. This period of 'Personal Rule' had generated a series of grievances and a sense of grievance, both felt strongly in London; and Parliament turned on Charles' ministers and policies. The MPs elected to the Long Parliament from London, Westminster and Southwark were Puritans, while a clandestine press operating in London in 1640–41 printed works produced by the

Scottish Covenanters as well as books intended to challenge the position of the Church of England. These publications were significant, as rates of literacy was well above average in London. About 15,000 Londoners signed a petition presented to Parliament in December 1640 that called for an end to bishops. Such pressure was judged undesirable by royalists and led to criticism of London opinion as sectarian, unruly and lacking social quality, charges contested in the capital.

In an atmosphere of mounting crisis, in which London crowds played a vocal and vigorous role, Charles sacrificed one of his key ministers, Thomas Wentworth, 1st Earl of Strafford, who was suspected of authoritarian tendencies. A visitor to Westminster wrote about the 'multitudes of people' that flocked there in May 1641 during Strafford's trial'.[2] His execution, which owed much to the threatening pressure of large crowds, meant that Parliament was the first to resort to violence in the mounting crisis. Subsequently, the need to raise an army to deal with a major Catholic rising in Ireland in November 1641 polarised the situation. Dissension over who was to control this army exacerbated tensions over parliamentary pressure for a change in Church government, with the Puritans gaining strength in December's elections to the Common Council, and two new London petitions against bishops.

Charles resorted to the use of force, invading Parliament on 4 January 1642 in order to seize the 'Five Members' (and one peer), his leading opponents; but they had already fled to the City by river, the most convenient way thence from Westminster. The House of Commons followed, sitting in the Guildhall for a week, while the City's Common Council elected a Committee of Safety charged with defending the City and by-passing the Court of Aldermen, among whom Charles still had supporters. There was no chance of Charles seizing his opponents in the City and when, on 5 January, he appeared at the Guildhall to ask the Corporation for help in bringing his six opponents to trial, he found scant support. As he left, the crowd made its hostility clear, while Sir Richard Gurney, the Mayor, was assaulted. Rumours that evening of a royalist attack led, despite Gurney's opposition, to the mobilisation of the Trained Bands, and much of the population, in defence of the City.

As both sides prepared for war, Charles left London – for the last time except as a prisoner – on 10 January in order to raise funds and out of fear for his safety and, especially, that of his wife in the face of ugly and threatening demonstrations in Whitehall. London was not alone in its central political importance: Paris, too, played a key role, in the *Frondes*, the rebellions in France in 1648–53, while Barcelona, Constantinople, Lisbon, Moscow and Naples also took centre stage in the political turmoil of mid-century.

Charles's departure also weakened the royalists in London, for example the members of the Inns of Court who had demonstrated in favour of Charles in Whitehall in 1641, as well as those royalists dependent on the City. The Committee of Safety took over control of the Trained Bands from the royalist Mayor, and in March 1642 the Common Council

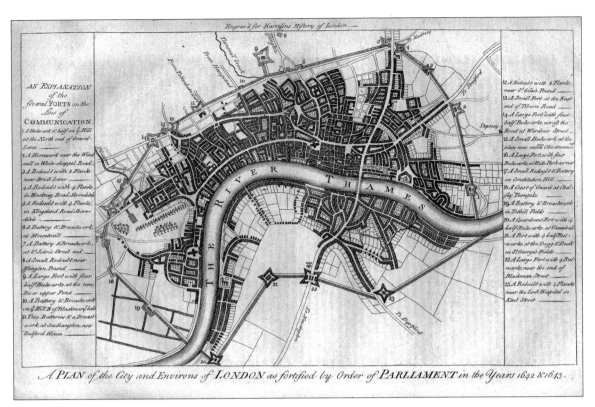

A PLAN of the City and Environs of LONDON as fortified by Order of PARLIAMENT in the Years 1642 & 1643.

established its ability to take decisions without the support of the mayor and aldermen. Charles's departure left the royalists in the fleet in a weak position, too, and this was exploited in March with the replacement of royalist captains by more politically reliable and experienced seamen from the mercantile marine. An attempt to restore royal control over the navy was thwarted that July. London was to be crucial to the naval dimension of the war. Gurney was sent to the Tower in July and replaced in August.

Later in 1642, having narrowly defeated the main parliamentary army (which included no fewer than 10,000 Londoners) at Edgehill in Warwickshire on 23 October, Charles advanced on London, but this did not prove a decisive drive. Moving in from the west, Charles captured Brentford (then a town in the country) on 12 November, but, the following day, his army's advance was checked at Turnham Green. This was one of the most decisive dates in London's history. The parliamentary army had been able to return to London from Edgehill, and Charles found himself greatly outnumbered, by a largely London force, at Turnham Green, then to the west of London. He failed to press home the attack in what were difficult circumstances, and retreated to establish his headquarters at Oxford. Charles's best chance of winning the war had passed. The closest parallel of similar significance was the stopping at Valmy in 1792 of the Prussian advance on Revolutionary

During the Civil War parliamentarian London was fortified by a vast encircling complex of walls and forts, but a royalist attack never came. Their rapid subsequent removal helped ensure that walls defined London's later street plan far less than in cities such as Vienna.

IMAGE COURTESY OF DAVID HALE, MAPCO

Paris in the face of a larger defending army. After Turnham Green, royalist advances were never again to challenge the parliamentary heartland of London and the South East. London's support was particularly important at this stage of the war, with a municipal loan of £100,000 in September 1642, as well as donations by Londoners, and the weekly assessment introduced in London in November, all providing much of the finance for the parliamentarian cause.

An eleven-mile-long defence system was rapidly constructed for London, an earthen bank and ditch with a series of 28 forts and two outworks. It was never tested in action, but was a testimony to the resources available for the parliamentarian cause, as well as the anxiety created by the king's advance in November 1642 and by the sack of Brentford. Sites of forts along the wall included the Old Kent Road, the Elephant and Castle, the Imperial War Museum, Vauxhall, Millbank, Hyde Park Corner, Great Russell Street and Great Ormond Street. The area included was much greater than that of London's medieval walls and recorded the extension of London in the meanwhile. A large area to the south of the river was also included, as was Westminster and the built-up area to the west of the City. Although work on the defences began in late 1642, it was largely pushed through during the following spring. This was a formidable undertaking. Much of the work was completed voluntarily, the Venetian ambassador claiming that 20,000 citizens worked without pay; but the City authorities did have to pay for some of the work, and special taxes were raised accordingly. Neither the royalists nor any other parliamentary city was able to match this effort, although no other city had such an extensive perimeter to protect.

The royalist plan for 1643, of concentrating their forces on Oxford and then advancing on London, failed. Instead, the royalists captured Bristol and unsuccessfully besieged Gloucester. The Trained Bands were the key element in the parliamentary army under the Earl of Essex that relieved Gloucester on 6 September, and then at Newbury, on 20 September, thwarted the royalist attempt to block their return to London. Subsequently, the Trained Bands were important in blocking the royalist advance into Sussex in December and January 1643/44. However, war-weariness led to problems with reliability among the parliamentary forces in November 1643 and, even more, the early summer of 1644. By then, there had also been demands for peace in London. Problems with the reliability of local forces helped lead Parliament to create a national army, the New Model Army.

London's defence was not simply conducted on land. The navy, under the command of Robert, 2nd Earl of Warwick, helped maintain the commercial buoyancy of London, and this achievement was crucial to the revenues on which the parliamentarian cause depended. London's importance was increased by the royalist capture of Bristol in 1643. The royalists challenged London's commercial position by licensing a large number of privateers, which made the parliamentary fleet's task of commerce-protection difficult. The parliamentary navy was also operationally important, especially in making it possible to supply isolated strongholds such as Hull, Lyme Regis, Milford Haven, Pembroke and Plymouth. Their retention by Parliament made it difficult for the royalists to exploit local strength and successes, and to concentrate their forces on targets closer to London. The parliamentarians could afford the loss of Bristol, but not the possibility of that of London.

Moreover, unlike most other major English towns, London was not besieged, which reinforced the message of very strong parliamentarian control. Because it was not besieged, London, unlike most other urban centres, was unscathed by the war: there was no loss of life and no destruction of property. The parliamentarians emphasised the centrality of London: they reported events in letters to London, and it was from London that orders were issued for the deployment of regiments and the army.

The support of London, the wealthiest place in the country, was important to parliamentarian victory, which was finally achieved in 1646. In the meanwhile, the country had had a rival capital at Oxford, to which Charles had retreated after he was rebuffed at Turnham Green. As an alternative centre of government, Oxford said much about the nature of the two regimes, and also indicated London's strength, both in this respect and more generally. Dominated by the royal court, Oxford was a garrison-capital, but the city could not offer the royalist cause either the resources or the organisational strength provided by London. These resources were a matter not only of money but also of manpower and productive capacity.

London was also the centre of the parliamentarian press. The abolition of Star Chamber in July 1641, part of the collapse of Charles I's authority, had led to an explosion of publication in London, the press feeding off the increased politicisation of the 1640s. The leading parliamentarian newsbook was *Mercurius Britannicus*, but after the removal of royal censorship the overall number of publications burgeoned. Within the churchyard of St Paul's in mid-century could be found the premises of bookseller and publisher George Thomason. Before his death in 1666 Thomason had assembled a collection containing perhaps as many as three quarters of all the pamphlets and tracts published in England – most in London – during the Civil War period. Now in the British Library at St Pancras, Thomason's invaluable collection totals a remarkable 22,000 different volumes.

Having defeated Charles I, who surrendered in 1646, the victors then fell out with each other in particular disputes over Church organisation, the payment of arrears to the New Model Army, and relations with Charles. Angry with Parliament on all three of these counts, the army occupied London on 3 August 1647. Some 18,000 troops marched through the streets and, by the end of September, the City defences had been destroyed in a powerful display of the army's determination to enforce control. London, where the Presbyterians, dominant on Common Council, were drawing closer to the royalists, was not to be permitted a separate military identity or destiny, as the City authorities had sought to do that summer.

The following summer, the army, increasingly dominated by its most successful general, Oliver Cromwell, fought the royalists and Scots in the Second Civil War. This war involved conflict in the South East, but the royalist force that was raised in Kent was blocked in June when it advanced first on Blackheath and then on Bow Bridge. Benefiting from control of London, the parliamentary forces proved adept at dealing with the royalist rising.

The navy, however, was divided in part as a result of the unpopularity of its commander from 1647, the radical Colonel Thomas Rainsborough, and twelve warships blockaded the Thames on behalf of Charles. The ability to exert pressure on London was a key point. Yet, without control of an anchorage, and threatened with a squadron under Warwick, who had returned to command on behalf of Parliament, the royalist ships lifted the blockade and sailed to Holland.

The army followed up its victory in the Second Civil War by purging Parliament in Pride's Purge that December, in order to stop it negotiating with Charles. The commanders then pressed on to ensure the trial and execution of Charles for treason against the people. In front of a shocked crowd, he was beheaded, on 30 January 1649, at the centre of royal power, outside the Banqueting House in Whitehall: Charles walked through the House under the glorious painted ceiling by Rubens he had commissioned, before proceeding out of one of the windows to his execution. Ironically, in the winter of 1647–48, Charles had planned a major redevelopment of the palace at Whitehall that would have incorporated the Banqueting House. The palace was designed to have a river frontage of 850–900 feet, as well as an imposing façade on the other side. This scheme was a key instance of Charles's interest in glorifying himself against the backdrop of London. Another example were his unrealised plans to rebuild London Bridge, much of which was destroyed by fire in 1633.

The choice of a site outside the Banqueting House for what was a very public execution was intentionally symbolic. Not only was an overthrown king to be killed, as had happened to Edward II, Richard II, Henry VI and Edward V, but this was to be a public act, as none of those episodes had been, and the centrepiece of the end of monarchy. Charles, however, was not executed at the Tower in order to avoid the need for a procession through London.

This purging of the monarch was to be accompanied by the end of the royal presence in the capital. In part, this entailed the removal of royal coats of arms and other devices. The statues of Charles and his father at the west end of St Paul's were demolished, as was that of Charles at the Royal Exchange, although the equestrian statue of Charles now in Whitehall was hidden until the Restoration by burial in the churchyard of Covent Garden. There was also a more specific change in status and function for the royal centre of Westminster. Charles, meanwhile, was buried at Windsor, not Westminster. His execution in London increased royalist denunciations of the city which, to the Bishop of Down in 1649, was 'the great City spiritually Sodome where our Lord was crucified'.

Ironically, Oliver Cromwell, the parliamentary general who governed as Lord Protector from 1653 to 1658, in turn created a court that had a quasi-royal structure, and this court was also located in the centre of government: London. He even welcomed foreign ambassadors in the very heart of the royal palace of Whitehall, the Banqueting House. As another return to authority under Cromwell, most of the London press was banned, and from 1655 only two newsbooks were authorised: both were published in London.

Alongside political uncertainty, there was religious disruption and social tension, the last leading to political radicalism as with the Leveller and Digger movements. The Levellers' movement, which came to the fore in 1647 and which owed much to the leadership and support of Londoners, called for male suffrage, and this programme was pressed in the Putney Debates held by the General Council of the army. Suppressed by the army's leaders, the Levellers were succeeded by the True Levellers, or Diggers, who, seeing private property as the consequence of the Fall (the exclusion of Adam and Eve), pressed the people's rights to common property. The Diggers tried to dig the common on St George's Hill in 1649 but were dispersed by the army and angry locals, suffering the same fate subsequently at Cobham. The Diggers' leader Gerrard Winstanley indicated the mobility of British society. Born in Wigan, he was apprenticed in London, but his failure in trade led to his becoming a Surrey cowhand. Social tension was also seen when the enclosure of sections of Enfield Chase in 1658 led to an organised incursion by local people and to conflict involving troops.

London's support for the parliamentary cause in the Civil War made it easier to preserve the essentials of its political and social structures. Thus, radical attempts to make the Common Council more representative of the freemen than of the liveries of the guilds were resisted successfully.

London, however, had more influence during the regime of the Rump Parliament in 1648–53 than under Cromwell, who was a Huntingdonshire gentleman with no particular affinity for the city. The Rump made commercial protection a key plank of its policy, and built up the navy to this end. This greatly helped London's commercial position as part of a broader attempt to boost national trade. Of particular long-term importance were the Navigation Acts of 1650 and 1651, which excluded other powers from the trade of the English colonies and restricted most of the trade of England, Wales and Ireland to nationals. Groups of City merchants sought political influence in order to exploit commercial opportunities. Puritan London merchants focusing on colonial trade helped to frame commercial policy.

Colonial trade also led to a major change in the city's social scene, with the opening of the first of London's coffee-houses, in St Michael's Alley, Cornhill, in the early 1650s. Established by a trader with Turkey, Daniel Edwards, who supplied the coffee – 'this Newfangled, Abominable, Heathenish Liquor' as it was described by one member of an initially hostile public – the premises were run by his exotically named Armenian servant Pasqua Rosée. Within a decade there were over 80 coffee-houses in London.

Cromwell's Protectorate was less favourable to London's commerce, as he embroiled Britain in a war with Spain that hit trade as well as leading to a serious financial burden. By the time of Cromwell's death in 1658, social tensions and disaffection were both grave. He had made one important change to the composition of the city's population when, in 1656, he legalised the return of Jews to England. By 1662 there was a synagogue with a congregation of a hundred in Creechurch Lane, and by 1677 this population had doubled, with a new synagogue at Bevis Marks in Aldgate ward.

The occupation of London in 1660 by George Monck, the army commander in Scotland, brought to an end the republican interregnum. This occupation was supported by the threat of another royalist blockade of the Thames, although it would be mistaken to see Londoners as playing no role in the end of the Interregnum. Instead, from 1659, the political instability of the Interregnum after the death of Cromwell, not least due to the weakness of his son and short-term successor Richard, combined with the strains created by government policies, had led much of the capital's populace to support a return to

Sir Hamo Thornycroft (1850–1925), was the scion of a renowned family of sculptors (see also page 15). He produced several public sculptures, including those of General Gordon on Victoria Embankment and this, of Oliver Cromwell. Depending on one's point of view, Cromwell can be seen as dictator, regicide or principled country squire, perhaps even as England's most important Member of Parliament. Not surprisingly, then, the erection of statues to the parliamentarian general provoked opposition as well as support. One statue in Warrington, Lancashire, reportedly aroused the grave displeasure of Queen Victoria, while the Conservatives on Manchester Corporation described the Liberals' intention to erect a statue of Cromwell on Deansgate (on the site of the first casualty of the Civil Wars) as 'a preposterous whim'. Remarkably, then, London's statue takes centre stage at Westminster, right outside Westminster Hall where Charles I was tried. Mindful of Cromwell's historical legacy in Ireland, the Irish Nationalist Party objected furiously to public money being used for the statue, and so, in 1899, it took its place here thanks to the generosity of the wealthy Liberal peer Archibald, fifth Earl of Rosebery, Chairman of London County Council from 1889 to 1890 and Prime Minister from 1894 to 1895.
PHOTOGRAPH: CARNEGIE 2009

monarchy. The leaders of London's Dissenters preferred monarchy to religious sectarianism which had expanded greatly in London in the 1640s and 1650s with the collapse of episcopal authority.

Monck restored a moderate Parliament, which recalled Charles II, the eldest son of Charles I, while the corpse of Cromwell was exhumed and hanged at Tyburn, the ancient place of execution for common criminals. The restoration of the monarchy was popular. John Evelyn wrote in his diary:

> On 29 May 1660, Charles II entered London with a triumph of … horse and foot, brandishing their swords and shouting with inexpressible joy; the way strewed with flowers, the bells ringing, the streets hung with tapestry, fountains running with wine; the mayor, aldermen and all the companies in their liveries, chains of gold, banners; lords and nobles, everyone clad in cloth of silver, gold and velvet; the windows and balconies all set with ladies, trumpets, music and myriads of people flocking the streets and ways as far as Rochester … I stood in the Strand and beheld it and blessed God. And all this was done without one drop of blood … it was the Lord's doing'.

This synagogue, which is tucked behind Bevis Marks in Aldgate, is the oldest in Britain still in use, having been built in 1699–1702 to cater principally for the Spanish and Portuguese Jewish merchant community in that area.

PHOTOGRAPH: CARNEGIE, 2009

The day was also that of Charles's birthday. Maypoles destroyed under Cromwell were re-erected, while a new Bear Garden was built in Southwark after the Puritan prohibition of bull- and bear-baiting was lifted. The king's return helped bring activity and prosperity to Westminster. For his coronation on 23 April 1661, Charles had a great processional entry from the Tower via the City to Westminster, passing through four large triumphal arches erected for the day. Musicians and choirs performed along the route, and cakes and wine were given to the crowd.

Popular joy, however, did not solve political problems; nor did it last. Legislation against Nonconformists hit their worship and ended the possibility of their holding office, leading to an intolerance that created problems for many Londoners. Control over the world of print was also reimposed. Under legislation of 1662, printing was strictly limited to the master printers of the Stationers Company of London and the university printers. Only twenty of the former were permitted, and vacancies were filled by the authority of the Archbishop of Canterbury and the Bishop of London, who were troubled enough by the dissemination of heterodox opinions not to support a relaxation in the control of printing. Thus, London's control was mediated through a conservative ecclesiastical structure which ensured that only certain circles in London benefited from the system. What to outsiders might appear monolithic control by London was in practice a very divided and divisive situation.

This reimposition of royal and ecclesiastical control was to unravel over the following three decades, but, in the meanwhile, Londoners were offered two harsh reminders of the vulnerability of human society. The first of these came in 1665, with a brutal and rapidly spreading visitation of bubonic plague, which hit London hardest. The early seventeenth century had already seen several outbreaks – in 1603, 1625 and 1636 – which killed over 60,000 people in total, but the 1665 epidemic was worse still. The long, hot summer of 1665 helped in the spread of the disease, which hit hard from April. As deaths mounted, red

A plague broadsheet showing nine scenes relating to the Great Plague of 1665. 1. The sick at home; 2. Shutting up the houses (once the plague had infected one member of a family, the house would be locked to prevent the disease spreading); 3. Fleeing London by boat (10,000 people camped on boats in the Thames to avoid infection); 4. Fleeing London by land (the king and court fled to Oxford, and many wealthy citizens took refuge in the countryside); 5. Carrying the corpses; 6. Carrying the dead in carts; 7. Burying the dead; 8. Funeral procession; 9. Return to London.
MUSEUM OF LONDON

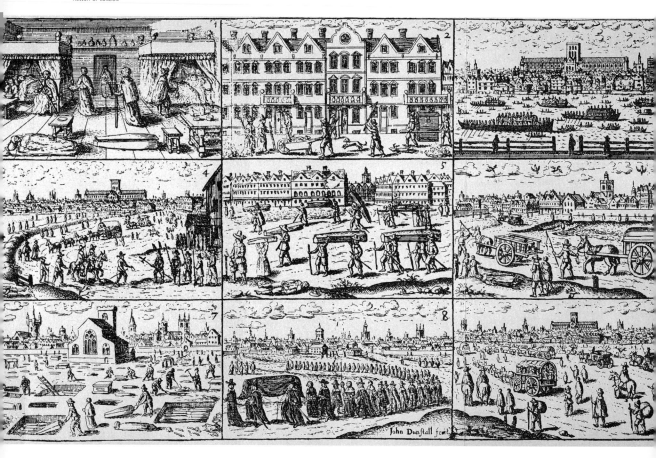

Samuel Pepys' diary entry for 22 November 1665 notes: 'This day the first of the Oxford Gazettes come out, which is very pretty, full of newes, and no folly in it.' The *Gazette* was first published during the plague year in Oxford, where Charles II had resorted for safety and where, in such a provincial backwater, courtiers felt in need of a source of news. When the court returned to London, so did the newspaper, taking from that time the name *London Gazette*. Within a year it was able to carry a sober but harrowing account of the spread of the Great Fire of London. This edition of 3–10 September 1666 not only catalogues the progress of the fire, but was probably the first written account to claim that 'care was not taken for the timely preventing the further diffusion of it, by pulling down houses, as ought to have been', and noting also that 'Divers Strangers, Dutch and French were ... apprehended, upon suspicion that they contributed mischievously to us, who are all imprisoned ...' The *London Gazette* may, to this day, be a medium of official record – to be 'gazetted' is to have one's bankruptcy or insolvency announced to the world – but the reporting in this early issue contains a good amount of sound journalistic enquiry and gripping narrative.

CARNEGIE COLLECTION

THE LONDON GAZETTE.
Published by Authority.
From Monday, Septemb 3, to Monday, Septemp 10, 1666.

crosses were painted on the doors of infected houses in a fruitless attempt at isolation. The bills of mortality recorded 97,306 deaths. Dead paupers were thrown into large burial pits, such as one at Tottenham Court. Many citizens fled the city, including the wealthy, most physicians and a large number of the parochial clergy, which was a serious issue as many of the churches were thronged in response to the crisis. London's economy was also in ruins. Public places were closed, sports banned, and a 9 p.m. curfew imposed. Commerce collapsed, with fairs, such as Bartholomew Fair in Smithfield, prohibited. The attack did not abate until the November frosts.

Contemporaries could not know that the Great Plague of 1665 was to be the last major outbreak in the city. Mutations in the rat and flea populations were probably more important in preventing a recurrence of plague than clumsy and erratic public health measures, or alterations in human habitat thanks to construction with brick, stone and tile. Yet, all this lay in the future (the building changes in large part due to the Great Fire) and, in 1665, it was easy to see the Great Plague as a result of divine displeasure. During the Plague the royal court moved to Oxford, which served merely to demonstrate London's importance, for there was no way in which Oxford could serve as a viable capital other than as a crisis measure. While at Oxford, Sir Roger L'Estrange used royal-delegated monopoly powers to publish the *Oxford Gazette*, as the sole newspaper. Yet, in February 1666, when the court returned to London, the newspaper moved with it and became the *London Gazette*, or *Gazette* for short.

Thereafter, smallpox, which killed Charles II's younger brother, the Duke of Gloucester in 1660, and Mary II (the wife of William III) in 1694, replaced plague as the most feared disease in London. Immunity was low, not least because a more virulent strain began to have an impact in the second half of the seventeenth century; from this time the fatality rate of smallpox continued to rise. Smallpox was airborne and far more contagious than plague, though less fatal. Smallpox was particularly serious in London, where it became endemic as well as epidemic. As proximity was important in its transmission, it was particularly deadly within the family or household group, and to infants and children. Smallpox was also socially selective, as the poor lived at a much higher population density than did the wealthy. In addition, smallpox viruses remained viable for up to a year and could be contracted via clothing or bedding; and the poor, less able to afford to destroy clothing and bedding after a death, were again more vulnerable to smallpox; they were also less likely to be able to wash their hands after defecating and urinating, which increased the chances of contaminated food and gastric infection; both acute diarrhoea and dysentery were killers. Another century was to pass before inoculation against smallpox, especially the Suttonian method from about 1768, and, from 1796, the safer alternative of vaccination, were in place to lessen the chance of attack.

Charles II's statue stands in King's Square, later known as Soho Square. This stone statue has not weathered well.

Meanwhile, just twelve months after the height of the Great Plague, a second great calamity struck the capital. The Great Fire raged for four days from 2 September 1666. Loss of life was tiny compared to the Great Plague, but the destruction of property was terrible. Much of the great medieval City was lost in the flames. Beginning in Thomas Faryner's bakehouse in Pudding Lane, near London Bridge, as a result of the failure to extinguish an oven properly, the fire quickly took hold among the tightly packed wooden buildings. It destroyed or severely damaged St Paul's Cathedral, the Guildhall, the Royal Exchange, 87 churches, 44 livery halls, and about 13,200 houses, burning 373 of the 448 acres within the ancient city walls and another 63 acres to the west. The strength of the fire, fanned by the strong easterly winds, was such that it was able to cross the Fleet river, and this spread

proved feckless early hopes that the fire would be only minor. Partly as a result of those hopes, the necessary measures to create effective fire-breaks by pulling down houses were not taken until late.

Charles II and his brother, James, Duke of York, took an active role in fighting the flames, filling buckets and encouraging the fire-fighters, and there was success in preventing the spread of the fire, not least by the use of gunpowder to create fire-breaks, which saved the Tower, but the blaze swept on, defying the generally inadequate responses. It was only finally stopped on the night of 4–5 September when the wind dropped, which permitted the fire-fighters to rally and dowse the flames. The fire left the City devastated. Far more damage was inflicted than in the Blitz of 1940–41, although only five people died in the Great Fire, which anti-Catholic propaganda blamed on the Catholics.

Old St Paul's – not for the first time – had been ravaged by fire: 'Thus lay in ashes the most venerable Churche, one of the antientest Pieces of early Piety in the Christian

Very few people are recorded as having perished in the Great Fire of 1666, but in terms of physical destruction this was a terrible week in London's history. This oil painting shows the scene at the height of the fire, with St Paul's about to be engulfed.

A PLAN OF LONDON:

Containing twenty five Churches only, reserved on their old Foundations, with all the principal Streets almost in the same part they formerly were, and Spaces for all the rest of the Houses, Lanes, and Alleys of note, according to the Dimensions following. Though by reason of the narrowness of this Plan the measures are not exact.

	Feet		Feet		Feet
The Key.	80	St Pauls to Cheapside	45	Pater noster Row	40
Thames Street.	40	Guild Hall to Cheape.	60	Lombard Street.	40
Fleet Lane.		Aldersgate Street to the Thames	40	Old Bailey from Smithfield to Blackfryars	35
St Bridge.		Exchange to the Thames			
Ludgate Hill.	50	and Moorgate	40	Warwick Lane to the Thames.	30
Holborn to Aldgate.	55				
Bridge to Bishopsgate.	50			All the Streets leading from Cheapside to the Thames	30

Described by J. Evelyn Esq. F.R.S.

Thamesis Fluvius

1. Fleet Street.
2. Fleet Conduit.
3. Shoe Lane.
4. St Bridge.
5. Ludgate Hill.
6. St Sepulchre's.
7. Bridewell.
8. Temple Bar.
9. St Dunstan's West.
10. Temple.
11. Temple Lane.
12. Fleet bridge and Channel.
13. Old Bailey.
14. Ludgate.
15. St Martins.
16. Newgate.
17. Christ Church.
18. Physicians College.
19. St Andrew's.
20. Baynard's Castle.
21. St Pauls.
22. The Wharf or Key.
23. Queen Hyth.
24. Bridge Market.
25. Belingsgate.
26. Custom House.
27. The Tower.
28. The Bridge.
29. St Magnus.
30. St Peter's.
31. Pauls Wharf.
32. Old Fish Street.
33. Watling Street.
34. Cheapside.
35. Lothbury.
36. Bread Street.
37. St Martins.
38. St Anthelins.
39. Alhollows the Less.
40. St Michael Hill.
41. St Mary Abchurch.
42. Alhollows Barking.
43. St Mary's Abchurch.
44. Alhollows Fenchurch Str.
45. Leaden Hall.
46. St Michaels.
47. Royal Exchange.
48. St Mary's Woolnoth.
49. French Church.
50. St Margarets and New Throckmorton Street.
51. St Olaves.
52. Bow Church.
53. Guild Hall.
54. St John Evangelist.
55. St Alban's Wood Str.
56. St Michaels Wood Str.
57. St Michaels by Pater noster Row.
58. Sion College.
59. Aldersgate.
60. Criplegate.
61. Moorgate.
62. Bishopsgate.
63. Aldgate.
64. Market where stood the Stocks.
65. Cheapside Market.
66. Gracechurch Str. and Market.
67. Lombard Street.
68. Tower Street.
69. Fish street Hill.
70. Threadneedle Street.
71. Basinghall Street.
72. Aldermanbury.
73. Coleman Street.
74. Wood Street.
75. Bartholomew Lane.
76. St Martin's Lane.
77. Pater noster Row.
78. Bow Lane.
79. Wallbrook.
80. Ivy Lane.
81. St Austin's.
82. Warwick Lane.
* Piazzas.

A PLAN of the City of LONDON

World,' as John Evelyn mourned. Ironically, just two years earlier Charles II had appointed commissioners – among whose number had been Evelyn and Christopher Wren – whose task had been to supervise a major restoration of the medieval cathedral. Wren's detailed plan for this had been accepted just before the Great Fire cleared the way for the brand-new baroque cathedral so familiar today.

In the aftermath of the fire, Charles II issued a declaration promising that London would be rebuilt better than ever, and would 'rather appear to the world as purged with the Fire … to a wonderful beauty and comeliness, than consumed by it'. He also declared that a handsome vista would be created on the river bank by banishing smoky trades which might mar the view.

John Evelyn, Peter Mills, Christopher Wren, Robert Hooke, Richard Newcourt and Valentine Knight then produced plans for rebuilding London as a consciously modern project and to a more regular plan, the pattern followed in other leading European cities, and one that reflected the favour of the period for dramatic, long streets and rectilinear town plans. Evelyn urged the value of zoning, especially the removal of noxious trades from areas of polite habitation. Wren proposed a city with two central points, the Royal Exchange and St Paul's. In his scheme, ten roads were to radiate from the former, while a piazza in front of St Paul's was to be the focus of three key routes in the western part of the city. The city was laid out in his plan in a grid dependent on the major through-routes, with piazzas or rond-points playing a key organisational role. The river was to be faced by a 'Grand Terras'. Wren's plan influenced John Gwynn's 1776 proposal for a replanning of the entire city. Evelyn was also interested in piazzas, while Hooke (who later became City Surveyor) and Newcourt each proposed a regular grid.[3]

Resources and will, however, were lacking, and the existing property rights of individuals were one of the chief stumbling blocks to an organised replanning. The need for a rapid rebuilding was paramount. As autumn nights drew in, the homeless camped in fields in Islington, Highgate and Moorfields, while mercantile and other activities were relocated. The rebuilding involved tapping the resources that could be readily raised by property-owners. Despite the work of the Fire Courts which adjudicated competing claims to land, there was no equivalent to the commissioners empowered by Parliament to organise the replanning and rebuilding of Warwick after the devastating fire there in 1694, an expedient that proved particularly successful in that case. The Rebuilding Acts for London of 1667 and 1670 were far more restricted in their scope, although they dispensed with the requirements of the trade guilds in order to aid rebuilding and also sought to limit the danger of a new fire by stipulating that buildings should have no projecting windows and should have, at most, four storeys. Houses were to be built out of brick and to be uniform in their frontages, and these regulations acted as the model for large-scale urban building elsewhere in England. The fire also encouraged the taking out of insurance policies.

In London, existing property rights ensured that by and large boundaries did not change, while existing roads were also preserved. The opportunity was taken to reduce the number of parishes, while numerous streets were widened. The sole new street, however, was King Street and on from that Queen Street, which created a new route from Guildhall to the river. Designed by Wren and the scientist Robert Hooke, the Monument to the Fire followed in 1677. The new Royal Exchange, an Italianate building with arcades, had already been built in 1669 by Edward Jarman; it was to be destroyed, again by fire, in 1838.

As King's Surveyor of Works, Wren had to be content with designing the dramatic new St Paul's, much of which was built in the 1700s, becoming the key work in the English Baroque. Wren was also responsible for designing 51 London churches, for long a highpoint of London's architectural heritage, although, challenged by Victorian redevelopment and by German bombing, only 23 remain. Like its medieval predecessor, St Paul's towered over the city, and thus provided a key point in vistas from elsewhere in

The main frieze on Christopher Wren's and Robert Hooke's 202-feet high Monument to the Great Fire of London. At the foot of one inscription a sentence referring to 'Popish frenzy, which wrought such horrors [i.e. the Great Fire]' was added in 1681, during the Exclusion Crisis, but deleted in 1830, soon after Catholic Emancipation.

PHOTOGRAPH: CARNEGIE, 2009

London and from the suburbs, but the absence of any coherent new plan to the rebuilding of the rest of the city ensured that St Paul's could no more provide a clear centre to the new London than any of the other buildings in the city. Moreover, Wren's plan for the canalisation of the river Fleet, so as to provide space for more wharves, failed, and the river, instead, became a sewer which was to be covered over in 1733. The canal and the rebuilding of the churches and public buildings was financed by a coal tax.

The rebuilding in the wake of the Great Fire, which may have cost close to £6 million, left a city that was considerably more attractive visually than that after the air attacks in the Second World War. Moreover, beyond the reach of the Great Fire, much of medieval and Tudor London survived the seventeenth century, only to be destroyed by the Victorians and the Blitz.

It took time for London to be repopulated. Some 80,000 people had fled and, by the end of 1672, a quarter had not returned. The lower cost of living in the Middlesex suburbs was cited as one reason, because taxes in London were higher and indeed had increased further due to the costs attendant on new churches, the paving of streets and drains. As a

Sir Christopher Wren's baroque masterpiece. The overall height of 365 feet is impressive, but would have been dwarfed by the reputed 489-feet high spire of the great medieval St Paul's. The modern cathedral is also somewhat shorter but wider than the medieval St Paul's.

PHOTOGRAPH: CARNEGIE, 2009

result, in 1673, the City, mindful that over 3,000 of its new houses were unoccupied, took steps to ease the burdens on new freemen.

Yet, there was a reluctance in the City to understand the extent to which Londoners now had alternatives as to where to live, and indeed that citizenship was not the only way to the privileges of London life.[4] The City's loss of control over the identity, and thus interests, of London and Londoners was to become a more prominent theme in succeeding decades. This theme, the emerging distinction between the City proper and a far bigger London, remains highly significant to this day, albeit with the key distinction now being the Greater London Authority area and the wider region.

The threat posed by fire was seen again when the Inner Temple was hit hard in 1677, while the royal palace in Whitehall burned down in 1698, with only the Banqueting House saved. The king, William III, did not rebuild Whitehall as a royal palace, and, from then, there was a divergence between the centre of government in Whitehall and the royal residence which, instead, became Kensington or St James's.

During the reign of Charles II (1660–85), London was not only the site of battle with plague and fire. To moralists, there was also the challenge from laxity, more specifically a sexual permissiveness that was a reaction to Puritan zeal. Engine, a maid in Edward Ravenscroft's play *The London Cuckolds* (1681), explained:

> This employment was formerly named bawding and pimping, but our Age is more civilised and our language much refined. It is now called doing a friend a favour. Whore

Lambeth Palace from across the river, by Hollar. Known as Lambeth House until 1658, the building was castellated in the fashion of an earlier age, with the entrance via Morton's Tower (c.1490), built by John Morton, archbishop from 1486 to 1500. The role of the river as a means of communication is readily apparent in this view. There is still a small pier in more or less the same location today.
© HISTORICAL PICTURE ARCHIVE/CORBIS

is now prettily called Mistress. Pimp; friend. Cuckold-maker; gallant. Thus the terms being civilised the thing itself becomes more acceptable. What clowns they were in former ages.

Characters like Engine helped explain the attacks on the alleged profanity and immorality of the stage, for example by the non-juror cleric Jeremy Collier, in his pamphlet *A Short View of the Immorality and Profaneness of the English Stage* (1698). Such agitation led to government pressure on the London playhouses the following year.

Meanwhile, in contrast, in Thomas Southerne's play *The Wives' Excuse* (1691), marriage to a callous husband was presented as imprisonment. As a reminder of the harshness of life, a Dutch visitor in 1662 witnessed the treatment of a woman convicted of murdering her husband, a crime treated with great severity and scant consideration of any provocation there might have been:

> we saw a young woman, who had stabbed her husband to death … being burned alive … She was put with her feet into a sawn-through tar barrel … A clergyman spoke to her for a long time and reproved her, and said the prayer. Then faggots [sticks] were piled up against her body … and finally set alight with a torch … and soon it was ablaze all round.

Far less harshly, just over half of the thieves committed to Bridewell in 1642–58 were women, while, as an instance of female exclusion from many activities, women were largely barred from coffee-houses, as, indeed, were the poor.[5] In practice, however, there were women involved in responsible economic positions. For example, in the 1690s and 1700s, Elizabeth Hervey was the London 'agent' of her family's cloth manufacturing business in Taunton. Such activity, nevertheless, was of limited interest to most commentators, who found London a tempting stage for the culture wars of the age.

The sense of London as uniquely sinful was a frequent theme of moralists. Prostitution was indeed one of the major industries there, and, more generally, there were the many possibilities for adventure and the independence of anonymity that the city offered and that moralists deplored. Intimate personal information from and about individuals becomes more common in the eighteenth century, but there is no reason to doubt that what it indicates were equally pertinent for the seventeenth. Two clear themes are the dangers posed by the venereal diseases of Londoners, and the contrast drawn between metropolitan vice and rural activities. Thomas Steavens noted:

> I was indiscreet enough to desire the employment of Miss Sally Clerk, a young lady who sells oranges at Drury Lane Playhouse; and she cruel enough to consent to it, in short

an unnatural flame on my side, and a still more unnatural one on hers had made such a bonfire of my body that I was obliged to apply to mercury.[6]

Indeed, in 1710, Zacharias von Uffenbach noted the large number 'walking with masks before their faces … they are generally harlots, of whom there is a vast number here especially by night in the streets'.[7] In August 1749 Major Thomas Gage wrote from the family seat:

> I have been in Sussex only about four or five days; though I made all possible haste to leave London, which was grown most intolerably stupid and dull. The only way I could devise to divert myself was with a wench, who has obligingly given me a pretty play-thing to divert me in the country, in bestowing a most generous clap upon me. I call it generous from its copious flowings, which I am endeavouring with the assistance of injections and purgations to put a stop to … One Tomkyns, a surgeon in London, advertises to have medicines sent him by one Monsieur Daran, surgeon to the French King.[8]

'Civis's' articles on prostitution, which appeared in the *London Packet* in 1787, dealt with a topic that received very little attention in the press. Civis condemned infant prostitution and pressed for legislation against seduction.

In contrast, in 1750, Henry Harris reported from London about the attitude of Mary, Dowager Lady Savile to her son, Sir George, later a prominent politician:

Sir Christopher Wren's Portland stone Temple Bar (1669–72) has now been re-erected in Paternoster Square in the shadow of St Paul's Cathedral. It was the successor to a more modest wooden structure with a prison above that had stood at the westernmost point of the City's authority, where Fleet Street became the Strand. (Similar, non-defensive chain and timber structures had stood on other roads into London, including Holborn, Smithfield and Whitechapel.) This was not one of the gates of the ancient city wall, but well beyond, on the way to Westminster: as the London-born wit once wrote in *Punch*: 'Temple Bar has always seemed to me a weak point in the fortifications of London. Bless you, the besieging army would never stay to bombard it – they would dash through the barber's.' There had apparently been plans to rebuild the medieval bar under Charles I, for in the *Remembrancia* there is an order, dated 27 April 1636: '… directing certain Aldermen, the Recorder, and Inigo Jones, Esq., His Majesty's Surveyor-General, to confer touching a convenient gate to be built at Temple Bar, and report to the Council thereon.' Traditionally monarchs stop at Temple Bar, where they are received by the Lord Mayor and formally invited, or allowed, to enter the City.

PHOTOGRAPH: CARNEGIE, 2009

We have here a young, sucking knight of the Bath, upon whom the fame of this curious taste will stick more closely. A very sober, demure, bible-faced spark he is – never misses the sacrament, and being well white-washed from all sin, but Whit-Sunday he began a new score in a stable yard with the waiter at Mount's Coffee-House'.

Three months later, Harris added:

Lady Savile has taken her young twig of Sodom into the country, and, by way of weaning him from that unnatural vice, takes great pains to coker him with every Abigail in her house, and all the milk maid cunts in the neighbourhood.'

Homosexual activity was treated harshly, not least the 'molly houses' (male brothels) that were raided in 1698, 1707 and 1726. The raid on Mother Clap's molly house in 1726 led to the execution of three men and to the publication in 1729 of *Hell Upon Earth: or the Town in Uproar*, which attacked homosexuality in the city.

During the 1670s, there was also much disquiet about the morality of the royal court, and virulent suspicion that its laxity extended to tolerance of Catholics. George Larkin's pro-government *Publick Occurrences Truly Stated* referred to 'the confiding coffee-houses, where the grave men puff out sedition'. Anxieties led, in 1678, to the controversy over what was called the Popish Plot. An adventurer, Titus Oates, claimed that there was a Catholic plot to assassinate Charles and replace him with his Catholic brother, James, Duke of York, later James II. Charles had no legitimate children, and thus James was his heir. The mysterious murder of Sir Edmund Godfrey, the London magistrate who took Oates's evidence, as well as the discovery of suspicious letters in the possession of James's former private secretary, inflamed concerns and helped the plot to become sensational news.

In a political atmosphere made frenetic by rumour and hard-fought elections, the Popish Plot, in turn, became the Exclusion Crisis (1678–81). This was an attempt to use Parliament to exclude James from the succession and to weaken Charles's government. London was a centre for support for anti-Catholicism and for Exclusion, support associated with the Whigs, the first English political party and one that, in large part, looked back to the same groupings and tendencies that had opposed Charles I. Whig common councillors

Sir Christopher Wren based the dome of St Stephen Walbrook on his original plan for St Paul's. The dome is immediately supported by eight arches which lie at 45 degrees to a cross-shaped arrangement of twelve Corinthian arches. The Lord Mayor serves as one of the churchwardens.
PHOTOGRAPH: CARNEGIE, 2009

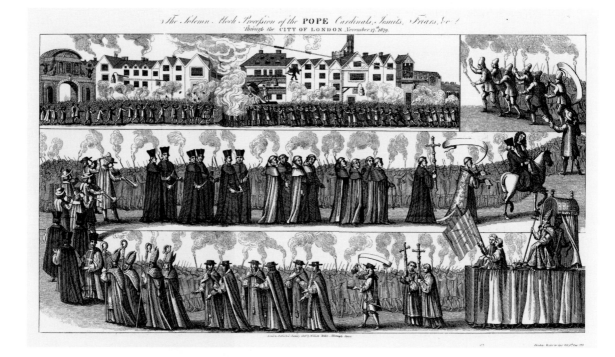

The Solemn Mock Procession of the POPE Cardinals, Jesuits, Friars, &c
Through the CITY OF LONDON November 17.th 1679.

The Pope-burning procession through the City of London in 1679 featured, among other things a depiction of a priest 'giving *Pardons* very Plentifully to all those that should *Murder* Protestants, and proclaiming it *Meritorious*'.

tended to represent parishes with a strong sense of Nonconformism that harked back to Puritanism.[10] London was also the centre of press activity. The establishment of the Penny Post in 1680 facilitated the transmission of information and the distribution of publications from London.

The Whigs' loyalist opponents were termed Tories, and they argued that Exclusion threatened the social order and might, indeed, cause another civil war. The association of London with the Whigs led Charles II to summon the new Parliament to Oxford in 1681. He correctly felt that it would be more under control there, in the royalist capital of the Civil War, than in London. Oxford was never again to have such a role.

The cause of Exclusion failed in 1681, in part because most of its supporters did not wish to push it to the point of violence, but also because Charles was more skilful than his father, and also retained control of Scotland and Ireland. Charles then launched a reaction. As an important component, royal influence over town corporations, especially London, was strengthened, and this new control was used to remove political opponents. In 1683 the charter of the City was abrogated, undermining the Whigs' position. Municipal rights were thus bound up with Whig policies including toleration of Nonconformists. Moreover, the Whig newspapers were stamped out.

At the height of this civic turbulence, a chill reminder came that politics could often be overshadowed by natural events. On this occasion it was frost, rather than fire, that became newsworthy. The great freeze of 1683–84 was the longest in which the Thames froze over. During the little Ice Age from the fourteenth to the eighteenth centuries the river froze on several other occasions. In 1536 Henry VIII had travelled on the river by sleigh, and hackney carriages were said to have plied their trade on the ice. Such freezes were aggravated by the greater width of the river, the many arches of London Bridge, and the fact that the stream generally moved more slowly than today. Frost fairs were held upon the ice, John Evelyn noting that 'Streets of booths were set upon the Thames … all sorts of trades and shops furnished and full of commodities'.

Control over London helped ensure that Charles, in the last years of his reign, had more sway over his kingdom than any of his predecessors since Henry VII. There was also a crisis in London's governance, with the City authorities forced to declare a moratorium in 1683 as a result of its long-standing cumulative deficits. At the same time, as a reminder of the diversity of London opinion, Tory crowds turned out in force in support when James, Duke of York returned to London, burning effigies of Jack Presbyter and of the Whig leader the Earl of Shaftesbury. Yet there were still Whigs in London, and the city remained very divided.

James II's more dogmatic and inflexible stance totally squandered the legacy left him by his brother Charles. Indeed, James helped ensure that opposition to his policies for autocracy and Catholicisation drew in much of the political nation. London played a major role in this opposition, as James's attempt to use the formal levers of power repeatedly clashed there with a strongly held sense of loyalty to national and Protestant liberties. In September 1685 Henry Compton was suspended as Bishop of London for refusing to suspend John Sharp, rector of St Giles-in-the-Fields who had criticised Catholicism from the pulpit.

The situation seemed all the more more threatening and urgent in 1685 as Louis XIV's abrogation of Protestant rights in France had resulted in a flood of Huguenot refugees into London. The Huguenots, who by 1690 had increased to about 8–10 per cent of the city's population, were to become important to London's character, settling in particular to the east, especially in Spitalfields where they played a major role in manufacturing, notably in silk-weaving. Their arrival expanded the city physically in this direction. Other Huguenot areas of settlement included Soho, Leicester Fields, Chelsea and Wandsworth. By the late 1690s, there were 45 Huguenot churches in London, about a quarter in Spitalfields, with others in the City and to the west of the City. The Huguenots highlighted the issue of immigration, but there were other migrant flows into the city. One major one was that of Scots, and in 1665 the Royal Scottish Corporation, a charity to support needy Scots in London, received its charter.

There were tensions in the short term as a result of the Huguenot influx, notably pressure on housing and competition for jobs, especially to lower-paid workers and to the Companies of Silkweavers and Cabinetmakers, and these tensions led to some discrimination and violence, including riots in 1675 in part due to the pressure on silk workers created by the use of new looms. The Huguenots were accused of working for lower wages. However, their new skills and techniques helped in the development of a damask and brocade industry in Spitalfields, while paper-making and work with gold and silver also benefited. The government tended to favour the Huguenots and, in the long term, they were to integrate well into London society.

By accentuating the already cosmopolitan character of the city, the arrival of the Huguenots emphasised London's difference to the rest of the country. New ideas came with them, as well as unfamiliar foods, including caraway seeds, garlic, oxtail soup and pickles. Their Protestantism was not that of the Church of England, although some Huguenots preferred it to Nonconformity.[11] Many of the Huguenots looked to Amsterdam, a key site in their diaspora. Indeed, intellectual and cultural links with the Low Countries were to increase as a result. By comparison, there was no real linkage between London and Hanover while the Hanoverian dynasty were on the British throne, from 1714 to 1837.

The Frost Fair on the Thames at Temple Stairs, January 1684. General view of the frost fair showing line of booths, coaches, sledges, sedan-chairs and groups of people on the ice. The round Temple Church can be seen in the centre-right background.
MUSEUM OF LONDON

Trafalgar Square accommodates the statues of two Stuart kings whose disastrous reigns were brought to an end at least in part because of the opposition of London. The equestrian portrait of Charles I now looks wistfully down Whitehall to the place of his execution, while this rather preposterous representation of James II in the attire of ancient Rome stands outside the National Gallery. One of only two known statues of the king, this one has been attributed to the studio of the London-based woodcarver Grinling Gibbons. Contemporary with James's brief reign, it was originally sited at the Royal Chelsea Hospital built by his father Charles II. In 1947 the Tory Lord Lloyd suggested in the House of Lords that a more 'central location' be found for the statue. Lord Henderson replied that this 'temporary' site had been allocated in Trafalgar Square, and that the Royal Fine Art Commission would try to find a new site 'when the new Government Offices in Whitehall are completed and the adjoining gardens are laid out' (*Hansard*, 18 Dec. 1947). No such site was found, and James II waits to this day to find a more accepting place at the heart of the British state.

PHOTOGRAPH: CARNEGIE, 2009

James II's pressure on Protestant London was demonstrated in the winter of 1687–88 when the three questions about favouring tolerance for Catholics put to all parliamentary candidates and magistrates were also put to members of the London Livery Companies: 3,500 members were expelled for failing to concur. Meanwhile, Catholic schools were founded in London; a Benedictine monastery was established in Clerkenwell; and Catholic priests in the city sought to recruit Anglicans.[12] The birth of a Prince of Wales on 10 June 1688 – later to be the Jacobite claimant 'James III' – suggested that the new pro-Catholic order would prevail, rather being than a temporary interlude before James's Anglican daughters, the childless Mary and then Anne, succeeded him.

On 30 June London was the centre of a massive demonstration of opposition to James, when the acquittal of the seven bishops (Archbishop Sancroft and six bishops), tried in Westminster Hall for refusing to support royal wishes on religious tolerance by reading the Declaration of Indulgence, was greeted by a great outpouring of public joy, including a large number of bonfires. The importance of London in public opinion during James's reign was emphasised by the way both James and his opponents sought to win over popular opinion by publishing tracts and books about such episodes. In turn, the acquittal was to be memorialised when the Palace of Westminster was rebuilt following the fire of 1834, as E.M. Ward's fresco was included in the Commons' North Corridor.

In November 1688 James's first cousin and son-in-law, William III of Orange, husband of his daughter Mary as well as the key political figure in the United Provinces (Netherlands), invaded with a Dutch army, in order to protect Protestantism and traditional liberties, and to ensure that Britain lined up against Louis XIV. Compton, the suspended Bishop of London, was one of the 'Immortal Seven' who had invited William to invade. Landing at Brixham, William marched on London, control of which – just as with William I in 1066 – was seen as crucial for the success. James deployed his forces at Salisbury, but his nerve failed, and the resistance dissolved. In turn, William refused to halt his march on the city in order to allow negotiations to proceed, as the Tory leaders (who were less unfavourable to James than were the Whigs) would have preferred, and James fled the capital, tossing the Great Seal of England into the Thames from London Bridge in the vain hope, perhaps, that the country would plead for him to return because no Parliament could be called without it. With James gone and William still outside London, fear of the London mob and of complete anarchy led to the Archbishop of Canterbury and leading peers taking control of the city.

Captured and returned to London, James was finally driven from it by Dutch pressure. Moreover, James's captors had to encourage him to flee a second time by leaving him unguarded. The report of William's arrival at St James's Palace in the *London Courant* linked demonstrations of support with the ideology of the new order. The Prince arrived,

> attended by a great number of persons of quality in coaches and on horseback, while multitudes of people of different ranks crowded the highways, echoing their joy from all hands in the loudest acclamations of welcome, which was more entirely testified by the cheerfulness and serenity that sat in all peoples countenances, to whom either true religion or liberty are of any value, all such ascribing their deliverance from popery and slavery to the courage and conduct of his Illustrious Highness, next to the providence and power of the Almighty. Nor were the exterior testimonies of ringing of bells, bonfires at night etc wanting to testify a general satisfaction at the coming of His Highness'

James's flight enabled William and Parliament to claim that James had deserted the realm, and, on that basis, Parliament offered the crown to William and his wife Mary in 1689. They were crowned by Compton. William's success was such that in 1715 the Jacobites initially planned to repeat his scheme to seize power with a landing by 'James III', the Stuart claimant, in the south-west of England, where there was to be a major rising, followed by a march on London.

The new political order from 1688–89, the Revolution Settlement, was one that suited powerful London interests as well as an increasingly defined and potent self-image of the city as a modern, commercial centre. In particular, the establishment of the Bank of

England in 1694, and its central role in public finances, provided a key junction between government and capital, and one in which London acted as the focus for, and anchor of, national financial activity. This role matched the theatrical accounts of London as a city of energy and flux. In his successful play of 1696, *The Relapse*, John Vanbrugh referred to London as 'that uneasy theatre of noise'. This was a theatre, however, that could have a violent side, as in 1711–12 when the young gentlemen of the 'Mohock Club' brawled and were held to slit the noses of victims and other such activities. A major attempt to improve public order occurred in 1697 when the privileges of Alsatia (see page 95) were abolished, although it took a long time to make the area orderly.

The Revolution Settlement produced a very different political world to that of James II, one that centred on London. Parliament had not met for most of the period 1682–88, but now was created a parliamentary monarchy with a practical requirement for annual sessions of Parliament and, after the passage of the Triennial Act of 1694, of elections at least every three years. Moreover, the lapsing of the Licensing Act in 1695 led to the end of the control over the number of printers by the Stationers' Company and of pre-publication censorship, and was followed by the expansion of the press. Some of the new papers spread London's influence across England. Papers such as the *Flying Post*, *Post Boy* and *Post Man*, all of which first appeared in 1695, were published on Tuesdays, Thursdays and Saturdays when the Penny Post left London. At once, this postal service enabled the new papers to meet both metropolitan and provincial demand and to establish their claim to be a national voice. The first daily paper, the *Daily Courant*, appeared in London in 1702.

The improvement of the road system assisted postal services. In 1663 the first turnpike trust was created on part of the Great North Road, while the first section of the London–Norwich road was turnpiked under an Act of 1696. A national turnpike network was not a reality until the mid-eighteenth century, but, in the meanwhile, communication links had already been improved, in part driven by the needs of serving the London market. The growth of the London-focused transport network had significant commercial and economic implications.[13] In 1702 John Evelyn visiting Helston in Cornwall, noticed 'where we dined was the Royal Oak Lottery which one could hardly have expected to have found in a country town so remote from London'.[14]

London also benefited from the improvement of its river links. The improvements on the Thames between Oxford and London had a major impact upon the supply of food, wood and other commodities to the capital. Similarly, the Wey navigation between the

The Bank of England, which, despite the name, is the central bank of the United Kingdom, was established in 1694. The funded national debt, guaranteed by Parliament, and based on the bank, enabled the borrowing of hitherto unprecedented sums, and at low rates of interest.
PHOTOGRAPH: CARNEGIE, 2009

Thames and Guildford (1653) – the first major river navigation which included extensive new sections of canalised waterway to avoid the more treacherous and winding parts of the river – was predicated on the booming trade in grain and timber from west Surrey to London. Commercial traffic on what is now known as the Wey and Godalming Navigations ceased only in 1983.

A new political order meant new palaces. At Hampton Court and Kensington, William III demolished earlier work and built anew. Wren remodelled Hampton Court for William with scant concern for the Tudor fabric: he designed the Baroque Fountain Court which was surrounded by two sets of state rooms because William and Mary were joint monarchs. As a consequence, there were two royal staircases and so on. The impression was dramatic as befitted both the grandeur of a ruler seeking to establish his position as king, and the Baroque style. The King's staircase glorified William, the murals, by Antonio Verrio, presenting him as Alexander the Great. The enfilade of the king's state rooms were similarly designed to exalt William, not simply with the three throne rooms, but also with the large state bed. On the ground floor, in contrast, William's living quarters were far more modest, in keeping both with his character and with the emphasis on display under the public gaze. A palace nearer London was also required, and, with Whitehall unacceptable because its damp and smog exacerbated William's asthma, he bought the Earl of Nottingham's house in Kensington for £20,000 and had that greatly altered, not least with a series of reception rooms.

Political attention and contention were focused on the competition for office between Whigs and Tories, but this competition also related to a host of issues in dispute, including religious toleration, Church government and foreign policy. The London press ventilated these issues, as did the developing world of the coffee-house. Most of the contention was peaceful, but the attack by Tory, High Church mobs on Low Church meeting houses in London in the Sacheverell Riots in March 1710 showed the possibility of violence. Sociability was also related to politics, and, in the 1710s, London's political clubs supervised electoral efforts. Events in London, moreover, provided important episodes for the public politics reported and debated in the press. Thus, the elections of London's MPs were seen as of particular significance, while the Common Council elections also attracted attention. This attention extended to foreign commentators, as with the French envoy dwelling in January 1716 on Tory victories in the Common Council elections.[15]

These were also years of war, with large-scale war being waged with France from 1689 to 1697 and from 1702 to 1713, the Nine Years' War and the War of the Spanish Succession. These conflicts led to unprecedented government expenditure, which put considerable pressure on the London money market, as did the need to finance military operations abroad, and thus transfer specie. War encouraged the growth of London, both the formal military organisation of government in London and the informal military support systems organised from the city. The *Observator* of 10 June 1702 commented on the public's interest in the war:

> 'Tis an easy matter to pull down pallisades, to attack half-moons, bastions, and counterscarps, in the coffee-houses of London and Westminster, and to bomb citadels and castles with quart bottles of wine in a tavern, where there is seen no smoke but that of tobacco, nor no shot felt but when the reckoning comes to be paid.

Such commentary was potentially subversive both socially and politically. In Delarivier Manley's novel *Secret History of Queen Zarah and the Zarazians* (1705),

> apprentice boys assume the air of statesmen before they have learned the mystery of trade. Mechanics of the meanest rank plead for a liberty to abuse their betters, and turn out ministers of state with the same freedom that they smoke tobacco. Carmen and cobblers over coffee draw up articles of peace and war and make partition treaties.[16]

More critically, London was seen as the centre of a moneyed interest that many regarded as disruptive. In his pamphlet *The Conduct of the Allies* (1711), Jonathan Swift offered the classic Tory critique of financial activity and speculation, specifically 'undertakers and projectors of loans and funds' seeking 'to create a moneyed interest'. Similarly in his pamphlet *Thoughts on the late Transactions of respecting Falkland's Islands* (1771), Dr [Samuel] Johnson, another Tory, was to refer to the 'sudden glories of paymasters and agents, contractors and commissaries, whose equipages shine like meteors and whose palaces rise like exhalations'.

This Tory presentation of London drew upon Cavalier and Anglican disquiet about the city during the seventeenth century, and, in many respects, was the latest iteration of the critique associated with the Exclusion Crisis. This was also a time when the money market was developing rapidly in what came to be termed the Financial Revolution. The funded national debt, guaranteed by Parliament and based upon the new Bank of England, enabled the borrowing of hitherto unprecedented sums and at low rates of interest. To its critics this monied interest was a threat – political, economic and cultural – to landed society and the values it represented. To them, it appeared that commerce was replacing virtue. In this London was very much a threat, with the city seen not only as a particularly conducive sphere for the activities of those pursuing the quest for power but also as aiding their endeavours. Moral and paternalistic attitudes towards wealth clashed with the reality of new money. Indeed, in 1696, as an alternative to the Bank of England, there was a politically pointed (and unsuccessful) attempt to found a Land Bank, using landed wealth as a credit source.

Reprising the complaints about usorious London merchants in the Tudor century, London was seen by critics as a site and source of false values, financial, political and sexual. It was where everything was for sale, as with the notice in the *London Journal* of 27 November 1725 for Thomas Rogers, 'Agent for Persons that buy or sell merchandises, estates etc.', who was willing to meet customers at the Rainbow coffee-house in order to discuss the purchase and sale of estates. Indeed the landed élite came to London to raise capital by mortgaging property (as well as to be close to the stock market),[17] while bankers bought status and land. For example, Sir Richard Child, later 1st Earl Tylney, had Wanstead House built in 1714–20; it was demolished in 1822. James Brydges, first Duke of Chandos, who made his money as Paymaster General, built a magnificent house at Canons, but the house and contents were auctioned and dismantled for building material soon after Chandos' death in 1744: the cost had proved too great and an estate praised by Alexander Pope survives now in the name of a Tube station (Canon's Park) and in part as the site of a girl's school, the North London Collegiate School.

In some respects, the critique of London was anachronistic, as commercial values and the money economy were scarcely new, while intermarriage between merchant society and the nobility had increased from the 1590s. Social divisions were permeable and status was open to negotiation and adjustment. Indeed, as far as control over land was concerned, the disruption attendant on the Reformation was far more acute than that linked to the Financial Revolution. Yet the link between money and power appeared to critics to be closer than ever before, and the speculation associated with financial assets appeared to challenge reality and value.

Within London, there was a different, but related, development as the guilds, which had become brotherhoods of wealthy merchants by the sixteenth century, increasingly, in turn, became associations of the wealthy (and worthy) committed to charity, education and clubability, but without any real accountability.[18] This transformation removed an important vertical strand in the city's socio-political fabric, contributing to a Tory critique from within London of the Whig dominance of the city world of money and privilege.

From both within London and from outside the city, there was also concern about the metropolis as the destination of immigrants. After the Huguenot influx came that of German Protestants fleeing Catholic persecution, especially in the Palatinate, the source of the 'Poor Palatines'. By 1709, over 13,000 Palatine refugees had reached London. About 6,500 were housed in army tents on Blackheath, about 5,100 in the navy's ropeyards at Deptford, and 1,400 in the warehouses of Sir Charles Cox, a Southwark brewer and MP.

Alongside the importance of London to Britain's governance and politics came its growing role in a developing global economy. As far as Britain was concerned, transoceanic voyages began from Bristol and later from Liverpool, but London came to play the key role, both in trade and, more generally, in the commerce and culture of the British

Atlantic. Theatre productions reflected these new trans-oceanic links. In Shakespeare's *King Henry VIII* (1613), a London porter wonders why there is so much noise: '... have we some strange Indian with the great tool come to Court, the women so besiege us?' Ironically, the Globe Theatre burned down during the first production of this play as a result of the thatch catching light after cannon were fired to mark an entry by the actor playing the king. In Philip Massinger's play *The City Madam* (c.1632) the villain is ready to sell his sister-in-law and nieces to the heroes who are disguised as 'Indians' seeking women for sacrifice.

London's commercial role had unattractive aspects, notably in the trans-Atlantic slave trade, in which the English had participated from the 1550s. The Company of Adventurers of London Trading to the Ports of Africa (the Guinea Company), which was granted a monopoly by James I in 1618, only traded to the Gambia in 1618–21 before abandoning the unprofitable trade. Another group of Londoners dominated the Scottish Guinea Company, founded in 1634, which operated on the Gold Coast, but the company had only limited success. Their role was a reminder of the place of London capital in many concerns. The Company of Royal Adventurers Trading into Africa, chartered in 1660 and reformed as the Royal African Company in 1672, was more successful in this cruel trade, and London dominated Britain's slave trade until the 1710s when it was superseded by Bristol, which, in turn, was to be superseded by Liverpool.

The regulatory framework that had maintained London's control was dismantled in 1698 by the Ten Per Cent Act, so named because the merchants were granted permission to trade to West Africa as long as they paid a 10 per cent duty to maintain the company's forts. As a result, the African trade was freed from the control of the Royal African Company whose position had been undermined after the Glorious Revolution which led to a decline in government support. The Ten Per Cent Act legalised the position of private traders, and made shifts in the relative position of ports far easier, helping lead to the rise of Bristol.

Another example of seeking to circumvent London privileges came in the 1690s with the rearming of the army with flintlocks equipped with socket bayonets instead of matchlock muskets and pikes; to get round the monopoly of the London gunsmiths, which acted as a drag in a situation made urgent by the Nine Years' War, the Ordnance Office employed their Birmingham counterparts.[19]

The company structure, however, was preserved for trade with South and East Asia, as well as in the case of the Hudson's Bay Company. Each was controlled from London. The East India Company, founded in 1600, came to form the basis of Britain's Indian empire. A joint-stock concern, the company reflected the strength and sophistication of London's commercial and financial circles, and it contrasted with the far greater state direction of most continental trading companies. In 1609 James I came to see the launch of the company's ship *Trade's Increase*. Joint-stock companies also operated within the

British Isles, including the London Lead Company extracting lead from the Pennines in the 1660s.

London's commercial position reflected the dynamism of its traders. The value of London's imports from the East India Company and the English plantations nearly doubled from the 1660s to the end of the century, while the percentage of London's total imports by value from these areas rose from 24 to 34 in the same period. Such statistics in part reflected the rise in direct trade, rather than using intermediary traders, especially the Dutch, and intermediary ports. This rise in direct trade was a result of the legislation of mid-century, the Navigation Acts of 1650 and 1651, which were reprised in the Navigation Act of 1660 and the Staple Act of 1663. Moreover, London's role in the British economic system was enhanced by the prohibition of exports direct from the colonies to foreign markets and, instead, the requirement that they be exported to England or one of its colonies. Not only were British entrepreneurs protected from foreign competition by the Navigation Acts; they also benefited from the absence of local tariffs. The value of London's docks led Valentine Knight, in his proposal for rebuilding the City after the Great Fire, to suggest building a canal from the Thames via the heart of the City to the Fleet river in order to provide additional space for wharves.

Ship-building, another activity in which the Thames played the major role in this period, was helped by legislation in 1660 that all foreign-built ships in English ownership be registered. Two years later, the purchase of Dutch ships (the principal source of imported ships) was hindered when an Act decreed that ships of foreign build not registered by that date were to be deemed alien and to be subject to alien duties. In 1698 Peter the Great of Russia came to the Royal Dockyards at Deptford on the Thames, as well as to the United Provinces (Netherlands), in order to see ship-building in process, as he searched for foreign models for the industry he intended to establish. Ship-building reflected the powerful role of the Thames, not only in shaping London and in its transport links, within and outside the city, but also in its economy.

Around the time of Peter the Great's visit, London's — and Britain's — first commercial wet dock was constructed. The dock, originally called Howland Great Dock, predated Thomas Steers' Old Dock at Liverpool by a decade or so. It later came to be known as Greenland Dock because of its links with the whaling industry, and it was significantly extended at the end of the nineteenth century. Built by the Duke of Bedford on the southern bank of the Thames in Rotherhithe in 1695–98, the Howland Great Dock was used by the East India Company initially as a safe anchorage and ship repair facility rather than as an unloading dock (unlike that at Liverpool); its real significance was as the first of many Thames docks that were excavated from the riverbank downstream of the ancient port near the Tower, part of a gradual, on-going migration of facilities towards deeper water and cheaper land to the east.

The Thames had always been central to London's experience, for water, for transport, for trade and for ship-building. As Antonio Canaletto's painting of *The River Thames on Lord Mayor's Day* (1747–48) indicates, the river was also very important to the City's ceremonial, in this case showing an annual riverine procession of the City's leaders.

Helped in part by Dutch investment after the Glorious Revolution of 1688–89, investment which constituted an important aspect of a growing Anglo-Dutch co-operation, London's role in the multi-centred trading system was becoming more prominent. Direct trading

This section of Stanford's 1862 map shows the Thames at Millwall on the Isle of Dogs (*top right*), where Brunel's *Great Eastern* was built (see page 242) and, on the south bank, the Royal Dockyard at Deptford not long before it ceased to be operated as such. King Henry VIII had set up these dockyards, as well as those downstream at Woolwich, to build and refit royal vessels, although Chatham was more important at most periods. There has long been a bridge where the river Ravensbourne joins the Thames at Deptford Creek, and it was here on 17 June 1497 that Cornish rebels under blacksmith Michael Joseph (An Gof, 'The Smith'), and lawyer Thomas Flamank were defeated by the forces of Henry VII. After the battle, also known as the Battle of Blackheath, the rebel leaders, in time-honoured fashion, were hanged at Tyburn, while their aristocratic ally James Touchet, seventh Baron Audley, was beheaded on Tower Hill. Their heads were mounted on spikes on London Bridge. Deptford Creek's other major claim to fame is that on 4 April 1581 Queen Elizabeth I knighted Francis Drake aboard the *Golden Hind* when it was moored here after he had returned from sailing around the world in 1577–80. This scene was subsequently memorialised in the epic of national heroism and expansion. On the Isle of Dogs side of the river one can just make out the small dry dock (Tyndal's Dock) on Ferry Road which features in the 1930s' photograph on page 329.

CARNEGIE COLLECTION

required more capital resources and expenditure and a more sophisticated organisational structure, but this trading enabled the British, essentially in the shape of London merchants, to bear the bulk of the transaction costs themselves and also to take much of the profit. This process can be seen with the India trade, which was largely financed with returns for bullion that could be obtained only from profits on other trades, for example the export of light draperies to the Mediterranean and of sugar to Hamburg.

The profitability of these trades and the role of the Anglo-Dutch link helped provide a financial strength that underlined London's importance politically. Linking politics and finance, Scottish historian Robert Wodrow noted in 1724 of the leading minister:

> Mr Walpole at present manages all. He has raised his reputation and interest exceedingly by his dealings with the Dutch. The monied people there have a high value for him, because of his appearances in the end of the Queen's [Anne's] reign in favour of liberty, and are willing to trust their money in his hands at three per cent. This put him in case to deal with the three great companies in England, the Bank, India, and South Sea, and to bring them to his own terms, as to the national debt, and being thus in case to guide these three, and consequently the House of Commons, he is got to the head of affairs, and is become absolutely necessary to the King.[20]

More generally, London benefited from being an emporium, such that, far from being compartmentalised, the British trading system had important financial as well as economic interdependence. Indeed, British re-exports rose from £2.13 million in 1700 to £2.30 in 1720 and £3.23 million in 1750, as imported goods, such as tobacco from the Chesapeake (Virginia and Maryland) or sugar from the West Indies, were re-exported to continental Europe, notably to entrepôts such as Hamburg and Livorno.

The importance of trade led to the appearance of specialist newspapers. In 1696, Edward Lloyd, a coffee-house keeper, published a tri-weekly, *Lloyd's News*, containing much shipping news. During Anne's reign, other relevant newspapers included *Proctor's Price-Courant*, the *City Intelligencer*, *Robinson's Price-Courant* and *Whiston's Merchants Weekly Remembrancer*. Imports also affected the material culture and structures of sociability of London, as with tea-pots and coffee-houses and the patterns of behaviour linked to the consumption of chocolate, coffee and tea. New codes of conduct were thereby set in London, such as differences between men and women in their consumption of the new drinks. In turn, London audiences saw themselves depicted on stage in these contexts, as with John Philip's play *The Inquisition* (1717), the action of which opened in Child's Coffee-house in London. Exports, meanwhile, took London goods across the world. When Peter Macskásy, a Transylvanian landowner in modern Romania, died in 1712, his effects included 'a pair of London summer gloves'.[21]

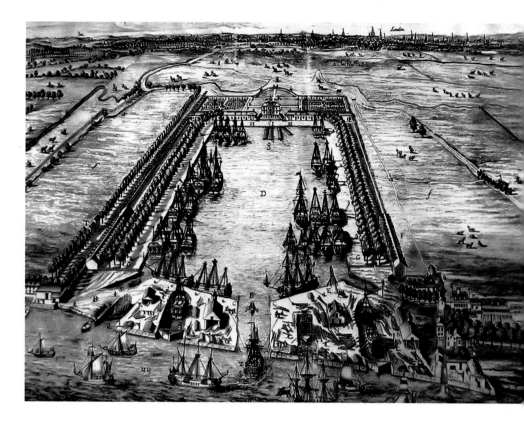

A view of the Howland Great Wet Dock in 1717, the first enclosed dock on the Thames. The dock was built on the Rotherhithe loop in the river Thames, and London can be seen in the far distance out to the west. At first it was not planned to unload goods at the dock itself – there were no warehouses, and it lay a considerable distance from the port in and around the Pool. Instead ships for the East India Company sheltered here before unloading upstream at the Legal Quays. There were also ship-repair facilities here, seen in the foreground.

CARNEGIE COLLECTION

London also remained an important centre of manufacturing, especially in the luxury trades and in cloth finishing, both high-value activities. Other industries included ship-building, needle-making, and industries focused on serving the growing population of the city. Among these were slaughterhouses, brewing, sugar-boiling, soap-boiling, glue-making and kilns. Commercialisation was seen in the case of Oliver Cromwell's wife Elizabeth who wished to brew her own ale in Whitehall, only to have to accept Morning Dew, a new London ale. The Bear Garden in Southwark was replaced by a glassworks in the 1680s. The difficulty of moving and preserving products such as beer and meat contributed to the location of these industries in the London area.

As a result of these industries, pollution in and around the City was considerable. Tanning, which required urine and faeces, soap-boiling and glue-making, all aspects of the processing of dead animals, were noxious. In turn, this pollution helped affect the geography of the city, reflecting and contributing to the lack of appeal of particular areas. Many of the noxious industrial processes, for example tanneries, were located south of the Thames. Just south of Westcheap lies the City ward of Cordwainer, in which John Stow had found 'Cordwainers, or Shoemakers, Curriars, and workers of Leather dwelling …' But such artisans now bought the leather they worked from the new centre of the tanning industry, downstream of the City, at Bermondsey, where tidal streams on the south bank of the Thames were utilised to good effect. By the eighteenth century it was said that as much as one third of the country's leather was being tanned in Bermondsey. There were also lime-kilns in Limehouse and Bankside. Such industries affected others requiring clean air or water, so that by the 1680s the dyers were moving from Southwark to Crayford as they dried the finished cloth in the open and could not afford the proximity of industries producing noxious fumes.

Industrial sites both revealed specialisation and yet were also flexible, as energy sources, especially water-power, and premises could be reused for other purposes. This was particularly seen with the Wandle, one of the tributaries of the Thames. A centre of water-powered grain milling in medieval and, even more, in Tudor times, this valley also became the setting of a greater range of industries including the printing and dyeing of textiles. Just as there was residential differentiation within London, so there was also industrial. Many of the more polluting industries were on the south bank, whereas, to the east of the City, there were new industries such as silk-weaving, as well as other manufactures that benefited from a cheaper and less regulated working environment than that in the City. Nevertheless, some industry continued within the City, for example printing.

Within Britain, the economic links of the Tudor age continued and new ones were created, accentuating London's role in a developing national economy. The first shipload of Cheshire cheese reached London in 1650. By 1664, more than fourteen cheese ships

This elaborate spire which rises above the relatively austere classical body of St George's Bloomsbury (1720–30, consecrated 1731) carries the figure of George I (in Roman toga surmounted by lightning conductor), as well as sculptures of lion and unicorn. The church, one of the earliest in London with a portico, was the last of Nicholas Hawksmoor's six London churches, which in recent times have entered popular fiction as the focus for the architect's supposed devil-worship and theistic satanism. The assertive bulk of Hawksmoor's work, seen also in his St George-in-the-East, Wapping (built 1714–29), encapsulated Baroque values of scale.

PHOTOGRAPH: CARNEGIE, 2009

were sailing from the North West, and by the 1680s over fifty. Return cargoes from London helped to transform the regional economy in the North West and elsewhere. Cheese also came to London from Somerset via Bristol. Feeding the city's growing numbers depended on agricultural expansion in England (as yet little food was imported), and also on greater organisational efficiency. Food was relatively bulky and costly to transport and preserve, so Kent and the Thames valley were key early sources of crops, fruit and vegetables for London. Hops and malt were produced in Kent and East Anglia to provide the beer and ale that were more crucial than today due to the lack of clean water, the difficulty of providing fresh milk, and the restrictions upon, and the cost of, wine imports. Animals came from further afield due to the practice of droving: walking them to near London, fattening them up, and slaughtering them to provide fresh meat. Cattle and sheep were driven from as far as Scotland and Wales, while geese and turkeys were walked from East Anglia.

As another instance of the city's role as the focus of production and trade within the country, coal from the north-east of England continued to be shipped from Newcastle. Between the mid-sixteenth century and 1800 the output of the North East coal mines increased by a factor of more than sixty. By 1682 seventy per cent of the coal shipped from the river Tyne – sea-coal – went to London. When the Scots invaded England in 1644, one of their objectives was to secure coal supplies for their parliamentary allies in London as Newcastle was then under the control of the royalists. The Scottish capture of the city that year, therefore, was very important to London.

Across the period as a whole, water transport was particularly favoured for the movement of heavy or bulky goods, which was very significant for London as it could be supplied by both maritime and river routes. For example, at the start of the eighteenth century cloth was generally taken from Stroud to London by Thames barge from Lechlade. London was also the focus of wagon routes, not least because many cross-country routes were poorly developed. London's organisational strength was also important in ensuring that merchants across England sent goods to London to be distributed elsewhere in England. Increasingly and to an unprecedented extent, the city of London and its immediate region acted as a focus and a hub, dominating national as well as regional commerce.

By the end of the period, London, which benefited visually from the rebuilding after the Great Fire, was also displaying clear signs of confidence in the naval success and imperial destiny of the country. In part, this was a matter of London's place as a setting for the projects of government. For example, the naval role was celebrated in the Royal Hospital for Seamen for which the Tudor palace at Greenwich had been rebuilt. By 1663, Charles II had decided on a major rebuilding of the palace. The initial work was carried out by John Webb, but the scheme was transformed into one for a Royal Hospital for Seamen, appropriately situated near the Thames. Executed by Wren, who was also responsible for the Royal Hospital in Chelsea for ex-servicemen, the result was a masterpiece of the English Baroque. In 1708, James Thornhill was commissioned to paint the Great Hall, and by 1712 he had provided a triumphant ceiling work, proclaiming British power. William III and Anne were shown bringing Peace and Liberty to Britain and Europe. The subsequent painting at the end of the hall made reference to naval success and power, a list of naval victories appearing as part of the group portrait of the Hanoverian royal family.

Very differently, the extent to which London was changing, while yet retaining traditional features, was captured in Marco Ricci's painting *A View of the Mall from St James's Park* of about 1710. The Mall was a walk where fashionable society went to see and be seen, to intrigue, to flirt and to proposition. The park contained three avenues for pedestrians and, in the 1700s, Queen Anne's gardener, Henry Wise, planted 350 limes to provide shade. In his painting, Ricci has Wren's St Paul's in the distance and shows London society on display, but this is also a world with cattle grazing in order to provide the city with milk. Elizabeth Cromwell had kept cattle there. The large number of women depicted in Ricci's painting reflected the extent to which many public places were not segregated. Another take on the scene is provided by the information that Bird Cage Walk in the park was a major centre for gay sex.[22]

An emphasis on trade and grand buildings does not capture the flavour of London life in this period. Instead, the earthy quality of manners emerges frequently. The *London Mercury* of 11 February 1721 reported:

A certain last-maker in Butcherhall-Lane being resolved to divert himself after a new method ran into the Sign of the Three Birds, and called for the landlady, who, immediately attending, he called her a bitch and fell a laughing. The woman, surprised to know his meaning, stood mute, while Dick persisted in his tone, calling her bitch and bitch of bitches, and as she kept such a house, ought to stand the censure of her customers; the woman, who was infinitely, above the saucy language of his scandalous tongue, resenting his ill manners by calling him rascal. Dick to prove to the contrary before forty people, pulls down his breeches to stand search. The gentlewoman of the house absconded with great confusion; but a lusty butcher woman broiling her supper, having more courage than the former, she swore she would try the event, and catches hold by his trickstaff with a pair of steak tongs with which she was turning her meat, and shook him while he roared out like a bull, and ran away as fast as he came, and hath been seen no more. The woman swore she believed he was a rascal by her manner of feeling.

Another theme was the growth of a public, entrepreneurial culture defined by the market. Public concerts became more frequent, those organised by John Banister in 1672 being the first such to be advertised. The role of advertising was enhanced by the expansion of the press from the 1690s, and this, in turn, helped create the sense that music performed for, and paid by, the public was normal. Henry Playford, who succeeded his father as an active publisher of music, founded, in order to broaden his position in the music market, a tri-weekly concert in 1699 at a coffee-house where his music could also be sold, and established a club for music practice. In his preface to the fourth edition of *The Second Book of the Pleasant Musical Companion* published in 1701, Playford linked improvement and sociability, both key themes in London's culture:

> The design therefore, as it is for a general diversion, so it is intended for a general instruction, that the persons who give themselves the liberty of an evening's entertainment with their friends, may exchange the expense they shall be at in being sociable, with the knowledge they shall acquire from it.

Meanwhile, the spatial differentiation noted at the beginning of the chapter was becoming more apparent with the development of the West End. This differentiation was also a cultural one, captured repeatedly in plays across the period that portrayed a rivalry between 'citizens', who lived in the City, and 'gentlemen', who increasingly lived in the West End. The citizens could be criticised for greed or praised for industry and honesty, and the gentlemen praised for nobility or criticised as vicious seducers especially eager for the wives of merchants. London recorded and propagated these tensions, and each of these images contribute to the impression it created.

CHAPTER 6

Earth has not any thing to shew more fair:
Dull would he be of soul who could pass by
A sight so touching in it's majesty:
This City now doth like a garment wear
The beauty of the morning; silent, bare,
Ships, towers, domes, theatres, and temples lie
Open unto the fields, and to the sky;
All bright and glittering in the smokeless air.
Never did sun more beautifully steep
In his first splendor valley, rock, or hill;
Ne'er saw I, never felt, a calm so deep!
The river glideth at his own sweet will:
Dear God! the very houses seem asleep;
And all that mighty heart is lying still!

WILLIAM WORDSWORTH

LONDON DOMINATED THE GAZE of the Georgian public. In mid-century, Antonio Canaletto, with his splendid canvases, used the talents he had developed depicting Venice in order to show the resplendent glories of modern London, as Marco Ricci had done earlier in the century. A modern pride in London was expressed in Canaletto's views, with recent or new buildings, such as St Paul's Cathedral, Greenwich Observatory, Westminster Bridge, and the new west front of Westminster Abbey playing a prominent role. This pride was also expressed in John Rocque's important map of 1746 and in the presentation of London as a new Rome.

The centre of all, 1714–1815

'Old Somerset House from the River Thames', c.1746–50, by Canaletto. The old Tudor and Jacobean house was eventually demolished in the 1770s to make way for the new house that was built right on the riverbank. The artist gives us a very detailed portrayal of several Thames watermen, some apparently in livery, along with their small rowing boats or 'wherries', of which there were thousands on the river at this date, providing a water taxi service across and along the stream.

A less grand view, but one that accurately captured the city's expansion, was offered by Richard Wilson in his *Westminster Bridge under Construction* (1744), with the blue openness of the river Thames and the sky being spanned by the new bridge. Canaletto's *A View of London and the River Thames* of about 1746–47, produced for Prince Lobkowicz, who had visited the city in 1745, similarly depicts work on the bridge, which obviously impressed contemporaries.

In 1700, London had more than half a million people – more than all other English towns put together – and in 1800 more than a million. Although London's share of the national population did not rise during the century, by 1800, thanks to the growth in the latter, its population had doubled, to make it the most populous, and wealthiest, city in Europe or the Americas (and the third most populous in the world), and it was over ten times larger than the second city in England. Indeed, in 1805, George III, who had a markedly conservative view about social values and structures, referred to 'the overgrown metropolis'.[1] It has been calculated that, from 1650 to 1750, the increase of London's population (from about 400,000 to about 675,000), along with the relatively high rate of mortality in the city, were such that the city absorbed half of the natural increase in population in the whole of the rest of England. At the same time, though large, London was compact, especially north to south, and did not yet suffer from congestion and sprawl comparable to those of the following centuries.

An unsought testimony to London's importance was that conspiracies and invasion schemes centred on it. In 1722, the Atterbury Plot, a conspiracy on behalf of 'James III', the Stuart claimant to the throne, was blocked by prompt governmental action, including the creation of a large army camp in Hyde Park. The Jacobites had planned to exploit disaffection in the Guards and co-operation from the City Corporation, among whose senior ranks were a number of supporters, in order to seize the Tower, the Royal Exchange and the Bank of England, an indicative choice of key points. It was then intended to raise disaffected groups of the London population, the Southwark Minters, the Westminster mob, and the Thames watermen. Once London fell, the counties were to be raised. However, the government's firm response overawed London and frustrated the plans for rebellion.

In 1743, when planning an invasion by supporting French troops, the English Jacobites again presented control of London as the crucial objective. Maldon in Essex was selected as the landing place because it would permit a march on London without having to cross the Weald, the Downs and the Thames. In the event, a Channel storm thwarted the French invasion attempt mounted in 1744, an attempt that was planned to include a landing at Blackwall. In December 1745, James's son, Charles Edward Stuart, Bonnie Prince Charlie, having invaded Scotland, advanced on London from Edinburgh, knowing that he had to seize the city in order to secure the Jacobite position.

Although the Jacobites never came within 150 miles of the city, this crisis threw light on the politics and anxieties of London as never before during the century. Sir Dudley Ryder, the Attorney General, noted in his diary on 3 December 1745, 'people in great pain for the City ... Papists suspected of an intended rising as soon as the rebels are near London.' The following day, William, Duke of Cumberland, second son of George II and one of his leading generals, advised that 'without alarming the City the infantry that is about London could be assembled on Finchley Common'.[2] A force of 4,000 troops was gathered there.

It was unclear, however, what London itself would do. William Hewitt suggested to the Duke of Devonshire, a keen supporter of the government, that little could 'be hoped for from the common people about London', whom, he claimed, would rather 'be disposed to join in plundering than defending the property of other people'. In contrast, the London weavers offered 1,000 men to the royal troops. After the Jacobites retreated from England to their defeat at Culloden the following April, there were popular demonstrations of

These drawings of London's gates were made in 1756 for Maitland's *History of London*. In the Roman period there were just four main gates in the city walls – from west to east Ludgate, Newgate, Bishopsgate and Aldgate – with two more allowing direct access into the fort, one of which remained in use as Cripplegate after the fort was disused, and, later in the Roman period, a gate at the northern end of London Bridge and another city gate at Aldersgate. Moorgate was not built until the fifteenth century. All of the gates had rooms above, many of them used as prisons. By latter half of the eighteenth century they had lost any defensive role they might have retained from an earlier period and were all demolished.

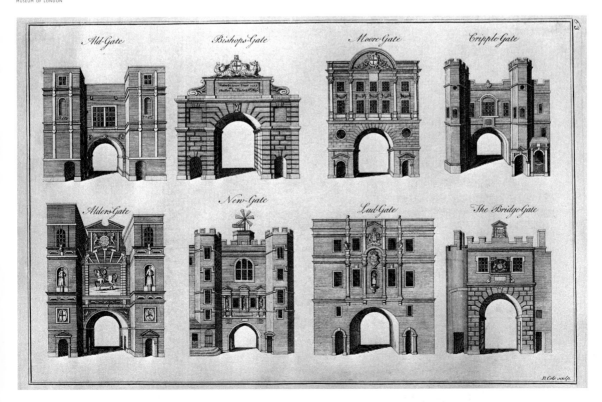

loyalism in London, including the breaking of unilluminated windows, but the situation was less clear-cut during the crisis itself. In the event, an absence of support within the Jacobite army for pressing on in the face of a lack of English support or French action, ensured that, on 6 December 1745, Charles Edward had to turn back at Derby. Earlier in the crisis, George II reviewed the city's militia units in St James's Park. In 1751–53, as a further sign of London's strategic position, the Jacobite Elibank Plot focused upon attempting a coup in the city.

In the 1745 crisis, the government suffered from having just one centre of power. When, in contrast, the French, Bavarians and Saxons had attacked the Habsburgs in 1741, Maria Theresa had been able to retire from Vienna to Pressburg (Bratislava), the capital of her kingdom of Hungary, while her enemies had to choose whether to advance on Vienna or Prague, the capital of the Kingdom of Bohemia. They chose and took Prague, but Maria Theresa was able to continue fighting. Similarly, during the War of the Spanish Succession (1701–14), Philip V of Spain had lost Madrid to the British-backed claimant 'Charles III', but he was able to fight on, as was Frederick the Great of Prussia when he briefly lost Berlin during the Seven Years' War. In each case, their army was the centre of their power.

Such was the unique importance of London, however, that there was little doubt that, if George II had lost London in 1745, his regime would have collapsed. Some of his supporters would probably have wished to fight on, especially in Ireland where there were both troops and concern about the maintenance of the Protestant ascendancy. Moreover, it is difficult

Westminster Bridge under Construction, painted by Richard Wilson in early autumn, 1744.
TATE GALLERY

Canaletto's View of the Thames and Westminster Bridge, c.1746–47. This view was painted from the south-east, with Westminster Abbey, complete with its new west front, prominent on the skyline to the left, and Lambeth Palace bottom right.
BRIDGEMAN ART LIBRARY

to see the Duke of Cumberland accepting Jacobite success without a battle. However, without London, the logistical and financial infrastructure of the military establishment would have collapsed. Pay and supplies would have become a problem for Cumberland, doubtless encouraging desertion among his soldiers and helping to dictate his strategy. It is probable that there would have been a measure of support from the English Jacobites for Charles Edward had London fallen; although, more significantly, it is likely that, as in 1642–43 during the Civil War, the fall of London would have affected the British fleet, disrupting its supplies and influencing the determination of some officers, which, in turn, would have assisted French plans for an invasion. It was readily apparent that government finances would have been hit by a march on London. On 1 October 1745, Edward Weston, an Under-Secretary in the Northern Department, observed: 'The Association of the Merchants has saved the Bank [of England] for a time, but I doubt not the first ill news will raise the same spirit again.'[3] In the event, the bodies of Jacobite traitors were to be displayed in London after the rising as also in 1696, 1716 and 1723.

The city's role was not only crucial at moments of national crisis. Instead, this role drew on London's prominence across a broad range of national activity. Throughout the eighteenth century, London's vitality and dominant position owed much to its place in finance, trade and industry. London-based insurance companies, such as the Sun Fire Office, as well as the banks, were able to organise business throughout England by delegating the work to agents in other towns with whom regular contact could be maintained.

The capital also led the way in national societies and voluntary movements, such as the SPCK and the Societies for Reformation of Manners; London parishes were more important than others in the Church of England. The bishopric was a key position, held from 1723 to 1748 by Edmund Gibson, whose influence was such that he was known as 'Walpole's Pope'. Gibson was buried in All Saints, Fulham, remarkable for being the resting place for no fewer than nine London bishops. In the diocese, there were many preachers, readers and lecturers, and a high level of clerical activity. Although there was non-residence and pluralism on the part of some of the clerics, levels of daily celebration and services were high, and the clergy had a pronounced view of their duty. London also played a central role in Dissent and in new religious developments, such as the Fetter Lane Society established in 1738 by a group of Anglicans seeking a society for religious observance. London was also the headquarters of Freemasonry, a new movement that proved particularly influential among the Whig élite.

London was also the centre of government, the law and consumption, and its position in the world of print became even more important as a shaper of news, opinion and fashion. Most new periodicals were launched in London, including, in 1788, the *Family Magazine; or a Repository of Religious Instruction and Rational Amusement – Designed to counteract the pernicious tendency of immoral books*. It was not simply a contrivance of the plot that has

London's most important eighteenth-century cartographer, John Rocque, was the son of Huguenot immigrants. This section of his map of 1746 shows Mayfair under development. The name derived from a fair held on the site of Shepherd's Market (*bottom right*). Also visible is the Chelsea Waterworks' reservoir in Hyde Park.
MUSEUM OF LONDON

Henry Fielding in *Joseph Andrews* (1742) send Parson Adams to London in order to get his nine volumes of sermons published. Even Welsh publishing was dominated by London presses, while St David's Day was more celebrated in sermons and at Court in London than in Wales. London newspapers circulated throughout England, and were also crucial sources of news and opinion for the provincial press.

The turnpike and postal systems radiated from London. Stage-coaches regularly left London inns such as the George at Southwark, a new stage of Southwark's role as a terminus for overland journeys, as with Chaucer's pilgrims. On 19 June 1773 *Jackson's Oxford Journal* reported:

> The difference in the number of stage coaches, etc. travelling on the Western road, within these few years, is not a little remarkable. About ten years ago there only passed through Salisbury in the course of a week, to and from London and Exeter, six stage coaches, which carried six passengers each, making in the whole (if full) 36 passengers. At present there constantly pass, between the above places, in the same space of time, 24 stage coaches, carrying six passengers each and 28 stage chaises, carrying three each making in the whole, if full, 228 passengers'.

Travel was made faster as a result of the road improvements carried out by turnpike trusts, and comfort was enhanced by the replacement of leather straps by steel coach springs, and by the introduction of elliptical springs. By 1750, a sizeable network of new turnpikes radiating from London had been created. London and north-west England were well linked, with the road to Chester and both roads to Manchester turnpiked for most of their length. A direct coach service from Kendal to London began in 1760. The time of a journey from Manchester to London fell from three days in 1760 to twenty-eight hours in 1788, while average speeds between London and Birmingham rose to fifteen miles an hour.

The frequency of links also increased. The first regular Norwich–London coach service taking less than a day started in 1761, and by 1783 there were 25 departures a week from Norwich to London, as well as two departures of stage wagons carrying goods. London to Bristol and Birmingham services became more frequent in the 1740s. By 1788 the Pickford family was sending a wagon from Manchester to London every day bar Sunday.

The new and improved roads made it easier for Londoners to travel into the surrounding countryside, and this led to the publication in 1790 of John Cary's *Survey of the High Roads from London to Hampton Court* and twenty-five other places around the metropolis, a volume divided into forty strips covering, for example, London to St Albans in three maps. This work was reissued in 1799, 1801 and 1810, and drew attention to 'the numberless villas' outside London. There was also road-building in London in order to improve circulation and maintain access. Most significant was 'The New Road' opened in 1756 in order to improve access from the west toward the City. The route is now followed by the Marylebone and Euston Roads.

River links, however, remained important for freight. For example, it cost 33s. 4d. (£1.67) a ton to move goods by road from London to Reading in 1792, but only 10 shillings by water. Improved communications by road and canal during the century led to a greater uniformity of English prices, with these being set in London. A letter in the *Newcastle Journal* of 19 July 1740 referred to 'London which place governs the value of all grain in England'.

The vital energy of London was captured across the arts and provided the context for much of national culture. Under the shadow of St Paul's Cathedral were published accounts of the diversions of the capital, such as James Ralph's *The Touchstone: or, ... Essays on the Reigning Diversions of the Town* (1728) and Henry Fielding's *A Trip through the Town* (1735), as well as a particular genre of unbottoned travelogues, for example *A Trip through London: Containing Observations on Men and Things, viz ... A remarkable rencounter between a bawd and a sodomite ... of a person of quality's clothes sold off his back in the Mall by auction, by his valet de chambre ... of the Exeter 'Change beauties ... practices of petty-foggers exposed* (1728).

London was significant in influencing notions of urban life, and in providing both setting and topics for cultural activity. As a subject, it was the most striking in the country until the cult for landscape late in the century led to a marked shift in preference from urban elegance to sublime landscape, a change that was to provide the background for a harsher view of the city as a physical environment. London's role was seen in the titles of works, for example poetry, such as John Gay's *Trivia: or The Art of Walking the Streets of London* (1716) and Samuel Johnson's *London* (1738), and also in the divided response to the metropolis. The Whig playwright Nicholas Rowe, in his *The Tragedy of Jane Shore* (1714), presented a London merchant acting an honourable part, in support of 'the commonities of mankind', in opposition to a vicious nobleman.

Throughout the eighteenth century, London was presented by some as a site of liberty, trade and progress; others viewed it in terms of moral, political and economic disorder and dissolution. Urban living served, as so often, to delineate, if not define, issues and alignments. Whigs tended to take the former view, looking favourably upon London, as progress, while Tories focused more upon

Fire, bombing and redevelopment over the centuries have inflicted terrible destruction on the legacy of timber-frame building in and around London. A rare survivor in Southwark is this galleried coaching inn, the George, just behind Borough High Street. The inn is shown on a map of 1542 (page 89), but was largely rebuilt after a fire in the 1670s.

PHOTOGRAPH: CARNEGIE 2009

London as problem. In the Tory Alexander Pope's *The Rape of the Lock* (two versions, 1712, 1714), the witty satire about a lack of values, encapsulated by Belinda's expenditure, was set in London polite society. Pope was the son of a London linen-draper.

It was not necessary, however, to be a Tory in order to criticise London. There was disquiet, indeed, across the political spectrum. Joseph Yorke, a well-connected member of the 'Old Corps' Whig establishment, wrote in 1763:

> Don't you think that the overgrown size of our metropolis is one of great cause of the frivolousness, idleness and debauchery of our times. I have often wondered that the legislature has not long since laboured to put bounds to its increase, for it is really too big for the good observance of the law or the gospel.[4]

Concern about public morality in London helped lead to George III's proclamation in 1787, 'For the Encouragement of Piety and Virtue, and for the Preventing and Punishing of Vice, Profaneness and Immorality', and to the activities of the Proclamation Society to which this gave rise.

At the same time, London was also the site for the re-iteration of narratives of national identity and history. For example, the epilogue in praise of the Reformation spoken at the

Kenwood House, Hampstead. The original house was extensively remodelled in the eighteenth century by Robert Adam (1728–92), a Scottish architect also responsible for work on other stately piles, such as Lansdowne House in Berkeley Square, Osterley (Hounslow), Syon House (Brentford) and Northumberland House on the Strand.

opening of the New Theatre in Goodman's Fields was disseminated through its publication in the *Weekly Journal: or, The British Gazetteer* of 8 November 1729:

> When Britain first from Monkish Bondage broke,
> And shook off Rome's imperious galling yoke,
> when truth and reason were no longer chained
> In Popish fetters, and by Priests explained,
> then wit and learning graced our happy Isle.

The Londoners rioting in 1780 in the Gordon Riots against the Catholic Relief Act were acting out such views and reflecting the suspicion of Catholics that had been seen at the theatre in Goodman's Fields in 1731 in 'an entertainment at the close of the play relating to Father Girard and Miss Cadiere', an account of seduction in France by a Jesuit confessor.

Meanwhile, both Tories and Whigs sought to woo London. Thus, in 1721, Thomas, 3rd Earl of Strafford, a prominent Tory, was urged to dine with the Lord Mayor in order to

The Mob destroying & Setting Fire to the KINGS BENCH PRISON & House of CORRECTION in St Georges Fields.

'give life to the honest part of the City. It has often been practised by another party [the Whigs] (with too much success) in this manner to keep up the spirits and support their interest here.'[5]

While London's political support was enlisted, the city changed physically. The expansion into the West End seen during the reign of Queen Anne (1702–14) continued, and led to the building of grand houses as well as a larger number of homes designed for the fashionable. The street-plan of the West End was filled in and also spread. Thus, Fitzroy Square, in the angle between the Tottenham Court Road and the New Road (now the Euston Road), was begun in the 1790s to a design by Robert Adam. At that stage, there was little development to the north of the New Road; on the other side of the road, indeed, opposite where Cleveland Street joined it, could be found Kendal's Farm. To the east of the Tottenham Court Road south of the New Road, there were still empty fields in the 1790s. As with other periods of the city's history, much of the building on the edge was speculative development.

Further south in the West End, the construction of grand houses reaffirmed the aristocratic stamp on that part of the city. Devonshire House was built in the 1730s, Chesterfield House in 1747–52, and the new Norfolk House in 1748–56. This move of the nobility west from the Covent Garden area closer to the royal palace at St James's was an important realignment socially and politically as well as being part of a major shift in land-use. The Haymarket, originally the source of feedstuff for horses, was cleared for development in the early eighteenth century.

The new houses joined those in rural areas close to London in providing a setting for display and elegance. For example, Robert Adam redesigned not only Northumberland and Lansdowne Houses in the built-up area, but also Syon House, Kenwood and Osterley, then in the country, now in the area of the Greater London Authority. Much work was also put into the grounds of these and other houses, for example that of Lord Burlington at Chiswick. Adam designed a large, pedimented Doric orangery for Osterley Park in 1763–64, and this complemented the Doric temple with Rococo interior plasterwork already in place. At South Lodge in Enfield Chase, where he held the lease from 1747 to 1753, William Pitt the Elder added a temple dedicated to Pan, as well as a garden pyramid.

As leading aristocrats built or rebuilt grand houses, such as Burlington, Carlton, Canons, Derby and Spencer Houses, they not only reaffirmed the links between city and country, crown and élite, but also affected urban society. Patterns of behaviour were moulded by the example of wealth, and the development of the West End was crucial. The aristocratic world of the West End involved sumptuous events. On 2 January 1735, for instance, the Earl of Jersey held a grand entertainment at his house in Grosvenor Street for the birthday of Frederick, Prince of Wales. It was attended by the Dukes of Newcastle, Portland and Richmond, the Earls of Pembroke and Scarborough, Sir Robert Walpole (the

Prime Minister) and foreign diplomats. The churches of the West End were fashionable, too, especially St George, Hanover Square, and St James, Piccadilly.

At the same time, this aristocratic stamp caused tension within London. In the *Covent Garden Journal* (1752), a periodical by Henry Fielding, many of the essays were devoted to the cause of good behaviour, both against specific abuses, such as gambling, adultery and an interest in pornography, and against the general problem of selfish and improper conduct, while much of the satire was directed at the abuses of the polite world. 'People of Fashion' were criticised for their behaviour and their attitudes, and were presented as dangerous role models for tradesmen, a long-standing theme and one in which the Puritan-related criticism of the seventeenth century was reformulated. 'Reflector' in the *London Evening Post* of 8 April 1762 condemned 'that ruinous prevalence of following the fashions of the Court which now infects the citizens of London'.

This social tension arose in part from the uneasy neighbourhood of the City and the West End while it was in London that a self-conscious bourgeoisie was most clearly developed.[6]

The magnificent Crimson Drawing Room at Carlton House, the Prince Regent's town house between Pall Mall and St James's Park, specially fitted out for Princess Charlotte's marriage to Prince Leopold of Saxe-Coburg in 1816.

MUSEUM OF LONDON

LEFT

St George, Hanover Square, was one of a dozen or so churches built in the early eighteenth century under the auspices of the Commission for Building Fifty New Churches. For 36 years Handel lived on Brook Street nearby and worshipped in St George's.

ABOVE

The interior of St James, Piccadilly, a Wren church consecrated in 1684. Both of these churches were in fashionable districts of the city.

PHOTOGRAPHS: CARNEGIE, 2009

Home House, 20 Portman Square, was built between 1773 and 1776 for Elizabeth, Countess of Home. English Heritage regard it perhaps as Robert Adam's finest surviving town house, while in *England's Thousand Best Houses*, Simon Jenkins describes it as 'Adam's urban masterpiece'. It is now a private members' club.

PHOTOGRAPH: CARNEGIE, 2009

Fielding indeed saw London in terms of a corrupt court and aristocracy at its West End, with their commerce in vice, and the more acceptable commercial metropolis. The interplay between the two was a major theme in literature, and also in Hogarth's caricature series. London was a setting for villainy for many artists and writers, for example of the snares that bedevil William Booth in Fielding's novel *Amelia* (1751). William Wordsworth's Preface to his *Lyrical Ballads* (1798) asserted the pernicious consequences of the move to the cities, although in his sonnet 'Composed Upon Westminster Bridge' in 1802 he praised the beauty of Thames-side London at dawn.

There was also a more light-hearted, but still edged, dimension. Visiting the Haymarket Theatre in 1786, Sophie von La Roche noted a hostile interplay of fashionable spectators with the rest of the audience, and with the actors also responding rapidly:

four ladies … entered a box during the third play, with such wonderfully fantastic caps and hats perched on their heads, that they were received by the entire audience with loud derision. Their neckerchiefs were puffed up so high that their noses were scarce visible, and their nosegays were like huge shrubs, large enough to conceal a person. In less than a quarter of an hour, when the scene had changed to a market square, four women walked onto the stage dressed equally foolishly, and hailed the four ladies in the box as their friends. All clapped loud applause.

She also noted the actors defending the value of the stage: 'After this delightful performance I saw the players hold a kind of trial and support the motion, "That it is the duty of the stage to condemn social evils, and to seek improvement through the medium of its wit".'[7]

Beyond the West End, there was a development of suburban residences in the Thames valley where the wealthy could enjoy more space, as well as hunting. Thus Walpole, the leading minister from 1720 to 1742, had not only his Norfolk stately home at Houghton, but also, in the 1710s, two houses in London, one on Arlington Street, the other, with more land, at Chelsea. In 1722 he purchased another house at Chelsea for £1,000. This house took him out of the bustle and smell of London and gave him some semi-rural calm. Chelsea was also near both the royal palace at Kensington and – easily reached by boat across the Thames – the hunting pleasures of Richmond, where Walpole had a hunting lodge and kept a pack of beagles. An official residence in Downing Street was offered by George II in 1731, but Walpole did not occupy it until 1735. Both his wife, Catherine, and his mistress (and second wife), Maria, were the daughters of London merchants, and Walpole installed Maria (when mistress) at Richmond, where he spent the weekends. As Prince of Wales, the future George II gave his mistress Henrietta Howard £11,500 to build and furnish an appropriate house, the result being the Palladian-style Marble Hill House at Twickenham, where the banks of the Thames were lined by such properties.

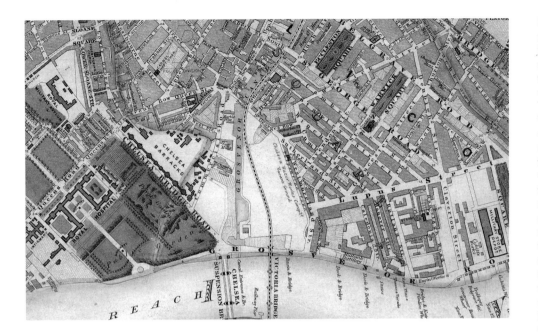

In the 1720s a new scheme for the supply of water for west London was devised. The Chelsea Waterworks Company was set up to extract water from the Thames, a 'canal' being dug from the river as far as the later site of Victoria Station. By the time Stanford's map was drawn in the 1860s, the Grosvenor Canal (*centre*) was more or less redundant. Prohibited from 1852 from drawing water from the Thames for domestic use, despite the introduction of sand filtration, the water company's former ponds were now marked as 'vacant ground', part of which had been used to build the London, Chatham and Dover Railway line to Victoria in the 1850s.
CARNEGIE COLLECTION

Chelsea remained a lightly built-up area at the close of the century. Indeed, past Westminster there was only limited development along the river, and places such as Parsons Green were villages, surrounded by market gardens. The same was true south of the river of villages. In the case of Tooting, for instance, the five or six miles from Charing Cross were easily sufficient to isolate the village from the bustling Georgian conurbation; though located on a major route which had been in use since Roman times, Tooting remained surrounded by the still quite extensive tracts of Tooting Common, Wandsworth Common and the open fields and common at neighbouring Mitcham. Major development did not encroach significantly here for many years. At the same time, there was a degree of ribbon development from Lambeth, especially in Clapham, just as Kensington and Knightsbridge were characterised by ribbon development north of the Thames. Alongside farmland, especially pastures and meadows providing milk and hay, in this outer belt, there were market gardens, for example in Stockwell, as well as clay and gravel pits to ensure supplies of bricks and gravel for construction and new roads.

At the same time that the West End was being created, other areas further east were also developed, especially Spitalfields, while some parts of the city, such as Clerkenwell, became less fashionable; a process that was paralleled in Paris with the decline of the Marais, which was also to the east of a city where the west was being built up and becoming fashionable. Meanwhile in London, the financial and economic importance of the city led to significant artistic work there. In 1725–27, Sir James Thornhill, the first native artist to be knighted, provided painted decorations for the ceiling of the New Council Chamber in

The west towers of Westminster Abbey, designed by Nicholas Hawksmoor, the abbey's Surveyor-General from 1723 until his death in 1736, and completed in 1745.

the Guildhall, offering Baroque themes and images, with the oval medallion in the centre providing a personification of the City of London as a young woman attended by Pallas Athena (symbolising wisdom), Peace, Plenty, and two cherubs. George Dance the Elder (1700–68), Surveyor to the Corporation of London, designed the Mansion House begun in 1739, and the Excise Office in Broad Street near Bishopsgate (built on the site of Tudor almshouses built by Sir Thomas Gresham). Dance's son, also George, succeeded him as Surveyor, and was responsible for the rebuilding of Newgate Prison.

Robert Taylor (1714–88) did sculptural work on the façades of the Bank of England and the Mansion House, before becoming an architect. As architect to the Bank of England, Taylor made extensive additions in neo-classical style, including wings on either side of the original façade. In turn, reflecting the range of London life, his London work included the Stone Buildings for the lawyers in Lincoln's Inn, as well as a house in Piccadilly for the Duke of Grafton. Many of his clients had City interests. As an instance of the prominence that could come from architecture, Taylor became sheriff of London, was knighted and left a large fortune.

Government was also a source of building commissions. William Kent, Architect to the Board of Works, was responsible for designing the new Horse Guards, the headquarters of the army's staff. The earlier, late seventeenth-century, building was demolished in 1749 and a new building begun in 1750. The supervision of the project was in the hands of John Vardy, who had worked with Kent since 1736. Kent also produced a design for a royal palace at Richmond, but this only got as far as the creation of a model in 1735. Indeed, neither George I nor George II were great builders, any more than Queen Anne had been. Nevertheless, Anne enhanced Kensington with an Orangery by Nicholas Hawksmoor, while George I was responsible for extensive work on Kensington Palace, including the completion and decoration of Colen Campbell's new state rooms, richly painted by William Kent. George was also a patron of George Frederick Handel, whose *Water Music* was first performed on the Thames in 1717, as part of an evening of entertainment for the king, and in order to ensure that ceremonial and élite sociability focused on him and not on his heir, the future George II, with whom George I was then in severe dispute. Similarly, Handel's *Dettingen Te Deum* was first performed for George II in 1745 at St James's Palace; his *Music for the Royal Fireworks*, again for George II, followed in 1749.

George II's daughter-in-law, Augusta, the widow of Frederick, Prince of Wales, employed Sir William Chambers to adorn the gardens of her house at Kew, and in 1757–62 he erected a number of buildings there in oriental or classical styles that had a great impact. Augusta's son, George III, purchased Buckingham House in 1762 and had it considerably altered by Chambers. It was called Queen's House, and later Buckingham Palace. In Richmond Park, George III replaced the ornamental landscaping carried out under George II by the contemporary, natural look popularised by Lancelot 'Capability' Brown.

Although the eighteenth century is not generally seen as a period of religious energy, this view is mistaken, and the period certainly left London with an important legacy of churches, in addition to the completion of Wren's St Paul's. It is true that when the Commission for Building Fifty New Churches in London and Westminster, established in 1711, was abolished in 1758 owing to the inadequacy of its principal source of funds, the coal duty, it had authorised the construction of just twelve churches. Nevertheless, several architects produced major works, including St Mary-le-Strand, St Peter's Vere Street, St George-in-the-East and St Martin's-in-the-Fields by James Gibbs, St John's, St John's, Smith Square, by Thomas Archer, and St Botolph's, Aldgate, St Luke's, Old Street and St Leonard's, Shoreditch, by George Dance the Elder. The sums involved could be considerable. St Giles-in-the-Fields (1731–34) by Henry Flitcroft cost £10,000 and his St Olave, Southwark (1737–39) £5,000. These churches also had an impact elsewhere. The engravings of St Martin's-in-the-Fields in James Gibbs' *Book of Architecture* (1728) influenced designs elsewhere. The churches, moreover, were linked with a vibrant religious culture in London, for example the music produced by organists, such as Henry Purcell, organist of Westminster Abbey (1680–95).

The physical creation of London was an evolutionary, piecemeal process, with much development taking place out of existing housing types and traditional layouts. And, like today, maintaining, changing and upgrading the structure of houses made them perfectly suited to a society of consumption geared towards continual renewal and replacement. As in modern London, too, this was also a process that reflected and sustained social distinctions both within and between communities. Gradual but important shifts in the social character of districts could, over time, become easily discernible. The nature of these distinctions could also be seen in open spaces within London in the eighteenth century. Squares, such as Hanover Square, laid out

Dating from 1762 and designed by the Swedish-born William Chambers, the Chinese pagoda at Kew is an original feature of the ornamental gardens. Wooden dragons, painted gold, used to adorn the outside of the structure, but rotted away over time. The pagoda is over 160 feet high and provides a striking landmark in the south-east part of the gardens. Chambers, who taught the future George III architectural drawings, fixed the cultural pattern of the Orient for contemporaries with his *Designs of Chinese Buildings, Furniture, Dresses, Machines and Utensils* (1757). He was also the author of a successful *Treatise on Civil Architecture* (1759). The plan he produced in 1715 for a Richmond Palace fell victim to the projected cost and to the difficulty in securing the necessary land. A smaller palace, begun in 1770, was abandoned in 1779.

PHOTOGRAPH: CARNEGIE, 2008

between 1717 and 1719, were a key element in the development of the West End. They tended to be public, rather than private, arenas until the 1720s. Then the emphasis came to be on exclusivity; open spaces were enclosed, laid out as gardens, and restricted to residents; this change – Georgian gentrification in all but name – helped to further a process of social exclusion.[8]

Communication routes over the river Thames were improved hugely in the eighteenth century, proclaiming at the same time the importance of London and the availability of resources to undertake the task. Several river ferries were replaced by new bridges, in what was a major development reflecting greater human control over the environment, as ferries were subject to river conditions such as ice and other adverse weather. The first new bridge was built at Datchet, near Windsor, in 1706; demolished in the 1850s this is the only Thames bridge no longer to exist. Datchet was followed by Putney (1729), Westminster (1739–50), Walton (1750), Hampton Court (1753), Kew (1758–59), Blackfriars (1760–69), Battersea (1771–72), and Richmond (1774–77). Although it challenged the passenger traffic by ferry, the building of Westminster Bridge markedly helped development on the south bank, but, as a reminder of potent social tensions, the ½d. toll demanded from those who crossed Blackfriars Bridge led to a riot.

Another view of the river was provided in *The Thames during the Great Frost of 1739–40* by Jan Griffier the younger, a landscape painter who practised in London. Griffier was the younger son of a Amsterdam painter who settled in London in the 1660s and painted many Thames-side scenes. The elder son, Robert, also painted London scenes. The family's careers reflected the close links between London and Amsterdam, and the openness of London's culture to foreign influences.

A more serious problem was posed by the quality of the drinking water. River water in London was often muddy, while pump water there was affected by sewage. Typhus was one result; the disease was partly responsible for a rise in winter mortality in London in the first half of the eighteenth century. More generally, the proximity of dunghills to humans was hazardous to health. Privies with open soil pits lay directly alongside dwellings and under bedrooms, and excrement flowed on and beneath the surface through generally porous walls. Mary Scarth, the raker of the parish of St Giles-in-the-Fields from 1705 to 1723, was paid £400 by the parish and employed twenty horses, four carts and five men to move the excrement from cesspits to farmers seeking manure – a trade similar to that carried out along the Leeds and Liverpool Canal from Liverpool to the market gardens of south-west Lancashire – and which underlined London's varied significance for the surrounding region.

Disease was not the sole killer. Dearth was also a problem. In London, high grain prices tended to increase the incidence of epidemic diseases and deaths among middle and older age groups. The London printer Edward Owen noted in 1757: 'Bread is getting so excessive dear … which makes it go very hard with the poor, even in the City.' The issue of food prices serves as a reminder that, although London's development was in part as a centre of finance, trade, consumption and leisure, the living conditions of much of the population were far from easy.

London's role as a centre of leisure was significant both for the capital and in helping set national patterns of behaviour and aspiration. The amount of fixed, specialised investment in leisure in the city rose greatly, with the opening of theatres, pleasure gardens, picture galleries, auction houses and the ubiquitous coffee-houses. The range of establishments reflected the vitality of the metropolis, and also the intellectual and cultural ambitions at stake. As the world's first national museum of its kind, for instance, the British Museum was created by Act of Parliament in 1753. The Museum acted as though it were an encyclopaedia, with the sequence of rooms, their layout, and the juxtaposition of objects within them providing a means of understanding relationships within the world of objects and specimens. In 1784 12,000 people visited it, although the rules banned children and sought to prevent 'persons of mean and low degree' from gaining access.

Across the arts, meanwhile, London provided venues, performers and audiences, as well as entrepreneurs seeking to produce multiple links between them. Changes in any of the artistic factors of production could alter the cultural world. For example, the enlargement of Covent Garden in 1792 and of Drury Lane in 1794 led to theatres that were less intimate and, instead, more conducive to the drama of spectacle. These changes in the London theatres interacted with those in national taste, as they proved especially conducive to the fashion for Gothic drama in the 1790s, as well as to the increase in payments to playwrights, and the profits of theatre owners and lessees.

Profit and public came together in pleasure gardens such as Ranelagh and Vauxhall. Their popularity reflected the density of London's population and the resulting proximity of suburban facilities. These were places to see and be seen, eat and meet, set and spot fashions, and find spouses or whores, but also showpieces for all kinds of art and major sites of entertainment, especially of music. In the season, Vauxhall, which was developed from 1728 by Jonathan Tyers, had two programmes of music each evening, featuring music by leading composers. Johann Christian Bach wrote songs for Vauxhall in the 1760s and 1770s. George II was insulted at Ranelagh in 1742 while walking with his mistress:

> The last time the King was at Ranelagh Gardens he had this joke cut upon him, *viz.* two young fellows were walking by the King, one said to the other, 'where shall we sup?'. T'other made answer, 'At the King's Arms.' 'Oh,' says t'other, 'that's too full' (for the Countess of Yarmouth was with him). 'At the King's Head, then.' 'Oh, no,' says he, 'that's very empty.' On which the King made out of the Gardens directly, as well as the young fellows, and they say it caused a great disturbance.'

London's unparalleled diversity and the entrepreneurial search for profit gave rise to a great variety of diversions. Alongside Vauxhall came other pleasure gardens, such as Marylebone, and a total of 64 such gardens are known to have existed in London at this time. There was an attempt to match services to the varied pockets of consumers, as entrepreneurs such as Daniel Gough at Marylebone sought to mesh emulation with distinctiveness. Gough, also a tavern keeper, himself reflected the range of the service industries devoted to catering for public tastes. Assembly rooms provided an inside equivalent to pleasure gardens, most obviously with James Wyatt's Pantheon in Oxford Street, a grand assembly room completed in 1772, although it was to fall victim to fire.

As well as pleasure gardens, there were parks. Several of the West End parks had been in existence for centuries, often as royal hunting grounds. In the 1730s Queen Caroline supervised her Royal Gardener Charles Bridgeman in the reworking of the ancient Hyde Park, dividing it into two parts, Hyde Park and Kensington Gardens. It was Bridgeman who built the dam and sluices over the Westbourne stream to create one of the first

Hyde Park as it was in the middle of the Victorian era. It has been a park since Tudor times, when Henry VIII acquired the land at the dissolution of the monasteries. It was maintained as a royal hunting estate until just before the Civil War, when it was finally opened to the public as a park. The Serpentine was formed by damming the river Westbourne.
CARNEGIE COLLECTION

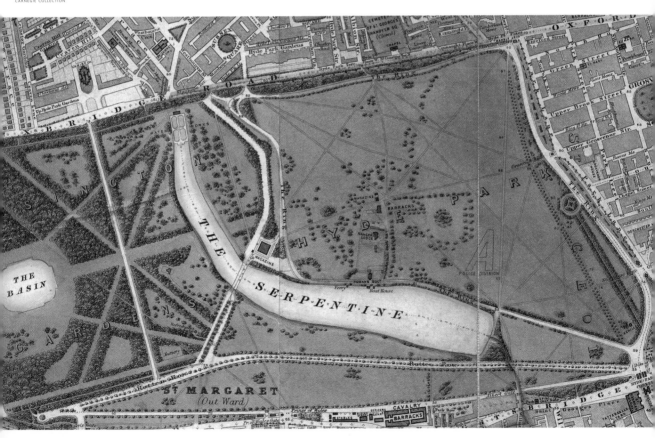

naturalistic lakes, The Serpentine, between the two parks. Before this time artificial lakes had been much more formal affairs, a good example being André Mollet's 850-yard seventeenth-century 'canal', in neighbouring St James's Park. Part of this enormous body of water was reclaimed in the 1760s to make way for Horse Guards Parade, and the rest was transformed by John Nash in the mid-1820s into the curving lake we see today. The development of a vista culminating in Buckingham House was also part of the park's transformation.

The pull of London attracted talent not only from abroad, for example Handel, Mozart and Haydn, but also from the provinces. Alongside the famous, came a host who were instrumental in making changes in their particular fields. London offered opportunity for the able, ambitious and energetic (as well as for many others), and, as throughout its history, some of the talented it attracted rose to the top. For example, the great surgeon William Hunter (1718–83), educated at Glasgow and Edinburgh, went to London in 1741 and became a noted anatomical lecturer, and, in 1768, the first Professor of Anatomy

The centrepiece of Ranelagh Gardens in Chelsea was a 37 m wide Rotunda which was used from 1742 until its final closure and subsequently demolition in 1803. Ranelagh was more expensive and more socially select than Vauxhall, as Horace Walpole extolled in 1742: '[Ranelagh] … has totally beat Vauxhall. Nobody goes anywhere else – everybody goes there. My Lord Chesterfield is so fond of it, that he says he has ordered all his letters to be directed thither. If you had never seen it, I would make you a most pompous description of it, and tell you how the floor is all of beaten princes – that you can't set foot without treading on a Prince of Wales or Duke of Cumberland.' The central column of the Rotunda contained fireplaces and a chimney to heat the building in winter.

to the Royal Academy. His younger brother, John, rose to be head of the surgical profession in London. Anna Maria Garthwaite (1690–1763), the well-educated daughter of a Lincolnshire parson who came to London in about 1730, was one of the leading silk designers, producing and selling an average of eighty designs a year. Born in Whickham, County Durham, the son of a music-master, William Shield (1748–1829) was a key figure in northern musical life, the leader of the Durham theatre orchestra and the conductor of the Newcastle concerts, but, in 1771, he moved to become a violin player in London. He began an active life in metropolitan musical life, including being composer at Covent Garden, which, in turn, was to lead to becoming master of musicians in ordinary to the king in 1817, and to burial at Westminster Abbey in 1829. As an instance of the degree of inflow, fewer than a third of the clergy in the London diocese came from the area, and, instead, many came from Wales, the West Country and Yorkshire.[10]

Those from abroad who visited but did not stay, such as Montesquieu and Voltaire, were also impressed by London, commenting on its cosmopolitan character, which they traced to religious toleration. For Georg Christoph Lichtenberg, the London of the 1770s was an exciting centre of civilisation, where he could meet Priestley or Banks and see Garrick on the stage. In turn, London was influenced by the Continent. Cultural, stylistic, intellectual and religious fashions and impulses crossed the Channel and were taken up in London. These included Italian opera and French cooking and card games. The morning levée and toilet was introduced into London from France, as was the umbrella. A large number of French artists also practised in London. Maurice Quentin La Tour, a portrait painter admired by Hogarth, had a successful visit in 1723. The draughtsman Hubert Gravelot worked in London from 1733 to 1745 and, as a teacher at the St Martin's Lane Academy, trained a whole generation of British artists, including Gainsborough. The portrait painter Jean Van Loo arrived in London in 1737 and spent a lucrative five years taking commissions from resentful English rivals.

Culture, indeed, was a sphere of competition, a field of patronage and a commodity of vital importance to London's craftsmen, much of whose production was destined for the domestic luxury market. Foreign craftsmen were seen as rivals. Ten tailors, three gilders, three embroiderers and one dancing master were among those on the list of thirty-six French Catholics living in Westminster which the French chargé d'affaires handed the British government in June 1722.[11] There was much hostility to cosmopolitanism, and, in this, London acted as a metropolitan forcing house of political, social and cultural tensions, a role that has been of continuing significance over the centuries. In the shape of John Gay's English-language ballad-operas, especially *The Beggar's Opera* (1728), London was the scene for the development of an indigenous reply to Handel, then a composer of operas in the Italian style. There were also riots against French actors, as in 1738, 1739, 1743, 1749 and 1755. At the Haymarket Theatre in 1738, the audience 'interrupted with hissing, catcalling, ringing small bells, knocking out of candles, pelting etc.', leading the actors to quit the stage.[12]

London, indeed, was the centre of cultural competition with France. The Anti-Gallican Association was founded in 1745 'to oppose the insidious arts of the French Nation' and 'to promote British manufactures ... discourage the introduction of French modes and oppose the importation of French commodities'. Attempts were also made to encourage British production of good quality bone-lace in order to compete with French imports, and the French invention of *papier maché* for decorative work – a threat to the livelihood of carvers – was condemned. In London, the same period saw Hogarth's vigorous espousal of the cause of British art, although Hogarth himself had been affected by French influences.

From the 1760s, organised cultural anti-Gallicanism abated somewhat because of the ebbing of the Rococo style and the less obvious influence of French culture in the age of Sir Joshua Reynolds, co-founder and first President of the Royal Academy of Arts from 1768 until his death in 1792. Greater national self-confidence after victories in the Seven Years' War (1756–63) and the direction of metropolitan artisanal political interest towards domestic politics, were also important. Nevertheless, attacks on French cultural influence remained frequent. In 1779 Robert Henley Ongley, a very wealthy London merchant, told the House of Commons that 'the French had contributed not a little to the increase

The baroque Painted Hall at Greenwich Hospital. In 1824 a naval gallery was opened in the room, where pictures of naval battles and admirals were hung. The hospital itself closed in 1869 and the buildings were converted into a naval training facility, the Royal Naval College, which in turn closed in the 1990s.

NATIONAL MARITIME MUSEUM

of divorces, by the introduction of their petit maitres, fiddlers and dancing masters, who had been allowed to teach our wives and misses to allemande, and to twist and turn them about at their pleasure.' The world of London music, however, remained closely linked to the Continent. Mozart visited in 1764, and Carl Friedrich Abel and Johann Christian Bach launched a successful annual concert series in 1775.

London's development greatly influenced that of other British and colonial cities, not least because of the importance of image. In the *St James's Chronicle* of 6 August 1761, George Colman argued that the improvement in transport had pushed the example of London to the fore, a situation similar to that experienced later with railways, steamships, motor transport and aircraft:

> Stage-coaches, machines, flys, and post-chaises are ready to transport passengers to and fro between the metropolis and the most distant parts of the kingdom ... the manners, fashions, amusements, vices, and follies of the metropolis, now make their way to the remotest corners of the land ... The effects of this easy communication have almost daily grown more and more visible. The several great cities, and we might add many poor country towns, seem to be universally inspired with an ambition of becoming the little Londons of the part of the kingdom wherein they are situated: the notions of splendour, luxury, and amusement, that prevail in town, are eagerly adopted; the various changes of fashion exactly copied; and the whole manner of life studiously imitated ... every male and female wishes to think and speak, to eat and drink, and dress and live, after the manner of people of quality in London.

Taste and emulation focused on London. Facilities for, and patterns of, social activity responded to the example of London, which was presented as the benchmark for conditions elsewhere. The Royal Academy of Arts helped to develop a national style that the provinces and colonies sought to emulate.[13] Moreover, London craftsmen were in demand across the country. The Rococo silver basket in the dining room at Wallington in Northumberland was made by John Jacobs in 1750, while Thomas Bromwich (d. 1787), a noted metropolitan maker of cabinets and paper-hangings, was commissioned to produce a *trompe d'oeil* wallpaper scheme for changes to the Long Gallery at Wentworth Woodhouse in Yorkshire.

London's publications spread designs, as in *Household Furniture in Genteel Taste for the Year 1760 by a Society of Upholsterers, Cabinet-Makers, etc. Containing upwards of 180 Designs on 60 Copper Plates. Consisting of china, breakfast, side-boards, dressing, toilet, card, writing, clan, library, slab, and night tables, chairs, couches, french-stools, cabinets, commodes, china shelves and cases, trays, chests, stands for candles, tea kettles, pedestals, stair-case lights, bureaus, beds, ornamental bed-posts, corniches, brackets, fire-screens, desk, book and clock-cases, frames for glasses, sconce and chimney-pieces, girandoles, lanthorns, chandalears, etc., etc., with scales.* This book included designs by Robert Manwaring, William Ince, John Mayhew, Thomas Chippendale and Thomas Johnson. Later, in about 1790, Thomas Sheraton (1751–1806) from Stockton established himself in London and began publication of a series of manuals of furniture design. Thanks to such books of designs, fixtures, fittings and furniture became more standardised, and London fashions had a national scope.

The literary equivalent included works such as Charles Vyse's *New London Spelling Book* (1776). The norms of the language were set in London, although this could involve contradictions. Thus, John Walker's *Pronouncing Dictionary of English*, which was published there, provided 'rules to be observed by the natives of Scotland, Ireland and London for avoiding their respective peculiarities'. Influence, however, only operated up to a point. For example, provincial silversmiths, such as those in Exeter, were influenced by London designs, but also produced work with unique features. It would be a mistake to ignore the capacity in the provinces both to preserve local practices and to take initiatives. In part, moreover, London's impact was itself a product of its openness to influences from outside, both within Britain and from further afield.

The price of culture was higher in London than in most of Britain. For example, the cost of portraits in London and Bath was not matched elsewhere. Nevertheless, many aspects of London's culture were copied in provincial and colonial towns. For example, London's squares were imitated in cities such as Bristol, as well as in Rittenhouse Square in Philadelphia. Moreover, the social basis of London's development, a major expansion in the middling orders and a growing practice by the rural élite of spending part of the year there, was matched in regional capitals such as Norwich and Nottingham, in country centres such as Warwick, and in developing entertainment centres – particularly spa towns – such as Tunbridge Wells and Bath. A young Samuel Johnson (not the great Dr Johnson), described a modest subscription assembly at Islington that he visited and danced at in 1775:

> This assembly is quite a sociable meeting where the greatest part of the company is known to each other, and very like ours, a dancing room and a cold room, tea about 10, and breaking up about 12, two or three fiddles, a tabor and pipe, and I believe a hautboy, and a horn, admittances 5 shilling, twelve or fourteen couples, but generally I believe nearer to twenty, minuets and country dances, two or three handsome ladies, one very handsome, one very good natured man (Captain Shirley) to unite the company together, and this I think a recipe for an agreeable assembly. All kinds of liquors such as punch are included.

Gentility and equality were thus fused. The assurance of the former made it possible in theory for the company to set aside status and to act as equals, sidelining the concerns about social fluidity that played such a corrosive role in mixing. Indeed, London helped promote the interaction of bourgeois/middle-class and aristocratic thinking and values, and did so more successfully than in the seventeenth century, in part because religious and political tensions were less prominent. The virtues and values summarised as 'sensibility' were frequently contrasted with the commercialism and crassness of new money.

At the same time, the extent to which London offered different prospects to those of landed society was captured by George Lillo in his play *The London Merchant* (1731), which deliberately focused on ordinary people. 'A London apprentice ruined is our theme,' declared the prologue. In the dedicatory preface to the printed version, Lillo claimed that tragedy did not lose 'its dignity, by being accommodated to the circumstances of the generality of mankind ... Plays founded on moral tales in private life may be of admirable use.' A London in which there was much social differentiation was the context for this remark. In Joseph van Aken's painting of *Covent Garden Market* (c.1726–30), social distinctions were reflected in clothes and in positioning, with maids and servants depicted in drab colours, often standing behind brightly dressed ladies purchasing fruit and vegetables, literally and metaphorically in the shadow of their mistresses.

More generally, the variety of London society was captured in the very diverse roles of women. They could be prominent, dominating the lottery held by Thomas Coram's Foundling Hospital for nominating to places, and also playing an important role in the debating societies that developed from the late 1770s, while there was also involvement in less genteel activities. On 5 September 1759, *Lloyd's Evening Post* reported:

> On Monday night was fought at Stoke-Newington, one of the most obstinate and bloody battles between four noted bruisers [boxers], two of each sex; the odds, before the battle began were two to one on the male side; but they fought with such courage and obstinacy, that at length the battle was decided in favour of the female.

Prostitution was the fate of many women. Decorated tiles showing explicit sexual positions – probably from a brothel or gentleman's club – were discovered following a fire at the Cheshire Cheese pub in 1962. One depicts a woman lying on the ground holding a rope that passes over a pulley and controls a wickerwork cradle in which a seated man is apparently being lowered onto his consort's waiting dildo. An important homosexual 'subculture' also existed in London, with its own vocabulary, dress-codes, rituals and geography.

By European standards, London's social conventions were not rigid. The Comte de Gisors was surprised, when visiting the city in the 1750s, to find young women of quality paying visits alone without loss of reputation, but the French ambassador told him that it was the English habit to trust daughters to do this.[14] In 1763 a later French ambassador was

Covent Garden Piazza and Market, as painted by Joseph van Aken from the side of St Paul's church around 1730, a century after the area was first laid out. The West End – outside the ancient City limits – has since Tudor times been by far the most important area of London's development.

described as not having been long enough in post 'to learn that the ladies here had much rather trudge up and down the stairs by themselves, than be escorted by anybody'.[15] A degree of freedom had consequences in terms of relations with men. Prior to mid-century, the majority of actions for divorce brought in the London Consistory Court were brought by women against their husbands for cruelty, but, thereafter, the notion of romantic marriage and domestic harmony came to prevail among the prosperous, and the practice of divorce for incompatibility grew.

The social world that fostered demand for new buildings and spaces was complemented by the wealth of a growing economy, and by entrepreneurial activity, to provide many opportunities for artistic skill. Aesthetically and practically, the transfer of classical ideas to houses, churches and public buildings was not easy, as the prototypes were mostly ancient temples and baths, and it proved necessary to design a new architectural grammar for design and ornamentation. This need encouraged a recourse to books of designs. Yet, anglicised classical ideas transformed architectural style.

The aspect of London changed hugely over time. After the Great Fire of 1666, timber and thatch were seen as dated, unattractive, non-utilitarian and, increasingly, indeed, non-urban, as were long-established but irregular street patterns, and ferries, rather than bridges.

Instead, the city's appearance was reworked by and after the rebuilding following the Great Fire and the expansion of the West End. Urban improvements were almost invariably propagated by, and paid for, by the urban élite and the seasonal visitors from landed Britain, and these improvements produced new urban images and practices that reflected increased social polarisation. In contrast, the large-scale redevelopment of poor urban districts by local authorities lay well in the future. The resulting cityscape was one in which those who lacked gentility seemed out of place. As a consequence, alongside issues of different access to cultural facilities, came those of social acceptability.

Improvement was political in its broadest definition, reflecting a concern with the urban environment, a confidence that it could be improved, and a determination to act. London, indeed, appeared to be one of the principal products of human activity, the section of the environment most amenable to action, and the place where society was open to regulation. This view and practice reflected interacting functional, moral and aesthetic criteria and requirements that were aspects of the cultural activism of the eighteenth century.

Alongside official edifices, the new stone and brick buildings offered definitions of urban function, with an emphasis on leisure and retail and, more generally, on private space open to those who could pay – such as shops and subscription rooms – rather than spaces and

One of the very few buildings in the west of the City that survived the Great Fire, 17 Fleet Street boasts some fine Jacobean plasterwork dating from a rebuilding of 1610 and a street-facing balustrade at third-floor level. Despite various claims of association with Cardinal Wolsey and Prince Henry, son of James I, the building appears to have been constructed and probably mainly used as a tavern, at various times known as The Prince's Arms and The Fountain.

PHOTOGRAPH: CARNEGIE, 2008

places open to all, such as market places and churches. Increasingly the buildings could be seen and admired into the evening, as the night was more thoroughly lit after the introduction of street lighting. In 1716, the City's shops were instructed to hang a lamp outside their premises from six to eleven o'clock in the evening. Before gas lighting, and, later, electricity, transformed the situation, however, the change between day and night was far more abrupt than is the case today. As Hogarth's *Night* indicated, night-time offered different sensations, experiences and dangers, and, as a result, the role of moonlight was much more important than now.

The public buildings of the period greatly contributed to the fabric of society. Five voluntary hospitals, for example, were opened in London in the early eighteenth century: Westminster Infirmary (1719), Guy's, in Southwark (1725), St George's, originally at Hyde Park Corner (1733) and the London (1740) and the Middlesex Infirmary (1745). At the same time, the purposes of medical and other charitable foundations revealed the poor state of social welfare, the failure of family networks to care for all the destitute, and the grim nature of much of life. In London, charitable donors sought to provide adequate care for lying-in women and their babies, to rescue the all-too-numerous orphaned and abandoned children, and to rehabilitate those driven by poverty into prostitution. The term 'hospital' was also used for institutions concerned with the destitute, such as the Magdalen Hospital for the Reception of Penitent Prostitutes which was established in Streatham in 1758.

This statue is of Thomas Guy (1645–1724), son of a Thames lighterman. He became a book and Bible seller who amassed a fortune from printing and investments. In his will he left more than £200,000 to the hospital that bears his name. In this way he joined a long list of benefactors to London's hospitals, many of which were based around or run by monastic or religious organisations. The largest of the medieval London hospitals was St Mary without Bishopsgate (known as St Mary Spital), whose foundation near the City bars in 1197 was helped by a grant of land by one Walter Brunus. To the north-west of the City was the hospital of St Bartholomew, founded in 1123 by a courtier of Henry I, while in Southwark St Thomas's had been run by Augustinians since the twelfth century. In the 1530s, Henry VIII's dissolution of these monastic establishments brought much of the land and facilities into royal ownership. While Barts was 'refounded' by Henry (see page 99), St Thomas's was continued through the patronage of the City of London after Edward VI had relinquished the property. St Mary Spital, meanwhile, closed, much of its land being redeveloped by Henry VIII into the Old Artillery Ground in the appropriately named Spitalfields (see also page 98). Thomas Guy had been a governor and benefactor to St Thomas's before setting up his own hospital nearby to provide more beds.

PHOTOGRAPH: CARNEGIE, 2009

Thomas Coram's Foundling Hospital, established in 1739 and in full occupation by 1753, was a testimony to the harshness of London life, as many of the foundlings given up to care were not illegitimate but the children of couples who could not cope with sustained poverty and the impact of savage crises. The hospital thus testified as much to the problems of the poor, as to illegitimacy, and, during the Seven Years' War (1756–63), as many as sixty per cent of the children were legitimate. In contrast, from 1801 the hospital accepted only illegitimate children.

Other problems of London life also emerge from the study of the hospital. Death rates there could be as high as eighty per cent, but, as a reminder of the need to use sources carefully, they could also be low for the period, in part due to a care for foundling health and diet which included the dispatch of the children to nursing women outside London, where chances of survival were held to be higher. This was an important link between London and the provinces: the foundlings were sent to rural wet-nurses for the first five years of their lives, before being returned to London for education and for placement in apprenticeships.[16]

A far less benign situation was captured by Hogarth in the last painting in *The Rake's Progress* (1733–34), when he showed the insane at Bedlam being visited by fashionable ladies. Moreover, the London Lock Hospital founded in Grosvenor Place in 1746 for sufferers from venereal disease put an emphasis on moral reform and excluded repeat cases. In addition, institutions, charities and local authorities struggled to cope with the consequences of poverty and the pressures it placed on individuals and families. Thus the St Marylebone workhouse, built in 1752, was swiftly found to be inadequate, and another was begun in 1775. Designed to hold 300 paupers, it was holding 1,000 by the 1790s.[17]

London's role and image were made more prominent by the greater importance of provincial towns within their particular regions, as the city was thus seen to exemplify a national trend. Urban economies were helped and made more prominent by the growing commercialisation of life and by the rise of professions such as law and medicine. Moreover, in a world of 'things', where increasing numbers could afford to purchase objects and services of utility and pleasure, towns played a central function as providers of services, as much as of commercial and industrial facilities. The dynamic character of urban life was also seen in the number of town histories published, while the idea of town life as the cutting-edge of civilisation very much affected the perception of London, as did the growing sense of Britain as the successor to ancient Rome, with London the modern equivalent of that great city.

Changes within London, therefore, were not only aspects of the shaping of the city by its interaction with the wider world, but were also played out under the gaze of a nation that saw London either as synonymous with the country or as a hindrance to it. Thus, alongside complaints from other trading cities, especially Bristol, about the monopolistic character of London's privileges, the reiterated stress on the city's commercial importance ensured that its trade was generally seen as synonymous with that of the country. London merchants were able to press the government on policy, and also discussed matters with foreign envoys. In 1727 Hamburg's representatives in London prompted merchants to present a memorandum to George II, while in 1788 prominent London merchants told the French envoy that they were against government schemes for changes in Polish frontiers that would see Danzig (Gdansk) become Prussian.[18] In 1748 the government deciphered the report of a Spanish agent about discussions with London merchants concerning the need for bringing the war with Spain to a close.

London's commercial and maritime role was celebrated in the triumphal works produced in the capital. John Bacon's statue of George III in the courtyard of Somerset House depicted him in a Roman costume, holding the rudder of a ship attended by a majestic lion and above a colossal figure of Father Thames. In James Barry's paintings for the Society for the Encouragement of Arts, Commerce and Manufactures executed between 1777 and 1783, the figure of Father Thames was presented as a reborn Neptune. In the third edition of his influential *Universal Dictionary of Trade and Commerce* (1766), a work that first appeared in 1751, Malachy Postlethwayt, an active writer on economic issues, added a dedication to George Nelson, the Mayor, and to the aldermen and councillors of the City, that included the passages:

In this, the eighth and final tableau of Hogarth's *The Rake's Progress* (1733–34), the unfortunate Tom Rakewell, a young man who follows a path of vice and self-destruction after inheriting a fortune is seen in the Bethlem Royal Hospital, the lunatic hospital better known as Bedlam. By this stage Tom had already enjoyed the services of the Rose Tavern prostitutes in Covent Garden, been arrested for debt and married a one-eyed hag for her fortune. This he gambled away, only to be arrested and confined to the Fleet debtor's prison before going mad and ending up in Bedlam, where two fashionable ladies have come to view the lunatics.

SIR JOHN SOANE'S MUSEUM

London tradesmen appear to constitute the very active soul of the commerce of the whole British state; and they are an essential medium between the merchant, the country shop-keeper, and the consumers ... Of such high concernment are the London tradesmen to the whole traffic of the nation, that all our native commodities and manufactures almost of every sort, more or less, centre at first in London, and amongst the London tradesmen, brought to them from all the inland manufacturing and trading towns; and are afterwards sent again from London to the several different trading towns and cities throughout the kingdom, where those commodities and manufactures are not made or produced. The countrymen sheer their sheep, sell their wool, and carry it from place to place; the manufacturer sets it to work, to combing, spinning, winding, twisting, dyeing, weaving, fulling, dressing, and thus they furnish their numberless manufactures in the whole woolen branch. But what must they do with them, if London did not take them

Bacon's 1789 bronze statue of George III in the courtyard of Somerset House. George is depicted holding the rudder of a ship and stands above a colossal figure of Father Thames presented as a reborn Neptune. As in Rome, where Father Tiber is an ancient symbolic figure, the derivation of the phrase (Old) Father Thames comes from the centrality of the river to the city's origin, fortunes and growth. Father Thames is usually depicted in ruddy middle age with a beard, as here as well as on the PLA building (see page 307) and on a statue far upstream at St John's Lock, Lechlade, Gloucestershire.

PHOTOGRAPH: CARNEGIE, 2009

first off their hands, and the London tradesmen, warehousemen, factors, and wholesale dealers, did not vend and circulate them amongst the London merchants, as well as to all the remoter parts of the nation? London is the grand central mart'.

The city was also the forcing house for new developments. Thus, the insurance industry focused on London, where companies included the Sun Fire Office, Royal Exchange Assurance and Phoenix Assurance, founded in 1708, 1719 and 1782 respectively. Moreover, in 1773, a group of brokers subscribed towards the acquisition of a building which became known as the Stock Exchange.

London's commercial importance was seen in the economic news carried in the press. Shipping and grain were the early staples. In 1716 the *Supplement to the Weekly Journal* promised readers that it would provide them with information of ships arriving at and leaving London, a service common to many newspapers. Reports on grain prices were also found in most newspapers. The prices invariably mentioned were those at Bear Key, the Bear Quay, where grain was landed and where a major corn market had been established. These prices, and the value of the leading London stocks, were also carried by many of the newsletters used by early provincial papers as a major source of information.

The *London Evening Post* of 30 March 1762 devoted much of its attempt to publicise its contents to its economic news, offering

an exact table of the current prize of merchandise ... an account of the arrival of British ships at, and their departure from the several ports of the habitable world ... the several courses of exchange, the prices of gold and silver, of stocks of corn at the Corn Exchange ... and of other articles of a like nature. All notices given in the *Gazette*, with lists of bankrupts, and such other matters as may be useful to the public.

By the 1790s, London papers which in no way specialised in economic news, such as the *Express* and the *Telegraph*, were providing in every issue nearly a column of information (a formidable amount when, for tax reasons, papers were only four pages long) on London markets ranging from the price of butter and hides to that of tallow and sugar.

London's economic importance was also displayed in the columns of the provincial press. By 1774 the *Kentish Gazette* was regularly providing half a column on the prices in the London markets. The *Newcastle Chronicle* in 1787 provided a description of the condition of the London markets as opposed to a mere list of prices. The 'Market Herald' carried in the *Chelmsford Chronicle* in 1792 gave the London prices of grain, flour, seed, leather, raw hide, meat, tallow, coal, hay, straw and hops. *Woolmen's Exeter and Plymouth Gazette* of 30 November 1809 provided London grain, meat and leather prices. The *Sherborne Mercury* in 1837 offered reports on Smithfield, as well as the local cattle market.

These prices were significant because goods needed to be purchased from London, but also because the city was by far the largest market for producers elsewhere; indeed, London set the tone and prices for markets across Britain. The dependence of London on outside supplies was captured in a painting by Robert Dodd (1748–1816) of a collier brig discharging into lighters near Limehouse. The marine theme was also seen with Samuel Scott's *Sailboats on the Thames by the Tower of London* (1753), a painting that juxtaposed river and shore, with the Tower, the Monument and St Paul's Cathedral all visible.

London helped to mould a national economic space, although it is clear that specialisation for the London market was accompanied by the persistence of more local economic patterns. Most of the food for London's growing population came from within Britain. Welsh cattle were driven to Kent to be fattened for the London market, while cows were also driven south from Yorkshire. Fresh fish was brought from the Fens by wagon, the water in the butts changed nightly. From the introduction of powdered ice in 1788, large quantities of salmon were shipped direct from Berwick to London.

In turn, London markets affected agriculture elsewhere. Thus, in Cleveland, enclosure of both open field arable and commons owed much to the increase in pastoral farming for the London market. After 1769, when the Tees was bridged at Stockton, large quantities of Cleveland wheat were shipped from there to London. Good-quality butter was also moved to London by sea, for example from Malton via Scarborough, Whitby and Hull.

Some industrial processes were dangerous to workers or hazardous to public health. Dressing and tanning leather polluted water supplies and, as a result, was located on the banks of the river Wandle south of the Thames, and away from the City. London remained very important as a manufacturing centre, not least in brewing and flour milling, each aspects of food processing reflecting the size and appetite of the city's population. When Thomas Jefferson, the future American president, came to London in 1785, he visited the Albion Flour Mill, a steam-powered mill at the southern end of Blackfriars Bridge which made a considerable impression on him. This showcase for steam power, however, was burned down in 1791, to public rejoicing by 'the mob'. In 1750, David Hume, a key figure in the Scottish Enlightenment, noted, 'The manufactures of London, you know, are steel, lace, silk, books, coaches, watches, furniture, fashions ...'[19]

Greater energy efficiency did begin to make steam engines less expensive to run in London than hitherto, and therefore more viable as there was no local coal. Energy prices in London – based predominantly upon coal, rather than wood as in Paris or peat as in Amsterdam – were in fact very low by international standards even before the industrial revolution, helping to heat the homes of Londoners as well as fuel the early development of industrial processes. Nevertheless, opportunities in London in commerce and the service sector ensured that manufacturing did not dominate its economy, even though some plant, such as the major breweries, were substantial. Moreover, certain industries were affected by serious industrial disputes, although this did not prevent their location in London. After the violent silk-weaving strike of 1768–69, peace was restored only once the Spitalfields Act of 1773 brought an unusual degree of outside regulation of wages.

The human and environmental costs of urban and industrial development were increasingly clear. In 1714 the French envoy complained repeatedly about the effect on his breathing of the coal smoke that enveloped London.[20] An essay, 'Observations on the method of burying the parish poor in London, and on the manner in which some of the capital buildings in it are constructed and kept, as two great sources of the extraordinary sickliness and mortality, by putrid fevers, so sensibly felt in that capital; with hints for the correction of these evils', originally in the *Gentleman's Magazine*, and re-published in the *Annual Register* for 1776, criticised the dangerous stench from corpses that were buried in shallow graves, the hazards of crowded hospitals and public buildings, and the general lack of pure air: 'In this city, where coal fires are principally used, with the inflammable, mephitic, and other matters thrown out, probably an acid is decomposed, and exhaled from the sulphur in the coal.'[21]

Despite such warnings, relatively little was done to improve the situation. It would be mistaken to think that there was no care and were no improvements prior to the mid-nineteenth-century movement for reform, but the existing urban structures proved unable to cope satisfactorily with the rapid growth of the period.

Political developments and divisions excited more attention, especially when the city

William Beckford (1690–1770) was a radical Member of Parliament for the City of London, twice Lord Mayor who had become fabulously wealthy as a slave-owning sugar tycoon in Jamaica and later by pursuing business in the City. Horace Walpole once said of him, 'Under a jovial style of good humour he was tyrannic in Jamaica ...,' but he was well liked in the City, partly because of the lavish banquets he laid on here in the Guildhall. The Corporation of London had long enjoyed the unique privilege for a city authority in being able to make addresses in person to the monarch, and as Lord Mayor (as well as an MP for London) in 1770 Beckford, on the occasion of presenting a petition about the neglect of an earlier petition, harangued George III on the supposed misdeeds of his ministers, an unacceptable step that was said to have enraged the king. Beckford had died of a cold within a month of his outburst, but his reputation led the City authorities to vote this statue of him in the Guildhall, inscribed below with the text of what was believed to be his speech, which was, in fact, impromptu.

PHOTOGRAPH: CARNEGIE, 2009, WITH THANKS TO THE CITY OF LONDON

Westminster election hustings at Covent Garden, with St Paul's church in the background. In the eighteenth century, Westminster, where the franchise lay with resident male householders who paid the poor rate, had the largest urban electorate – about 12,000 – in the country. In London, where the franchise was restricted to the livery, it was the second largest, at about 7,000 voters. Westminster was a prestige constituency, and the government made major efforts to secure the election of sympathetic candidates.

was affected by disturbances and riots, as with the Sacheverell Riots in 1710, the Excise Riots in 1733, the Wilkesite troubles in the 1760s, and the dramatic Gordon Riots of 1780. There was an underlying volatility in the city that could spill over into political complaint, in words and deeds. In 1736 William Pulteney, a leading opposition politician, reported one such complaint directed against George II's mistress, the Hanover-born Amalie Sophie Marianne von Wallmoden:

> One Mrs Mopp, a famous she bone-setter and mountebank, coming to town in a coach with six horses on the Kentish Road, was met by a rabble of people, who seeing her very oddly and tawdrily dressed, took her for a foreigner, and concluded she must be a certain great person's mistress. Upon this they followed the coach, bawling out, 'No Hanover Whore, no Hanover Whore'. The lady within the coach was much offended, let down the glass, and screamed louder than any of them, she was no Hanover whore, she was an English one, upon which they all cried out, 'God bless your Ladyship', quitted the pursuit, and wished her a good journey.[22]

Thus, Mrs Mopp reprised Nell Gwyn's patriotic claim under Charles II not to be French, a sentence that can be variously reordered without losing this meaning. When Wallmoden did arrive, the crowd greeted her with cries of 'Hanover Whore'.

Political and religious radicalism and political criticism were particularly associated with London, as they were to be until the development of radicalism in the heartlands of the Industrial Revolution, such as Manchester, Sheffield and South Wales. In 1762, as we have seen, Elizabeth Montagu was shocked by the extent of critical sentiment in London.[23] Yet, as Lady Charlotte Watson-Wentworth pointed out that year, when referring to criticism of the Prime Minister, John, third Earl of Bute, the impact could be dulled by repetition:

> Lord Bute was furiously hissed in the City and the Mob called out Pitt for Ever, but no great stress can be laid upon that, the Lord Mayor would have thought the whole parade incomplete, if the day had passed without proper hisses and huzzas.[24]

At any rate, ministers and indeed monarchs monitored London politics. In June 1723 Sir Robert Walpole reported 'Some of the City gentlemen dined with me on Tuesday, and it was then agreed that Sir Richard Hopkins and Mr Feast should be desired to stand for sheriffs'. In the event, George I was particularly pleased by the election of the sheriffs.[25] The election of MPs from London, Westminster and Middlesex was regarded as especially important. In December 1741, government defeats in the Commons on the Westminster election petition were seen as particularly damaging, while the inability of the king to have sympathetic MPs for where he lived was noted by foreign diplomats. George II was further concerned in 1752 when an opposition printer was acquitted in London. The Duke of Newcastle, the First Lord of the Treasury, commented on George's concern about 'this spirit in the juries and the City which the King had flattered himself was almost entirely spent, and at an end; and indeed there were great appearances of it.'[26]

There were also attempts by government to control or limit disaffection. These included steps against the freedom of the press, such as the Juries Act of 1730, as well as moves to manage the political system. The City Elections Act of 1725 defined the freeman franchise as narrowly as possible, and imposed an aldermanic veto on the actions of the more popular and Tory-inclined Common Council in order to limit the volatility and independence of popular London politics. However, the Common Council often sought to restrict the authority of the aldermen.

Criticism of the government was frequently raised. In 1730, the Dowager Countess of Portland observed of the popular abuse of the Walpoles:

> There is not an evening, that there is not some paper cried about the street, good or bad, of Robert hatch, Robert hangman, Robert the coachman etc. or something of this kind, which shows what a spirit he has to defend himself against.[27]

Three years later, London played a key role in the opposition to the government's proposal for changes in the excise regulations. The nature of excise powers challenged suppositions about the constitution and the character of British liberties. Excise officers and commissioners were seen as arbitrary figures unconstrained by jury trials. Demonstrators in London paraded wooden shoes, the symbols of supposed French slavery. On 6 February 1733, Henry Goodricke observed, 'The rising tempest of an excise makes a furious roar in this town',[28] and on 10 April the government majority fell to seventeen on what turned out to be the key division, an opposition motion to hear by counsel a petition from the City of London critical of the scheme. Next day, the legislation was dropped. London, which had played a crucial role in its defeat, was illuminated in celebration, and Walpole was burned there in effigy. Indeed, although Walpole sought to build up support in London, he did not have any particular feel for London politics, still less the ability to woo metropolitan opinion. London took a major role in organising opposition activities to his government in 1733 and 1738–42.

The range of disaffection in London was considerable. In July 1736, when London workers rioted against the employment of cheaper Irish labour and had to be dispersed by the militia, Walpole wrote to his brother:

I sent several persons both nights to mix with the mob, to learn what their cry and true meaning was, and by all accounts the chief and original grievance is the affair of the Irish, and so understood by the generality of the mob, but in several others the Gin Act was cried out against, in some few words of disaffection were thrown out, and one body of men of about eight were led on by a fellow that declared for Liberty and Property. It is said that money was dispersed both nights, but that does not as yet appear to be certain, but although the complaint of the Irish was the first motive, the Jacobites are blending with it all other discontents, endeavouring to stir up the distillers and gin retailers, and to avail themselves of the spirit and fury of the people.

The following month, he reported on the prospects of disorder in London from the Gin Act:

what seems to me most probable is that the lower sort of brandy-shops, whose poverty secures them from the penalties of the law, may continue to sell in defiance of the law, and in hopes that nobody will think it worth their while to prosecute them, for what they cannot possibly recover.

London seemed to be under control only precariously. In September 1736 troops were deployed there to prevent planned disturbances over the Act, and Walpole wrote:

the murmurings and complaints of the common people for want of gin and the great sufferings and losses of the dealers in spirituous liquors in general have created such uneasiness that they will deserve a great deal of attention and consideration, and I am not without my apprehensions that a non-observance of the law, in some, may create great trouble, and a sullen acquiescence and present submission in others, in hopes of gaining redress by Parliament, may lay the foundation of very riotous and mobbish applications when we next meet.[29]

More bluntly, troops were used to deal with riots in 1768 and 1780. These deployments reflected the strength of dissidence in London. In the 1760s popular radicalism combined with the consequences of economic strain. The unwillingness of the House of Commons to accept the bitter attacks of John Wilkes was a key issue. Expelled from Parliament in 1764, he was elected for Middlesex in 1768, only to be imprisoned for blasphemy and libel and expelled from the Commons. Three times re-elected by Middlesex in 1769, Wilkes was declared incapable of being re-elected by Parliament, and his opponent was declared elected, a thwarting of the views of the electors that aroused anger. Wilkes was the focus of more widespread popular opposition to the government and a measure of radicalism that led in 1768 to riots in London.

That year, Elizabeth Grenville was concerned about her husband's safety amid 'the tumults and disorders' in the city ... God grant you safety in the midst of a wild, tumultuous and daring mob.'[30] Already in 1763 there had been resistance in London to the burning of Wilkes's seditious paper *The North Briton*: 'Mr Harley, the Sheriff, no sooner appeared with the paper to give it up to the all devouring flames, than the mob among themselves immediately with the faggots already laid for the conflagration, drove Mr Harley back into his chariot [carriage] with the loss of some blood on his part.'[31]

The Wilkesite controversy provoked a considerable degree of politicisation in London, which led to a different social politics, prefiguring the situation with the rise of Labour in the early twentieth century. Thus in Surrey, there was the rise of Joseph Mawbey, a Vauxhall vinegar distiller who became MP for Southwark (1761–74), a baronet (1765) and, eventually, despite opposition to him as a parvenu, MP for Surrey (1775–90). Mawbey benefited in elections from the willingness of freeholders to ignore the county's 'natural' leaders, and from the electoral strength of the London suburbs within Surrey.

In London a group of radicals, including John Horne Tooke and John Sawbridge, established in 1769 the Society of the Supporters of the Bill of Rights. This society supported not only Wilkes but also political reform, specifically shorter parliaments and a redistribution of parliamentary seats to reflect the population. This programme was continued by the Constitutional Society established in London in 1771.

George III (r. 1760–1820) was much criticised by London radicals. Indeed, when he

Smithfield on the north-west of the City was used for St Bartholomew's Fair, a cloth and meat market made famous by Ben Jonson. This eighteenth-century painting shows the fair in full swing. The fifteenth-century tower of St Bartholomew the Less rises about the houses to the left.
MUSEUM OF LONDON

drove to Parliament in 1771 to give his assent to a number of Bills, he was hissed, and an apple was thrown at his carriage. In turn, George was concerned about the electoral situation in London and Westminster, writing in 1774 to John Robinson, the Secretary to the Treasury and the government's Mr Fixit,

> Had the City affairs been managed with as much activity prior to Mr. Robinson's being in office as he does, the Court of Aldermen would not have been composed of a majority favourable to so disgraceful a member as Mr Wilkes, Mr Robinson having fully stated the state of the mayoralty and the meeting at Guildhall for proposing candidates for the county is very agreeable ... it may be seen that riots will be attempted; Mr Robinson will therefore keep the peace officers in the way during the Westminster Election.[32]

The political attention of Londoners extended to foreign countries. In 1768, for instance, a large public subscription was organised in favour of the Corsicans resisting French conquest, a step that led to complaint by the French foreign minister.[33] Yet, there was also a less pointed engagement with the outside world, one that reflected interest not partisanship.

At Bartholomew Fair in 1733, representations of Louis XV and his queen were displayed. Three years later, 'the gentlemen of the name of Brown in and about this City had a grand entertainment at the Spread Eagle Tavern; when, among other healths, they drank to Louis XV (Bourbon) King of France, as chief of the clan.'[34]

In part, the use of troops to preserve public order reflected the absence of an effective police force. In 1785 a Bill was introduced in Parliament to create a single, centrally controlled police force for London, in place of the existing local ward and vestry constables and watchmen. However, this Bill, and a similar one in 1814, was defeated, due to opposition from local interests and fears about the consequences for liberty. Instead, local initiatives in policing owed much to entrepreneurship, as prominent and dynamic individuals saw opportunities and needs. In West Ham, for example, watchmen and constables earned reasonable sums from the reward system. The use of 'thief-takers' was rife, although abuse, as in 1745–54 when they fabricated crimes in order to collect rewards, was common.

The most famous thief-taker, Jonathan Wild, showed what was possible in the relationship between capitalism and crime. Born in Wolverhampton in 1683 and originally a buckle-maker, Wild gravitated to the vortex of opportunity in London. Once in the world of crime, he moved from the established techniques of extortion and protection rackets to develop the trade of receiving stolen goods. Sidelining the fences by paying thieves a higher price for stolen goods, Wild used newspaper advertisements and other methods to resell them to their original owners. He also profited from the rewards for turning in criminals, including members of his own gang. In the early 1720s Wild destroyed rival gangs such as the Spiggott, Hawkins and Currick gangs. Hanged in 1725 for receiving stolen goods, Wild achieved continuing fame as a character type. He was the model for 'Peachum' in John Gay's *The Beggar's Opera* (1728), and his career was even compared to that of the Prime Minister, Walpole.

Crime in London seems repeatedly to have risen after wars ended, because men accustomed to fight were demobilised without adequate provision in a metropolitan labour market in which un- and under-employment were chronic. More generally crime reflected desperation, and, as in other periods, London's economic growth and importance were matched by poverty and despair. Yet, there were also periodic upsurges in social problems and crime. After the War of the Austrian Succession, there was believed to be a crime wave in the early 1750s. The long-serving Austrian agent Zamboni reported that, due to the rise in thefts and murders, London was unsafe both on the streets at night and even in people's houses, and that policing was negligent. Post-war demobilisation led to another reported crime wave in 1783–84.

Conversely, the outbreak of a war acted as a damper on crime because many desperate individuals enlisted. On the other hand, the statistical basis for such observations is not strong enough for definitive conclusions to be drawn, and it is possible that the lack of war news led the newspapers to devote more attention instead to local crime. A valuable source made recently available is the online database of more than 100,000 trials from the Old Bailey proceedings covering 1674 to 1834.[35]

In the face of periodic panics about crime waves, new solutions were sought, and it would be mistaken to argue that policing was in a dire state prior to the establishment of the Metropolitan Police in 1829. In the 1750s, for example, John Fielding (half-brother of the novelist), an active JP despite his blindness, organised mounted police patrols by his Bow Street Runners in and around London; this initiative was funded by the government. Efforts were also made to deal with the problem of low rates of criminal prosecution, for before public prosecution was introduced it was up to the victims themselves to decide to prosecute; not surprisingly many did not do so for reasons of expense. This led in the late 1750s to the foundation in London of a prosecution association, in which subscribers agreed to fund prosecutions. The 1792 Middlesex Justices Act extended the model of Bow Street, a court under stipendiary (paid) magistrates deploying a group of professional police officers, to other parts of London.

Convicted criminals faced the possibility of capital punishment, although extensive use of transportation of convicts to the colonies – North America until the War of American Independence and, from 1788, Australia – ensured there was less need for the 'bloody code', while the Penitentiary Act of 1779 led to a further diminution by encouraging imprisonment. In London, the forcing-house of change in the system of punishment, there was a declining dependence on crude terror. The number of those hanged there was far lower in the late eighteenth century than in the early seventeenth century. The percentage of those sentenced to death in London and Middlesex who were actually executed had declined from 72 in 1753 by more than two thirds in the 1780s.

Crime in London reflected the spread of the money economy and the extent to which it centred there. In 1784 Charles Price, nicknamed Old Patch, was able to circulate £200,000 in forged notes. He used high-quality paper and inks and, to escape detection, maintained three households (and wives). Moreover, much smuggling served the London market, and indeed it was insured there, which was a reflection of the role of London merchant capital in its financing. The game trade, which flourished in the second half of the century, in part through the developing network of coach services, also focused on London.

Profit was also made from the struggle against crime, not only by thief-takers but also thanks to the letting out to operators of sites near the gallows at Tyburn. Public executions upon the 'Tyburn Tree' were one of the major and free public shows in London. In 1746 Thomas Harris, a London lawyer, wrote to his brother:

This has been one of the most entertaining weeks for the mob … yesterday (which was the top of all) Matthew Henderson was hanged, at whose execution all the world (I speak of the lowlife division) were got together; and he did to the great satisfaction of the beholders, that is he was dressed and in white with black ribbons, held a prayer book in his hand and, I believe, a nosegay.[36]

In practice, the social élite joined in finding such occasions of great interest; some, indeed, justified attending the spectacle for the moral edification it might provide.

Moral misdemeanours also attracted attention. Robert Trevor wrote from London in 1729 about a notorious adulteress:

Private persons have not escaped the notice and censures of our licentious press; nor can even the grave bury poor Lady Abergavenny's shame, every syllable of whose name, and every particular of whose life are hawked about the streets as articulately as old cloaths etc.

Billingsgate market in 1808, from Ackermann's *The Microcosm of London*. Billingsgate was the city's principal fish market and unloading point.

Tyburn Tree, seen here in William Hogarth's depiction of *The Idle 'Prentice Executed at Tyburn*, was a triangular gibbet upon which up to 24 felons could be hanged at the same time, although only one instance is recorded when this was done, in 1649. The crowd could be large and boisterous: in *The Chronicles of Newgate* (1884) Arthur Griffiths described them as a 'ribald, reckless, brutal mob, violently combative, fighting and struggling for foremost places …' The *Gentleman's Magazine* of 7 March 1783 recorded just one instance: '… executed at Tyburn … John Kelly, for robbing Edward Adamson in a public street, of sixpence and one farthing.'

CARNEGIE COLLECTION

Those who had been condemned to execution at Tyburn made the painful journey from Newgate prison on Monday morning, usually on the back of a cart and sometimes sitting upon their own coffins. The journey could take up to two hours, with a stop at the church of St Sepulchre-without-Newgate (*left*) for a blessing, following by a pause for a last drink of ale – 'one for the road' – at the hospital of St Giles-in-the-Fields or, later, at the Bow Tavern. The prisoners, according to Henry Fielding, were subjected to public humiliation in order to 'add the punishment of shame to the punishment of death'. The exact site of the Tyburn Tree is unclear, although a pavement marker has been placed near Marble Arch. Parts of St Sepulchre date from the fifteenth century; it is one of the largest parish churches in the city, with an attractive three-storey porch. It used to stand on Snow Hill, just outside Newgate, hence its name, but now fronts the approach to Holborn Viaduct, which replaced the little stone bridge over the river Fleet in 1869. In 1605, the merchant and tailor Robert Dow gave £50 to have a handbell rung outside the cell of the condemned at midnight before an execution. The bellman of St Sepulchre (where the Newgate handbell is still on display) would ring bell and issue the warning:

> … Examine well yourselves in time repent,
> That you may not to eternal flames be sent.
> And when St Sepulchre's Bell in the morning tolls
> The Lord above have mercy on your soul.

In the early eighteenth century it was estimated that up to 100,000 spectators resorted to the area to watch the proceedings. Execution processions to Tyburn finally ended in 1783.

PHOTOGRAPH: CARNEGIE, 2009

The discovery of an admiral's wife in a Charing Cross brothel in 1771 also provided good copy. Prostitution was always newsworthy, as in 'The Frenchman's Blunder', a poem published in the *Moral and Political Magazine of the London Corresponding Society* (1796), which began,

> A Frenchman, lately come to town,
> Quite gallant, gay, and debonair,
> Rambling one ev'ning up and down,
> Pick'd up a nymph both frail and fair.

A sense of the liveliness of London life was captured by Henry Fielding in his *Life of Jonathan Wild* (1743), a work that captured the attraction of celebrity and the ability to coin it, as well as Londoners' interest in seeing their city depicted. *En route* to meeting his beloved Laetitia, Wild

> accidentally met with a young lady of his acquaintance, Miss Molly Stradle ... Miss Molly, seeing Mr Wild, stopped him, and with a familiarity peculiar to a genteel town education, tapped, or rather slapped him on the back, and asked him to treat her with a pint of wine at a neighbouring tavern ... the young lady declared she would grant no favour till he had made her a present.

London poet and painter William Blake (1757–1827), meanwhile, published a poem simply entitled 'London' at the height of the French Revolution in 1794:

> I wander through each chartered street,
> Near where the chartered Thames does flow,
> And mark in every face I meet,
> Marks of weakness, marks of woe.
>
> In every cry of every man,
> In every infant's cry of fear,
> In every voice, in every ban,
> The mind-forged manacles I hear:
>
> How the chimney-sweeper's cry
> Every blackening church appals,
> And the hapless soldier's sigh
> Runs in blood down palace-walls.

But most, through midnight streets I hear
How the youthful harlot's curse
Blasts the new-born infant's tear,
And blights with plagues the marriage-hearse.

Unlike Wordsworth, who was to be pleasantly surprised at the view from Westminster Bridge eight years later (page 166), Blake could see clearly behind the façades and the marble vistas of the Georgian city. For him London contained throngs of poor or disadvantaged human beings who understood only too well – and had come to accept – the life of misery, hardship and hopelessness which was their lot.

A focus on London can lead to a lack of attention to the city's wider significance within Britain. This significance was becoming more complex and intense, for example in finance. Banking houses, single-unit partnerships with unlimited liability for their losses, developed in London and the provinces, especially in the second half of the eighteenth century. Moreover, an inter-regional credit structure based on London was established, ensuring that local economies were very much linked to the situation in London, as well as to each other via London. The foundation of a bank clearing house in Lombard Street in 1775 led to a great improvement, as banks were allowed to balance credits and withdrawals by a ticket system.

London also continued to play the key role in Britain's overseas trade, and, with the shift of centrality in European commerce from the Netherlands to Britain, this trade was more significant than hitherto. London's role in foreign trade was practical and cultural, entrepreneurial and institutional, and these roles interacted with the situation within Britain. Thus, London helped secure the influence of commercial considerations upon national policy.

There was a bleak side, however, to this prominence. For example, in 1750–79 the port of London recorded the second largest number of slave-trade sailings: 869, compared to 1,909 from Liverpool and 624 from Bristol. Moreover, the shipping of slaves was part of a complex trans-Atlantic trade, including that of colonial products back to Britain, and this trade depended on credit. The role of finance, especially on the sugar commission business, ensured that London, where it was centred, was as heavily involved in the slave trade as Liverpool. More generally, the growth in the numbers, assets, skills and functions of London's business community was important to Britain's successful participation in the Atlantic economy.

Key individuals spanned the worlds of commerce and government, lending a London focus to policy. William Baker (1705–70) was a prime example of the London merchant-politician. The eldest son of a London draper, he was very active in trading with North America, not least with New York, and was also a major entrepreneur, buying land in

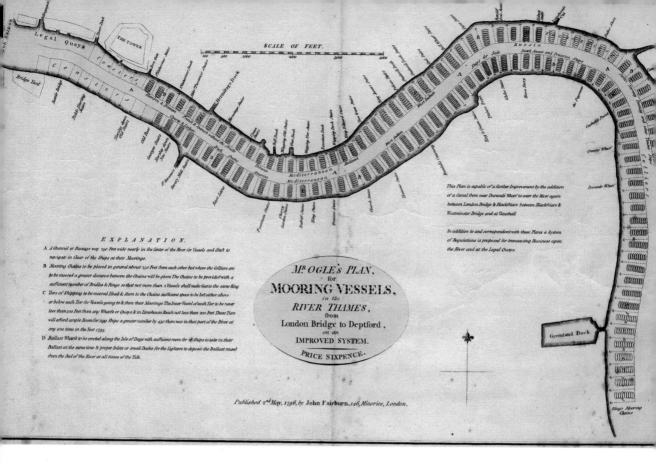

Mr OGLE'S PLAN,
for
MOORING VESSELS,
in the
RIVER THAMES,
from
London Bridge to Deptford,
on an
IMPROVED SYSTEM.
PRICE SIXPENCE.

Published 2nd May, 1796, by John Fairburn, 146, Minories, London.

Edward Ogle's plan of 1796 for rationalising mooring in the river to deal with the increasing number of vessels. His scheme was not implemented; indeed, the river wharves resisted all such attempts at rationalisation.

NATIONAL MARITIME MUSEUM

Georgia and South Carolina. A director of the East India Company, with short gaps, from 1741 to 1753, he was its Chairman in 1749–50 and 1752–53, as well as Deputy Governor of the Hudson's Bay Company from 1750 to 1760 and its Governor from then to his death. An alderman of London from 1739, and an MP from 1747 to 1768, he bought a country estate in 1757 and was knighted in 1760. Baker also played a role as a government contractor, victualling and paying troops in Nova Scotia from 1746. Baker was also regularly consulted by ministers on colonial matters, and was considered as a possible head of the Board of Trade in 1765.

Personal links and networks such as these, and the extent to which they reinforced each other, were enduring features of the city's élite, helping make London central to national policy-making. This was a time when London was the capital of the world's strongest empire, and Londoners in many ways played a disproportionate role. For example, the weakness of the short-lived Bath–Granville ministry in 1746 was indicated when the City withdrew a loan offered to the previous Pelham ministry. The major financial interests had close links with the Pelhams, and in wartime there was a desperate governmental need to keep loans flowing to the government. Partly due to the City, therefore, George II was forced to yield over government policy to Henry Pelham and his brother, Thomas, Duke of Newcastle, who had resigned in order to force his hand. They returned to office.

Foreign trade also helped encourage interest in the outside world. In his 1730 play *Rape upon Rape, or The Coffee-House Politician*, Henry Fielding was able to satirise the fears of the London tradesman Politic, who is so concerned about reports of international developments that he neglects threats to his daughter's virtue, knowing that the audience would share the joke:

> Give us leave only to show you how it is possible for the Grand Signior [Sultan] to find an ingress into Europe. Suppose the spot I stand on to be Turkey – then here is Hungary – very well – here is France, and here is England – granted – then we will suppose he had possession of Hungary – what then remains but to conquer France, before we find him at our own coast.

Interest in the outside world was, as ever, reflected not only in the careers of Londoners but also of those who came to London. For example Dean Mahomet (1759–1851), an India quartermaster with the Bengal army of the East India Company, came to Britain in 1784, married an Irish woman, became an assistant to Sir Basil Cochrane at his vapour bath in London, established the Hindoostane Coffee House in the capital in 1810, and subsequently opened Mahomet's Baths, which was patronised by such leading figures as Sir Robert Peel.

London and Londoners were also affected by the abrupt political changes of the period. The American War of Independence (1775–83) divided opinion, with much initial support for the American cause, but also considerable anger and opposition to it. There

Francis Russell, the 5th Duke of Bedford, was responsible for the style of development that took place on his family estates in Bloomsbury. From the 1770s several squares were laid out, including Bedford Square (*left*), Woburn Square, Russell Square and Gordon Square. For more than a century Bloomsbury was one of the most fashionable addresses, before its social standing declined. Bedford House itself was demolished in the early nineteenth century.

PHOTOGRAPH: CARNEGIE, 2009

was also periodic pressure from Londoners for radical political changes. The Westminster Association pressed in 1780 for universal manhood suffrage, annual elections, the secret ballot and equal constituencies, a programme endorsed by the Society for Constitutional Information established in London in April 1780 by a group of Rational Dissenters including John Cartwright and Thomas Brand Hollis. This society printed a mass of material in favour of parliamentary reform, much of it circulated free of charge; to our knowledge there were at least 88,000 copies of thirty-three different publications between 1780 and 1783.

In 1780 pressure from the Protestant Association for the repeal of the 1778 Catholic Relief Act led to a challenge to order in the centre of empire in the form of the Gordon Riots. Already, in 1773, fear of accusations of crypto-Catholicism had led the Archbishop of Canterbury and the Bishop of London to block attempts by the Dean of St Paul's to commission religious paintings for the interior of the cathedral. Then, on 2 June 1780, about 50,000 members of the Protestant Association marched on Parliament to present the petition for repeal. The Justices of the Peace had only about seventy-six constables to control the crowds, but Parliament refused to be intimidated into repeal. The angry demonstrators initially turned to attack Catholic chapels and schools in Westminster and London, before threatening establishment targets such as the houses of prominent ministers and politicians thought to be pro-Catholic and of magistrates who sought to act against the rioters. The prisons were stormed in order to release imprisoned rioters, while distilleries and breweries were pillaged and the Bank of England threatened.

The riots reflected a popular Protestantism that was deeply suspicious of tolerant tendencies on the part of the élite. In the end, George III, who was unimpressed by the City authorities' response and 'convinced till the magistrates have ordered some military execution on the rioters this town will not be restored to order', summoned the Privy Council which empowered the army to employ force without the prior permission of a magistrate. George then sent in troops to end the riots. They did so, and, after the subsequent trials, 26 people were hanged. These riots, in which 210 people were killed in the streets and 75 died subsequently from their injuries, were to leave a lasting impact in Charles Dickens' novel *Barnaby Rudge* (1841). The riots occur halfway through the story and The Warrens, the house of Geoffrey Haredale, a central figure, is burned to the ground, while his daughter Emma, the heroine, is kidnapped. A hostile Dickens wrote of the rioters becoming 'wilder and more cruel', changing 'their earthly nature for the qualities that give delight in hell'.

St Paul's was to serve as the dramatic setting for the celebrations of George III's recovery in 1789 from what appeared to be madness. The thanksgiving service on 23 April was in marked contrast with the drama that was to unfold soon after for Louis XVI, as political crisis escalated to revolution in Paris that year. Henry, second Viscount

Palmerston recorded 'the entering into the church [St Paul's] was very magnificent, an avenue all through it being formed by Guards and Beefeaters in a double row and in the centre under the dome the astonishing mass of charity children piled up quite round. Their singing as the King came in and went out had a great effect.'[37] As with many London occasions, reports and engravings spread accounts of the service. A sense of majesty emerges clearly from illustrations such as Edward Dayes' two views of the interior of the cathedral that day, and Robert Pollard's mezzotint of the same.

A pronounced division of opinion in London nevertheless arose as a result of the French Revolution; initially, in London, there was a marked upturn in radicalism, so that the radical London Corresponding Society, founded in 1792, grew in size and prominence. Indeed, Edmund Burke's famous critique of radicalism was entitled *Reflections on the Revolution in France, and on the Proceedings in certain Societies in London relative to that event* (1790). Concerned about the possibility of insurrection, the government moved troops nearer to London in late 1792. A major effort was also made to mobilise loyalist support, and this, too, centred in London. On 20 November 1792 the Association for Preserving Liberty and Property against Republicans and Levellers was launched there at a meeting at the Crown and Anchor Tavern. John Hatsell, the Clerk to the House of Commons, observed: 'This appears to me a better plan than trusting to the soldiery and brings the question to its true point – a contest between those who have property and those who have none.'[38]

Loyalist newspapers were launched, while opposition publications were suppressed by legal action. In 1792, for example, the *Argus*, a radical London paper, was brought to an end: its printer, Sampson Perry, was outlawed when he fled to France to avoid trial for libel. The presses were then used for a loyalist newspaper, the *True Briton*, launched in January 1793. When, that month, news reached London of London XVI's execution the play at the Haymarket came to an abrupt end when the audience shouted out 'No Farce, No Farce' and left. In 1794 plans for a national convention of radicals at London were disrupted by the arrest of the leaders of the reform societies, and in 1794–95 legislation, including the Seditious Meetings Act of 1795, made agitation for reform more difficult. Partly as a consequence, the membership of the London Corresponding Society declined. The proposal in 1794 that the society remonstrate to George III, outlining their grievances in the hope that he might dismiss the ministry was naïve, as was the alleged plot by the society to shoot the king with a poisoned arrow from an airgun. George's carriage was attacked by a mob *en route* to the opening of Parliament in October 1795, but thereafter London's response to the government was more orderly. The LCS suffered from its opponents' ability to smear the cause of radicalism as extremist and un-English.

In 1796 the general election was a triumph for the government in London, where the radical platform failed. Britain had been at war with France since 1793, and continued so for most of the period until 1815. On the home front, this conflict led to a lack of tolerance for radicalism and to a rallying to the Crown. Despite anti-war demonstrations in 1795, London, instead, frequently became a stage depicting loyalism, as when George III reviewed volunteers in Hyde Park on his birthday in 1799 and 1800, or with Nelson's funeral.

Nevertheless, as a reminder of the central position of London in the nation's politics, the naval mutiny at the anchorage of the Nore in 1797 was made more dangerous by the vulnerability of London to blockade, while in 1802 Edward Despard, a former army officer and disappointed petitioner, plotted to seize the Tower and the Bank of England and to kill George on his way to open Parliament. Betrayed by informants, the conspirators were arrested, tried and hanged. George, however, was sufficiently wary of London to urge the Home Secretary that Despard's trial be held in Surrey to avoid the independence of 'a Middlesex Jury'. The king's continuing concern with London politics had been shown in 1801 when he expressed his pleasure that Sir James Eamer had been proposed as Mayor, 'that alderman having uniformly conducted himself as a loyal subject and diligent magistrate'.[39] The City's loyalty to the established order was also displayed in 1806 with the address of thanks to George from the Corporation congratulating him

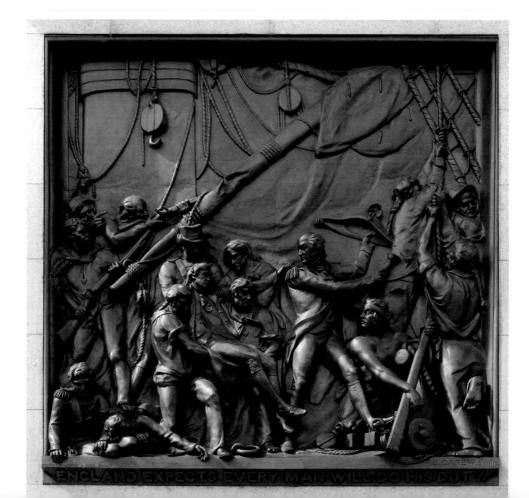

A great maritime power commemorates arguably its greatest naval commander: this relief by the Irish sculptor John Edward Carew is one of four that adorn the base of Nelson's 46-metre high column in Trafalgar Square. Carew also worked on Buckingham Palace and designed the statue of Richard Whittington (see page 5).

PHOTOGRAPH: CARNEGIE, 2009

for the 'decided support and protection given by him to the Protestant reformed religion as by law established'; in other words for opposing Catholic Emancipation.

The living conditions of the majority of the population remained bleak, even if by this date London workers – those in settled employment – enjoyed the highest wages in the world.[40] The Society for Bettering the Condition of the Poor noted of London in 1805:

> that many of the inhabitants of the more crowded parts of the Metropolis suffer very severely under infectious fever ... that in many parts the habitations of the poor are never free from the febrile infection; there being not only courts and alleys, but some public buildings, in which it has continued for upwards of 30 years past; – and that, by means of the constant and unavoidable communication which exists between the different classes of the inhabitants of the Metropolis, and between the Metropolis and other parts of the kingdom, this dreadful disease has frequently been communicated from the London poor to country places, and to some of the more opulent families in the Metropolis.

This was also a society that showed great cruelty to animals. In his *Autobiographical Notes*, Hogarth wrote that the 'cruel treatment of poor animals makes the streets of London more disagreeable to the human mind than anything what ever'.[41] In his engravings *The Four Stages of Cruelty* (1751), Hogarth depicted the torture of animals, for example the pushing of an arrow into a dog's anus. Moreover, in the same engraving a tired coach-horse is being beaten, while an exhausted lamb that has been driven too harshly to market is clubbed to death, and, as a reminder of man's inhumanity to man, a child playing in the street is being run over by a cart driven by a drayman who has fallen asleep.

This bleakness derived from a sense of cheapened life, both literally and figuratively. Alongside this, however, there were the opportunities created by entrepreneurial energy, opportunities that led to competition. For example, a troupe of dancing dogs had a very successful run at Sadler's Wells Theatre in 1784, and by 1785 there were two competing troupes. The dogs portrayed tradesmen and acted a series of scenes including the failed storming of a castle.

It was the unemployed, the unconnected, the newly arrived migrant, and young single women who were generally the most badly treated by the judicial system; they were most likely to be suspected of crimes and brought before JPs. The notebook of Henry Norris, a Hackney JP, reveals that he was honest, but had little sympathy with the plight of the poor and was rarely lenient, even when they were obviously in want. Over two thirds of the offences brought before him involved some form of assault, while allegations of theft or damage to property formed the second largest category. Justice before Norris and others was swift but rough. Without legal representation and the right to present their case to a jury, defendants were at the mercy of the JP.[42]

Thomas Lord's
cricket ground
at St John's
Wood in 1835.
Lord's first
ground had
been at Dorset
Square about
a mile to the
south-east; in
1810 it moved to
St John's Wood,
but construction
of the
Regent's Canal
necessitated a
final move, in
1814, to the St
John's Wood
Road site still in
use today.
BY COURTESY OF THE
MARYLEBONE CRICKET CLUB

Hackney was part of the in-between world of outer London, where settlements on or close to the outskirts of the City were greatly affected by its life. They were not only economically linked, but also places where Londoners could pursue leisure, as with Blackheath where cricket matches were played before big crowds from the 1730s, and annual archery tournaments were staged by 1770. Thomas Lord opened a new cricket ground near Regent's Park in 1787. It was moved to St John's Wood when that lease ended, became home to the Marylebone Cricket Club, and finally occupied Lord's current site in 1814. South of the river, cricket had been played on Kennington Common for at least 100 years before the Oval was laid out for the new Surrey County Cricket Club games in 1845. Proximity meant that, for many, two-way travel between London and its outskirts was a daily or weekly occurrence, and thus may be discerned the beginnings of what was to become a central feature of the capital's life and pattern of development: commuting.

Whether in or near London, the impact of hierarchy was felt at all levels. In the 1770s, John, third Duke of Dorset, was a key patron of cricket, notably as a supporter of the White Conduit Club which played at Islington Fields. The newspaper advertisements for the Handel concerts at Westminster Abbey in 1791 were headed:

By command and under the patronage of their Majesties; and under the direction of the Earl of Uxbridge, Honorary President [of the Royal Society of Musicians] Honorary Vice Presidents –

> Duke of Leeds
> Earl of Exeter
> Earl of Sandwich

Viscount Fitzwilliam
Lord Grey de Witton
Joah Bates Esq.

Bates, a Yorkshire-born musician, was the expert. Alongside the social politics of
London, it is pertinent, not least because the same was true of earlier and later periods, to
look at the tension between cosmopolitanism and xenophobia. If this tension was true of the
country as a whole, it was most acute in London, especially because, as today, the city was
the focus of immigration and of cultural expression. Anxieties were acute. Thus, having
a French hairdresser might seem the precursor of a Bastille in Hyde Park, and eating a
ragout an intimation of a conversion to Catholicism. A pamphlet of 1735, *Considerations
upon the Mischiefs that may arise from granting too much indulgence to foreigners, occasioned
by the late election of Broad Street Ward*, argued 'Our Beaumonde, our People of Quality
and Rank can relish nothing that is not of a French cast, which may in time be attended
with fatal consequences; since by imitating their manners and fashions, we may insensibly
fall into their vices.'[43] Eleven years later, when a French barber, resident in London, was
hanged in 1724 for the murder of his wife, a large crowd, mostly of women, uttered 'a
universal torrent of curses ... French Dog ... a bloody French cut-throat rogue ... French
Devil'.[44]

At the same time, London was increasingly a cosmopolitan city. In part, this was a
case of the reconceptualisation of Britain, a process registered by the Acts of Union with
Scotland and Ireland. After Union a considerable number of Scots did indeed arrive in
London. There were expressions of prejudice, but the Scots arrived without the tensions
arising from the arrival of Irish migrants, many of whom were Catholic. A large number
of the Irish migrants were also poor and congregated in the poorer end of town, notably
in the St Giles rookery. There were also more distinctive foreign immigrant communities
which contributed to the sense of London as foreign. The location of these communities
reflected the availability of property and the desire of immigrants to flock together and
benefit from community networks: Huguenots focused on Spitalfields, and Jews on
Whitechapel. This situation added a new level of variety and complexity to the social
differentiation of the city.

By the close of the period, new pressures and changes included an industrial world
different to the manufacturing of a century earlier and with transport links to match.
This was a world of new docks, and of iron plateways and railways, though not yet steam
locomotives. Much of the shaping of inner London was moving to completion, including
John Nash's works, especially Regent Street and the construction of Regent's Park. In
contrast, earlier schemes had not come to fruition, including John Gwynn's plan of 1766 for
a royal palace in the middle of Hyde Park and Spurrier and Phipp's 1794 plan for a Bath-

Much of Georgian London was built by small-scale speculative builders and developers such as George Barnes; the first tenant of this, 25 Brook Street, part of Barnes's small, -building development, was George Frederick Handel, who lived here from 1723 until his death in 1759. It was a modestly fashionable and convenient location for the composer.

PHOTOGRAPH: CARNEGIE, 2009

inspired circus in St John's Wood. London's development reflected a qualitative change in the building industry, with a greater standardisation of construction methods and the organisation of building firms. Expansion and rebuilding were designed not only to provide housing and benefits for the affluent, but also for the bulk of the population, with small, often wooden, houses being replaced with brick houses built in terraces.

The names Regent Street and Regent's Park reflected the patronage of George, Prince of Wales, Prince Regent from 1811 to 1820, later George IV, but the key element in patronage increasingly was the support of a wide tranche of society. Handel, who had worked at Canons, composing anthems for the Duke of Chandos' choir, had then moved to the public market of London, re-inventing himself from a servant of the rich composing 'Italian' operas, to the nationalistic author of English-language oratorios. Moreover, singers at the concerts in Vauxhall Gardens in the second half of the eighteenth century knew that their future engagements depended on the number of encores.

Yet, picking up a theme that still echoes strongly today, there was anxiety about the character and consequences of public taste, particularly that of whoever was assumed to be lower in social status than the observer or commentator. Thus, 'An Essay on the Present State of Music Among the Common People, and the Influence of Bad Music on Their Morals', published in the *Monthly Miscellany* of February 1774, asked:

What has made London a sink of filth and wickedness, one monstrous mass corruption. Why, the ballads that are chanted in every street and lane of the City ... a ballad-singer, standing in the chief place of concourse, with a crowded audience round him, inflaming their appetites and passions, winning his way into their hearts, by means of music often too sweet, and raising at his will the various devils of unbridled lust, shameless lasciviousness, discontent, sedition and unrest.

Moreover, looking toward demands for change later in the nineteenth century, London continued to be a centre for critical sentiment and opposition political activity. For example, in 1802, Sir Francis Burdett, a radical MP, stood in the general election for the prominent seat of Middlesex, against William Mainwaring, chairman of the Middlesex and Westminster Quarter Sessions, who had sat for the seat since 1784. Burdett had criticised the war with France and had complained about what he presented as the autocratic aspects of government, making a particular impact with his criticism of the treatment in the Coldbath Fields Prison in Clerkenwell of suspects denied the protection of habeas corpus. Mainwaring had resisted Burdett's inquiry into prison abuses. Burdett won handsomely, only for his election to be declared void in 1804. A contested election then led to the return of Mainwaring's son, but the result was amended to return first Burdett (1805) and then his rival (1806). In 1807 Burdett won again, sitting for Westminster until 1837, but he was sent to the Tower in 1810 for breaching the privilege of the House of Commons by publishing a contentious speech.

George III, who had opposed Burdett's election in 1802, complained in 1805 about an Address from London that 'outstrips its true line of duty'. He argued that no response could be made as he did not want to encourage 'haranguers on subjects not properly coming under their cognisance'.[45] This was a politics that was on the way out, as developments later in the nineteenth century were to show.

London from Greenwich Park by J.M.W. Turner (1775–1851). The son of a Covent Garden barber, Turner was educated at Soho Academy and the Royal Academy schools and worked largely in London, living in Queen Anne Street from 1812.

TATE GALLERY

7

I T W A S during the 'long' nineteenth century that London commanded its greatest significance for world history. Its streets and public open spaces were the prime setting for imperial drama. The state funeral in 1852 of Arthur, Duke of Wellington, the victor of Waterloo, was a solemn instance. As the *Illustrated London News* of 20 November 1852 declared,

> Wellington and Nelson sleep side by side under the dome of St Pauls, and the national mausoleum of our isles has received the most illustrious of its dead. With a pomp and circumstance, a fervour of popular respect, a solemnity and a grandeur never to be surpassed in the obsequies of any other hero hereafter to be born to become the benefactor of this country, the sacred relics of Arthur Duke of Wellington have been deposited in the place long since set apart for them by the unanimous decision of his countrymen. All that ingenuity could suggest in the funeral trappings, and that imagination and fancy could devise to surround the ceremonial with the accessories that most forcibly impress the minds of a multitude, all the grace that Royalty could lend, all the aid that the state could afford in every one of its departments, all the imposing circumstances derivable from the assemblage of great masses of men arrayed with military splendour and in military mourning, together with the less dramatic but even more affecting grief expressed by the sober trappings of respectful and sympathetic crowds, all the dignity that could be conferred by the presence of the civil and legislative power of the great and ancient kingdom; and, lastly, all the sanctity and awe inspired by the grandest of religious services, performed in the grandest Protestant temple in the world, were combined to render the scene, inside and outside of St Paul's Cathedral on Thursday last, the most memorable in our annals.

Such episodes lived in the memory of participants and spectators, and were retold through publications and illustrations, but a more lasting impression was presented by the

THE WORLD CITY, 1815–1914

Walking around London one can hardly avoid powerful reminders of the city's centrality in national and imperial events. The great hall of the Guildhall boasts enormous memorials to Nelson and Wellington, as does St Paul's Cathedral; Trafalgar Square has its Column; a major group of statues on Waterloo Place commemorates the Crimea; a Wellington Arch in Green Park; and there is this, Sir Francis Chantrey's equestrian statue of Wellington, erected in front of the Royal Exchange and the Bank of England in 1852. In fact it was not intended to honour his great military or political career. Rather, the City part-funded the statue out of appreciation for the duke's help in securing the passage of the London Bridge Approaches Act of 1827.

memorialisation of triumph in grand stone monuments and in names. Nineteenth-century London came to be the display-site of victories to a degree unprecedented in the nation's history. Trafalgar Square, begun in the 1820s on the site of the royal mews at Charing Cross, and completed in 1845, soared with Nelson's Column, which was topped by Edward Hodges Baily's eighteen-foot-high statue of the admiral. Baily's father had been a carver of ships' figureheads in Bristol. The bronze lions at the column's foot, sculpted by Queen Victoria's favourite painter, Sir Edwin Landseer, followed in 1867. The heart of empire was complete.

Meanwhile, Wellington himself had been commemorated with what was thought to be the largest equestrian statue in existence. Designed by Matthew Cotes Wyatt and cast from captured enemy cannon, this bronze was erected in 1846 on top of the triumphal arch at Hyde Park Corner, although it was thought disproportionately large and in 1883 was removed to Aldershot.

Less prominent statues included that on Carlton House Terrace of Frederick, Duke of York, the commander-in-chief for most of the Napoleonic Wars. In 1823 the Painted Hall of the Greenwich Naval Hospital was established as a national gallery of marine paintings to mark the services of the navy. George IV provided over thirty canvases from the royal collection, and the gallery was soon receiving up to 50,000 visitors a year. Names given to the very fabric of London came to echo imperial glories, with examples

During the nineteenth century the parks and avenues of western London were systematically filled with patriotic statuary and symbols of national and, later, imperial grandeur. George IV (r. 1820–30) gave the city not one but two triumphal arches, built mainly to provide grand entrances to his redesigned Buckingham Palace. Both arches – Marble Arch and Wellington or Constitution Arch – survive, although both have been moved from their original locations. Decimus Burton designed this, the Green Park Arch, in the 1820s. Twenty years later, the top of the arch was considered a suitable place for a truly enormous equestrian statue of the Duke of Wellington – right opposite the Duke's residence at Apsley House. Designed and built by London-born painter and sculptor Matthew Cotes Wyatt, the statue weighed 46 tons and looked hopelessly out of place on top of the arch. Much of London society ridiculed it; the arch – renamed Wellington Arch – could not easily support it; and Queen Victoria was said to disapprove of it. It could hardly be taken down while the duke lived, but in the 1880s, when the arch had to be moved for road-widening, the opportunity was taken to ship off Wellington's statue, where it still stands. The much smaller Wellington statue now near the arch is said to be small enough to fit under the belly of Wyatt's earlier horse. The four-horsed chariot – or quadriga – was added to the top of Wellington Arch in 1912.

PHOTOGRAPH: CARNEGIE, 2008

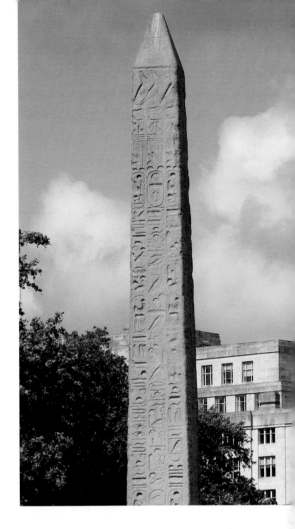

Cleopatra's Needle. This famous landmark has nothing whatever to do with Cleopatra. Rather, this ancient obelisk was erected in Heliopolis by the pharaoh Thutmose III 1,400 years before she lived. Paris had already acquired an ancient Egyptian obelisk in 1833, which the French dubbed l'Aiguille de Cléopâtre; and the cast-iron cylinder used to transport this obelisk to London was also nicknamed *The Cleopatra*. The name stuck. The hieroglyphs are not original either: these were added by Ramesses II around two centuries after the obelisks had first been erected. In all nineteenth-century great powers there were those keen to associate themselves with the greatest of ancient empires; in a similar way parallels with ancient Greece and Rome underlay the popularity of neo-classical architecture. Witness, for instance, the prominent 'Elgin Marbles' frieze around the top of the Athenaeum Club on Waterloo Place (see page 275).

PHOTOGRAPH: CARNEGIE, 2009

including Waterloo Bridge and Waterloo Station, opened in 1817 and 1846 respectively, as well as Waterloo Place. Prior to the battle, the first was to have been called The Strand Bridge.

The commemoration of victory was not without its criticisms, some of which focused on the social dimensions. On 1 August 1814, when a national jubilee was held to celebrate peace with France, the parks were opened to the people. Eight days later, however, Charles Lamb complained to William Wordsworth:

… all that was countryfied in the parks is all but obliterated … booths and drinking places go all around it [Hyde Park] … the stench of liquors, bad tobacco, dirty people and provisions, conquers the air and we are stifled and suffocated in Hyde Park.[1]

Here Thomas Schütte's colourful 'Model for a Hotel' (2007) adorns the 'fourth plinth' of Trafalgar Square. The National Gallery is in the background.

PHOTOGRAPH: CARNEGIE, 2009

British greatness was displayed in other ways. In 1820, Mehemet Ali, ruler of Egypt, presented an obelisk, now known as Cleopatra's Needle, to George IV. Transported half a century later from the sands of Egypt inside a great floating iron cylinder that almost foundered in the Bay of Biscay, the obelisk was erected atop the recently completed Victoria Embankment on the north bank of the Thames in 1878. The National Gallery was founded in 1824 and moved into its new building on Trafalgar Square in 1838; the gallery testified to the same urge to celebrate Britain's role.

London's interaction with the wider world was far wider and more varied. Founded in 1759, the Royal Botanic Gardens at Kew became a focus for research

based on holdings from around the world, while much missionary activity also centred on London. Thus, Robert Moffat, who, in 1816, became a missionary for the London Missionary Society (founded in 1795), went beyond the frontier of Cape Colony north into Namibia. There, he laid out a new mission station at Kuruman and translated part of the Bible into Sechwana.

Earlier, in 1787, a settlement based on London's blacks was established at Freetown in West Africa. Although some had come to England in the course of their working life, individually as seamen or as servants, the great majority who became involved in the Sierra Leone expedition were loyalists from the War of American Independence, discharged in England after the end of the war. Most were poor, in their twenties, and had lived in the East End. Since there were relatively few women among them, or among the previous black community in London, a significant number took white wives. The great majority of London newspaper items covering the expedition were sympathetic in tone. Combined with intermarriage and the good public response to the appeal for money to help poor blacks, this situation suggests that racial hostility may have been less common than has often been assumed.[2]

Indeed, foreign trade and cosmopolitanism had been such facts of life for so long in London that racial tolerance was more generally the norm than the exception. Colour was also employed as a device in comic works, as in Henry Bate's opera *The Blackamoor Washed White*, produced at Drury Lane in 1776.

At the same time as displays of interest and pride in Britain's global role, there were sharp social configurations in the imperial city, configurations underlined on the part of most commentators by a self-righteous belief in their moral character. Thus, Charles Booth's *Descriptive Map of London Poverty, 1889* ascribed a low moral status to the poorest residents: 'Lowest class, vicious, semi-criminal.' These residents were differentiated from 'Very Poor, casual. Chronic want', and from 'Poor. 18s. to 21s. a week for a moderate family'. Booth's social survey, which incorporated extensive field visits, followed earlier work by others including Henry Mayhew.[3] Booth (1840–1916), who had made money with the Liverpool-based Booth Steamship Line, was a noted statistician, indeed President of the Royal Statistical Society from 1892 to 1894. He doubted the 1886 report of the Social Democratic Foundation that a quarter of the working population were living in poverty, but instead found that the percentage was higher than he had anticipated, indeed 30.7, the vast majority as a result of poor wages rather than their own flaws. In particular, Booth, who

This illustration shows a production in progress in Theatre Royal, Drury Lane, shortly after the completion of the present building in 1812. A theatre had been on this site in Covent Garden since the 1660s, making it the City's oldest theatre. The building is now owned by Andrew Lloyd Webber and hosts mainly musical theatre

CARNEGIE COLLECTION

was bothered by the greatly different social condition in London, attributed poverty to the role of seasonal and casual labour, and the problems of child-rearing and old age without social welfare, and, as a result, he called for old-age pensions, a call that was to influence the Liberal government that gained power in 1905. His *Life and Labour of the People of London* appeared, in 17 volumes, from 1889 to 1903.

Booth also presented poverty as a threat to civil society. In his *Life and Labour of the People in London ... Poverty* (1889), Booth depicted

> The lowest class, which consists of some occasional labourers, street sellers, loafers, criminals and semi-criminals ... Their life is the life of savages, with vicissitudes of extreme hardship and occasional excesses ... their only luxury is drink ... From these come the battered figures who slouch through the streets, and play the beggar or the bully.

This unsympathetic view, conflating social and moral classifications in the worst of his eight categories, highlighted a sense of menace that can be glimpsed more widely in the remarks of commentators. This sense was linked to accounts of the East End as dark and criminous, accounts that flared into high anxiety with the much-reported murders of five prostitutes by Jack the Ripper in 1888 and the failure of the police to catch him. Whitechapel, the site of these killings, became a source of anxiety about the moral consequences of social deprivation,[4] an anxiety that led to calls for slum clearances.

It is possible to discuss social differentiation within London in very different ways, notably with a stress on exclusion or on inclusion in institutional and social practices. Thus, the London Palladium, opened in 1910, included facilities for gentlemen changing into evening dress, which underlined the extent to which public forums provided a stage for displays of difference. At a less exalted level, from the 1890s, theatre syndicates from existing music-hall managements built new venues, such as the 'palaces', for more 'respectable' customers who, of course, could be charged more. George V came to the Palace Theatre for a Royal Command Performance in 1912. On the other hand, it is possible to emphasise a more inclusive position, by stressing the degree to which the London working class in jobs had access to inexpensive forms of culture, such as the many music-halls and newspapers.

Photographer Henry Dixon wrote that this image of c.1875, 'shows a row of shambles, destroyed for the extension of the Metropolitan Railway from Aldgate to Tower Hill'. Dixon photographed many historic buildings, including Cloth Fair, as well as new building projects such as Holborn Viaduct.
MUSEUM OF LONDON

This painting by Emile Claus shows the nine arches of John Rennie's original Waterloo Bridge, opened in 1817, and demolished and replaced in the 1940s after some of the piers had been undermined by the increased flow of the river following the demolition of the old London Bridge in the 1820s. John Betjeman attacked the decision to replace the bridge, 'one of the last great works of a great age', drawing attention to arguments that it could have been saved, and suggesting that bureaucratic folly and a lack of artistic taste played roles in the decision.

The size of London's population grew greatly during the period, in part due to natural growth, but, in large part, as a consequence of migration, notably within the British Isles, but also from overseas. At the same time, London contributed to emigration of these times; indeed, Britain had net outward migration in every year from 1876 to 1914, the period for which statistics are most comprehensive. In the lean years of the 1880s, emigration was particularly important. There was a sense of greater opportunity to be had abroad, notably in the USA, the major destination for British emigrants, as still for many Londoners today, but also in Canada, Australia and New Zealand.

By modern standards, average death rates were high, but early marriage, in part as a result of economic opportunity, meant more children, helping births to outstrip deaths. Moreover, an improving diet, particularly after 1850, in part as a result of imported food such as North American grain, Argentinean beef, Australian mutton and New Zealand lamb, helped gradually to raise life expectancy. Thus the food brought to the London docks directly affected the life opportunities of the city's inhabitants. Yet, while the fertility level of a city with a largely young population pushed London's growth, immigration remained important.

Indeed, recently arrived Irish labourers, many responding to the crisis in Ireland caused by the Great Famine of the late 1840s, proved a particularly important component in the male workforce, notably in construction projects such as the railways. The largest Irish communities in Britain were always in London, even though in percentage terms many other places were far more Irish. The 1851 census revealed that 4.6 per cent of London's population was Irish-born, compared to 18.9 per cent of Liverpool's. In nineteenth-century

London, the large Irish communities were in central areas, such as St Giles, which, in one sense, were building on early modern Irish settlements, dating to at least the seventeenth century. In the late nineteenth century the Irish became concentrated in the East End.

Large numbers of Russian and Polish Jews immigrated from the 1880s until the Aliens Act of 1905, again very much focused on the East End, where the network of contacts and institutions established by recent Jewish immigrants encouraged fresh settlement. By the end of the nineteenth century, the number of Jewish immigrants in London had risen to about the same as that of the Irish, but, by then, the latter appeared less alien, not least because they spoke English. There was also Chinese immigration, especially to Dockland, while Indians from Sylhet (now part of Bangladesh), who were employed on merchant shipping, could also be found there. From the 1850s, too, a small African and Asian middle class established itself.[5]

These migrations caused a measure of social and political tension. The Clerkenwell explosion of 1867, a Fenian terrorist act, indicated the potential political issues posed by immigrants, in this case the Irish. So also did the 1858 riot in Hyde Park between pro-papal Irish and radicals in favour of Italian unification, a policy that was to lead to the Pope's loss of control over the Papal States of central Italy. In 1859–60, the strength of anti-Catholic views were shown in the anti-Ritualist demonstrations held in St George's-in-the-East in Wapping. In addition, local schoolboys were paid to pelt the curate, a notorious Ritualist, with eggs. Joseph Conrad, a Polish immigrant who became a naturalised subject while working in the British merchant marine, depicted a deadly world of Russian revolutionary anarchists and government agents in his novel *The Secret Agent* (1907), which included a bomb plot aimed at the Greenwich Observatory.

A small detail of the 2½ metre long 'Rheinbeck' panorama of London by an anonymous artist, c.1806–07. This detail shows the Legal Quays between London Bridge (*top left*) and the Tower (*bottom right*). The Customs House is clearly visible (*centre*), as is Billingsgate. The oval of open space behind the Tower is Trinity Square.
MUSEUM OF LONDON

This is J.C. Bourne's illustration of the stationary engine house under construction at Camden Town in 1837 for the London and Birmingham Railway, whose line from Euston to Birmingham was the first of London's inter-city connections. Parts of the route were opened before the whole was complete in order to facilitate travel to London for Victoria's coronation that year. The engine, which pulled trains by rope up the incline from Euston to Camden Town, was only used for six years, until 1844. It has been said that early locomotives were not powerful enough to haul trains up the slope, particularly as it had to rise high enough to pass over Regent's Canal near Gloucester Road, but this is not the case. Instead Parliament had not allowed the railway company to operate steam locomotives close to the city, a restriction that was soon relaxed and then ignored completely.

In part, notably with the Irish, London's growth was a case of the imperial exploiter partly taken over by immigrant groups from the empire, a process that was more generally to be the case from the 1950s. Yet the relationship was also more complicated because immigrants in turn played a role in the pursuit of imperial advantage. For example, in the 1880s and 1890s, Central and Eastern European Jews used London as a base for benefiting from the production of gold and diamonds in South Africa. The patterns of causation and influence were therefore complex, but there was a common feature of power and influence that was open to being taken over by outside groups. Indeed, this pattern has persisted into contemporary London, not least with the role of the 'non-doms', non-domiciled foreign residents.

Access to immigrants was related to London's capacity as the great absorber of the nation. As a result, the city was best placed to cope with those seen as unusual in any regard. This absorption was not so much a matter of inclusiveness as of the capacity, in the city's vastness, to find those with similar backgrounds, commitments and interests, thus creating a virtual community as well as a renewed identity for the individuals concerned. One aspect of the city's character was therefore the identity, or at least opportunity, that it provided for what was regarded as social and sexual deviance. Homosexuals, for example, were more likely to congregate in London, a situation that continued in the twentieth century. Indeed, I can recall being told by a psychiatrist in Newcastle in the 1980s that she advised suicidal homosexuals to move to London as they were more likely to find acceptance of their homosexuality there.

More generally, London's population was dynamic, not only in terms of its growth but also due to the steady, but uncounted, flow of people passing in and out of its boundaries. For example, the population of 958,863 in 1801 nearly doubled between 1801 and 1831, and again between 1851 and 1901, to reach 6,586,000 inhabitants. In comparison, the population of the borough of Liverpool rose from 83,250 in 1801 to 375,955 in 1851. In a period of major demographic expansion in the country, the percentage of the population of England and Wales living in London also rose, from 12 per cent in 1801 to 15 per cent in 1891. London headed the list of leading cities in Christian Europe, followed in 1800 by Paris (550,000), Naples (430,000), Moscow (300,000) and Vienna (250,000). London's population was indeed such that it became an index by which growth could be gauged: in 1798, for instance, Pest was termed 'the emergent London of Hungary'.

While much of London's growth was due to net in-migration, natural increase accounted for 85 per cent of all growth by the end of the century. The rate of increase was indicated by the rise in the population of the Greater London area from 5,572,000 in 1891 to 7,160,000 in 1911.

In comparison with the great northern cities such as Leeds or Manchester, London was not dependent on industry or large factories, but it had a richly variegated economy. Relatively few of its businesses employed large numbers, although the breweries, such as Charrington's in the Mile End Road and Watney's in Pimlico, did. Instead, most of the factories were 'sweatshops' in east London, near the docks and the Thames. Advanced technology still played a role both with them and in some of the engineering workshops. Workshops and small concerns prevailed, and 86 per cent of London employers in 1851 had fewer than ten employees.

Manufacturing and commerce were not the only large-scale employers. Indeed, in part due to the role of domestic service, women out-numbered men in London. This role coincided with a reduction in labour opportunities for rural women: in 1851, 229,000 women were employed in agriculture, but by 1901 this had fallen to 67,000. This decline was especially noticeable in areas where urban industrial development was least apparent, for example in southern England, the West Country, and East Anglia, all of which were prime sources of migrants to London. George Lansbury, a key figure in the London Labour Party in the 1920s, for example, had been born in East Anglia in 1859.

In general, migrants from other counties were attracted to London in inverse proportion to their distance from South East England. These migrants received far less attention than the Irish or those from the Continent, but they were more numerous. The Scots attracted less attention than the Irish, but in the 1860s there were about 40,000 Scots living in London, a figure that rose considerably over the following century.

Like their counterparts elsewhere, migrants to the metropolis were young, mainly in their twenties. Rural migrants tended to avoid London's inner city, where three quarters of residents were London-born, and many others were Irish and (especially later in the century) Jewish or Italian. Migrants were part of a highly fluid demographic situation. Mobility between residences within London, and into and out of London, was highest among casual labourers, whose job security was lowest. Moreover, among migrants, turnover in residences was high. At any rate, a large part of the working-class populace occupied the same housing for only a few months. Charles Booth discovered that 40 per cent of families in Bethnal Green had moved within one year.

By the later nineteenth century, London had cemented its position as the world's largest metropolitan centre. It was a magnet for people, a centre of political life, and a place whose cultural élite had European pretensions, but whose businesses were of world importance. As the administrative centre of Britain, London was also the hub of the world's greatest empire. Its waterfront thrived on a busy commercial traffic which saw London conducting

London attracted skilled artists and craftsmen, many setting up small workshops and tendering for lucrative commissions. Samuel Parker, 'Bronzist to his Late Majesty ... [George III]', operated from premises in Argyll Street, Westminster, and was engaged to work on the spectacular bronze gates for Marble Arch when it was first built in 1828. Around the same time Parker also made a balustrade for Buckingham Palace's grand staircase. Marble Arch, which originally stood in the Mall as the principal entrance to Buckingham Palace, has recently been restored, and the gates re-bronzed. This detail shows St George, depicted as an warrior of ancient Sparta, slaying the legendary dragon, a strange concoction of historical symbols – the virtue of England's national saint and the glories of ancient Greece – in which historical accuracy or anachronism were not major concerns.

PHOTOGRAPH: CARNEGIE, 2009

European and Empire traffic in a way that dwarfed even Liverpool's dominance of trans-Atlantic commercial activity.

The growth of British trade was accompanied by a major expansion in shipping and docks. A spate of dock-building took place in the first years of the nineteenth century. The first to open, in August 1802, were the pair of docks known as the West India Docks, which cleverly cut across the neck of the Isle of Dogs in order to provide entrances at both ends of the dock; the northern dock was used for ships unloading, while the southern, Export, dock was for loading. Meanwhile, the excavations for London Dock at Wapping, to the east of the Tower, had begun in 1801. Like the West India docks, this 20-acre dock was furnished with a comprehensive range of warehouses and was later extended to the east, in part to provide a second access from the river. Further downstream came the East India Docks, at the north-east end of the Isle of Dogs, in 1805. Then, on the southern bank of the Thames, not far from the old Great Howland ('Greenland') Dock, work began on the Surrey Commercial Docks in 1807.

This dock-building reflected the acute congestion on the Thames and its wharves in the 1790s, as overseas and domestic trade expanded. In 1800, just before the development of enclosed docks, some 1,800 vessels were being moored in the river, rising to 16,000 in 1824, while in the 1860s, no fewer than 1,717 sailing colliers were enumerated working the London coal trade from the North East, bringing almost 3½ million tons of coal each year to drive the industry and heat the homes of the capital. There were innumerable complaints of lengthy delays before a berth was available, all of which was exacerbated by the fact that whole flotillas of cargo ships would tend to arrive simultaneously when the winds and tides

The Prospect of Whitby in Wapping. There was a public house on this site in Tudor times, but it has changed its name from the Pelican, to the Devil's Tavern, and then to the Prospect of Whitby after a Newcastle collier that used to moor here. The current building is nineteenth-century.

PHOTOGRAPH: CARNEGIE, 2009

gave favourable sailing conditions. Vessels would moor in the river, their cargoes transferred to small, unpowered barges known as lighters which would take the goods to the wharves. Before steam tugs began to be used to tow the lighters, they were manoeuvred using only long oars known as 'sweeps' and by taking advantage of the tides and winds, a highly skilled job that required considerable knowledge of the 'set' of the tides.

Unlike at Liverpool, the building of the docks on the Thames was done by private companies rather than the municipal authority, and was generally undertaken in an unplanned, rather chaotic fashion. Despite the new docks, indeed, the river wharves continued to do brisk business. A major factor in this was the 'Free Water Clause', initially a provision of the West India Dock Act of 1799 and later applied also to the other dock schemes. This allowed 'lighters or craft entering into the docks … to convey, deliver, discharge or receive ballast or goods to or from on board any ship … or vessel.' The lightermen thus had free access to the docks, where they could unload ships and move the goods out into the river to be landed at the river wharves, all free of toll or charge. This system cost the dock companies dear and had a hugely detrimental effect on their finances, and also helped to preserve the bustling, congested and chaotic trade of the many river wharves and warehouses to an extent and in a manner not seen at any other British port.

Indeed, London's commercial role increased during the French Revolutionary and Napoleonic Wars (1793–1815) as the trade of other European maritime powers, especially,

Unloading into lighters in the Upper Pool of London. At one time there were as many as 6,000 lightermen at work on the Thames.

NATIONAL MARITIME MUSEUM

To this day canal narrow boats do occasionally venture on to the Thames, though rarely now on the tidal sections. In Thomas Hosmer Shepherd's view of the Limehouse entrance to the Regent's Canal in 1823, several barges are being manoeuvred into the Regent's Canal Dock (later renamed the Limehouse Basin), the terminus for the Regent's Canal. Thames lightermen were renowned for their skill in using the tidal currents and wind to move barges and lighters up and down the river. The canal's heyday came somewhat later than this view, with vast amounts of coal being shipped to fuel commercial and domestic fires as well as gasworks and, later, power stations, which could all be reached from the canal.

CARNEGIE COLLECTION

from 1795, the Netherlands, was hit by French occupation and/or alliance and the resulting British naval blockade. Amsterdam's role as a financial centre had already been greatly hit by the Anglo-Dutch war of 1780—84.

The importance of the Thames within Britain's commercial system was enhanced by canal construction, enabling greater quantities of goods to be transported to the city and port of London from elsewhere in England. For example, by the late 1760s London's first true canal, the Limehouse Cut, had connected the ancient River Lee Navigation with the Thames. More importantly, from the 1790s, the Grand Junction Canal provided a link between the Thames at Brentford and the Midlands that eliminated the need for the long river journey to Oxford to join the earlier Oxford Canal. A further connection was provided between the Grand Junction and the Thames at Limehouse Basin via the Regent's Canal, which was completed in 1820; both of these canals were incorporated into the later (new) Grand Union Canal in 1929 from London to Birmingham. The canals improved freight links, providing a valuable long-distance route to join the Thames system to the industrial heartland of the Midlands, as well as more local traffic within the London region. Regent's Canal in particular wound its way around parts of north London which were undergoing rapid development at this time. The canals provided an important trade route that encouraged industrial location, especially by making coal more readily available within London, and even with the coming of the railways continued to supplement the capital's transport infrastructure in an important manner.

More and larger docks were constructed after the Napoleonic Wars. In a major development involving the demolition of 1,250 houses and the uprooting of more than 11,000 inhabitants, the St Katharine Docks were shoe-horned into the space between the Tower of London and the London Docks, becoming in 1828 the furthest upstream of London's excavated docks. The small Poplar Dock was built in 1852 as a railway dock.

The City Road basin on the Regent's Canal, by Thomas Hosmer Shepherd, 1825. As this was the closest the canal came to the City, the basin (and its neighbouring Wenlock Basin, built in 1826) handled a large amount of local traffic, including coal, building materials and general merchandise.

MUSEUM OF LONDON

Regent's Park in 1862, showing the 'Collateral Cut' (the Cumberland Arm) of the Regent's Canal that used to run along the eastern side of the park from the main canal, past the Cavalry Barracks and up to the Cumberland Market which had become the capital's principal hay market from 1830 after the closure of the market at the more central but congested Haymarket. This section of the canal was closed in 1942 and filled in eight years later; only a short stub remains today. At the north of the park can be seen the Zoological Society Gardens, which were pioneered by Sir Stamford Raffles, the founder of Singapore, although he did not live long enough to see the Gardens open to members of the society in 1828. Shortage of funds being a perennial problem, the zoo opened its doors to the public from 1847 in order to raise money. Devotees of the anarchic radio comedy show I'm Sorry I Haven't a Clue will note Mornington Crescent, at the northern end of Hampstead Lane, whose Tube station has for over thirty years been the final destination for a game allegedly made up to confuse the show's producer: as presenter Humphrey Lyttelton said, 'Quick … Let's invent a game with rules he'll never understand.'

CARNEGIE COLLECTION

As the nineteenth century progressed and shipping increased in size and volume, new docks became ever larger and were built further downstream and in the marshlands of Rotherhithe. The Royal Victoria Dock of 1855 (the first of the 'Royal' docks) was able to cater for the large steamships of the day, and could handle massive quantities of goods; like Liverpool's Albert Dock it was a pioneer of hydraulic power for goods handling. Millwall Dock followed in 1868, the Royal Albert Dock in 1880, and Tilbury Docks, around twenty miles downstream, in 1886.

The total investment in this dock-building programme was formidable, as was the amount of work involved, while the royal nomenclature of three of the grandest docks reflected their grandeur as well as official endorsement of their purpose. The docks were key sites of imperial identity and interest. Competition was important to dock-building, with the East and West India Company building Tilbury to compete with the London and St Katharine's Company, which built the Royal Albert Dock. Tower Bridge, opened in 1894, had a 200-foot opening span that allowed ships up-river, but by this date the docks down river had taken most shipping activity away from the Pool of London.

The major expansion of dockyards reduced congestion in the Thames, making it easier to control trade and to cut pilfering from open wharves (many of the new docks were surrounded by high walls for this very purpose), and this expansion also responded to the needs of the larger iron and, later, steel merchantmen. Thus, the river system developed in response to the changes in the nature of shipping, revealing a dynamism seen in other aspects of the city's infrastructure and economy. London's waterfront housed at any one time more vessels than any other port in the world, and was a counterpart to the City's role in the financial architecture of the world.

Dock employment varied greatly. Some of the work was skilled and therefore fairly regular and well paid, but most dock work was poorly paid and casual. Until remarkably late many cargoes were handled by hand, and employment levels naturally fluctuated greatly with trade, as indeed did the nature of injuries suffered. Being hired on a daily basis helped create a hard working environment in the docks, and was to encourage a militancy that led to strikes in 1872 and 1889.

Charles Dickens described vividly the energy and scale of London's trade. In *Great Expectations* (1860–61), Dickens had Pip travel down the Thames and its

tiers of shipping. Here, were the Leith, Aberdeen and Glasgow steamers, loading and unloading goods … here, were colliers by the score and score … here …

The population statistics for the parish of St Katharine by the Tower read as follows: in 1821, 2,624; in 1831, 72. During the late 1820s the area had been extensively cleared of homes and parish church in order to allow the building of St Katharine Docks. This is the only remaining old warehouse, Ivory House, of 1858. Extensive vaults stored wines and spirits, while the warehouse above handled expensive imports, including ivory.
PHOTOGRAPH: CARNEGIE, 2009

was tomorrow's steamer for Rotterdam … and here tomorrow's for Hamburg … again among the tiers of shipping … hammers going in ship-builders' yards.

The river played a major role in his novels. Quilp, the villainous moneylender and smuggler in *The Old Curiosity Shop*, falls into the Thames near his wharf and drowns.

Even within Britain, maritime trade mounted a formidable challenge to other means of transport. Thus, in 1800, London received more than one million chaldrons (25.5 cwt per chaldron) of coal by sea, principally from collier boats sailing from Newcastle. Even in the 1850s, when the rail network was becoming well established, sea-borne coal was far more important to the capital than that brought across land: in 1855, for example, when tons were used as measurement, 3 million came by sea, compared with 1.2 million tons by rail. The ease of moving coal by sea was facilitated by the use of large steamships as well as the mechanisation of unloading. Only in 1869 was coal brought by sea to London matched by that moved by rail. In 1879, although 6.6 million tons of coal was transported to London by rail, some 3.5 million still entered the Thames by vessel. The victory of the railways was thus hard-fought and only occurred over a protracted period. Macdonald Gill's *Wonderground Map of London Town* (1914) shows a coalman at St Pancras Goods Yard, now the site of the British Library.

Through the Port of London increasingly came the food to feed London's growing numbers. Indeed, free trade, one of the key political issues of the nineteenth and early

The 'Royal' docks are not to be confused with the Royal Dockyards at Deptford and elsewhere. The 'Royal' docks were commercial docks given the royal stamp of approval rather than being owned by the Crown. All three can be seen in this aerial photograph of 1955, looking west with the Thames to the top left of the photograph. At the top in the distance can be seen one end of the first and largest of the Royal docks, the Royal Victoria (1855), while in the right foreground is the Royal Albert (1880). Both of these were built by private dock companies, but by the time the King Geoge V dock (*left*) was projected and built (1912–21) the docks were under the control of the Port of London Authority. Together, at 245 acres, the three Royal docks constituted the world's largest area of enclosed water. The King George V added 10 per cent to the capacity of London's docks, yet was to be the very last of the upstream enclosed London docks. Ships of up to 30,000 tons could use the facilities, the largest visitor being the liner *Mauretania* in 1939. The Royal docks closed in the 1980s, and along the central quay in this photograph was constructed the 'Short Take Off and Landing' London City Airport.

SIMMONS AEROFILMS

twentieth centuries, served both to cut the cost of Londoners' food and also to alter transport patterns to London. The end of protection for British agriculture came with the repeal of the Corn Laws in 1846, a measure that helped urban consumers rather than rural producers, and that had been pushed hard by urban lobbyists, notably in the Anti-Corn Law League. The impact of this repeal was accentuated by changes in the world agrarian system, notably the results stemming from the creation of long-distance railway systems, and from large steamships and refrigerated holds. As a result of the ability to move food rapidly without spoilage, agricultural production for London developed in other temperate climates. Canada was the crucial source of wheat, Argentina of beef, and Australia and New Zealand of wool and mutton. Australian frozen meat arrived in London from 1879.

At the same time, some of London's food came from the Continent, especially fruit and vegetables, grain from Germany, Poland and Ukraine, and Danish bacon by the end of the century. Yet, British sources remained significant. The market economy near London, for example in Essex, was long specialised to respond to its requirements. Fruit and vegetables from Berkshire, especially apples, pears and cherries, had become important in the London market from the second half of the eighteenth century. Moreover, now no longer known for its agriculture, Middlesex, including the rich soil on which Heathrow airport was to be built, was then a major centre of market gardening for London.

Aside from food-processing, for example sugar-refining, the docks provided the basis for a mass of industrial activity, not least as the docks came to be integrated into the railway system. The processing of other imports, for example of tobacco and timber, provided numerous jobs. The coal unloaded in the docks provided energy that was another encouragement for industry, including gasworks. In turn, the availability of coal, coke and gas encouraged the location of industries using their products, such as tar distilling and sulphuric-acid factories. Silvertown (named a rubber factory founded by S.W. Silver in 1852) and West Ham became major centres of the British chemical industry.

Notwithstanding the far-reaching industrialisation of northern England with the Industrial Revolution, London remained the largest centre of manufacturing throughout the nineteenth century, an activity that left literary form in novels such as Albert Smith's *The Struggles and Adventures of Christopher Tadpole* (1848), with its description of the many riverside factories in Vauxhall. There was extensive industrial activity across much of London, but some centres, for instance West Ham and the Wandle valley, were particularly significant. London's relative importance in manufacturing was to increase greatly after the First World War with the run-down of heavy industry elsewhere.

The Thames, however, was less important than hitherto for ship-building. The switch from timber was important as Britain had major competitive advantages for ships built of iron and powered by coal, but, although iron ship-building at Millwall and Blackwall flourished in mid-century, a new geography of ship-building came into being, with the focus on the Clyde, the Tyne and the Wear, each near centres of iron-working, and on the Lagan at Belfast. London ceased to be a major centre of ship-building, centred on Poplar and Deptford, although warships were still being built there in the 1870s, including for the Brazilian and Ottoman navies. The city's ship-building was also hit by the higher costs of industry in London, including higher wages and overheads.

This decline was of wider significance for London's economy, as it meant that it would not benefit from a heavy industry in which Britain led the world into the next century. The knock-on impact was also significant. Shipyards employed large numbers of people, as did ancillary concerns such as engine-makers and steelworks. Thus, London's downriver was never to become a centre of heavy industry. Had it done so, then the political complexion of the city might have been very different, perhaps with a much stronger hard-left component.

Returning to the Thames, a cosmopolitan maritime population – Chinese, Lascars (East Indians), Americans, Europeans – crowded the dock front, embarking on, or disembarking from, vessels. This was very much an environment moulded by man. In 1913, Arthur Sarsfield, a London crime reporter who, under the pseudonym Sax Rohmer, published the successful novel *The Mystery of Fu Manchu*, about a sinister Chinese master-criminal based in Limehouse, described a journey down the Thames, the 'oily glitter of the tide', and 'on the Surrey shore a blue light ... flicked translucent tongue against the night's curtain ... a gasworks'. The pollution noted by Rohmer had finally brought the fishing industry on the Thames to an end by the 1820s.

An emphasis on employment in industry and foreign trade runs the risk of failing to note the scale and range of jobs in the service economy, from bankers to milliners. Some of these jobs sustained London's high average wages and others serviced the consequences. Thus, the variety of the service economy also reflected the availability of casual and inexpensive labour. The combination of this service sector with manufacturing provided London with a greater economic resilience than that of economic zones that were heavily dependent on one particular sector.

As London sprawled outwards, areas of countryside were swallowed up by new suburban developments. John Walker's map of 1830 recorded villages such as Dulwich and Haringey in the countryside, but the situation changed rapidly. Although Ford Madox Brown's Hampstead was still surrounded by suburban greenery when he painted it in *English Autumn Afternoon* (1852–54), it had been fully rural thirty years earlier, when the poet John Keats had lived there. Twenty years later, Hampstead had been engulfed by more suburban settlements. As London's boundaries rolled out into the Home Counties, hitherto small towns and villages were swallowed up by its progress.

In 1829, John Claudius Loudon (1783–1843) published *Hints on Breathing Places for the Metropolis, and for Country Towns and Villages, on fixed Principles*. A Scottish-born landscape-gardener, Loudon came to London in 1803 and from 1826 published the *Gardener's Magazine*. His other monthlies included the *Suburban Gardener and Villa Companion* (1836). His impracticable plan was far too radical for the time, but it indicated the extent to which London's expansion was leading to fresh thinking, although this was not to become influential until Ebenezer Howard's garden-city movement in the late 1890s. Loudon proposed

surrounding London, as it already exists, with a zone of open country, at the distance of say one mile, or one mile and a half, from what may be considered the centre, say from St Paul's. This zone of country may be half a mile broad, and may contain ... part of Hyde Park, the Regent's Park, Islington, Bethnal Green, the Commercial Docks, Camberwell, Lambeth, and Pimlico; and it may be succeeded by a zone of town one mile broad, containing Kensington, Bayswater, Paddington, Kentish Town, Clapton, Lime House, Deptford, Clapham, and Chelsea; and thus the metropolis may be extended in alternate mile zones of buildings, with half mile zones of country or gardens, till one of the zones touched the sea.

Such ideas looked to the future. In the meanwhile, London's geographical spread reflected the development of commuting, with the railway helping to create suburbs and suburban environments. Prior to the railway, there had been important transport changes. As well as the canals already noted, there were many road improvements within London. Important new streets included Regent Street, which provided a route into the heart of the West End. Moreover, within the city, there were plentiful stage-coaches and hackney (four-wheeled) and hansom (two-wheeled) cabs. The large number of bridges across the river also facilitated access. New ones included Vauxhall (1816), Waterloo (1817), and Southwark (1819). These bridges were crucial to the opening up of south London. Settlement there greatly expanded in the nineteenth century, not least because much of south London was closer to the City and nearby areas to the west, such as the Strand, than the parts of west London into which development was spreading. The draining of marshland, for example in Waterloo, was also significant to the growth of south London.

The bridges owed much to the talent of John Rennie, whose career reflected the ability of London to attract able individuals, as well as the extent to which it was a centre of national and international enterprise. Scottish-born and educated, Rennie (1761–1821) came to London in 1784 to take charge of the works at the Albion Flour Mill, where he designed the steam machinery. Rennie then founded an engineering firm at Holland Street, Blackfriars, the base for work in London and elsewhere on docks, canals and bridges, including the London, East and West India docks, and Waterloo, London and Southwark bridges. He was buried in St Paul's. His eldest and second sons, George (1791–1866) and John (1794–1874), took over the business, and their works included the construction of the new London Bridge (1824–31), for which John was knighted, as well as railways in Britain and on the Continent.

Tunnelling was far less easy than bridge-building in the early nineteenth century, in part due to the problems of tunnelling under London and the Thames, and in part to the

This photograph of 1900 shows a row of horse-drawn hansom cabs outside Victoria station, District Railway (now the District Line). This type of low-slung, manoeuvrable cab was extremely useful in the congested London streets. Motor cabs began to be introduced from 1907, when over 700 were licensed. Cab owners had to pay a fee to be allowed to collect passengers from outside the station.

In the mid-1840s, we arrive in the age of photography. This image by the celebrated William Henry Fox Talbot, c.1845, shows the newly opened Hungerford suspension footbridge bridge built by Isambard Kingdom Brunel between Hungerford Market near Charing Cross and Lambeth to the south. This bridge was later replaced in 1864 by a railway bridge for the South Eastern Railway Company.
MUSEUM OF LONDON

limited explosives available in the period. The Brunels, nevertheless, managed to construct the Thames Tunnel between Wapping and Rotherhithe (completed in 1843), by burrowing with a purpose-built 'shield' and then lining the resulting tunnel. This method proved the eventual basis of much of the subsequent underground railway system.

At a more modest level, the London-born George Shillibeer (1797–1866), who had been trained as a coach-builder, introduced to London in 1829 the Paris system of omnibuses. He ran two from Paddington along the New Road to the Bank of England. In each omnibus 29 passengers could be carried, at a fare of one shilling. In 1834 Shillibeer established services to Greenwich and Woolwich. He was ruined by railway competition, which was much better capitalised, but in 1856 the London General Omnibus Company was founded, and omnibuses became a key element in the transport system. They were important in linking the railway termini and in supporting commuting.

Even before the application of steam technology, there had been the use of horses drawing wagons along rails. The Surrey Iron Railway Company, the world's first railway company and public railway, operated from Wandsworth to Croydon from 1803. Self-propelled steam locomotives transformed the situation. Indeed, London became the focus of long-distance train travel. Already, prior to the train, there had been a marked improvement in road transport within Britain, notably thanks to the work of Telford and

McAdam. Thus, by 1832, Edinburgh was 42 hours away. The situation, however, improved markedly with the spread of train services. Services from London reached Birmingham in 1838, Southampton in 1840, Exeter in 1844, Norwich in 1845, Ipswich and Bury St Edmunds in 1846, Plymouth in 1847, and Truro in 1859; although the national main-line system was not completed until the early 1870s.

At the same time, although London was the key centre of the rail network, it suffered, like Paris, from the lack of through-routes or a central station. This lack can be seen as a failure of planning akin to that seen after the Great Fire of 1666, but the disruption such a process of construction would have caused would have been massive. As it was, termini were built in the City itself – Farringdon, Cannon Street, Broad Street (closed in 1986) and Liverpool Street, while lines reached the Strand at Charing Cross. Moreover, there was massive destruction involved during construction, culminating with Marylebone, the last of the termini, the construction of which led to the destruction of Blandford Square.

Work on Sir Marc Brunel's Thames Tunnel began in 1823, using his patented tunnelling shield (bottom of picture), but a major flood in 1827 years later led to a delay before work was finally completed in 1843. It was used as a pedestrian route between Wapping and Rotherhithe, but, despite becoming a major tourist attraction, was never a financial success because of the enormous cost of construction. In the 1860s the tunnel was converted to use by the Underground, helped by the fact that it had been built with plenty of headroom as Brunel had originally intended horse-drawn vehicles to use it (bottom left image). Brunel had had sawmills in Battersea in the 1810s, when he had also experimented with steam navigation on the Thames. This series of explanatory drawings was made in 1827. The top-most image shows the tunnel in cross-section; the light blue of the river shows the high-water mark, and dark blue the level of the river at low water. The light blue within the right half of the tunnel and the right-hand shaft shows the extent of the flood in May 1827. The layout of the proposed warehouses, top left and right, show the favoured dockland 'canyon', which allowed convenient vehicular access between the warehouses behind the riverfront buildings; such a canyon, complete with overhead walkways, can still be seen today at Shad Thames.

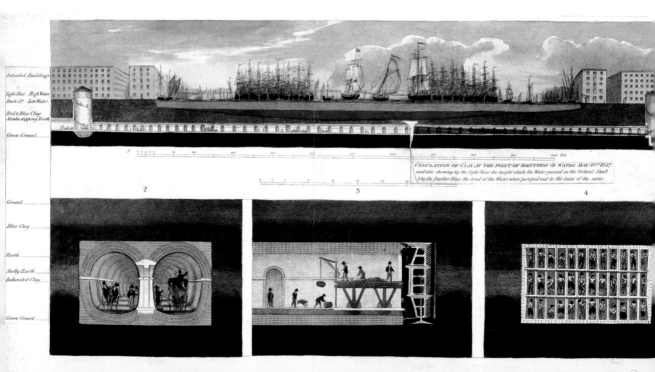

The shape of London also changed internally as railway lines both joined and bisected. Urban street patterns focused on the new railway stations. The major stations, such as Isambard Kingdom Brunel's Paddington, and Sir George Gilbert Scott and W.H. Barlow's St Pancras, were designed as masterpieces of iron and glass, in effect more lasting versions of the Crystal Palace built for the Great Exhibition of 1851. The stations each also had large railway hotels, such as the Great Western Royal Hotel at Paddington, opened in 1854, and the huge Great Central Hotel at Marylebone, which dates from 1899.

As a result of the trains, goods travelled to London more readily than in the past. The railway helped speed slate from north Wales towards London, which changed the townscape as this inexpensive, lightweight material became the prime form of roofing; indeed, rain-slicked slate roofs became a potent visual feature of the city. Food supply was also transformed. In the 1870s, the rail companies expanded London's market for milk, encouraging dairy farmers to produce 'railway milk', rather than farmhouse cheese. The railway also took Cornish broccoli to London, as well as spring flowers, first brought from the Isles of Scilly by steamer and then moved on by rail.

Attitudes to, and perceptions of, distance were transformed by the railway, while the horse ceased to define the possibilities of land travel. Unprecedented speeds of travel became possible and then commonplace. The *St James's Chronicle* of 30 March 1847

Railways dominate the Euston Road and King's Cross areas, as routes to the north of Britain radiate out from this point. The magnificent façade of St Pancras Chambers and station can be seen here, with King's Cross station beyond. Since 2007 St Pancras has been a terminus for Eurostar services to Paris and elsewhere.
WWW.LASTREFUGE.CO.UK

discussed the impact of rail travel on the human body. The new sounds and sights contributed to a powerful sense of change, which was overwhelmingly seen as progress. This sense of progress through change extended to the Underground. In 1862, William Gladstone joined the directors of the Metropolitan Railway on the first run over the full length of their new underground railway in London.

In fiction, the train allowed metropolitan sophisticates to take their manners and mores into the countryside. Employed frequently as a device, this idea reflected a sense of London as different and disruptive, as when Gwendolen Faifax visits Hertfordshire in Oscar Wilde's play *The Importance of Being Earnest* (1895) and Ethel Henderson comes to Sussex in H.G. Wells' novel *Love and Mr Lewisham* (1900). By train, Sherlock Holmes, and later Hercule Poirot, could descend from London to ferret out villainy, and Scotland Yard detectives could be sent to help provincial police forces.

Rail also increased London's centrality in the political system, not least by making it easier for politicians and journalists to travel, although that was already a facet of the pre-rail situation. For example, when he stood for the parliamentary seat of Tiverton in 1837, Palmerston made arrangements for the press to come from London, be well sited during his speech, lodged for the night, and for their return to London.

Rail made London more central in other ways. The railways needed standard time for their timetables, in order to make connections possible; and, in place of the variations from east to west in Britain, they adopted the standard set by the Greenwich Observatory as 'railway time'. From its offices on the Strand, the Electric Telegraph Company communicated Greenwich time from 1852: clocks were kept accurate by the electric

telegraph that was erected along railway lines. Moreover, an international conference of 1884 chose the Greenwich meridian as the zero meridian for global time-keeping and for the determination of longitude. The French eventually abandoned the alternative Paris meridian in 1911, and the Americans the Washington one in 1912.

The train moreover transformed postal services, which were organised from London, where, in 1840, the Penny Black, the world's first postage stamp, was released. Within London, the postal service encouraged the numbering of houses which had been started, by the late eighteenth century, to replace their designation by name. Entrepreneurship was private as well as public. In 1848, the first of what was to be the network of W.H. Smith railway bookstalls was opened at Euston station. Smith went on to become a leading London Conservative politician who supported the creation of the London County Council. The overall impression in London's life and features was one of change.

Commuting rapidly developed. Neither the long- nor the short-distance lines were built specifically for commuting. Nevertheless, an extensive network was soon in place. For example, rail services from London Bridge reached Deptford in 1836 and Greenwich in 1838, while the London to Croydon line opened in 1839, followed by lines to Margate in 1846, and to Southend in 1856. By then, the tolls on turnpikes no longer seemed viable and, in 1857, the Toll Reform Committee recommended their abolition on all tolls within six miles of Charing Cross. Their abolition rapidly followed.

The major rail lines also had a great impact on what became London suburbia, opening up areas for development. To take just one example, in 1838, the line to Southampton reached what is now Surbiton, leading to the building of housing estates around the station. As elsewhere, entrepreneurial activity played a key role, with, first, Thomas Pooley and, then, Coutts the bankers developing Surbiton. Largely because of rail-driven expansion, the population of the parish of Kingston, which included Surbiton, rose fivefold, from 7,257 in 1831, to 35,829 in 1881. In the 1890s the biggest building firm in London was Watts of Catford, a suburban firm. New rail lines continued to be built in the London area. The building of a direct route from London to Southend via Upminster, avoiding the Tilbury detour, opened in 1888, cuting the express journey time from 95 to 50 minutes, and was followed by an alternative route via Shenfield, opened in 1889. As a result, commuting from Southend into London rose rapidly.

The spread of suburbia and commuting moved people and groups apart; different areas of the city now accommodated and employed people from very different economic and social groups. This was a feature of life of which both Londoners and visitors were well aware. London and its hinterland were criss-crossed by isolines and the resulting gradients. The key perceived difference one was of acceptability: a complex matrix of class, cost, status and fashion. The results were noted by many, including the Swedish traveller Eric Svedenstierna, who spent two months there in the winter of 1802–03 in order to report on the British economy. He noted what was also to be apparent in Booth's maps, both variations by region among 'this far-flung and enormous mass of buildings', and also within them:

A traveller, who has business in the neighbourhood of learned institutions, and comes into contact with either scholars or with persons of rank, and must therefore lodge in the western part of London, must reckon upon no less a rent than one and a half to two guineas per week. For this rent one gets merely the room and its cleaning, and is therefore obliged to employ a servant who, if he is to be loyal, also receives one and a half guineas per week. Although it would be possible, even in this part of the town, to live fairly cheaply in certain tiny taverns or eating houses, it is almost a rule for a foreigner who is seeking good acquaintanceship, to visit the better taverns, where, even with all possible economy, one cannot eat for less than five English shillings per day. It is therefore necessary to reckon upon an expenditure of at least five guineas per week merely for

From the early years of the Underground travellers needed dedicated maps of the system to show the ever-expanding, changing and developing routes available. The nickname 'Tube', still in inverted commas on this map of 1908, was adopted widely from around 1900.

LONDON TRANSPORT MUSEUM

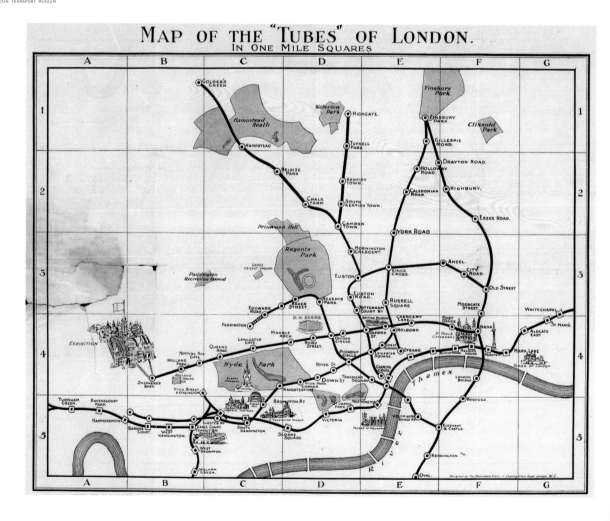

rent, service, and food, it one wants to live in this part of the town. On the other hand, in other, more outlying quarters of the town, one can have a respectable room, as well as service and meals, for half as much, perhaps for two guineas a week.[6]

Svedenstierna's city had been near the countryside, but this was not the case for much of the city a century later. The spreading extent of the city was indicated by the contrast between Washington Bacon's *New Large-Scale Ordnance Atlas of London and Suburbs* of 1888, which offered 25 four-inch maps, and the 1912 edition which provided 34, reaching out to Harrow, Chessington, Cheam, Purley, Selsdon, Farnborough and Orpington. Moreover, in areas already covered in the 1888 atlas, there were many new streets and houses, for example in Tottenham, Edmonton, East Greenwich, Hanwell and from West Ham to Barking and Ilford.

The spread of suburbia gave point to the establishment of parks, as new developments speedily surrounded new parks such as Victoria Park, as well as older ones such as Kensington Gardens. Indeed, in his song 'If it Wasn't for the 'Ouses in between, or, The Cockney Garden,' Gus Elen noted, 'With a ladder – and some glasses you can see the 'Ackney Marshes/If it wasn't for the 'ouses in between.' Nevertheless, the spread was not uniform in all directions. Indeed, as a residential city, London expanded more to the west than to the east, especially as far as the middle class was concerned. The central focus of London thus moved westwards. The sale of estates could facilitate development, as when most of the Spencer property in Battersea, Wandsworth and Wimbledon was sold in the late 1830s in order to relieve debts. The great builder Thomas Cubitt (1788–1855) played a key role in the development of Clapham Park as well as Chelsea, where he erected Belgrave and Lowndes Squares. Cubitt had begun with developments at Highbury and then Newington Green, Barnsbury Park and Bloomsbury. Most house-building, however, was small-scale, and a very large number of builders was involved, as one recent study of Wandsworth has made clear.[7]

The great suburban expansion inspired the Commons Preservation Society, founded in 1865, and a campaigning base of figures who were instrumental in the foundation of the National Trust in 1893–95, especially Octavia Hill and Robert Hunter. In 1875 Hill had failed in a campaign to save Swiss Cottage Fields from development. This concern looked toward interest in limiting the spread of the city, and, as part of this interest, to the garden-city movement. This call for the creation of autonomous towns surrounded by countryside in the South East was explicitly aimed at containing London's growth.

Transportation methods and patterns helped transform urban life. Individuals and groups who had hitherto travelled largely by foot now took the train. Thus, many members of City Masonic lodges in the 1840s had lived in Clerkenwell or Seven Dials, while their successors of the 1870s increasingly lived in Walthamstow or Wandsworth.

At the same time, rail travel reflected a social system stratified by wealth. There were three classes, with different conditions and fares. On the London to Brighton line, third-class carriages lacked roofs until 1852, and the passengers were exposed not only to the weather but also to the hot ash from the engine. Return fares on the line in 1845 were 21s. first class, 9s. second, and 5s. third.

The development of the rail system did not preclude an improvement of road links in and from London. These included not only new routes but also the upgrading of existing ones. New bridges included the Hungerford footbridge, designed by Brunel, while Westminster Bridge was replaced in 1862 and Blackfriars in 1869. New services were also created, in part linked to the train system. Trams – horse-drawn buses operating on rails – appeared in 1869, and by 1874 over sixty miles of track had been laid, although the trains carried more people. Another system of communications was offered by the London District Telegraph Company, established in 1859 and providing local services from a base at Charing Cross. The General Post Office built in King Edward Street in 1890–95 reflected the grandeur as well as the importance of London's role in communications.

The London of this period was painted in bold colours by a number of writers. Charles Dickens (1812–70) is the most prominent, and much of our image of the period derives from his novels, a process sustained by television adaptations, such as of *Little Dorrit* in 2008. In his day, Dickens' novels, such as *The Old Curiosity Shop* (1840–41) and *Little Dorrit* (1855–57), were very popular in the USA, as was his story *A Christmas Carol* (1843), and these works made everyone think that they knew London.

Yet, it is also necessary to note the prominence of other literary figures, and thus to appreciate the variety of images that were offered. In 1821, Pierre Egan launched *Life in London: Or, The Day and Night Scenes of Jerry Hawthorn, Esq., and his elegant friend, Corinthian Tom, accompanied by Bob Logic, the Oxonian, in their Rambles and Sprees through the Metropolis*, a shilling monthly that benefited from illustrations by Isaac Robert Cruikshank. George IV, who, in conscious emulation of Napoleon, sponsored the rebuilding of much of the West End by John Nash, accepted the dedication.

Life in London provided alternative scenes of high and low life with lively dialogue, and inspired imitations, including *Real Life in London* (1821–22), as well as prints, decorations on handkerchiefs and teatrays, and 'Tom and Jerry' fashions. The play *Tom and Jerry: or Life in London* (1821) enjoyed great success in Britain and America. A sense of London as a stage in life, an invigorating but not a lasting one, which is indeed the experience of many Londoners, was captured by Egan in his *Finish to the Adventures of Tom, Jerry and Logic*. Tom breaks his neck at a steeplechase, while Jerry returns to the country, marries his early sweetheart, and becomes a generous landlord. Jerry's fulfilment is rural in character.

Whereas Jane Austen (1775–1817) is noted foremost for her acute observation of provincial propertied society, and treated London as an aspect of this world, and Sir

Walter Scott (1771–1832) is noted for his historical works, Dickens deliberately addressed social conditions and urban society, specifically London. In his childhood, Dickens had experience of hardship in London. His father went to the Marshalsea Debtors' Prison in Southwark and, at the age of twelve, Dickens began menial work in Warren's blacking factory near Hungerford Steps. Later, he was employed as an office boy and a court reporter. Dickens' knowledge and understanding of London, both high and low, an understanding kept alive by frequent walks in the city, served him well in his *Scenes of London Life from 'Sketches by Boz'* (1836–37), in which London was subject as much as stage. The book's illustrations, by George Cruikshank, included troubling scenes of the public life of the streets: in *Monmouth Street*, children played in the gutter, which, given the limited sanitation of the period, could be a serious health hazard.

The overlap with Dickens' journalism was clear. Moreover, in 1849–50 the *Morning Chronicle* printed Henry Mayhew's accounts of the London poor. London-born Wilkie Collins, who was a regular contributor to Dickens' *Household Words*, used London as a sceptral setting for the first appearance of Anne Catherick, the woman in white, in his novel of that name published in 1859–60.

Much journalism also drew on the long-standing sense of London as particularly criminous, and therefore both fascinating and repellent. Indeed, prominent murders there excited great interest, both in London and more generally. In late 1823 much of the press focused on the 'Gill's Hill murder', in which William Weare, a London solicitor, was murdered at the behest of a well-connected, but somewhat shady, amateur boxer he had defrauded. There was also extensive coverage of the murder in chapbooks and ballads, including the immortal lines that amused Scott:

> They cut his throat from ear to ear,
> His brains they battered in,
> His name was Mr William Weare,
> He dwelt in Lyon's Inn.

Commenting on this case in its editorial of 6 November 1823, the *Birmingham Chronicle* was shocked to note the existence in London of 'a fraternity ... for the express purpose of robbery and murder'. London as violent and sinful was a message reiterated across the country. Thus, *Drewry's Staffordshire Gazette* of 2 August 1827 provided details of a London poisoning, while the *Sherborne Mercury* of 10 January 1837 devoted over a column to an item headlined 'Atrocious Murder in Ratcliff Highway. Examination of the Murderer.' This piece was followed by another item headlined 'The Edgeware Road-Murder'. Indeed, the press contributed to London's growing importance as a centre for crime and punishment, although this also rested on the development of the Metropolitan Police as well as on the role of the courts. This centrality was not only a matter of London's reputation and the press. London policemen were sent to the provinces to investigate crimes, while the London courts tried criminals for crimes that had been committed elsewhere.

The iniquities of London took many forms. The *Taunton Courier* of 2 March 1831 reported, under the heading 'London Advertising Money-Lenders':

One of these blood suckers has sent us an advertisement, which he requests may be inserted for a series of weeks. We have uniformly resisted the invitation of these fellows to allow our columns to become the vehicles of their depredatory practices.

Dickens was also harsh on the values of the city. Thus, in his novel *Little Dorrit*, society worships Merdle, a great, but fraudulent, financier, 'a new power in the country', while the government, in the shape of the Circumlocution Office, is callously inefficient. At dinner at Merdle's, 'Treasury hoped he might venture to congratulate one of England's world-famed capitalists and merchant-princes … To extend the triumphs of such men, was to extend the triumphs and resources of the nation.'

MICROCOSM dedicated to the London Water Companies

MONSTER SOUP commonly called THAMES WATER. being a correct representation of that precious stuff doled out to us

'Monster Soup', a caricature of 1828 by William Heath. Along the top it reads: 'Microcosm dedicated to the London Water Companies. Brought forth all monstrous, all prodigious things, hydras and organs, and chimeras dire.' The bottom title reads, 'Monster Soup commonly called Thames Water being a correct representation of that precious stuff doled out to us!'

In Merdle's case, the system is fraudulent, but, in practice, the city remained the centre of the growing and successful liberal international economic order. This was the world celebrated in paintings such as Edmund Walker's *The Royal Exchange and the Bank of England* (1852). Britain seemed central, and London directed both it and the world. The year before Walker's painting, James Wyld displayed a big model of the globe, 'Wyld's Great Globe', in a large circular building in Leicester Square. Gas-lit, and displayed until 1862, the globe was 60 feet high, about 40 feet in diameter, and the largest hitherto constructed. Wyld, who was an active parliamentarian, Master of the Clothworkers' Company, and a leading promoter of technical education, reflected a widespread confidence in British superiority and rule.

Whether rich or poor, however, everyone was threatened by the environmental situation. Fast-expanding, with a population unprecedented in British history, London proved a breeding ground for disease, a situation accentuated by the frequently appalling level of sanitation. The sewer system was particularly deficient, as large amounts of waste were discharged into the Thames without treatment, and up-river of where water supplies were obtained. In 1828 William Heath dedicated to the London water companies his caricature 'Monster Soup commonly called Thames Water', an illustration of the filth and life in the river. In law, the sewers were intended for the run-off of rainwater, and household waste was supposed to be collected in subterranean cesspools from which it was to be removed by local rakers who would sell it as manure to farmers. This system, however, collapsed as a result of the rising population and of the development and adoption of the flushing toilet, which washed effluent into the sewers with great efficiency. The water companies chose to ignore the degree to which they were providing contaminated water.

Repeating the situation with the Black Death, the spread of cholera from Asia was especially fatal. A bacterial infection transmitted largely by water infected by the excreta of victims, cholera struck first in the 1830s. The capital was hard-hit, with major outbreaks in 1831–32, 1848–49, 1853–54 and 1866, 10,000 Londoners dying of cholera in 1854 and 6,000 in 1866. It was in London that Dr John Snow, a leading anaesthetist noted as an advocate of chloroform, was able to carry out the research that enabled him to conclude, in his *On the Mode and Communication of Cholera* (1849), that the disease was transmitted not via 'miasma', or bad air, as was generally believed, but through drinking water contaminated by sewage, a problem that highlighted the state of the Thames. This research was supplemented, in a second edition published in 1855, by an analysis of the 1853–54 epidemic, and led to the closure of the public water pump in Broad Street in Soho, where a sewer was found to be leaking into the well. After this closure, the number of new cases of cholera fell. Snow also showed that the majority of the victims had drunk water provided by the Southwark

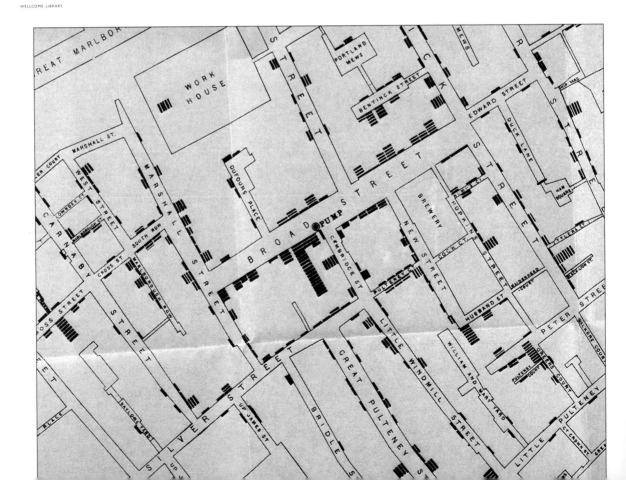

and Vauxhall Company which extracted water from near sewer outflows.

Snow is still celebrated in the name of a pub, the John Snow, in what has been renamed Broadwick Street; a replica of the street pump has even been sited nearby. The process by which Snow ascertained the means of transmission was typical of the research-based nature of public policy that proved so important to Victorian governance. This type of policy indeed was the very opposite to the world of the fictitious 'Circumlocution Office', and Dickens' depiction of an unreformed system was increasingly anachronistic. At the same time, such criticism was an aspect of the process by which the world of print in London served to focus reform tendencies. This process was more generally a characteristic of the public politics of the period. Agitation against slavery proved a good example.

Cholera was not the only killer. Typhus frequently spread from gaols such as Newgate to the wider population. Dysentery, diarrhoea, diphtheria, whooping cough, scarlet fever, measles and enteric fever were all

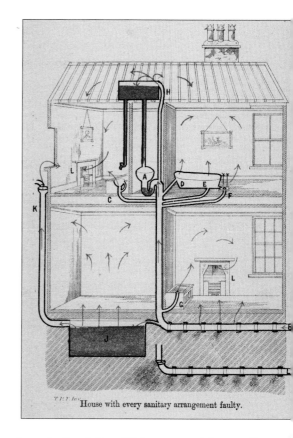

House with every sanitary arrangement faulty.

A 'house with every sanitary arrangement faulty', from Dr Thomas Pridkin Teale's *Dangers to Health* (1879).
WELLCOME LIBRARY

major problems, although thanks in part to vaccination, smallpox declined. In addition to diseases, the life of many was grim due to crowding, poor diet, hard working conditions and pollution. In *Peter Bell the Third* (1819), Shelley wrote 'Hell is a city much like London – A populous and a smoky city.' A more vivid comment was provided by the *Punch* cartoon, 'Father Thames Introducing his Offspring to the Fair City of London', of 3 July 1858, a response to the 'Great Stink' of that summer. In this facetious design for a fresco for the new Houses of Parliament, to replace those burned down in 1834, a filthy Thames, polluted by factories, sewage and steamships, presented figures representing diphtheria, scrofula and cholera to London. In *The Times* in 1855, Michael Faraday, a prominent scientist, had already described the river between London and Hungerford bridges as a 'fermenting sewer', a description that was accurate in both parts. The Houses of Parliament were also affected by smoke from the many factories in Lambeth on the other side of the river. Over-crowded cemeteries also remained a source of infection in inner London until the 1850s, whereas Paris had closed its central cemetery the previous century.[8]

With its population rising from just over one million in 1810 to over seven million by 1911, London therefore presented the most serious problem of public health in Britain but, from 1859, under the direction of the determined and effective Joseph Bazalgette, Chief

Engineer to the Metropolitan Commission of Sewers (a body established in 1847), an effective drainage system was finally constructed. As a result of the Great Stink, Parliament in August 1858 extended the powers of the Metropolitan Board of Works at the expense of the Office of Works and permitted the Board to raise £3 million. Fully completed in 1875, albeit at a sum greater than the original estimate but one financed by borrowing, this pioneering drainage system contained 82 miles of intercepting sewers. These took sewage from earlier pipes that had drained into the Thames, and transported it instead to new downstream works and storage tanks from which the effluent could be pumped into the river when the tide was flowing into the North Sea. A large number of steam pumping stations provided the power. The big one at Abbey Mills near West Ham, built in 1865–68, was an astonishing instance of the determination to disguise function, with the station's role concealed under Moorish towers and a Slavic dome. Storm-relief sewers followed from the 1880s. In part, the storm-relief system used London's rivers other than the Thames, completing the process by which these had been directed underground. This concealment of the rivers made their use for this sewage system acceptable.

Meanwhile, the 1852 Metropolitan Water Act obliged the London water companies to move their water supply sources to above the tidal reach of the Thames. This legislation was a comment on the failure both of the companies to respond adequately to the problems of dirty water (although they had begun to filter water) and of earlier public pressure, notably a Royal Commission of 1828. Subsequently, the Commissioners for Preventing the Pollution of Rivers pressed against sewage disposal in the Thames. The improvement in the water supply produced a large fall in mortality figures. Already by the 1820s, the annual average of baptisms was 7,000 greater than that of burials, ensuring that London no longer needed immigration to grow. Indeed, by 1874, the death rate per 1,000 had fallen, from a mid-eighteenth-century figure of 48 for London, to 18, compared to 29 for Leeds and 32 for Liverpool and Newcastle. As a sign of gradual but patchy improvement, the impact of the 1866 cholera epidemic was moderate in the western areas, where the drainage and sewerage systems had already been improved, but was still deadly further east. The growing population also posed a serious problem for water supplies. Early in the century the emphasis had been on shallow surface waters, but by mid-century there was a major use of boreholes sunk into the chalk aquifers under the London clay. From the 1860s, the Geological Survey produced information on falling water levels in these aquifers.

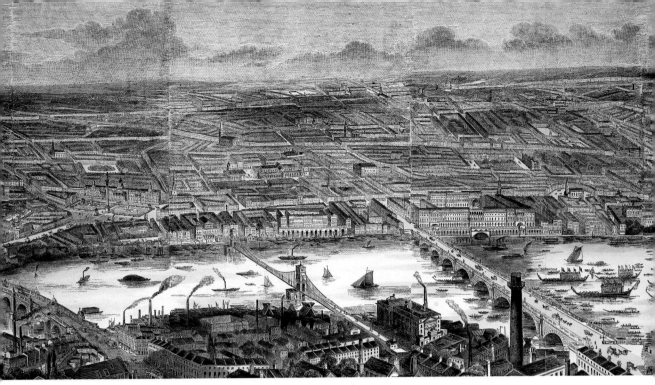

Mid-Victorian London attracted visitors, commentators, surveyors and artists from all over the world to marvel at the size, the bustle and the innovations of the first 'world city'. In just this one detail of this aerial view, we can see Brunel's original (pedestrian) Hungerford Bridge in the centre, with the substantial building of the Lion Brewery next to it on the south bank of the Thames, followed by the great 1826 shot tower where lead shot was made until the 1940s. (For the Festival of Britain in 1951 the shot tower was retained as a feature and surmounted by a radio beacon; it was demolished to make way for the Queen Elizabeth Hall.) Westminster Bridge is to the left, and Waterloo Bridge to the right. The Victoria Embankment has not yet been built, and Somerset House can be seen prominently right on the far riverbank; Trafalgar Square is to the left. On the south bank several chimneys belch smoke, and extensive timber yards line the riverside. The Thames is busy, while the bridges are a scene of activity. The decorated barges to the right might well include the Lord Mayor's state barge on its way to Westminster.

Like the pumps of the sewerage system, the new underground railway initially got their power from steam engines; and transport combined with public health to produce a new underground architecture that complemented the dramatic scenes above ground, notably with the tunnel for the District Railway built along the new Embankment between Westminster and the City. Artists captured the scale of the activity and satisfied public interest with impressions such as that in the *Illustrated London News* on 22 June 1867.

Other aspects of Bazalgette's work showed how man-made constraints were being stamped on the environment. He was responsible for the Victoria, Albert and Chelsea embankments: made of granite, these were very much constructions intended to endure. Within these embankments ran new riverside sewers, and they also limited the banks of the river Thames, and thereby improved its flow, as well as lessening the risk of flooding. In effect, the river was canalised, a process also seen in other European cities in this period. Thanks to these embankments, Bazalgette also created key new routes in London, including an attractive one between Westminster and the City. Streets were built at either end: Queen Victoria Street linked the Embankment to the Mansion House in the City, while Northumberland Avenue linked it to Charing Cross. New building sites were established, allowing for further building development. Bazalgette's works created other new routes, including new bridges across the Thames at Putney and Battersea, and the Woolwich steam ferry, and also helped transform parts of the city, in particular the in-between world of the river bank. Thus, the Albert Embankment, built on the south bank of the river, brought the local activities of boat-building and timber-yards to an abrupt end.

For many, the Victorian age is best exemplified by Tower Bridge, which was opened in 1894 and funded by the City Corporation (via the City Bridge Trust), offering a new lowest bridging point over the Thames, and one that aided the development of south-east London. This bridge was a testimony to mechanical power and applied technology. The hydraulic equipment that raised the bridge was supplied by the great Newcastle entrepreneur William Armstrong, who also provided the hydraulic lifts that enabled the Underground system to expand with deep stations such as Hampstead. The appeal of traditional architectural motifs in Tower Bridge helped explain its success in becoming a potent symbol of empire, but, alongside themes of continuity, it was the ability to devise and push through new solutions that was most impressive.

Public order was a key sphere of government activity. By 1820 the Duke of Wellington was sufficiently concerned about the possibility of disaffection among the Guards to recommend the creation of a special force, police or military, to control London. The 1820s were less disturbed by public agitation than the 1810s, but, alongside strong parliamentary opposition, there was a long-standing belief that London's policing was inadequate and ineffective. This argument was pushed hard by Sir Robert Peel, the Home Secretary in Wellington's Tory ministry, who pressed for a New Police. Peel conflated perceived threats from crime, radicalism and immorality, and had a hostile view of London as a centre for all three that required rigorous control. Passed in 1829, in part also to deal with corruption in existing police provision, Peel's Metropolitan Police Act created a uniformed and paid police force. This professional service was designed to maintain the law and to keep order, not only against radicals but also checking working-class immorality. Thus, despite being unpopular to those used to libertarian views about English freedoms, the police were a powerful weapon of middle-class dominance, as well as a desirable alternative to the army, which in northern England had frequently been called in by local authorities to quell social, political and industrial disorder, often with tragic consequences as at Peterloo in 1819.

The new Metropolitan force was controlled by the Home Office, and was initially made responsible for Marylebone, Finsbury, Tower Hamlets, Westminster, Southwark and Lambeth, an area within seven miles of Charing Cross. In 1839, under the second Metropolitan Police Act, this radius was increased to fifteen miles. By a separate Act of Parliament in that year the City, as so often, was excluded from these new, city-wide arrangements, and was given its own City of London Police Force, whose headquarters until 2002 were in Old Jewry. The Metropolitan Police force was 4,300 strong, and by 1839 crime rates had fallen markedly. Looking toward tensions still apparent today, the police force represented an overriding of the existing pattern of local control and also a cost that could not be controlled by the local authorities but was imposed as a police precept. Critics saw this as taxation without representation and had hoped that the Whigs would overthrow the Tory measure, but, instead, they strengthened it in 1839, in part as a force against radicals. As much of London opinion supported the Whigs, the new force became established. The creation, under the Poor Law Amendment Act of 1834, of poor law unions under elected Boards of Guardians also lessened the traditional role of parish vestries.

As the governance of London became more activist and regulatory, so the goal of the political groupings that controlled it increasingly became that of seizing the opportunity to push through policies, as much as the traditional objective of office-holding for personal profit and prestige. Partly as a consequence, the nature of power within London society was now discussed explicitly to a greater extent than a century earlier. The expanding middle class expected power and status, and was dubious of established institutions and practices that did not seem reformist or useful. Deference was eroded.

A similar process occurred in the great northern cities such as Leeds, Liverpool, Manchester and Newcastle, with reform linked to the growth of middle-class culture and consciousness. The basis of authority and the ethos of power in cities moved greatly from the traditional to the innovative. Ideas of reform and accountability were pushed hard, and the Anti-Corn Law League founded in 1839 was a symbol of, and platform for, middle-class aggression or, at least, assertiveness. Middle-class views and wealth stimulated a demand for, and process of, improvement, civic and moral, which was central to the movement for reform. This reform was directed as much against the habits of the poor as those of the Establishment. Each was judged vicious and backward-looking.

In part, this concern for reform drew on the long-standing sense of London as corrupt and corrupting. This image was reiterated in Victorian melodrama, although the plot of *London by Night* (1843), a work attributed to Charles Selby, was actually based upon Eugène Sue's *Les Mystères de Paris* (1842–43). In William Travers's *London by Night* (1868), a wicked French madame inveigled unsuspecting British virgins into her brothel, a plot that combined xenophobia with the frisson of London as the centre for debauchery. Both themes were to be taken forward in literature about Chinese opium dens in Limehouse. The sins of London revealed by press and police were far more wide-ranging in terms of the city's topography and behaviour, as the West End scandals of 1889–90 involving the clients and staff of a male brothel on Cleveland Street indicated.

Inherited privilege without purpose was also condemned in the press and in fiction. Thus, for example, London's development challenged conventional beliefs that certain areas were inhabited only by particular types of people, as, instead, it became necessary to define new, and to redefine established, neighbourhoods. In Anthony Trollope's novel *The Way We Live Now* (1874–75), Adolphus Longestaffe, the snobbish squire seeking both a loan and a railway directorship, had a town-house in Bruton Street:

> It was not by any means a charming house, having but few of those luxuries and elegancies which have been added of late years to newly built London residences. It was gloomy and inconvenient, with large drawing-rooms, bad bedrooms, and very little accommodation for servants. But it was the old family town-house, having been inhabited by three or four generations of Longestaffes, and did not savour of that radical newness which prevails, and which was peculiarly distasteful to Mr Longestaffe. Queen's Gate and the quarters around were, according to Mr Longestaffe, devoted to opulent tradesmen. Even Belgrave Square, though its aristocratic properties must be admitted, still smelt of the mortar. Many of those living there and thereabouts had never possessed in their families real family town-houses. The old streets lying between Piccadilly and Oxford Street, with one or two well-known localities to the south and north of these boundaries, were the proper sites for these habitations.

Such a hierarchy based on past values could not be sustained, and Trollope had no time for his fictional creation, who, indeed, is duped by the corrupt, but energetic financial protagonist. In contrast to Longestaffe, Lady Bracknell, the snobbish, but acute, fictional social observer in Wilde's satirical play about English social distinctions, *The Importance of Being Earnest* (1895), was keen to respond to the matrimonial prospects of money, and she noted that, to that end, it was possible to change the fashionable side of London squares. In her world, land was an encumbrance, made necessary by social position, and the true bastions of status were financial holdings.

Despite snobbish disdain for 'trade', social mobility was helped by primogeniture and the consequent need for younger sons to define and support their own positions, and also by the relative openness of marital conventions. These allowed the sons of land to marry the daughters of commerce and, less frequently, led to the daughters of land marrying the sons of commerce, a practice that cost less in dowries.

Like Longestaffe, the middle class also had a strong sense of place, of where it was acceptable to live, and of the conduct deemed appropriate in those areas. In contrast, immorality was criticised as debasing and unproductive. 'Morality', however, was not only a middle-class cause: self-improving artisans were also involved.

Similarly, reform agitation was not limited to the propertied. There was a radical fringe, at once subversive and satirical,[9] although it rarely turned to violence. In 1820, however, in the Cato Street Conspiracy, a small group of revolutionaries, many of them cobblers, under Arthur Thistlewood, planned to surprise the Cabinet at dinner, kill them, and establish a republican government. The conspirators were arrested and tried. Sentenced to death, Thistlewood declared at the end of his trial, 'Albion is still in the chains of slavery. I quit it without regret. My only sorrow is that the soil should be a theatre for slaves, for cowards, for despots.'

The strength of radical sentiment in London was revealed that year when the arrival of George IV's estranged wife, Caroline, was greeted with popular support by radicals keen to demonstrate the hypocrisy of the government and to use Caroline as a symbol of wronged womanhood, as well as by artisans opposed to the advance of a competitive market economy. George was sufficiently concerned about radical views to instruct the Home Secretary Henry Addington in 1821 to keep him informed about opinion in London.[10]

The royal drama was played out in London, where the government introduced a Bill of Pains and Penalties into the House of Lords to end the royal marriage on the grounds of Caroline's adultery and to dethrone her. In the event, the government felt obliged to abandon this campaign, but Caroline was successfully denied coronation.

George was determined that his coronation, held on 19 July 1821, should be an unprecedented occasion. A total of 12,532 diamonds were used in the setting of the crown, and George wore ornate clothes including, on his entry into Westminster Abbey, a black velvet hat carrying a large plume of ostrich feathers from which a heron's plume emerged, while his gold-bordered crimson velvet train was so heavy and long that nine pages were needed to support it. Caroline, in contrast, was refused entry, and the door was shut in

In 1813 John Nash prepared a 'PLAN ... of a STREET ... from CHARING CROSS to PORTLAND PLACE, leading to the Crown Estate in Marylebone [i.e. Regent's] Park'. This main part of this development, known as New Street and later as Regent Street, was a bold attempt to provide a major new north–south route and high-class shopping street. Many existing buildings were demolished, but existing property boundaries were respected in places. Thus, the sweeping bend north-west from Piccadilly Circus more or less followed the line of the pre-existing Marylebone and Titchborne Streets. Further north, Portland Place, running north towards New Road and the entrance to Regent's Park, was also retained. Nash was able to design the intervening stretch of his new street so that it could cross Oxford Street at right angles, at Oxford Circus, but this meant that it did not quite line up with Portland Place. The resulting kink, through the site of Foley House and its gardens, was softened by the focal point provided by All Souls, Langham Place, the only Nash building on Regent Street still standing today.

PHOTOGRAPH: CARNEGIE, 2009

her face. Soon after she died, and the passage of her body through London led to a riot in which the Life Guards fired on the rioters.

George supported John Nash's work of town-building, particularly the 'Royal Way' designed to link the new Regent's Park to George's palace at Carlton House Terrace near Pall Mall; this scheme, with the attractive sweep of Regent Street and the imposing Nash terraces alongside Regent's Park, is one of London's few successful large-scale schemes of town planning. It proved easier here in the West End to achieve the vistas that had been planned but not realised after the Great Fire of 1666. Earlier property rights had to be heeded, however, as is shown by All Souls, Langham Place, built in 1822–24. This church was a product of Nash being unable to continue the northward path of Regent Street as he might have wished. George IV's death in 1830 led to the abandonment of the rebuilding of Buckingham Palace; Nash took the blame for the cost and was sacked. William IV chose not to live in the palace and preferred, instead, to reside in the more modest Clarence House. Indeed, he proposed to Wellington that the palace be converted into a barracks.

Nevertheless, Nash's town-building captured the exuberance of the world-city of the age, the capital of the leading empire, and the setting for an energetic and questing society. Yet, at the same time, there were serious uncertainties both about how to manage and

As late as 1909, when this photograph was taken, hand work was still required in many trades. Here men take an interest in the photographer while women sit before large wicker baskets shelling walnuts in Covent Garden. The name 'walnut' derives from the Old English *wealhhnutu* – 'foreign nut' – and it was just one of dozens of exotic imports that came into Britain via the port of London. By this time many bulk cargoes such as tobacco, sugar and grain were being landed at Liverpool and elsewhere, but huge quantities of expensive goods still found their way to the capital.
© HULTON-DEUTSCH COLLECTION_CORBIS

govern a city unprecedented in extent, population, wealth and growth, and concerning the very consequences of this growth.[11]

The turn to violence on the part of radicals was far less common than the attempt to press for change while observing the constraints of the political system. Indeed, the pressure that culminated in the Great Reform Act, passed in 1832 by the Whigs, did not lead in London to the violence seen in Bristol, Derby and Nottingham. In the 1831 general election, all the four MPs elected from the City were keen supporters of the reform legislation. The 1832 Act fixed a uniform right to vote in the boroughs – all men occupying property, either by owning or renting, worth £10 per annum – which brought the franchise to the 'middle class'. As a result, London now had a large electorate. There were also five new constituencies – Tower Hamlets, Finsbury, Marylebone, Southwark and Lambeth – which ensured that London was less under-represented than it had been prior to 1832, although it still had too few MPs for both its population and its electorate.

Serious grievances, moreover, remained. In *The Man Wot Pays the Taxes*, a caricature produced in London, the hapless protagonist with broken shoes, exclaims 'In what better condition am I now that the Reform Bill has past. I have been obliged to rob my family to pay taxes.' Pressure for peaceful change was the case with Chartism, a large-scale and variegated protest movement of the 1830s and 1840s, which pressed, in the Six Points of the People's Charter, for universal adult male suffrage, a secret ballot, annual elections, equal parliamentary constituencies, the abolition of property qualifications for MPs, and their payment. Chartism's appeal, however, was varied. In London, the poor saw Chartism largely as a movement against taxes that hit them hard.

The political situation in London was also emphasised in some Chartist literature. Thus, the Second Chartist Petition, a demand for reform rejected by Parliament in 1842, noted, 'The borough of Guildford with a population of 3,920 returns to Parliament as many members as Tower Hamlets with a population of 300,000'. The latter figure was a testimony to the enormous expansion of the East End and to its very crowded character. The *Northern Star or Leeds General Advertiser*, launched in 1837, which was the leading Chartist paper, benefited commercially from its move to London in 1843, although the Chartists' pastoral form, for example the Chartist Land Company, represented a rejection of London urban life as well as the sense that London's urban existence was in some way 'unnatural'.

London was not to be the setting for any confrontation comparable to the anti-Catholic Gordon Riots of 1780. Prefiguring the situation during the General Strike, the Chartist uneasiness about any resort to violence ensured that there was no parallel to the Year of Revolutions on the Continent in 1848, while the scale of government preparations for disturbances in London was impressive. These preparations benefited from modern technology, as trains and the telegraph greatly increased the speed and effectiveness of the government's response. Thus, the Chartist mass-meeting on 10 April 1848 saw the deployment of over 8,000 troops and army pensioners, as well as the 4,000 members of the Metropolitan Police and the enrolling of about 85,000 special constables, including Gladstone, the future prime minister. Charles Grenville noted 'every gentleman in London is become a constable', although there were also working-class Specials. Thirty cannon were prepared at the Tower. The government was resolved to stop a mass procession taking the petition to Parliament, and to do so decided to stop the Chartists crossing the Thames. In the event, despite claims of half a million Chartists assembling on Kennington Common, the number was probably only 20,000. The violence that action against the Chartists could entail was noted by the Chartist poet John Leno:

> I saw a meeting announced to be held on the old tilting ground, Clerkenwell Green. The meeting was addressed by Sharp, Williams and O'Daly, the rostrum was a lamp-post. I was about to follow when an army of constables and detectives swept the Green. The people were terrified and fled. I was new to such sights, and I foolishly concluded that the people were cowards. Shortly after, I was standing on the pavement discussing the Irish question when a disguised policeman gave the order to move on. I said I saw no harm in thus speaking, and the reply was a shove. I still kept my ground when he commenced to belabour me with a truncheon, that he drew from his flannel jacket. This I stood till the blood fairly poured down my face. It was fortunate for him, or me, that I had no weapon of defence.[12]

In turn, the Chartists were blamed by critics for the disorder of that year.

In June, in face of renewed Chartist action, 5,000 troops were deployed, but, again, there was no fighting.[13] London's shift from Whiggery had already been shown in the 1841 election when two of the City seats were gained by the Conservatives, the successors to the Tories.

The absence of conflict did not mean a lack of political opinion, Londoners' awareness of international issues extended to far-away places. Workers were angered in 1850 by the visit of Julius Haynau, an Austrian general who had played an allegedly cruel role in the suppression of the 1848–49 Hungarian revolution. Haynau was set upon by a crowd of London draymen. Conversely, when the liberal hero of the same, defeated revolution – Lajos Kossuth – fled to England the following year, he was entertained officially by the Lord Mayor and Corporation of London, and thousands of Londoners cheered his procession through the city. In 1864, the visiting Italian liberal hero Giuseppe Garibaldi was similarly applauded by working-class crowds.

Reform was an aspect of the expansion of public politics. One of the many ways in which Victorian London was at the centre of life in Britain and its empire was the provision of the news. London newspapers created the images and idioms of nation and empire, shaped its opinions and lay claim to the title of the 'fourth estate' of the realm. Aside from its political function, the London press also played a central economic, social and cultural role, setting and spreading fashions, whether of company statements or through theatrical criticism. In what was an increasingly commercial society, the London press played a pivotal role, inspiring emulation, setting the tone, and fulfilling critical needs for an anonymous mass readership in a society in which alternative means of spreading opinion, such as the Church of England, appeared increasingly weak or redundant.

Many of Chartism's ideas, including democratic accountability, influenced popular Liberalism from the 1850s. The new socio-economic order was one that sat ill with traditional hierarchies, allegiances and practices. The failure of the Chartist programme was followed not by an end to working-class activism, but by a growth of interest in the working class building up its own institutions, such as a multitude of friendly societies and clubs, and in schemes for improving the physical and moral condition of working people through education and temperance.

Moreover, despite the fate of Chartism, officially sanctioned reform was a major theme in mid-century, and moderate reformers were in power, the Whigs, for instance, passing a Clean Air Act for London in 1853. The containment of the possible radical consequences of change proved central to the social politics of the period, while ideological and political strategies sought to confront what was seen as the troubling growth of democracy. Equally, the serious mismanagement of the Crimean War (1854–56), ineptitude that was amply covered and developed as a scandal in the London press, especially *The Times*, helped to boost middle-class values of efficiency in politics and governance at the expense of entrenched oligarchy.

This emphasis was linked to the movement of Whiggism to Liberalism in the 1850s and 1860s as, in acquiring middle-class support, the Whigs became a party fitted for the reformist middle class. Reform was central to their appeal. Reforming activism, moreover, was important in altering the urban landscape and in countering the worst ravages of social distress, as well as in introducing a broader pattern of improvement. Activism combined local initiatives with central supervision administered by inspectors, and the latter was an element of a major shift in the character of London's government, away from local control and toward that of the state.

It was symptomatic of the changing situation that the most dramatic display of initiative at mid-century, the Great Exhibition held in Hyde Park in 1851, did not owe its genesis to the city's traditional system of government. The Great Exhibition was seen as an opportunity to link manufacturing and the arts, in order to promote a humane practicality in which Britain would be foremost, and from which the British people and economy could benefit. Recent French national expositions were to be surpassed, while the Great

Exhibition was an opportunity to assert leadership at a time when the national élite felt challenged by Pope Pius IX's decision to restore the Catholic hierarchy in England. Indeed, 1851 also saw the passage of the Ecclesiastical Titles Act, which prohibited Catholics from assuming episcopal titles.

Supported by the Society for Arts, Manufactures and the Encouragement of Commerce, the Exhibition was planned in part by Prince Albert, the chairman of the royal commission that sponsored it. Seen as reflecting 'England's mission, duty, and interest, to put herself at the head of the diffusion of civilisation and the attainment of liberty', the Exhibition, in part, symbolised the arrival of a less fractured and more prosperous society, after the often divisive and difficult experiences of the 1830s and 1840s. It was a tremendous feat of organisation. Housed in a secular cathedral of cast iron and glass, boldly designed by Sir Joseph Paxton, the Exhibition was the first wonder of the modern world. Over three times the length of St Paul's, the Crystal Palace included 294,000 panes of glass. Six million visitors in 140 days were a testimony to the popularity of the Exhibition and the impact of rail travel: the city's population was 2.7 million in 1851. Class differences were readily discernible among the attending crowds, but social coherence was more notable. Moreover, this was the positive background to the Exhibition that succeeded in opening up minds to new possibilities.[14]

Crystal Palace was originally set up in Hyde Park for the Great Exhibition of 1851, but was moved south of the river, to a part of Penge Common at Sydenham Hill, three years later. It contained almost 1,000,000 square feet of space and was a wonder of its age. It was destroyed by fire in 1936.
© BETTMANN/CORBIS

The profits of the Exhibition appropriately led to the building of a series of museums and learned institutions in South Kensington, to the south of Hyde Park. The Museum of Science and Art, later called the Victoria and Albert, was followed by the Natural History Museum (1873–81) and, in 1907, by the Science Museum. The Royal College of Music and the Imperial College of Science were part of the same development, while the Royal Albert Hall (1870) was added by a private developer. The Albert Memorial (1872) in Kensington Gardens contributed to the townscape of knowledge, with Albert (put in place in 1876) shown holding the Great Exhibition's catalogue and presiding over industry and the arts. The Crystal Palace itself was moved to Sydenham in 1852, and championed by the railway baron Samuel Laing, but it hit repeated financial problems as its varied fare – concerts to dog shows, imperial festivals to balloon flights – attracted few. Partially damaged by fire in 1866, the building was totally destroyed by another in 1936.

The Great Exhibition had looked outwards, with London serving as a stage for national and international display. Another aspect of this role was the embellishment of Buckingham Palace: Edward Blore completed Nash's rebuilding of it in 1831–38, and, in the 1850s, added the east front for Queen Victoria. Less grandly, the National Portrait Gallery was opened in 1856.

At the same time as London's national role, there was a growing interest within London in the display of the city. This element had never been absent, but it became more notable in the nineteenth century as entrepreneurs responded to the increase in the size and wealth of the population. In 1787 the English portrait painter Robert Barker had patented his technique of perspective painting to present 360° views, and coined the term 'panorama' to describe it. He made a considerable fortune displaying the panorama of London he had painted as if from the roof of the Albion Mill, from 1792. In 1794, he constructed a successful 'Rotunda' in Leicester Square. This was followed in 1824–29 by the construction of the 'Colosseum' in Regent's Park in order to house Thomas Horner's panorama from the perspective of the top of the cupola of St Paul's, a view kept on display until 1848.

Meanwhile, the development of urban working-class leisure was away from traditional customs, and towards new mass, commercialised interests. Music-halls and football clubs were founded in large numbers. These sustained local patterns of sociability and identity, as they were grounded in, and maintained links to, specific communities and indeed served to foster their sense of community. Despite improvements in transport within London, such communities were readily apparent, especially at the level of the working class. Even as it forged ahead as world city, London could remain an intensely local and provincial place. Most working people in the nineteenth century wed spouses who lived within half a mile.

Institutions such as music-halls and football clubs were commercial and organised, and these new forms of leisure were both more capitalised and more open to regulation, so that they should not challenge the requirements of the established order. Regulation and containment were certainly at stake in the treatment of earlier forms of leisure, too. In 1854, pubs were forced to close at midnight on Saturday, and, except for Sunday lunch and evening, not to re-open until 4 a.m. on Monday. Drinking was also affected by the 1869 Wine and Beerhouse Act and the 1872 Licensing Act. As pubs were central to working-class communal experience, and alcohol lessened inhibitions, these changes were very much part of a more controlled society; although self-regulation was also a key theme, one that linked more decorous and passive opera audiences[15] to the behaviour of much of the working population.

Yet, a more coercive mechanism was also at issue, not least with the scrutiny of alternative entertainments: under the Vagrancy Act of 1824, and later laws, the police were able to arrest street entertainers. By the end of the century, these had become figures of the past. Instead, popular activities were regulated and standardised. The new policing of the period was much concerned about the moral threat of the urban environment and sought to bring order and decorum to the streets. Prostitutes, and particularly children who were involved, were especially targeted. This process was political,[16] and reflected in particular Victorian ideals of the respectable society.

The political character of reform was demonstrated in the nature of consultation permitted and encouraged. In essence, expertise ruled and was self-referential, while other interests, even those of the social élite, could be ignored. Thus, the building of Northumberland Avenue destroyed the town house of the Duke of Northumberland in 1874, while, as a stark demonstration of the determination to push through change, notable (and beautiful), churches and graveyards were swept aside for urban development. This destruction owed much to the merger of parishes as a result of the Union of City Benefices Act. All Hallows, Bread Street, rebuilt by Wren after the Great Fire, was demolished in 1876. All Hallows the Great, Upper Thames Street, also rebuilt by Wren, had its tower and north aisle also demolished in 1876, in order to permit the widening of Queen Victoria Street. The remainder of the church was demolished under the Act in 1893–94 as the site had been sold to a brewery company. Other churches destroyed included St Mary Somerset (1872), St Matthew, Friday Street (1881), and St Olave, Old Jewry (1888). Furthermore, the interiors of Wren churches were transformed. The cannibalisation of buildings extended to recent ones, cleared to make way for new edifices.

The rebuilding of the city was not undertaken to any master-plan of development, for, until the foundation of the London County Council, there was no local government body responsible for the capital as a whole. There was therefore no institution able to push through such a vision, while, despite the presence of bodies such as the Office of Woods and Forests, a body dealing with the Crown estate, the nature of British public culture was such that the central government could not readily take this role. London's

Major civil engineering projects abounded in the Victorian age. Queen Victoria was able to open both the new Blackfriars Bridge and Holborn Viaduct on the same day in 1869. The 'Holborn Valley Viaduct', seen here in a watercolour, c.1870, by W. Haywood, was built '… to avoid the dangerous descent of Holborn Hill … and form a spacious and pleasant thoroughfare connecting the City with that great Mediterranean of western traffic, Holborn and Oxford Street.' In this view carriages and cattle pass along Farringdon Street under the viaduct, which was built to span the valley of the river Fleet whose waters had by this date been culverted and ran as a sewer below Farringdon Street. Sir Miles Hobart, a one-time MP and prisoner in the Tower, had been killed in 1632, when his coach overturned on Holborn Hill, so perhaps the descent was as dangerous as *The Builder* magazine contended. The viaduct itself is a fine construction, although it eventually cost in excess of £2 million.

development in mid-century could not, therefore, match that of Paris or Vienna. Instead, the particular demands of individual interests, such as banks, played a key role. Moreover, where constructed, new streets did not add up to a whole system.

James Pennethorne, a Worcester-born architect who had become the principal assistant of his relative John Nash, proposed in the 1830s that a major thoroughfare be built from the far east of London to the far west, but his and other of his plans were deemed too ambitious and costly by the government, though they were the basis for New Oxford Street, Endell Street, Cranbourn Street and Commercial Street. Acts of Parliament were necessary to push through new schemes such as that of 1846 for the extension of Commercial Street to Shoreditch. It was only the establishment of the Metropolitan Board of Works in 1855 that provided a body able to push through new road schemes, such as Victoria Street and Charing Cross Road, and, indeed, the Board was to take up some of Pennethorne's earlier ideas, including Garrick and Southwark Streets. Nevertheless, Pennethorne's plans, especially those for bold streets, were generally only executed in part.[17]

The destruction of the old reflected a general dislike of past architecture, especially that of the eighteenth century, as well as the demand for new institutions. Ambitious and expensive new structures were built in grand Victorian style, including Holborn Viaduct (1869), which carried the road to the City over Farringdon Street and the culverted river Fleet, and which was built of elaborate cast iron and adorned with statues. New institutions played a key role in the regularisation of commerce. The massive Coal Exchange with its mighty rotunda was built on Lower Thames Street in 1847–49, followed by Billingsgate Market in 1850–53, and Smithfield Meat Market in 1867–68. The last also reflected the pressure for sanitary reform, as the new market was built on the site of the live cattle market which had been moved to Islington in 1855 by the City Corporation in response to demands for cleanliness.

The French illustrator Gustave Doré was paid the huge sum of £10,000 a year for three years to draw 180 plates to illustrate *A London Pilgrimage* (1872). This one is known as 'The Bull's Eye', in which three policemen pierce the blackness of the London night to illuminate a sundry group of poor Londoners. We know from many sources the depths and extent of poverty that existed in parts of London, where those without employment or proper accommodation – often recent migrants, ethnic minorities and vulnerable groups – could easily fall into a seemingly inescapable trap of dearth, disease and hardship. London was not unique, of course – Engels told similar tales of the cellar dwellings of Manchester – but the work of Doré among others focused upon the richest city in the richest country of the world. *A London Pilgrimage* was a huge commercial success, and images such as this quickly became the recognisable, if not quite the recognised, depiction of the London underclass. Even at the time, however, some felt that Doré exaggerated the suffering, or even made some of it up: it was a commercial venture, and Doré's images were designed to sell. The *Westminster Review* found it all rather distasteful: 'Doré gives us sketches in which the commonest, the vulgarest external features are set down ...'

This 1884 photograph shows a London chimney sweep with the tools of his trade. Popular historical commentary usually centres on the exploitation of small boys by Victorian scoundrels until nineteenth-century legislation prohibited (at least in theory) the use of children to climb up the flues. Writers such as Charles Kingsley and William Blake waxed lyrical on the theme, while in *Oliver Twist* Dickens created the evil Mr Gamfield, who 'did happen to labour under the slight imputation of having bruised three or four boys to death already'. By the time this photograph was taken, the image had changed to one of good-natured Cockneys, by then making use of the better-designed brushes shown here. Behind the sweep's trade lies a very important historical change that took place first in London, namely the shift from wood to coal as a fuel for domestic heating. Between 1400 and 1800 the price of wood in London trebled, while coal, mainly from Newcastle, barely rose in price and, per unit of heat, became much less expensive. This spurred on the development of efficient coal-burning fireplaces, with their attendant chimneys that now needed to be kept clean. In the nineteenth century there were at least 1,000 sweeps in London.

An interesting aside here is the tale of Australian author Pamela Lyndon Travers, who was so dismayed by Disney's adaptation of her novel *Mary Poppins* (1934) in 1964 that she refused to work with the Hollywood film company again. In part her displeasure centred on the use of non-English actors in the screen adaptation of her London-based fantasy: Bert the chimney sweep was played by the American Dick Van Dyke, whose cringeworthy attempt at Cockney has been voted in *Empire* magazine as one of the worst cinema accents of all time.

© THE FRANCIS FRITH COLLECTION/CORBIS

The development of joint-stock banking was important for the streetscape, as the banks required substantial premises, notably the big, high-ceiling, banking halls that took up prominent sites in the City, for example the City of London Bank on Ludgate Hill (1890). So also with the insurance companies, with Alliance Assurance having two large office blocks on St James's Street (1883, 1905), while the Prudential built a sprawling one on High Holborn (1895–1905). The grand bank and insurance headquarters provided not only physical accommodation, but also legitimation and authority for their new financial power and possibilities. As with the expansion of the City's financial sector over the last fifty years, this architecture helped provide a sense of solidity and authority for a financial world that was complex and appeared unstable. Architecture thus represented an affirmation of stability that appeared to provide symbolic capital. Such buildings also greatly increased the rateable value of the City, and thus its ability, under rate equalisation schemes, to finance local government elsewhere in London.

Other large buildings included department stores, such as the Civil Service Stores and Harrods; hotels, such as the Westminster Palace, Savoy, Carlton, Piccadilly and Ritz; and gentlemen's clubs, which created a distinctive world of masculinity in and near Pall Mall. The Ritz (1906) was the first major steel-framed building in London. It could not match

From Roman times to the modern day the centre of the City has been a place of markets, trading and the supply of provisions. Near Gracechurch Street is Leadenhall Market, which has been a market for, among other things, meat, poultry and game for at least 650 years since Simon Eyre, originally from Suffolk, but later Lord Mayor, built the first market on this site in 1446. Before that there had been a mansion on the site, its lead roof reputedly giving the area its name. The present, ornate Victorian building dates from 1881, and is similar to edifices in other cities such as Rome.

PHOTOGRAPH: CARNEGIE, 2009

BELOW

London has two Smithfields. East Smithfield lies just to the north-east of the Tower, just outside the city walls, and West Smithfield derived its name from the 'smooth field' just to the west of St Bartholomew's Priory and not far from the river Fleet. Of the two West Smithfield is the more famous on account of its ancient meat market. This aquatint shows a busy market in 1811. Many complained about the place, none more so than Thomas J. Maslen in 1843: 'Of all the horrid abominations with which London has been cursed, there is not one that can come up to that disgusting place, West Smithfield Market, for cruelty, filth, effluvia, pestilence, impiety, horrid language, danger, disgusting and shuddering sights, and every obnoxious item that can be imagined.' The noise and hubbub are also described in *Oliver Twist*: '… the whistling of drovers, the barking of dogs, the bellowing and plunging of oxen, the bleating of sheep, the grunting and squeaking of pigs, the cries of hawkers, the shouts, oaths, and quarrelling on all sides; the ringing of bells and roar of voices, that issued from every public-house; the crowding, pushing, driving, beating, whooping, and yelling; the hideous and discordant din that resounded from every corner of the market …'

MUSEUM OF LONDON

the vast Hotel Cecil (1896) on the Strand, which had 700 bedrooms and was said to be the largest in the world. This hotel was demolished in 1930, whereas London's largest theatre, the Coliseum, opened in 1904, is still in operation.

Working-class communities found their neighbourhoods, such as Kingsway, rebuilt or reorganised without reference to them. Slums that were rebuilt included Agar Town on the rail approaches to St Pancras and the Old Nichol rookery in Shoreditch. Agar Town was a shanty town rapidly built in the 1830s but without proper drainage. It was demolished to make way for St Pancras railway station in the 1860s. New Oxford Street was driven through the St Giles rookery in 1847. In the case of Kingsway, construction of the road was deliberately intended to destroy a neighbourhood judged criminous, degenerate, and out of control. Indeed 28 acres were cleared in 1900–05 in order to make way for Kingsway and the Aldwych, a hugely expensive scheme. The LCC played a major role in the project, not least as its powers were necessary to accomplish it. Slum-clearance was not only for the sake of new roads, with the LCC building the Boundary Street estate in what had been a slum section of Bethnal Green, as well as the Millbank estate on the site of the Millbank Penitentiary (prison).

Aside from the response to particular communities, the decision to tackle London's public health and slum housing essentially through engineering and clearance directed by administrators ensured that alternative responses, such as measures to alleviate poverty, were given much less attention. The focus was on sewerage systems and clean water, rather than on securing the availability of food and work, nor of income at levels sufficient to lessen the impact of disease. Cleared from a slum, the poor moved on to other poverty-stricken neighbourhoods.

An air of total respectability did not come immediately to Pall Mall. The western end contained fine houses, but the street was 'greatly disfigured by several mean houses of the lowest mechanicks ... interspersed in it ...' The Regent Street development and the closing of St James's Market helped improve the tone. Here we see Pallas Athene and part of the Elgin Marbles frieze on the Athenaeum Club, and the Reform Club, 104 Pall Mall.

PHOTOGRAPHS: CARNEGIE, 2009

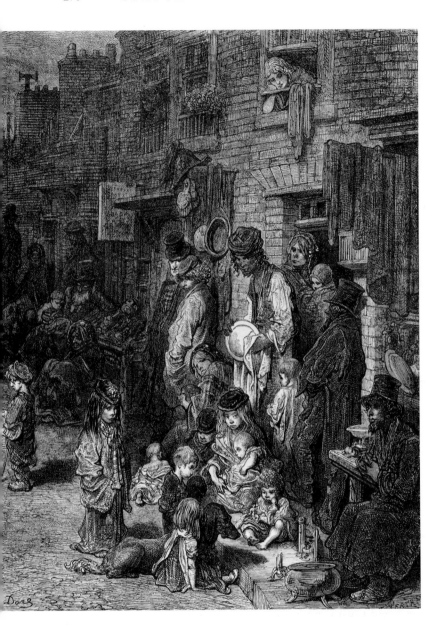

In *The People of the Abyss* (1903), the popular American writer Jack London wrote: '... For here, in the East End, the obscenities and brute vulgarities of life are rampant. There is no privacy. The bad corrupts the good, and all fester together. Innocent childhood is sweet and beautiful; but in East London innocence is a fleeting thing, and you must catch them before they crawl out of the cradle, or you will find the very babes as unholily wise as you.' During the nineteenth century the East End had progressively become the poorest, meanest part of London. Dorset Street in the Spitalfields 'rookery' was said to be the worst street in London, so bad that it was renamed Duval Street in 1904: 'There were pubs every few yards. Bawdy houses every few feet. It was peopled by roaring drunken fighting-mad killers.' Irish and Jewish immigrants found themselves amid poverty, distress, prostitution and unemployment. Russian actor Jacob Adler wrote, 'The further we penetrated into this Whitechapel, the more our hearts sank. Was this London? Never in Russia, never later in the worst slums of New York, were we to see such poverty as in the London of the 1880s.' This 1870s' engraving by Gustave Doré shows Wentworth Street, Whitechapel; it is a powerfully evocative image. This was the poor London known to readers of Dickens, and to those who were shortly to follow the full and gruesome newspaper reports of the unidentified murder of prostitutes who stalked this area and allegedly styled himself 'Jack the Ripper'.

The problems of the bulk of the population were starkly clear. In 1840, the death rate was 27 per 1,000 and the average age of death was 26.5. Henry Mayhew, in *London Labour and the London Poor* (1861–62), estimated that 10,000 of London's lodging houses were of the lowest sort, by which he meant places in which criminals and prostitutes resided. In the oft-reproduced engraving 'Over London by Rail', in Gustave Doré and Blanchard Jerrold's *London: a Pilgrimage* (1872), the houses are shrouded in smoke and overshadowed by the railway arches, and people are reduced to minor figures. Other prints showed the outside privies, smoking factory chimneys, and clothes drying in the polluted city, all of which contributed to sickness.

Pollution was a seemingly intractable problem. In his *A Morning's Walk from London to Kew* (1817), Sir Richard Phillips commented 'It must in a future age be … difficult to believe that the Londoners could have resided in the dense atmosphere of coal-smoke'. Indeed an increase in respiratory diseases in London in part countered the benefits stemming from action against smallpox and cholera. Air pollution contributed greatly to the fogs that frequently shrouded London, fogs that played a role in the details of life there, as well as a key and lasting role in the image of the city, one kept alive until the 1960s by British and Hollywood films such as *Gaslight*. Fogs were important in fiction, for example, in detective novels. Foreigners proved especially keen on using fog as a description of London. In 'The Regent's Park Murder' by the Hungarian-born Baroness Orczy, a short story set in 1907, John Ashley explains his being armed by saying 'I always carry a revolver about with me in foggy weather'. In *The Fog* (1901), a novel by the American war correspondent Richard Harding Davis set in London, the narrator describes being 'as completely lost as though I had been set down by night in the Sahara Desert'.

Paintings such as *The Pinch of Poverty* (1889) by Thomas Kennington provided a genteel view of poverty, while the children in Dorothy Stanley's *Street Arabs at Play* appeared well fed, but, despite such depictions, poverty was generally far harsher in its consequences. Indeed, the administration of the 1834 Poor Law system had faced serious problems in London, leading to a series of scandals over medical care and living conditions. As a result, the Metropolitan Poor Law Act passed in 1867 led to the establishment in London of large new Poor Law hospitals and asylums.

The plight of poor children moved crusading philanthropists such as Thomas J. Barnardo who, in 1867, founded the East End Juvenile Mission, the basis of what later became 'Dr Barnardo's Homes' for destitute children. From 1882 he sent some children to Canada for resettlement. Inspired by similar motives the Reverend Thomas Stephenson established near Waterloo Road a refuge for destitute children in 1869, the basis of the National Children's Home. In Whitechapel in 1865, meanwhile, William Booth and his wife Catherine launched the 'Christian Mission to the Heathen of our Own Country' and, thirteen years later, this became the Salvation Army. Initially focused on spiritual salvation, the Salvation Army's mission also became directed at social reform. William Carlile, an Anglican curate in Kensington, matched this by launching the Church Army in 1882, again linking evangelism and social welfare. Temperance was a key theme of the moral reformers. Emma Cons, who owned the Old Vic (formerly the Royal Coburg Theatre and then the Royal Victoria) from 1881 until 1912, provided decent entertainment on temperance lines.

The motives of crusading philanthropists have been queried in recent decades, but, however much philanthropy could serve the interests of spiritual well-being, curiosity

The Pinch of Poverty by Thomas Kennington (1889) did not provide a picture of smiling joy, but poverty was generally far harsher than this genteel scene might suggest. The flower-selling child is charming, but the cold pallor of her mother might just be indicative of tuberculosis.

and even personal aggrandisement, there was a drive both to offer relieving improvement and, in understanding the plight of the poor, to provide a more nuanced appreciation of the social environment. Yet, the moral panics about the plight of the poor that crusading philanthropy and journalism inspired, were, to a degree, replicated by unease about the willingness of philanthropists to compromise class and gender assumptions and roles in their charitable work.[18] Their focus was on the East End, which became more orderly as a result of the major effort for public improvement.

The City, which remained resolute in defence of its autonomy, and the surrounding parishes, were not affected by the Municipal Corporations Act, but legislation specific to London was passed in order to deal with the legacy of a large number of often competing local authorities lacking in consistent goals and coherent policy discussion and implementation. A particular problem was posed by the role of parishes as a basis for administration outside the City. Although they might have been sub-divided for ecclesiastical purposes, these parishes were significant governmental units deploying considerable staffs and budgets. Unlike the City, they were not answerable to a mayor or corporation, but instead to a parish vestry. The key element were the vestrymen who, from 1855, in a blow to long-standing oligarchical tendencies, were elected by an annual meeting. This system provided a strong sense of locality,[19] but was not really equal to the challenge of rising population numbers and also lacked coherence at the level of the city as a whole.

The view of public health as a disaster, real or incipient, made the existing system of government outside the City seem redundant. Based upon parishes but complicated by various precincts, liberties, boards and commissions, this was a system of local autonomy and independence and not of co-operation, a system that was reactive rather than pro-active, and one unsuited to deal with the major growth of the city's population. The City's system of wards also appeared inadequate. Although defended on the grounds of the value of self-government, these systems were no longer seen by national government as valid.

The Metropolitan Commission for Sewers had been established in 1847 by the Whig government at the behest of the ambitious public servant Edwin Chadwick, in part by abolishing six of London's seven commissions of sewers; only that for the City survived. The vestries opposed this restriction of local autonomy. As a result of the existence of the commission, London was excluded from the need to establish a Board of Health in the legislation passed the following year, an exclusion that also reflected the City's determination to maintain its autonomy. Nevertheless, Chadwick used the Board of Health to campaign for reform in London, creating contention over centralisation which was vigorously resisted by the vestries. In 1854, Chadwick was removed from the Board, which was wound up.

In reaction to Chadwick, the Metropolis Local Management Act of 1855 established the Metropolitan Board of Works. Its members were selected by the major local authorities. A powerful Metropolitan Board of Works was a necessary response not only to the problems facing the city but also to the increased scale of the private provision of services. Thus, in 1857 the gas companies moved from competition to an agreement on local monopolies. The Metropolitan Board of Works was the only real restraint on such activities. Yet, although the Metropolis Local Management Act clarified governance at the level of the city as a whole, it was only a partial reform and left the vestries in place. However, the Act standardised the way the vestries were elected and the qualifications for membership, as well as consolidating a number of smaller vestries into 'district boards'.

Looked at differently, the legislation was a response to the failure of Chadwick's drive for centralised government of London on the model of the Metropolitan Police Acts. His opposition to local authorities, and the variety and independence of opinions they represented, had fallen foul of these and more particularly of ratepayer opinion and the drive for more broad-based representative government. Two different models of reform

An official from Dr Barnardo's House pays a visit to Shadwell, 1920. Barnardo's was founded in the East End of London in the 1860s to provide care for poor children who had been orphaned in the wake of the cholera epidemic of 1866. Shadwell, like nearby Poplar, Limehouse and Wapping, was a sailors' community. As early as 1650 it was estimated that over two-thirds of Shadwell men were employed on the river, either in ship-building or as watermen or lightermen. By the nineteenth century the area was also home to a significant number of Indian and South Asian 'lascar' sailors who had been recruited to work on British merchantmen.

© CORBIS

had clashed and the political one, of ratepayer democracy, had prevailed over the statist one, at least in the context of the 1850s, a period defined by middle-class liberalism. This tension, however, was to be a key one in the subsequent history of London, albeit a tension complicated from the 1880s by the existence of a democratically elected governmental body for London as a whole.

In later periods ratepayer democracy and local accountability were to be put under great pressure from a dirigiste central state, notably with the Labour government of 1945–51. There were earlier intimations of such tension, for example with the dirigiste consequences of legislation such as the Metropolis Poor Law Amendment Act of 1867, which established the Metropolitan Common Poor Fund, and the Local Government Act of 1871. The former Act granted the Poor Law Board the power to nominate guardians to London Poor Law Boards and also to redistribute the cost of pauperism among the Poor Law Unions.[20] In turn, the policies of the government of Margaret Thatcher (1979–90) were to challenge notions of local accountability, not only at the level of London as a whole, but also of boroughs, such as Lambeth, that sought to follow different policies.

The Whiggish account of London's development assumes that a lack of central authority for the city held back progress, notably having a delaying effect on cleaning things up and providing for better conditions. This argument was also applied in recent decades, manifesting itself in support of the Greater London of regional planning. While there is clearly much force to this argument, it is also necessary to note the administrative and political problems posed by such authorities.

Initially the Metropolitan Board of Works had a restricted role – sewerage, drainage, roads, public spaces – but this changed gradually over time. Although Whitehall sought to exercise control by retaining direction over the acquisition of land and over large-scale expenditure, the Board, indeed, became the obvious repository for new functions. These included the Metropolitan Fire Brigade in 1865 (a response to the terrible Tooley Street fire in Southwark in 1861), parks in 1866 and tramways in 1870, as well as major roads and bridges, drains, the administration of the 1855 Building Act, and the naming of streets. Such functions reflected the sense that existing provision, especially in fire services, was

This small, inconspicuous memorial on Tooley Street, Southwark, is to James Braidwood. Braidwood had set up a municipal fire service in Edinburgh (where there is now a statue to this pioneering firefighter) in 1824, and he became the first director (from 1833) of the London Fire Engine Establishment. He distinguished himself in administrative reform, but also in fighting fires heroically. This memorial, appropriately, commemorates his death in June 1861 while combating the Tooley Street fire which consumed several warehouses, including Hay's Wharf, and raged for two days. Another heroic firefighter, Captain Eyre Massey Shaw, was to be commemorated in Gilbert and Sullivan's *Iolanthe*, first staged in 1882 at the Savoy Theatre which was built for their comic operas by the impresario Richard D'Oyly Carte: 'Oh, Captain Shaw! / Type of true love kept under! / Could thy Brigade, with cold cascade / Quench my great love, I wonder!'

PHOTOGRAPH: CARNEGIE, 2009

inadequate, and that the London area was the appropriate level of organisation. Fire services had been the responsibility of the Fire Engine Establishment, which was financed by the fire insurance offices. The growth of traffic led to pressure for road improvement, a measure combined with the clearing of 'rookeries' or slums. The bridge companies were bought out by the Board in the 1880s; tolls were lifted and new bridges built.

The emphasis on new engineered systems, like that on the clearing of slums, accorded with that of London's reforming middle classes, and was part of a wider mission to improve and regulate society in accordance with their interests. Regulation underpinned expertise, professionalisation and a process of establishing or raising standards that excluded others from participation, unless on acceptable terms.

Public spaces were defined and regulated. Commercial pleasure parks gradually passed away. The owners of Vauxhall Gardens went bankrupt in 1840; the Gardens reopened but finally went out of business in 1859, in part as a result of rowdyism among the changing clientele and in part due to the advance of industry.[21] The Recreation Grounds Acts of 1859 and the Public Health Act of 1875 supported the laying out of public parks as sites for improving public health and securing popular morals by bringing the recreations of the populace into contact with those of their supposed betters and also under the scrutiny of the police. Primrose Hill was bought as a park in 1842 and Battersea Park four years later. In Bow, Victoria Park, the site of which was purchased in 1841, was opened in 1845. Pennethorne, who was responsible for the design of Victoria, Battersea and Kennington Parks, as well as for the Albert Park in part realised by Finsbury Park, sought to offer lungs for the city, as well as urban accounts of country-house landscaping, lawns juxtaposed with carefully planned but apparently natural lakes and plantings of trees. Further afield, the Metropolitan Board secured Hampstead Heath, Clapham Common and Blackheath from development, while the City Corporation acquired Epping Forest in 1878 and Highgate Woods in 1885. Municipal parks and buildings also testified to the continued strength of local identities within London and to the desire to improve the local environment. Parks were filled with statues of the locally prominent; their bandstands served as a focus for orderly leisure; and their drinking fountains provided free clean water.

In time, public swimming baths came to complement the parks, as exercise became a more prominent theme, but much of the male population preferred to watch organised sport such as football. Based in London, the Football Association, formed in 1863 by alumni of Eton, Harrow, Winchester, Rugby and Cambridge University, sought to codify the rules. Increasingly popular, football was organised on a large scale from the 1880s, and London attendances increased markedly. In 1901, 111,000 spectators stood on the banking of Crystal Palace – the football stadium that hosted FA Cup finals from 1895 until 1914 – to watch Tottenham beat Sheffield United in the FA Cup final. Even more remarkably, perhaps, in 1913, 121,919 fans made very significant journeys to watch Aston Villa beat

Sunderland in the same competition. Other sports facilities became prominent on London's map, including cricket grounds and, in the suburbs, many golf courses. London also played a key organisational role. The Marylebone Cricket Club (MCC) played the key part in supervising cricket from 1788, when it issued revised rules, notably banning attempts to thwart a fielder making a catch. Over-arm bowling was introduced in 1864.

Souls as well as bodies required uplift and exercise. The reform of ecclesiastical provision was driven forward by concern about godlessness. Indeed, in 1828, when Charles Blomfield became Bishop of London at a time of marked challenge from Catholicism and Nonconformity, he pressed for the building of fifty churches in order to deal with the growth of London and with concerns about the lack of religious commitment, or apparent commitment or, at least, godly living of much of is population. Quantity appeared a key desideratum in facing the challenges of change. Already there had been some provision of new churches, as with Sir John Soane's St Peter's, Walworth (1823–24). The 1818 Church Building Act, which granted public money to a new Church Building Commission, led to an increase in the pace of building, but one that was opposed by Dissenters as well as by ratepayers worried about their contribution. Indeed, the cost of the new church at St Pancras led to particular bitterness. Church-building, however, continued. In the 1830s, Pennethorne designed churches in Albany Street and Gray's Inn Road.

An important area of reform in which Londoners led the way was the 'Women's Movement', a loosely organised pressure group largely populated by women from the wealthy middle class. The Society for Promoting Women's Employment was founded in 1859 by women who met in Langham Place. They pressed for their own interests, in the shape of the Married Women's Property Act, passed in 1870, as well as for those of women of a different background, in the shape of the campaign for the repeal of the Contagious Diseases Act, legislation aimed against women suspected of prostitution in towns with garrisons or naval bases. The society also called for female entry into the medical profession, a path blazed by Elizabeth Garrett Anderson (1836–1917), who became a licentiate of the Society of Apothecaries in 1865, before founding a dispensary and the first hospital completely staffed by women. I was born in the nursing home in Belsize Park named after her.

A different form of masculinity was challenged by the Royal Commission on the Livery Companies which reported in 1885 on what was then in effect a cosy world of socially conservative male clubbery. The Livery Companies then bore no relationship to the guilds from which they had evolved and these guilds, instead, were essentially represented by the early trade unions.

St Peter's Walworth, built of London stock bricks and stone facings and Ionic columns. Like much of the rest of SE17, the church was damaged during the Blitz but later restored. Sir John Soane also designed Holy Trinity, Marylebone around the same time, just after the Napoleonic wars.

PHOTOGRAPH: CARNEGIE, 2009

Yet, this process of local reform was very much affected, if not limited, by existing institutions, hierarchies and social assumptions. Most vestries did not respond to the possibilities, under the Public Libraries Act of 1850, to provide for rate-aided public libraries. The 1870 Education Act required a certain level of educational provision, introducing the school district in cases where existing parish provision was inadequate, and giving school boards, elected by ratepayers, the right to set rates to support non-denominational Board Schools. In place of the previous system, of Church and charity schools supplemented from the 1840s by the ragged schools, attendance at school was now compulsory between the ages of five and thirteen. This legislation was a major step, and the creation of the London School Board disrupted existing London hierarchies. This board, directly elected and covering the same area as the Metropolitan Board of Works (with the addition of the City), was the stamping ground for municipal reformers who, as Progressives, were to dominate the London County Council. New school buildings were erected across London and were an important indication of civic activism.

The Act, however, was resisted, not least because many were opposed to paying rates to support schools. In Ealing, tenacious efforts by the Church of England to protect voluntary education, and to resist the introduction of Board Schools, ignored the implications of rapid population growth, and left 500 children unschooled 25 years after the Act.

Despite such resistance, however, the more general process in London was one of the end of long-established distinctions, variations and privileges; and the furtherance of uniformity played a major role in the reform process, both as a goal and helping to anchor the process. Thus, for example, as far as the Church of England was concerned, there was a regularisation of the financial benefits of clerics, as Church livings were brought under central control and their emoluments standardised.

Legislative changes had ramifications across London, affecting different areas of life, but contributing to change. The introduction of open examinations for the Civil Service in 1870 was an important step in the move from patronage to merit, although the impact in terms of a change in social composition among office-holders was limited. The institutionalisation of Easter, Whitsun and Bank holidays in 1871 by the Bank Holiday Act, which provided holidays with pay, led to a growth in day-tripping from London. As a result, Southend grew rapidly as a seaside resort for East Enders, a development made possible by easy access by rail. The Liberal government of 1868–74 under William Gladstone, responsible for this legislation, was succeeded by the Conservatives under Benjamin Disraeli, who held power from 1874 to 1880. This was an administration that left most relevant decisions to London agencies, while rejecting, in 1874, the idea of a single municipal authority for London. Disraeli backed social reform, yet most of the legislation was permissive rather than compulsory, leaving decisions about implementation largely to local magistrates. Under Disraeli London was, therefore, spared the dictates of big government.

Disraeli's legislation brought far less benefit to the majority of Londoners than the titles of the Acts might have suggested. For example, the Artisans Dwelling Act of 1875 made urban renewal possible, by allowing local authorities to provide housing at the cost of the ratepayers, but its actual impact in terms of slum clearance was very limited. The attempt by the Metropolitan Board of Works to have an Act giving it control over the cost and quality of the gas supply failed in 1875 as a result of pressure from the gas companies, which, like their water counterparts, were influential in the Commons. The Board's attempt to gain control over the water supply was rejected in 1876. Apart from a lack of legislative improvement, London was hit hard by the serious economic depression that began in 1877. This depression had led, by the end of the decade, to a marked increase in unemployment and bankruptcies, as well as to much concern about slum conditions, and demands from many for a new municipal activism.

In contrast, other British cities followed different paths. Most notably, in Birmingham the former industrialist Joseph Chamberlain in his time as Mayor (1873–75) implemented many civic improvements which together constituted a new form of interventionist local government that included an extension of municipal ownership over utilities as well as early schemes of slum clearance.

The London electorate expanded greatly, both because of population growth and due to the reform of the franchise, a cause pressed actively in London by the Reform League. Indeed, there was a large-scale demonstration in Hyde Park on 6 May 1867, which included the carrying of a red flag topped by a cap of liberty, the symbol of the French Revolution. The right of the public to assemble in Hyde Park was one of the issues at stake.

The Second Reform Act (1867) provided the vote to all rate-paying male householders, as well as to the £10 lodgers in the boroughs. Hackney and Chelsea became parliamentary boroughs. The graduates of the University of London also gained a parliamentary seat. The 1885 Redistribution Act considerably increased the number of London seats in the Commons. In the event, the new electorate proved more conservative than many had anticipated, with London an area of Conservative strength in the national elections from the 1886 election until that of 1906, when it switched to the Liberals, helping take the latter to victory.

As a parallel development, there was a major expansion in the London press, one that reflected both a different legislative framework, with the abolition, between 1853 and 1861, of taxation on advertisements, newspapers and paper, and also a technological transformation centred on new printing presses and the continuous rolls of paper that fed them, as well as an entrepreneurial quest for new markets that reflected a sense of opportunity in London's social changes. The *Daily News* first appeared in 1846, and the advertisements for the paper published the following January found problems other than taxation responsible for the lack of expansion in the number of London dailies:

First, the capital required to be invested. Next, the various talents, knowledge and experience which must combine to produce the result. The number of the requirements have, in truth, occasioned something very like a monopoly – and monopoly always commands its own price ...a daily London newspaper remained, until the establishment of the *Daily News*, a costly luxury, in which only the wealthy could indulge. The *Daily News* looks for support, not to a comparatively few readers at a high price, but to many at a low price.

In the event, the number of daily morning papers published in London rose from 8 in 1856 to 21 in 1900, and of evenings from 7 to 11. Moreover, as an instructive response to the particular possibilities of new areas within the expanding city, there was a tremendous expansion in the suburban dailies. This contributed to the suburban sense of identity, and also to the rethinking of the areas affected by London's growth so that they thought of themselves as suburbs.

The repeal of the newspaper taxes permitted the appearance of penny dailies, especially the *Daily Telegraph*, launched in 1855, but they, in turn, were squeezed by the halfpenny press. The first halfpenny evening paper, the *Echo*, a supporter of municipal reform, appeared in 1868, while halfpenny morning papers became important in the 1890s, with

the *Morning Leader* (1892) and the *Daily Mail* (1896). The *Daily Telegraph* had a circulation of 300,000 by 1888, the *Echo*, 200,000 by 1870. In comparison, an eighteenth-century London newspaper was considered a great success if it sold 10,000 copies a week (most influential papers then were weeklies) and 2,000 weekly was a reasonable level of sales.

Thus, an enormous expansion had taken place, one that transformed London's public politics, and that matched the vitality of an imperial capital, swollen by immigration and increasingly influential as an opinion-setter within the country, not least because of the communications revolution produced by the railway, the telegraph and better roads. London newspapers increased their

The former Daily Telegraph building, Fleet Street, built in 1880. Launched in 1859 with the aim to be 'the largest, best, and cheapest newspaper in the world', the paper led the way for the penny dailies and by 1861 had a daily circulation of over 140,000 and by 1888 300,000. The Telegraph proved the most successful daily rival to *The Times*. The *Telegraph* had offices in Canary Wharf for a time, but the registered offices are now in Buckingham Palace Road, near Victoria.

PHOTOGRAPH: CARNEGIE, 2009

dominance of the national newspaper scene while, thanks to the train, these papers could arrive on provincial doorsteps within hours of publication. As an industry, the press, which underlined London's role in printing, also provided numerous jobs, and the creation of a Fleet Street industrial sector underlined the age-old phenomenon whereby particular areas of the city came to be differentiated by function.

The influence of the London press was also a matter of newspaper organisation and culture. Provincial dailies that were successful enough to invest in new printing technology and in a staff of reporters mirrored the internal organisation and developments of the London daily press. This replication facilitated the movement of individuals between the two, and also helped secure the position of the London press as the model to the remainder of the newspaper world.

The press played a major role in the growing relative importance and influence of the capital within the country and empire. *The Times* was read across the globe, defining world news from a London perspective. Thus, world news was London news. The national influence of the London press had influence alongside the railway and as part of a general pattern of improving communications. Similarly, the actions of the London exchanges were communicated through the telegraph, and centralised their role in business. All of this was symbolised in every railway station by the concept of 'the up train', meaning the train to London, and 'the down train'. Thus, train travel, the essential form of travel in the country, was thought of with regard to London, even if the traveller did not go there.

The improved communication system helped express London's growing significance across a range of activities. Not only the financial, insurance and banking centre of country and empire, it was also the place for memorials and commemorations, as well as the centre of the intellectual life of the country, with societies, libraries, the university (which was founded in this period), laboratories, and artistic sites, such as opera houses.

Politics was part of this process, but there was also a transforming influence on politics within London itself. As a result of electoral reform and the newly expanded public politics, political power was becoming more populist. Institutional reform accompanied the transition, as earlier governmental practices and political compromises seemed unacceptable and as both political parties sought to benefit from the change. In 1884, the Liberal government supported the London Government Bill, which proposed to establish a single authority for London, incorporating the City, the vestries and the Metropolitan Board of Works. Strong opposition from within London led, however, to the abandonment of the legislation.

In turn, the Local Government Act of 1888, a measure passed by a Conservative government, created county councils and county boroughs, with London being organised in terms of the new, directly elected London County Council (LCC), which covered 117 square miles. Nevertheless, the Conservative-dominated City retained the powers of a municipal borough and was excluded from the LCC area, while Greater London, the built-up area beyond the LCC, was also excluded. Householders and ratepayers (including women) had the vote in the LCC, while the Act replaced the traditional dominance of local government by municipal corporations and Justices of the Peace, and amounted to a revolution in local government, notably in the shape of democratic accountability. The LCC also took over the functions of the Metropolitan Board of Works; indeed, in some respects it was a continuation of the Board. In 1904, in a major consolidation of authority and power, the LCC took over the functions of the London School Board.

The first elections to the new body were held in 1889 and led to victory by the Progressives (or Liberals). The first chairman of the LCC was Archibald, first Earl of Rosebery, a prominent Liberal, who went on to become Prime Minister in 1894. As chairman from 1889 to 1890, Rosebery proved a critic of slum-landlordism. More generally, the LCC – the world's largest municipal authority – took an activist role in trying to expand its powers and improve London life, a role based on a strong sense of mission and a capacity to produce information on which policy could be based.

The politics of London were also transformed as the Conservatives benefited from the long-term expansion of the middle classes, and became an increasingly urban- and suburban-based party. In this, the Conservatives profited from the perceived radicalism of Gladstonian Liberalism, which drove the newly anxious middle classes, ironically the beneficiaries of the meritocratic reforms of the first Gladstone ministry, into the Conservative camp. The Conservatives, in turn, had become a party defending the property of the many, rather than social privilege. In 1882, Robert, third Marquess of Salisbury, later Conservative Prime Minister, wrote of the rise of 'a great Villa Toryism which requires organisation'. This middle-class move away from the Liberals in part reflected a reaction based on self-interest, namely opposition to the spread in the power and activity of local government, which led to new commitments, not least by school boards, pushing up municipal rates. As also with subsequent rallies to the Conservatives in London, rising tax demands pressed on a society that, in the 1880s, was less buoyant and, crucially, less confident economically, than it had been. Salisbury, Prime Minister from 1885 to 1886, 1886 to 1892 and 1895 to 1902, himself derived most of his disposable income from urban property, including London slums.

London's electoral weight itself had increased due to the Redistribution of Seats Act (1885), which was designed to leave the number of MPs proportional to the voting population, although some seats such as rapidly growing Croydon had a disproportionately large electorate. Whereas 25 Liberal MPs had been elected from the London area in 1892, in 1895 the Unionists (Conservatives allied with Liberal Unionists who had abandoned Gladstone over Ireland) won 53 seats compared to 8 for the Liberals. These results reflected the strength of a metropolitan Conservatism that was separate from the more suburban villa-dom. The former was the product of the appeal of Conservatism to significant working-class and lower middle-class interests.[22] Indeed, London was on average markedly Conservative in the period 1885–1910. Working-class support for the Conservatives in London owed something to opposition to immigration, to support for drinking (threatened by Liberal support for temperance), and to the backing of workers who had a degree of rights in their work, for example costermongers who saw their pitches as freeholds.[23] Similarly, the Convocation of the University of London, which, from 1868, elected the university MP, switched, after 1886, from Liberal to Liberal Unionist.

Prefiguring the situation for the Greater London Council faced by the Conservative government of Margaret Thatcher in the 1980s, the Conservatives under Salisbury were worried by the radicalism of the LCC. which was held by the Progressives from 1889 to 1895. In these years, the LCC pushed through the Blackwall Tunnel, the free Woolwich ferry and the building of a council housing estate at Boundary Street, while the Progressives became more radical in their language, composition and policy, and also pressed for greater attention to be given to the East End.

In 1895 the LCC elections saw a move toward the Moderates (or Conservatives), but the Progressives regained their majority in 1898. In turn, Conservative concerns led, in 1899, under the Government of London Act passed by the Conservative government, to the transfer of several of its roles to twenty-seven new metropolitan boroughs, alongside the City of London.

With marked parallels with the late twentieth century, notably over the privatisation of municipal services, the Conservatives had complained about the extent to which the LCC employed labour directly on public works schemes, which they presented as undercutting private businesses. There was also tension within London between prosperous areas, such as Westminster and Kensington, which were angered by what they saw as the need to finance less affluent areas, such as Deptford and Poplar. This need stemmed from the Metropolis Rate Equalisation Act passed in 1894 by the Liberal government, which had established a uniform rate across London, including the City, redistributing the yield in proportion to the population. In response, the prosperous areas pressed for the separate borough status they gained in 1899, Kensington leading the call. Thus, in weakening the LCC, the Conservatives also served their local interests. In the event, the Conservatives, now called Municipal Reformers, gained control of the LCC in 1907, retaining it until 1934, and in 1921 there was to be a similar dispute about the impact of large-scale outdoor relief to the poor in the Labour East End stronghold of Poplar as the other boroughs refused to contribute towards the cost. As a major mark of civic pride as well as a functioning headquarters, County Hall was designed for the LCC by Ralph Knott in 1909, although it was not to be completed until 1933.

The establishment of the metropolitan boroughs created under the Act of 1899 also brought to an end the situation in which parishes such as St Mary's Islington and St Pancras had been major administrative units. Indeed, both became boroughs, and, while the LCC was responsible for mains drainage and the fire service, the metropolitan boroughs replaced the parish vestries and district boards of work as the key local tier of government. The new borough of Westminster was soon also given the designation of city.

Politics was becoming more class-orientated, and the social order could be harsh as well as inegalitarian. A London campaign against street prostitution, launched in 1883, came to an end, in 1887, amid public complaints and parliamentary questions about the blackmailing of poor prostitutes, bribery of the police, and police harassment through arrests. By then, the Metropolitan Police were commanded from Scotland Yard, which had been bought for them by the Home Office in 1886 for £186,000.

A radical political current was also coming to the fore, one that had survived from Chartism, notably with the socialistic Chartism of the Irish-born James 'Bronterre' O'Brien (1805–64). Radical clubs were most active in London and provided the background for the First International Workingmen's Association in 1864, the Reform League demonstrations of 1866–67, the Manhood Suffrage League in the mid-1870s, the agitation, in the early 1880s around the refusal to allow an avowed atheist, Charles Bradlaugh, to take his seat in the House of Commons, the Socialist revival in the 1880s, and the major London demonstrations in 1887.

On 13 November 1887 – 'Bloody Sunday' – a meeting called by the Metropolitan Radical Association in protest against the government's failure to tackle unemployment was banned. Large numbers of police sought to block the entry of the march into Trafalgar Square, which led to a violent clash involving over 400 arrests and about 200 casualties, including two deaths. The previous year, riots by the unemployed in central London included attacks on expensive Piccadilly stores. There were rumours of widespread unrest among the south London poor.[24]

In turn, radical pressures from within the Liberal Party were supplemented, in London and elsewhere, by the creation of more explicitly working-class movements, both political and industrial. The development of trade unions reflected a new, more adversarial and combative working-class consciousness. There were major strikes in the London gasworks and docks in 1888–89, which helped radicalise the local Progressives, and, in 1900, the Labour Representation Committee, the basis of the Labour Party, was created.

Over the following decade, the Labour Party increasingly defined radical politics and Labour developed strong local roots, especially in the East End. Electoral victories, such as those of Keir Hardie in West Ham, South, in 1892 and of the Poplar politician Will Crooks at the Woolwich by-election in 1903, became more frequent, and radical issues were therefore presented in Parliament. As the first Labour mayor of Poplar and as MP, Crooks advanced the cases for unemployed workers and a minimum wage. Labour's support and activities were strongest in the East End, and far weaker in west London, which was far more integrated into the service sectors of the economy. The politics of the left thus added yet another layer of spatial differentiation within London, as well as contributing to the politicisation of the more engaged parts of the working population, as can be seen in the town meetings held in places such as Battersea.[25]

Yet, Labour also made fewer inroads in the LCC area than in the North, and in the 1906 general election only won Deptford and Woolwich; the East End remained in Liberal hands. The strength Labour was to show in London after the First World War and the introduction of universal male adult suffrage in 1918 was not yet apparent.

However, the rise in trade union and Labour activity led to new public occasions and displays, as with the May Day Procession in Central London in 1912. Photographs of the scene show large numbers of mostly male walkers, smartly dressed with jackets, ties and collars, escorted by the police. Brass bands were in attendance. At the same time, Docklands, in 1911–12, faced serious labour problems as a result of Syndicalist agitation.

More radical views were also disseminated. In 1885 the group variously termed the 'Hampstead Marx Circle' or 'Hampstead Historic Society', which included George Bernard Shaw and Sidney Webb, began meeting to discuss the work of Karl Marx. Two years later, an English translation of *Das Kapital* was published in London. Webb's *London Programme* (1891) pressed the Progressives to expand LCC powers to include control over gas, water, transport and the building of public-sector housing.

Greater radicalism contributed to, and in part reflected and sustained a sense of doubt, if not a crisis of confidence, in late-Victorian society. The demand for reform was matched by a pressure for security, the two combining to produce an uneasiness about present and future that fed into debate about the condition of the people. Concern about the extent of London's poverty, and the associated social problems, encouraged enumeration and analysis, led to calls for public action, and promoted charitable missions. Clement Attlee, Labour Prime Minister from 1945 to 1951, was converted to socialism by visiting, in 1905, Haileybury House, a boys' club in Stepney run by members of his old school, and he took over as manager of the club two years later.

Economic issues contributed to the feeling of doubt, if not crisis. By 1900, American and German competition was pressing hard on British industry, which hit London greatly as it was a major centre of manufacturing. The strength of the modern, technically advanced German chemical industry, for instance, affected the coal-based chemical factories of the East End. Yet, although Britain fell to being the third-ranking industrial state, she still dominated the service sector of the world economy, a sector that, with globalisation, was growing greatly in size and importance. This dominance increased London's influence within Britain as that sector was directed from the City and grew greatly there, the business on the Stock Exchange for example increasing substantially in the 1860s. From the 1870s,

New York became a key financial centre that was to challenge London, but London's was the busiest stock exchange in the world throughout the century, and that at a time when the ability to raise investment income was of steadily greater global importance. The London financial world benefited enormously from the expertise and connections it deployed, which were a product of unrivalled accumulated experience, excellent communications, and a willingness to accept skilled immigrants.

Organised through London, Britain was the leading overseas investor in the world, notably in the USA but also across the empire, as well as outside it. For example, £600,000 was raised in London to finance the construction of the Paris–Rouen railway line in 1843, and £5.5 million in 1851 for the far longer St Petersburg–Moscow line. London and Britain were able, therefore, to benefit from economic growth elsewhere. Sterling, from the 1820s, on the gold standard (fixed against other currencies on the basis of its value in gold), was the major currency used in international trade and finance and, as such, the international reserve currency in a global financial system that relied on a fixed exchange rate regime. The export of vast quantities of investment capital from the 1820s, including to the USA and Latin America, where it was fundamental to economic development, played a crucial role in the rise of the City as the leading world financial centre, as well as defining the character of such a centre.

Overseas income as a percentage of British gross domestic product rose from 2 per cent in 1872 to 7 per cent in 1913, the sum invested, moreover, being far more than for any other European country. In 1914, 43 per cent of the world's foreign investment was British, and, as an important index of its global role, Britain was also the sole state in Europe selling more outside the Continent than in European markets. The service sector was crucial to the economic strength of the country, for invisible earnings more than offset the deficit on Britain's external trade. The inflow of interest on investments helped to maintain a strong balance of payments, and thus to keep up the exchange rate of the pound sterling. Global commodity prices, shipping rates and insurance premiums were all set in London. London's financial strength helped ensure its political influence in Britain and overseas.

The global trading system was speeded up by steamships and telegraphs, in both of which Britain led the world, and each of which was organised from London, and this system benefited greatly from the fall in shipping freight rates. The opening of the Suez Canal in 1869 also helped by reducing the sailing distance from London to India by about 4,500 miles and also cutting the distances to points further east, such as Singapore and Shanghai. This led to a marked cut in freight costs and an increase in trade to the Indian Ocean and the Far East, so that direct trade between London and the Persian ports, for instance, tripled between 1873 and 1878.

The responsibility of the London service sector for the wider character and subsequent problems of the British economy has been much debated. Management failure has been linked to mistaken investment strategies, and it has been argued that the institutional providers of investment in the City, especially the banks, shared in a culture of complacency and gentlemanly amateurism. This problem has been traced to a series of inter-related cultural norms and practices, such as a suspicion of expertise and technical skills, which inhibited efficiency and encouraged false patterns of investment. London indeed was the prime site of what has been called gentlemanly investment, although such criticisms are difficult to prove or quantify.

More specifically, it has been suggested that there was a preference for investing in well-established companies rather than in developing sectors. Risk or venture capital was thus insufficient and too expensive: interest rates were too high. Furthermore, aside from this pattern of industrial investment, there was also a preference for non-industrial investment, both on the 'money markets', for example in British and foreign government bonds, and in housing. Even when there was investment in industry – old or new – much of it was poorly directed because of an absence of sufficient professionalism in information flows within the capital market. Moreover, much investment was short-term, responding to myopic institutional shareholders unwilling to commit sufficiently to long-term investments. Similar charges were to be made about the City in the late twentieth century and 2000s. In contrast, it has been suggested that American and German capital markets were more effective in providing large flows of investment income for technologically advanced industries before the First World War, such as cars, chemicals and electrical engineering.

London itself was being physically transformed, as the housing stock responded to the pressure of the rapidly growing population. The city had a vast array of housing types, which was unsurprising for a sprawling metropolis built up over the centuries. The classic terraced house – that utilitarian type of dwelling which still dominates much of London – was rare in the 1830s and also beyond the means of poorer working-class families. It was not until the 1860s that the terraced streets we know today were being built, and many date from after that. By the 1870s, a standard version of working-class housing was the two-up-two-down 'through terrace' – with its access at both front and rear, sometimes with a small garden or back yard, and of solid construction and adequately ventilated. Increasingly, this was becoming the standard dwelling. Moreover, the quality of this housing improved in the 1900s, not least with better insulation. Under the 1894 London Building Act, window area had to equal to or greater than a tenth of the floor area in all new rooms intended for human habitation. Nevertheless, many of the poor and casually employed still lived in one-roomed dwellings, tenements, back-to-backs, rookeries and courts, and would continue to do so until the Second World War. Many of their walls ran with damp; sanitation was often primitive; and poorly swept chimneys contributed to the fug in many homes.

The traditional terraced house was a great improvement on the back-to-backs, the lodging-house and the damp cellar in which all-too-many had lived. Terraced houses were built at a time when covered sewerage systems and adequately piped clean water were being included in new residences. Indeed, from 1875 it was mandatory to provide lavatories in new houses. These houses, with their separate rooms, enabled greater definition of the spheres of domestic activity, from chatting or reading to eating or sleeping, all of which had implications for family behaviour and gender roles.

Terraced houses were usually built in straight streets. This pattern replaced an earlier style of layout frequently described in terms of a warren. This earlier style has been difficult to keep clean or to light because it contained so many self-enclosed alleyways, closes or courts. In contrast, the straight streets of terraced houses, equally apportioned and relatively spaciously laid out, were easier to light and to provide with supplies of gas, water and drainage. This situation was true not only of areas as a whole, but also of individual properties. The removal of the Brick Tax in 1850 encouraged the large-scale use of bricks in construction, and their use helped keep damp at bay. Similarly, the end of the Wallpaper Tax in 1861 affected the interior of London houses. William Morris established a wallpaper manufacturing business in the Wandle valley in 1881. Technology also played a role, as in the provision of inexpensive linoleum from the mid-1870s as an effective floor-covering. A different type of housing was provided by mansion flats, which became important in parts of west London, though also in Bloomsbury.

At every level, new homes met the demand for self-improvement and status. An important aspect of London, which clearly defined manners, customs and social attitudes, was the desire of the lower-middle-class shop-owner or clerk to retain what he had. The petit-bourgeoisie were at the same time jealous of their superiors, but even more horror-struck at the thought of sinking back into the mass of their inferiors, a prospect made more apparent because there was no residential segregation. The poor in London lived across the city, for example in the Potteries area of Kensington,[26] not least in order to enable them to serve the needs of the prosperous. The result was a complex pattern of wealth and poverty, one that added local variations to the more general contrasts between, in particular, West and East Ends.

The social politics of the petit-bourgeoisie were important to London's trajectory, and looked toward the expansion of suburbia after the First World War. The embodiment of the view of the petit-bourgeoisie was George and Weedon Grossmith's *The Diary of a Nobody* (1892), the story of Charles Pooter, a fictional lower-middle-class clerk from Holloway. The Pooters rent a house rather too close to the railway line (the landlord lets it go cheap because of the noise), and fill their lives with the snobberies they imagine to be typical of a slightly higher class. Delivery men and servants they can ill afford are made to use the rear entrance of what is, in fact, a rather modest town house. The idea of maintaining an abode slightly too expensive for Pooter's salary typifies the anxieties of this much-parodied class which lived in suburbs such as Camberwell, Hackney and Islington.

In contrast, there was less pretension in the activities recorded by the rector of Bethnal Green in 1895:

> a vast majority of the men in your district will have spent their Sundays for the last twenty-five years and their fathers before them, in the following way: they will have lain in bed till about eleven or twelve, having been up early all week; they will then go round when the public-houses open, which they do at one; they will have what they call a 'wet' till three … they will then have dinner, the great dinner of the week, which the missus has been preparing all the morning. Then comes a lie down on the bed in shirt sleeves until five, with a pot of beer and *Lloyd's Weekly*; then follows tea, and after tea a bit of a walk round to see a friend or a relation; then fairly early to bed to make up for a very late Saturday night.

This was another view of the world of work depicted more heroically in Ford Madox Brown's painting *Work* (1863), the navvies of which were based on those Brown saw working in Hampstead. A harsher note was struck in Andrew Mearns' tract *The Bitter Cry of Outcast London* (1883), which exposed conditions in the Mint rookery, Southwark.

This social commentary, however, found few echoes of the stage. The theatre was dominated by actor-managers such as Henry Irving (1838–1905), who became lessee and manager of the Lyceum in 1878. There, his emphasis was on the opulence and drama of production, not the novelty of the play, and he shunned the work of George Bernard Shaw with its preference for radical debate. The London-based 'long-run' system replaced the high-cost permanent companies, necessary for a repertory (range) of plays, with long runs of single plays, for example Brandon Thomas' upper-class comedy *Charley's Aunt* (1892). The success of this approach could best be secured by undemanding plays by new stars, such as Irving's leading lady Ellen Terry, spectacular productions with an emphasis on scenery and music, familiar plots and uncontentious approaches. Augustus Harris, manager of the Theatre Royal at Drury Lane from 1879 until 1896, set the tone with spectaculars featuring avalanches, earthquakes, horse-races and snowstorms.

This system did not encourage adventurous drama, but brought profit to managements, encouraging investment in new theatres, such as the Prince of Wales (1884), Her Majesty's (1887), and the Lyric (1888). The Savoy Theatre was built by the impresario Richard D'Oyly Carte to take advantage of the success of Gilbert and Sullivan's comic Savoy Operas. This profitable theatrical world persisted until the cinema made a major impact from the 1910s. For the years prior to Shaw and Oscar Wilde, this period did not leave many plays that are still performed today. Musical comedy with a modern setting flourished with *The Gaiety Girl* (1893) by George Edwardes, and from 1894 at the Gaiety Theatre he brought on a new version of this popular work each season. His 'showgirls' were largely recruited from the middle-class suburbs, and some were able to translate starring roles into marriage into the aristocracy.

Nevertheless, there were 'social problem' plays, not least those by Sir Arthur Wing Pinero (1855–1934). Born in London, the son of a lawyer, he became an actor and writer of farce before considering the harsh position of women in British society. The most effective play, *The Second Mrs Tanqueray*, first performed at the St James's Theatre in 1893, has the protagonist reveal her past to prevent the marriage of her step-daughter to her seducer, before committing suicide to save the family from shame. Others included *The Notorious Mrs Ebbsmith* (1895) and *Iris* (1901).

There were equivalent paintings, too, such as George Frederic Watts' *Found Drowned* (1849–50), a reference to the lists of women, mostly prostitutes, found dead in the Thames, and Luke Fildes' *Applicants for Admission to a Casual Ward* (1874). On the whole, however, the London art world provided the comfortable art its purchasers expected: portraits (on which Watts specialised), family scenes, landscapes, or the historical and exotic works produced by Frederic, Lord Leighton (1830–96) and Sir Lawrence Alma-Tadema (1836–1912). Elizabeth Butler made her name with battle scenes.

Their success ensured that artists were able to purchase homes in smart areas such as Kensington, Holland Park, where Leighton lived, and St John's Wood where, amid Victorian villas, Alma-Tadema created one decorated on the model of Pompeii. The sums paid for paintings were a reflection of the opulence of London and the breadth of its art market. The traditional pattern of talent coming to London where it thrived was also shown: Leighton was born in Scarborough, Alma-Tadema in the Netherlands, Ford Madox Brown in Calais, and William P. Frith (1819–1909), noted for his painting of Paddington Station, was born in Yorkshire. Watts, in contrast, was London-born, as was Sir Edwin Landseer (1802–73) who specialised in painting dogs and deer, and William Morris (1834–96), whose work and ideas transformed the art of house decoration and furniture. Art had links with the Continent, not least as a result of the entrepreneurial activity of gallery owners such as the Belgian-born Ernest Gambart who, in mid-century, founded a French Gallery in Pall Mall. In the second half of the century, London became the centre of the world's commercial art market.

London was more advanced as a centre of music than of drama, in part because it was more open to Continental influences. Joseph Haydn had been a great success on his visits in 1791–92 and 1794–95, writing *The Creation* for London. Spohr was invited over in 1819 by the Philharmonic Society, which also commissioned Beethoven's Ninth Symphony. Rossini had mixed success, but made much money in 1824, and Weber composed his opera *Oberon* for Covent Garden in 1826, only to die of tuberculosis in London soon after the successful opening. Johann Strauss the Elder and his orchestra came over for Victoria's coronation in 1838 and was extremely successful, and in 1847 Verdi produced his new opera, *I Masnadieri*, at the new Royal Italian Opera at Covent Garden, winning a good response. Continental pianists, such as Franz Liszt in 1827, Henri Herz and Sigismund Thalberg, were very popular in London. Offenbach's operettas reached London in the 1860s, and Strauss's *Die Fledermaus* in 1875. Edward Dannreuther introduced the concertos of Chopin, Grieg, Liszt and Tchaikovsky to London audiences and organised Wagner programmes, while Hans Richter gave a series of annual concerts in London from 1879 until 1897. In 1911, Diaghilev's *Ballet Russe* also came to London.

Music-hall was more robust than theatre. It had variety – song, music, acrobatics, dance – and emphasised an interaction between performers and audience. Charles Morton, who founded the Canterbury at Lambeth in 1851, is seen as 'the father of the music-hall'. The London Pavilion followed in 1861. Music-hall was performance art; although the songs were printed and sold in large numbers, the printed version could not command the impact of singers such as the Great MacDermott, Dan Leno, Harry Lauder or Marie Lloyd. They and other singers acted songs such as 'Oh, Mister Porter', 'A Little of What You Fancy …', and 'The Galloping Major' (who gallops so much his new wife returns to her mother), to suggest a sexuality that was banished from other forms of public culture.

Indeed, Marie Lloyd (1870–1922), though 'the Queen of the Halls', was not socially acceptable and was not invited to perform at the Royal Command Performance in 1912, responding by adding to her posters 'Every performance given by Marie Lloyd is a command performance by Order of the British Public'. Yet, this was big business, whereas the individual music of street entertainers was ended by the Vagrancy Act of 1824 and subsequent police action. Indeed, control of the streets, a continual theme in London's history, was so policed that even the Salvation Army was technically liable to prosecution.

Music-hall lent itself to the new cinema. On 20 February 1896, the first films seen by a paying public in Britain were shown at the Regent Street Polytechnic, with 54 people paying a shilling each to see a sequence of short films by the Lumière brothers, a show also seen in the Empire, Leicester Square, a fortnight later. Jack Hunt, a private in the Scots Guards, described, in a letter to his brother, the British entry into Pretoria in 1900 during the Boer War: 'When we marched into the market square headed by Lord Roberts to raise the flag they took our photo by the cinematograph so I expect you will see it on some of the music-halls in London.'[27]

Empire was indeed staged actively, in music-hall, melodrama, blackface minstrelsy and exhibitions such as *The Empire of India* staged in London in 1895, or the *Stanley and Africa* exhibition five years earlier. Over 2.5 million visitors thronged the naval exhibition on the Thames embankment from May to October 1891.[28] In 1900 large London crowds, many of them clerks and medical students, applauded the relief of Mafeking in South Africa from Boer siege.

New theatres and music-halls were an important aspect of the expanding cultural infrastructure. So also were the museums and art galleries that proclaimed London's civic pride and cultural status, and offered improvement. The civic building is a major part of the cultural heritage of the nineteenth century.[29] In the twentieth century, especially during the post-1945 Modernist vogue, Victorian architecture was much castigated, and many buildings were destroyed, neglected or left stranded amid a new world of concrete and cars. Those destroyed included the Coal Exchange and the Entrance Arch at Euston

Roughly coincidental with the arrival of the motor car, the practice of pedestrians standing in silent reverence as a funeral cortege went by gradually died out. Here such an event is taking place at one of the busiest places in the capital: right outside the Euston Arch which used to act as principal entrance to the station. As reported at its opening in 1837, this was 'the Grand Avenue for travelling between the Metropolis and the midland and northern parts of the Kingdom … [and] the Directors [of the London and Birmingham Railway] thought that it should receive some architectural embellishment. They adopted accordingly a design of Mr Hardwick's for a grand but simple portico, which they considered well adapted to the national character of the undertaking.' Despite concerted and increasingly desperate attempts to save it, the portico was demolished in 1961 as part of the modernisation of the terminus for what had become the main west-coast rail line to Scotland. Many of the stones were used to fill a hole in a bed of the river Lea, which historian Dan Cruickshank rediscovered; the Euston Arch Trust which he founded is seeking to have the arch dug up and re-erected as part of a new Euston station revamp.

Nothing now remains of the London and Birmingham's London original terminus at Euston. The entrance lodges (1870) and war memorial seen here were both later additions. The Great Hall of the station (1849) was demolished at about the same time as the great Euston Arch which stood between the lodges, and the statue of the railway's engineer, Robert Stephenson, by Baron Carlo Marochetti, was consigned to the modernist piazza outdoors after the demise of the Great Hall.

Station, while the Midland Grand Hotel at St Pancras was left to rot, until recently restored as a giant apartment complex. Nevertheless, a large amount survives in central London, and these buildings remain an aspect of the culture that can be readily approached.

The early decades of the nineteenth century witnessed a variety of architectural styles. Neo-classicism was particularly important. The neo-classicism of the late eighteenth century drew heavily on Roman models, but that of the early nineteenth was dominated by Greek Revival, including the Doric and Ionic orders. Architects such as William Wilkins, Robert Smirke, C.R. Cockerell and H.W. Inswood all made lengthy trips to Greece.

Neo-Gothic was also highly influential, especially in ecclesiastical architecture, while the case was pushed hard by Augustus Pugin (1812–52), an architect who saw Gothic as the quintessentially Christian style. His arguments and designs hit home at the right moment as, after a long period in which relatively few new churches had been built, there was a period of massive church-building. This owed much to London's geographical expansion and to a determination to resist what many at the time saw as 'Godless London'; meanwhile, Catholic Emancipation in 1829 was followed by the building of many Catholic churches. Influential architects in the Gothic Revival included Sir George Gilbert Scott, William Buterfield, G.E. Street, Norman Shaw and Alfred Waterhouse. They were active in building and 'restoring' churches. Butterfield's work includes All Saints, Margaret Street (1859). There was also much secular building in the Gothic style, especially from the 1850s as it replaced Greek Revival. Scott's work included the huge Midland Grand Hotel at St Pancras (1865–71) and the Albert Memorial (1872), while other prominent buildings included George Edmund Street's Royal Courts of Justice on the Strand (1874–82) and Waterhouse's Holborn headquarters for the Prudential Assurance Company (1895–1905).

Yet Gothic Revival did not enjoy an unchallenged ascendancy. Displaying the eclecticism that was a feature of the period, Sir Charles Barry (1795–1860) worked in both Gothic (Houses of Parliament finished in 1860) and Greek Revival styles, but also developed a neo-Renaissance style, using Italian palazzi as models. This neo-Renaissance style was also employed by other architects, such as Gilbert Scott in his Foreign Office building. These grand buildings were central to the competition between the leading European cities as, in the full glare of publicity, they vied to hold the best exhibitions, build the most glorious monuments, develop the most impressive infrastructure, and so on.

The elaborate patterned brick-Byzantine tower of Westminster (RC) Cathedral, just off Victoria Street, which is clearly visible from vantage points such as Primrose Hill to the north. The main structure took just eight years to build following the laying of the foundation stone in 1895, but the interior decoration is still incomplete.

PHOTOGRAPH: CARNEGIE, 2008

New forms of transport and industrial technology ushered in new types of functional architecture and construction. The most famous single building in this category was probably Paxton's Crystal Palace, but railway stations and, more generally, iron-fronted commercial and industrial premises recorded and helped popularise new styles. The current east and west buildings of Smithfield Market were finished in 1868 at a cost of nearly £1 million. Functionalism took many forms. The Central Criminal Court, known as the Old Bailey after the street in which it is situated, built in 1907 on the site of Newgate Prison, contains not only eighteen courtrooms, but also Dead Man's Walk, the route to the gallows, which was designed with the arches becoming progressively smaller in order to stop the prisoners looking back.

A similar institutional legacy is seen in areas such as education. Thus, the London School of Economics was founded in 1895, in part thanks to help from the LCC, while, in 1902, the LCC and the University of London jointly founded the London Day Training College to provide training for elementary teaching. It became the Institute of Education in 1932, a research centre now partly divorced from the needs of the city, like all too many of the institutions founded there.

Returning to comfortable theatrical London, audiences were not used to seeing the plight of poorer Londoners depicted, and a lack of understanding of this plight was generally linked to a lack of engagement. At the same time, social missions to the poor of the East End, for example that based in Toynbee Hall, testified to a personal commitment to action that drew together disparate religious, paternalistic and radical socio-political themes. These looked toward the engagement with improvement over the following century, an engagement that encouraged central and municipal government action, but often without much understanding of the dynamics of local communities.

London, meanwhile, was being changed through improvements in transport. The volume of traffic reflected the intense web of connections that made up London life. In 1899 Sir J.W. Barry estimated that eight horse-drawn buses a minute would pass an observer on Tottenham Court Road,[30] an intensity that posed the problem of disposing of manure. The application of new power sources was important to transport, first electricity and then the internal combustion engine. Electricity permitted the improvement of the tram network; London's first electric tramway was established in 1901, running from Shepherd's Bush to Acton. Electric trams were quicker and carried more passengers than horse trams and cost less than buses.

As earlier with the trains, however, there was scant cohesion among the tramways that spread rapidly until the beginning of the First World War. The LCC was responsible for central sections, with private operators such as Imperial Tramways in west London, and boroughs such as East Ham active in the east. The trams of Metropolitan Electric Tramways served areas of north London, for example Barnet, that were to be greatly developed when the Underground system spread outwards. By 1914 the LCC services were carrying close to two-thirds of London's tram passengers. Toward the close of the period, the spread of suburbia was given greater energy by the development of electric train services, as well as by the establishment of bus networks. By 1913 London had 1,000 motor buses.

With such mounting transport pressure, the principal purpose of London's streets came to be as a means for circulation rather than for sociability, household tasks, leisure, manufacturing, trade and shopping. This change, which was a fundamental aspect of the difference between cities and smaller settlements, helped in the breakdown of communities

A garden-seat horse bus operated by W.S. Birch & Son, seen in front of the National Gallery in 1897. George Shillibeer had begun the first horse bus service in 1829, while Thomas Tilling began a service from Peckham to Oxford Street with just one horse bus in 1850.

within London: communities of shared space, as opposed to the shared activities of, for example, religion or sport. People were subordinated to outside purpose, with the utilitarianism of an emphasis on improved traffic taking precedence over other goals; and this emphasis was linked to the regulation of public space and activity by the police. The ability of residents to affect the use of public space was limited, a situation that remains the case today.

Within the more central area, which was too crowded to permit overground railways, the Underground system provided new transport links. The first underground railway in London – indeed the world – was the Metropolitan Railway, which linked Bishop's Road, Paddington, and Farringdon in the City, a distance of just four miles, and was

The early steam-operated underground routes needed open-air sections at regular intervals to reduce smoke build-up in the tunnels, and in this photograph we can see that numbers 23 and 24 Leinster Gardens in Bayswater have been demolished during the construction of the District Line in the 1860s to make way for such a vent. The façades of the houses were rebuilt as two dummy houses to match the rest of the street, with painted windows, blocked front doors and no letter boxes.

MUSEUM OF LONDON

London honours in public sculpture not only monarchs and generals, but civil engineers such as James Henry Greathead (1844–96), whose statue near Bank Station was unveiled in 1994. Greathead designed the tunnelling shield that made it possible to tunnel the deep 'Tubes' of the expanding Underground system. The first application of his technique, whereby a 2-ton cylindrical 'cutter' was forced through the soil by hand-screw, thus forming the tunnel and simultaneously protecting the workers, was the Tower Subway. This was designed and built in 1868–69 as a sort of shuttle service under the Thames, from Tower Hill to Tooley Street in Southwark, in which a stationary engine drew a single car on rails from one side to the other, arguably making it the world's first 'railway' that was completely underground. It did not catch on, and the Tower Subway was used instead for pedestrian traffic from 1870 until it was made redundant as a means of crossing the river by the building of Tower Bridge just downstream in 1894. The Tower Subway tunnel still carries water mains and communications cables under the river; the Subway 'entrance' which can still be seen near the Tower is not original.

PHOTOGRAPH: CARNEGIE, 2009

opened in 1863. It was built close to the surface using the 'cut and cover' method of tunnel construction and, as the trains were steam-hauled, had to tackle the problem of how to ventilate the tunnel and remove the smoke. The trains were also gas-lit. With its low fares compared to the horse-drawn bus, the new line was very popular, and the system spread, with separate companies constructing individual lines. Relations were not always good, with the Metropolitan Railway having poor ones with the second line, the Metropolitan District Railway. Nevertheless, the Inner Circle (now the Circle Line), which incorporated part of both systems, was completed in 1884. No other British city had an underground railway until Glasgow opened one in 1896.

The spread of the Underground was helped by the replacement of 'cut and cover' by the use of a tunnelling shield, the basis of the deep-bore 'Tube' tunnels, the first of which opened between Tower Hill and Bermondsey in 1870. Eschewing steam-haulage, it was cable-operated. The Tube system was also used to construct the City and South London Railway between King William Street in the City and Stockwell, which opened in 1890, now the City branch of the Northern Line. It was the first underground electric railway in the world. This line was followed by the Waterloo and City Line (1898) and the Central London Railway (the Central Line) between Shepherd's Bush and Bank (1900). The existing District and Metropolitan Railways switched to electricity, with the Circle electrified in 1905. The great success of the Central Line encouraged the building of other lines, notably the Bakerloo, Piccadilly, and Hampstead to Charing Cross lines, with the key figure being Charles Tyson Yerkes, an American financier of dubious practices but boundless energy. The Northern line ran from Angel to Clapham in 1901. The Piccadilly, opened in 1906, initially ran from Hammersmith to Finsbury Park, making it the longest line that fed commuters and shoppers from western London into the West End. Sensing the possibilities of expanding London, Yerkes planned an extension for the Charing Cross, Euston and Hampstead Railway (also known as the Hampstead Line) to Golders Green, which opened in 1907. However, there was no large-scale expansion of the system into Docklands. In 1909, another American, Gordon Selfridge, opened the West End's largest department store, one that occupied an entire block of Oxford Street.

New and existing transport systems created multiple links within London, bringing new possibilities for individual parts of the city. The population of Acton increased from 3,000 in 1861 to 38,000 in 1901, while that of St Pancras, over 100,000 in 1831, had nearly doubled by 1861 and by 1901 was 235,000, although, by then, its growth had ceased as areas further from the centre became the centre of growth. By 1901 the parish of St Mary's, Islington, had a population of over 330,000. The fastest growing urban areas in 1891–1901 were inner suburbs: Walthamstow and West Ham, the latter a major centre of manufacturing as well as a county borough, and both linked to central London by the transport system.

In *Anticipations* (1901), the novelist H.G. Wells wrote positively about the role of satellite towns, of the suburbs and of transport networks making possible the expansion of cities into large metropolitan spaces. The suburbs were explored anew in Wells' feminist novel *Ann Veronica* (1909), by when many women were using the safety bicycle introduced from 1885, as well as the more comfortable pneumatic tire added in 1890, to visit the suburbs and the countryside. In turn, the possibilities created by commuting – along with the higher rental yields of office buildings in the centre – contributed to the marked fall in the City's residential population – from 112,000 in 1861 to fewer than 38,000 in 1891.

London's greater size led to disquiet, both within and outside the metropolis. Nevertheless, this expansion was generally applauded as an attribute of an imperial city that was a force for progress in past, present and future. A close correspondence between national destiny and metropolitan activity was frequently asserted. In part, this argument rested on the association of London with commerce and activity, and not with parasitical consumption. Thus, Charles Pearson, in his *Historical Maps of England during the First Thirteen Centuries* (1869), noted of the civil war of Stephen's reign (1135–54), that whereas 'the Empress Matilda, who represented the not infrequent combination of a legitimate title and an oppressive government', drew her support from the upland, conservative west, Stephen was backed by London 'and the commercial towns of the east'. Similarly, in the 1260s, 'London and the south and east were with the great constitutional leader De Montfort', while in the Wars of the Roses the Yorkist party, which on the whole was that of good government, 'received partisans from the same district as De Montfort'. Similar comments were made about the English Civil War of 1642–46. Thus, London's position was clearly located in terms of a nineteenth-century view of progress through the limitation of royal authority. London also served as the setting for an exemplary national history, as with Daniel Maclise's paintings. *Wellington and Blücher at Waterloo* (1866) and *The Death of Nelson* (1864), both in the new palace of Westminster.

The widespread concern for social welfare embodied within late-Victorian values helped ensure a significant amelioration in living conditions, especially the decline of epidemic disease. This had already begun before medicine had the expertise to influence their morbidity and mortality directly. The supply of clean water was important. Typhus had virtually disappeared by the 1890s; typhoid was brought under partial control; and death rates from tuberculosis and scarlet fever declined. Improved diet, thanks, in part, to a significant fall in food prices, played an important role in the decline in mortality rates, while medical advances, not least the replacement of the 'miasma' theory of disease by that of 'germs', helped. Variations in rates of mortality between registration districts, nevertheless, persisted, with a noticeable, though not invariable, relationship between life expectancy and population density. The only infection seriously to affect adults by 1900 was tuberculosis, but the childhood killers were still rampant. The burial records of the Bonner Hill cemetery in Kingston indicate that over the period 1855 to 1911, one third of all burials was of children aged four or under. Diphtheria and measles were particularly serious killers, but neither was tackled adequately by medical provision, and the situation was exacerbated by the number of damp houses.[31]

The varied living standards charted by Charles Booth in his maps of London had many consequences. Affluent workers, benefiting from the low price of food, provided a key support for the growth of consumerism in London, which affected both the world of things and leisure activities. The cinema joined the music-hall, and food outlets multiplied, the first permanent Lyons teashop being founded in 1894. Low pay, casual work and underemployment ensured, however, that many in the urban working class could not share in these benefits.

Social welfare was pushed in the early twentieth century by the Liberal government in power at the national level from 1905, in large part in response to concerns about the 'condition of the people'. Free school meals (1907) were

The May Day procession along Kingsway in 1912.
GETTY IMAGES

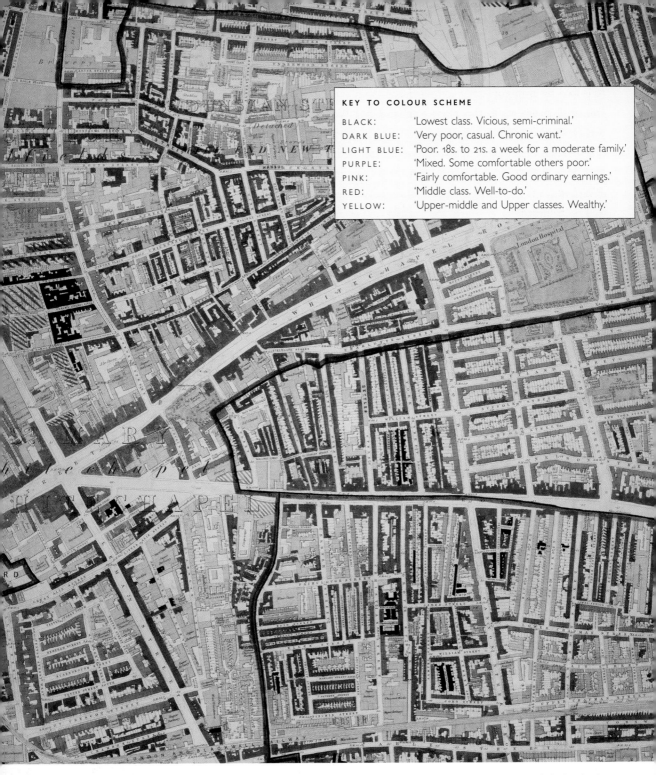

Sheet number 28 of Charles Booth's 'Maps Descriptive of London Poverty', the most distinctive product of his 'Inquiry into Life and Labour in London' (1886–1903), showing Spitalfields, Wapping and Whitechapel. The pockets of black stand out clearly; these constituted what were described as 'the lowest class … some occasional labourers, street sellers, loafers, criminals and semi-criminals. Their life is the life of savages, with vicissitudes of extreme hardship and their only luxury is drink'. As in northern industrial cities of the period, many of these areas of greatest poverty were to be found in 'courts' behind the street frontages (such as those, lower centre, just to the west of Cannon Street Road). Better-off shopkeepers and residents lived along the main streets. The Booth map for Belgravia, by complete contrast, contains extensive swathes in bright yellow.

followed by non-contributory old-age pensions (1908), labour exchanges (1909) and the National Insurance Act (1911), which provided for sickness and unemployment assistance. This policy was linked to a growing institutionalisation seen in the construction of schools, workhouses and asylums. By 1914, a basic national network of infant and child welfare centres had been created, while health-visiting was expanding. Educational authorities had been responsible for the medical inspection of school children.

Far from unconstrained capitalism, this was increasingly a regulated society. In opposition to the building of the high-rise Queen Anne's Mansions, the LCC secured parliamentary legislation, the London Building Acts of 1890 and 1894, designed to restrict the height of new buildings. The Liberals enjoyed considerable success in London in the general elections of 1906 and 1910, although the Municipal Reformers (Conservatives) won the LCC elections in 1907, 1910 and 1913, in part in reaction to the great increase in the rates stemming from the earlier policies of the Progressives, notably the Aldwych/Kingsway scheme, and expenditure on schools and on the attempt to create a public steamer service on the Thames.

The national government's reliance on public solutions was seen in the docks, where excessive supply, after the opening of Royal Albert Dock in 1880 and Tilbury in 1886, led to financial problems and to the establishment in 1908 of the Port of London Authority which took over all the docks (though not the river wharves) and become a major employer and landowner. The Authority also took over the management of the river from the Thames Conservancy Board which had gained control over this from the City Corporation in 1857. The Port of London Authority, a Whitehall-controlled quango, was similar to the Metropolitan Water Board that had taken over London's water supply from the water companies in 1904. Neither function was entrusted to the LCC.

Social welfare was not designed to provide comfortable living standards. Alfred Doolittle, the fictional London dustman in George Bernard Shaw's play *Pygmalion* (1914), remarked: 'We're all intimidated. Intimidated, ma'am: that's what we are. What is there for me if I

The tiered spire of Christopher Wren's church, St Bride's Fleet Street, is reputed to have been the inspiration for the traditional wedding cake, but, as confections go, few can beat the pomposity, self-confidence and sheer exuberance of the former Port of London Authority building on Trinity Square, with a resplendent Old Father Thames looking out over his watery domain. Despite the crucial role of the port to London's economy and life, the city had to wait until 1908 for a single authority with responsibility for the tidal river and the docks. The PLA's offices have followed the main focus of the port downstream, and are now opposite Tilbury docks, in Gravesend.

PHOTOGRAPH: CARNEGIE, 2009

chuck it but the workhouse in my old age? I have to dye my hair already to keep my job as a dustman.' Indeed, his industry was increasingly organised on a large scale, as local authorities, running their own dust removal departments via borough engineers, confronted the vast amounts of rubbish being produced, as well as strident pressure from ratepayers.[32]

London's development served more directly as an opportunity to debate the character and future of the country. In his novel *Tono-Bungay* (1909), H.G. Wells criticised the rural tradition in national culture, attributing the chaotic sprawl of the city to the degree to which the values of the ruling elite were still essentially feudal and non-urban. He also found the fake archaism of Tower Bridge to be indicative of a cultural failure to celebrate industrial function. Despite being built in the late 1880s, and right up to date in terms of technology – with stationary steam engines powering hydraulic accumulators to raise the bridge's road platform – Tower Bridge had indeed rapidly been treated as a representation of 'Olde London'. Wells's commitment to urban planning influenced the Labour Party. He also offered a vision of a London destroyed by Martians in his novel *The War of the Worlds* (1897), which, like Matthew Shiel's novel *The Purple Cloud* (1901), reflected the combination of uncertainty about the future and a fascination with the lurid.

As a sign of a changing agenda, however, Emmeline Pankhurst, a prominent campaigner for votes for women, was arrested outside Buckingham Palace in May 1914. She was a co-founder of the Women's Social and Political Union which was designed to force public attention onto the issue of extending voting rights to women. The suffragette movement was an aspect of a more general articulate and public challenge to gender roles. On the other hand, the practical impact of the idea of the 'new woman' is easily overstated, even for middle-class (let alone working-class) women. Instead, the idea of separate spheres, with women running the home and family, displayed both resilience and adaptability. Moreover, in the world of work, women mostly moved into the low-skill, low-pay 'sweated' sector, and were generally worse treated than men, a practice in which the trade unions co-operated with the management. The Bryant & May's matchgirls' strike in 1888 reflected growing anger with harsh working conditions.

Nevertheless, there was an incremental process of change. Thus, whereas the London Government Act of 1899 excluded women from the vote for the new metropolitan boroughs, in 1907, another Act gave women the vote in local elections. The process was also seen in

Emmeline Pankhurst is taken away by a policeman after leading a group of suffragettes in an attempt to present a petition to the king at Buckingham Palace, 1914.
© BETTMANN/CORBIS

education, with women admitted to London degrees in 1878, and with Westfield College founded for women in 1882 and Royal Holloway College, which opened in 1886.

The years immediately before the First World War marked a certain high-point in London's grand imperial history. The city was right at the centre not just of the nation-state, but of an unprecedented global empire. And, just at the same time as Pankhurst was being arrested, this centrality was made manifest by the creation of a great processional route. In one sense London was fortunate in having space between the City proper and the heart of royal and imperial authority at Buckingham Palace – just as there had always been physical and functional distance between London and Westminster – to allow the building of The Mall, the redesigned ceremonial avenue from the refronted Buckingham Palace to Trafalgar Square, finished in 1913 (as a memorial to Queen Victoria whose statue commands the *rond-point* in front of the palace). The route from The Mall into Trafalgar Square was opened by Admiralty Arch, and Whitehall had grand new ministerial buildings, notably the New War Office (1899–1906) and the New Public Offices (1899–1915). Already, London had provided the setting for Victoria's Golden and Diamond Jubilees in 1887 and 1897. Prominent visitors, such as the Khedive of Egypt in 1900, were entertained by the Mayor and Corporation of the City. London appeared eminently well suited to being the capital of the world's largest empire.

Admiralty Arch on the Mall (1912) bears a Latin inscription translated as 'In the tenth year of King Edward VII, to Queen Victoria, from most grateful citizens, 1910'. The Mall was conceived as Britain's great ceremonial route, with at one end Buckingham Palace's new façade and the enormous Victoria memorial, and Admiralty Arch at the other. Both the arch and the memorial looked back to Victoria's reign, and one can form the distinct impression of a whole generation looking to the past. The arch also forms a huge physical barrier between the royal Mall, with its national and patriotic focus, and the commercial hub of the City of London, a distinction and tension that have been consistent themes for centuries.

PHOTOGRAPH: CARNEGIE, 2009

8

THE MASSIVE EXPANSION OF SUBURBIA was the most obvious impact of these years on the London area, more so indeed than the bombing which created such destruction during the Second World War (1939–45) and which was responsible for some of the iconic images of London, including one famous photograph showing clouds of dust and smoke parting to reveal a sunlit, undamaged and defiant St Paul's Cathedral amid the devastation during the great German raid of 29 December 1940.

Bombing had also been a factor in the First World War (1914–18), when German airships (Zeppelins) and, later, aircraft concentrated on bomb raids of London. These raids inflicted damage and diverted considerable British military resources to anti-aircraft defences. Blackouts were imposed to make German targeting harder, bringing home to civilians the 'total' character of the war, as opposed to the losses to families and communities experienced at the Front. John Monash, an Australian army commander, wrote back to his wife from London in 1916:

> You can hardly imagine what the place is like. The Zeppelin scare is just like as if the whole place was in imminent fear of an earthquake. At night, the whole of London is in *absolute darkness* … All games and museums are closed – nothing but war-work everywhere … everything is at famine prices. Nothing is going on – in the shops, in the streets, anywhere – that has not a direct bearing on the war. Martial law everywhere – no private motors allowed, no functions, no racing … Nothing I had read conveyed to me any idea of how the war had taken hold of the whole British nation, and how every man, woman and child were bent on the one sole purpose, to prosecute the war in every form of activity.

The war was much harsher for many Londoners with German names and antecedents. They were subject to public hostility, including riots in 1914, on the outbreak of war, and 1915, after the sinking of the *RMS Lusitania*. The most prominent Londoners with

Troubled Glories, 1914–1945

IT IS FAR BETTER
TO FACE THE BULLETS
THAN TO BE KILLED
AT HOME BY A BOMB

JOIN THE ARMY AT ONCE
& HELP TO STOP AN AIR RAID

GOD SAVE THE KING

A Zeppelin
caught in the
searchlights
above London, a
poster of c.1917.
MUSEUM OF LONDON

German roots, the royal family, renounced all German titles and honours, and felt it politic in 1917 to change their family name from Saxe-Coburg-Gotha to the much less controversial Windsor.

Public acceptance of the war effort was shown in the spontaneous appearance of street shrines set up to commemorate those who had died for their country or to record the names of those who had gone to serve. Such shrines were the site of a popular religiosity that indicated the strength of wartime devotion. The first shrine we know of was established in Hackney in 1916, and many others followed, particularly in the East End. A large shrine was erected in Hyde Park in August 1918, prompting 100,000 to visit it within a week, with many leaving floral tributes there.

The Germans followed up their Zeppelin attacks with aircraft strikes in 1917 because they wrongly believed, possibly due to reports by Dutch intelligence, that the British public were on the edge of rebellion. The first (and deadliest) aircraft raid on London was a daylight one, on 13 June 1917, in which bombs from fourteen planes killed 162 people and injured 432, including a direct hit on a school that killed sixteen children. This raid led to a public outcry as well as much talk of London being in the front line, and was met by the speedy development of a defensive system involving high-altitude fighters based

Men in London
discuss the
closing of the
Stock Exchange
and the
announcement
of a 4% bank
rate, July 1914.
The outbreak
of the war
brought great
uncertainty to
the financial
centres of the
world.
© HULTON-DEUTSCH
COLLECTION/CORBIS

at airfields that were linked to observers by telephone. This response led to heavy casualties among the German Gotha bombers, and to the abandonment of daylight raids.

More seriously, the rationale of the German air campaign was misplaced because, far from hitting British morale, the bombing led to a hostile popular response. This position remained the case even in the winter of 1917–18, when the Germans unleashed four-engine Zeppelin-staaken R-series bombers. The alarm raised in sections of British civil society by German air attacks, nevertheless, encouraged post-war theorists to emphasise the potential of air power, which led to fear about the consequences for London of any future war. This fear led to the mass evacuation of children when war broke out anew in 1939, as well as the preparation then of a large number of coffins.

In the First World War, Londoners had been more seriously, if indirectly, threatened by the German submarine (U-boat) assault on Britain's maritime supply routes. They shared this challenge with the rest of the United Kingdom, but were also particularly affected due to London's role in maritime trade and to the city's total dependence on food grown elsewhere. On 9 November 1911, Winston Churchill, the newly appointed First Lord of the Admiralty, had told the Lord Mayor's banquet:

> The maintenance of naval supremacy is our whole foundation. Upon it stands not the Empire only, not merely the great commercial prosperity of our people, not merely a fine place in the world's affairs. Upon our naval supremacy stands our lives and the freedom we have guarded for nearly a thousand years.

In the event, German submarines sank 11.9 million tons of Allied shipping in the First World War. By the spring of 1917, when the Germans launched a campaign of unrestricted submarine warfare designed to bring Britain to its knees, British leaders were pessimistic about the chances of success against the submarines. However, attempts to enhance food production in Britain succeeded, as did the introduction, in May 1917, of a system of escorted convoys. Eighteen months later, the defeated Germans accepted an armistice from the Allies.

The shape and activity of the city was affected by the war, notably with the growth of munitions production and military hospitals on the edge of the city, for example in Enfield and Edmonton respectively. These tended to be located on new sites, although by the end of the war, the long-established Royal Arsenal at Woolwich employed over 80,000 people. As a more general impact, the pace of pre-war residential development and of the improvement of the transport infrastructure both slowed greatly or stopped during the war.

The First World War, however, did not have an impact on London comparable to that which stemmed from the expansion of suburbia. In his *English and the Octopus* (1928), the architect Clough Williams-Ellis berated builders and planners for their destruction of the countryside and what he called 'the common background of beauty'. In the case of London, expansion amounted to a vast new city in its spreading suburbia, a city that was far greater in scale than the 'arden cities' such as Letchworth built in the countryside. The sprawl was aided by lax planning regulations, as well as the break-up of aristocratic estates, in part due to death duties (which also led to the sale of London properties), the low price of land, and the post-war agricultural depression which encouraged farmers to sell land in order to survive. London became Greater London. Indeed, in the inter-war

J.R. Scott's 'Victory Arch' – exit number 5 on the rebuilt façade of Waterloo Station – remembers the railway company's many employees who fell in the Great War.

PHOTOGRAPH: CARNEGIE 2009

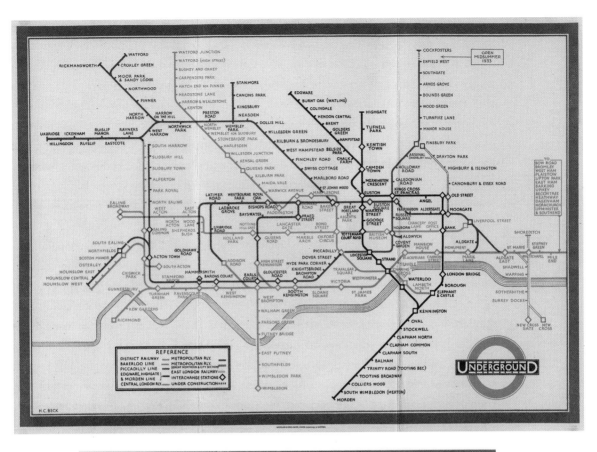

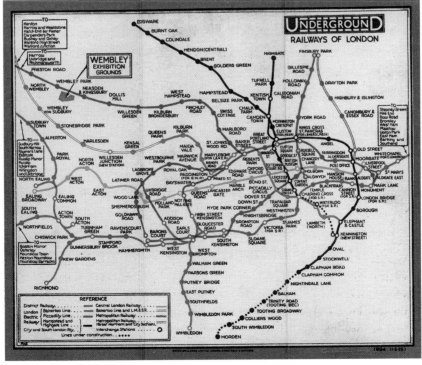

Beck's (1933) (*above*) and Stingemore's (1927) maps of the London Underground.

years Greater London housed, and thus provided, more than one third of the population increase of the whole of England and Wales.

Between 1921 and 1937, on the other hand, the population of inner London fell by nearly half a million. There were particularly steep falls – of over 16 per cent – in the City (the largest percentage fall), Stepney, Poplar, Bethnal Green, Shoreditch, Finsbury, Holborn, Southwark, Bermondsey and Camberwell. The housing in much of this area was old, lacking in what were now considered basic amenities such as running water and electricity, and frequently relied on shared cooking and washing facilities. The growth of municipal housing outside this inner area, combined with changing labour markets, were important in these falls, which interacted with a transformation in the culture of working-class communities, not least as the successful moved to suburbia. Within the LCC area, only Hampstead, Wandsworth, Lewisham and Woolwich had an increase in population.

In contrast, the population of Greater London, the area covered by the Metropolitan Police District, grew from about 7,252,000 in 1911, to about 8,203,000 in 1931, and to about 8,700,000 in 1939, about a fifth of the nation's population. This was a greater percentage than that in earlier ages, although it is important to note that the Metropolitan Police District is larger than what became Greater London after 1965 with the formation of the Greater London Council as the District includes substantial areas of what are still Surrey, Hertfordshire and other neighbouring counties. Particularly marked inter-war population rises occurred in Harrow, Hornchurch, Romford, Hendon, Epsom, Ewell, Chislehurst, Sidcup and Bexley. The growth south of the river owed much to the electrification of the Southern Railways, and to the new railway suburbs it encouraged, though Merton and Morden grew as a consequence of the southward extension of the Tube. Physically, the city sprang forward, for example from Hampstead to Edgware.

The influence of London between the wars was felt even further afield as people commuted long distances. Population growth was no less rapid in places such as Woking, Brentwood, Watford and Maidenhead, which lay well beyond any administrative definition of Greater London. This growth was particularly marked in the area of the Southern Railway, and accelerated with its 1930s electrification to outer south-east England, for example the Portsmouth line in 1935–37.

To support this spreading city, the Underground railway system became a widespread over-ground to the west, north and east of London; and, to a limited extent, also to the south of the Thames. The 'sub-surface' lines (as opposed to the 'Tube', the deeper, bored tunnels) already reached well into the country by 1914. The first Tube extension into greenfield areas was the Northern Line extension from Golders Green to Edgware in 1923–24, a project that was supported by Treasury money in order to help reduce unemployment. This line was followed by the Metropolitan to Watford, Amersham and Uxbridge in 1925, the Metropolitan (later Bakerloo) to Stanmore in 1932, the Piccadilly to Cockfosters in 1933, and then another Northern Line branch to Barnet. Each of these lines organised an important section of London's expansion, while also providing a local pattern of housing and shopping, as well as areas that were to a degree bypassed. South of the Thames, the Northern Line reached Morden in 1926.

The Tube was also responsible for the transformation of London's image, with the 1931 map of the system by Henry (Harry) Beck, an electrical draughtsman who worked for the Underground. This map was inspired by electrical circuit diagrams, and depicted the various Tube lines diagrammatically and as being straight. Prior to Beck's innovative and arresting work, maps presented by London Underground were designed to be accurate in terms of distance and direction. The first such map, produced to show all the Underground lines, as opposed only to those of an individual company, was issued in 1908. This map depicted the lines superimposed upon a central London street map, the same pattern that was used for maps of overground railways, such as Macaulay's *Metropolitan Railway Map* (1859). By the 1920s, the street-map background had been dropped from the Underground map, as with that by Fred Stingemore (1927).

In turn, using a topological structure, and abandoning scale, Beck, imagining that he was using a convex mirror, expanded the central station area for the sake of clarity. He also shrank the apparent distance between suburbs and the inner city, implying that peripheral destinations, such as Morden and Edgware, were within easy travelling distance of central London: thus, movement there did not appear to be a case of leaving London. Instead, the ease of travel into the centre was emphasised, a visual effect that was encouraged by the use of straight lines on the map for the individual Tube services. Beck's map was rejected in 1931 as too revolutionary, only to be accepted in 1932, and first printed in 1933 as a card folder. Subsequently the design was used by London Transport for both station wall maps and pocket versions. Describing his task as turning 'vermicelli into a diagram', Beck produced updated versions until 1959, but the copyright was held by the London Passenger Transport Board and he was embittered by the limited returns he enjoyed.

Different fare tariffs on the Underground played a role in the development of the linked housing system, for the Tube was consciously presented as integrating housing, transport and work. Fare tariffs helped, for example, to ensure that Edgware grew more rapidly than Stanmore, from where the fare to the city centre was higher in the 1930s.

A new governmental structure was established for transport and one that created a common experience for London, although the area covered was far larger than the London County Council area. The London Passenger Transport Board (or London Transport) was formed in 1933 as a result of the London Transport Act, by bringing together Underground lines, tramways and buses. The creation of the board carried forward the 1931 London Passenger Transport Bill advanced by the Labour London politician Herbert Morrison while Minister of Transport. Moreover, the Conservative-dominated National

Government introduced the New Works Programme (1935–40) as a further means to help with unemployment; the programme included the extension of the Northern Line to High Barnet and Mill Hill East, and also saw substantial lengths of the ex-Great Western Railway and ex-London and North Eastern track handed over to London Transport; thus the Central Line now reached to Ongar. The 17-mile tunnel between East Finchley (on the High Barnet branch) and Morden was, at the time of its construction, the longest continuous tunnel in the world.

London Transport was run from 55 Broadway, a proto-skyscraper at St James's built in 1927–29 for the London Electric Railway Company with attractive step-backs and external sculptures. The latter included 'Day' and 'Night' by Jacob Epstein and the 'Four Winds' by artists including Henry Moore.

South of the Thames, however, Southern Railways (created by amalgamation in 1923), the only rail company that electrified on a large scale, served London's massive expansion and remained outside London Transport. This difference encouraged a sense of 'South of the River' as different. When I was growing up in north-west London in the 1960s, the Tube, both the Northern and the Bakerloo lines, took me 'into town' but, partly because it did not go much into south London, I rarely went there. The excision of south London from public attention was also seen in the version of the popular board-game Monopoly that was produced for London. Based on a one-day trip to London in 1935 by the managing director of the Leeds firm of John Waddington, this game excluded any railway station south of the Thames, as well as any road there bar the Old Kent Road.

Built in the 1920s right on top of St James's Park Tube station, Charles Holden's 55 Broadway was the headquarters of the London Electric Railway Company.

LONDON TRANSPORT MUSEUM

With new Art Deco-style stations and the attractive advertising it sponsored, the Underground system encouraged a sense of pride. Charles Holden's new underground booking hall for Piccadilly Circus Tube station, which includes a number of well-signposted subway exits for pedestrians (1925–28) was followed by his work on a number of new stations, particularly on the Piccadilly Line, such as Chiswick Park (1932) and Turnpike Lane (1932). His work helped inspire the Moscow metro. Serving the new suburbs, the Underground system was much used. By 1934 the city's public transport system was attracting 416 million passengers annually. Road construction and commuting were also important. Buses competed actively with trams. In 1930 the LCC introduced the comfortable

and quick 'Feltham' trams, but the greater flexibility of buses ensured that London was soon planning to close its tram routes by 1941.

Meanwhile, in part as a measure to help tackle unemployment, arterial roads were constructed in the 1920s and 1930s, for example the Great West Road from Gunnersbury to Hamwell, and the Eastern Avenue from Wanstead to Romford. Many of the advantages of the new arterial roads were very rapidly lost, however, because weak planning powers, especially before the 1935 Ribbon Development Act, meant that the new highways were almost immediately edged by housing and cluttered with innumerable junctions and other impedimenta, which slowed traffic and recreated congestion.

Bolder schemes were on offer. Sir Charles Bressey, the Ministry of Transport engineer who investigated traffic problems in central London in 1936, proposed a programme of massive road-building, including large roundabouts and big flyovers. In the late 1930s, the Modern Architectural Research Group envisaged huge raised arteries more than 200 feet broad, crossing London at rooftop level, carrying trains and buses, while the streets below were to be handed over the private cars.

In turn, Patrick Abercrombie's *County of London Plan* of 1943 proposed a large number of new roads, including three orbital routes: A, which ran around inner London; B, which was further out, for example crossing the Thames to the east from the Isle of Dogs to

The grand circular booking hall of Piccadilly Circus Tube station, by Charles Holden.
PHOTOGRAPH: CARNEGIE, 2009

Deptford; and C, along the North and South Circular roads. In turn, radial roads were to join these rings and to provide routes from the centre to the major trunk routes in south-east England. His *Greater London Plan* of the following year proposed six ring roads, including E Ring, much of which is followed by the recent M25, as well as ten radial roads, six airports and a dozen new towns. Abercrombie argued that fast through traffic must be separated from local traffic, as London, he claimed, was composed of cellular communities which should be carefully nurtured and, to that end, sealed from the main roads round them. These plans foreshadowed the Greater London Council's commitment in the 1960s and 1970s to a motorway box for London.

Cars and roads led to new smells, as well as 'the sound of horns and motors' of T.S. Eliot's poem *The Waste Land*. The visual context of life was affected, with signs, lamp-posts and traffic lights, because the impact of motor vehicles on pedestrian behaviour had to be controlled by the development of safety measures, a need earlier seen with the horse-drawn trams. The first traffic roundabout in London was constructed at Parliament Square in 1926, five years after the last horse-drawn fire engine was withdrawn from service. Roads led to new boundaries and commands, to zebra crossings and to the flashing safety lamps called Belisha Beacons after the Minister of Transport. As a mark of the impact of cars, the *A–Z Atlas and Guide to London and Suburbs* appeared in 1936, the work of Phyllis Pearsall who had walked all 23,000 London streets researching her pioneering book.

Cars also affected crime, as well as the image of London which in film was frequently realised as the setting for crime stories, a situation that remains true of television schedules to this day. The spread in the 1930s of large numbers of affordable cars with reliable self-starter motors, so that it was not necessary to crank up the motor by hand, led to a wave of 'smash and grab' raids, as criminals took advantage of the new technology. Greater mobility also changed the pattern of crime. In response, the Metropolitan Police experimented with mounting ships' radios in cars, and was able to develop a fleet of Wolseley cars thus equipped with which to launch an effective response.

Industry continued to move out of the centre of London. Initially after the First World War, this was a continuation of the pre-war movement to the east (West Ham) and to the Lea valley in north-east London, but in the 1930s there was a new geographical focus, one that marked a major change in the spatial distribution of employment in the London area. This focus was also an aspect of the prosperity and growth of the decade, both of which are often neglected as writers continue to emphasise the severity of the Depression. The Great West Road became the site of a series of spacious factories that, with their use of electricity, were very distant from the smoke-shrouded world of dockland manufacturing and from the workshops of inner London. Aside from large-scale factories, such as those manufacturing Smiths crisps, Gillette razors and Curry's cycles, and the Hoover factory built in 1932–33 (all consumer industries), there was a host of small manufacturing works

In an interesting commentary on the good communications links of the river Thames, the Ford Motor Company's principal reason for its costly relocation from Trafford Park (despite the Manchester Ship Canal) to Dagenham in the 1920s was the importance of better access to the sea, for exporting vehicles as well as importing raw materials. This is a Model Y Ford, a smaller car deemed suitable for the Depression years. At Dagenham over 150,000 of these were built in the 1930s.
MUSEUM OF LONDON

on the Park Royal estate, built on the former showground of the Royal Agricultural Society; and comparable development along the North Circular Road at Colindale and Cricklewood. In east London, Ford's car factory at Dagenham was also a major site.

An instructive contrast from 1936 was that between the unemployed workers of Palmer's shipyard on the river Tyne, who drew attention to their plight with a march on London – the Jarrow March – one of 34 unemployed workers' national protest marches on London during the 1920s and 1930s; and, on the other hand, the new Carreras cigarette factory opened at Mornington Crescent in London employing 2,600 workers. The massive growth in light industry in the South East, including Greater London, was the main reason for the dramatic population movement from areas such as the North East, the North West, and South Wales. After 1918, most Irish immigrants landing at Liverpool went straight on to London, and did not think about staying in Lancashire, their traditional emigrant destination.

The docks remained a centre of London's activity, and were still the most important in the world.

> The river sweats
> Oil and Tar
> The barges drift
> With the turning tide

noted Eliot in *The Waste Land*. This was the river of the Oporto Wharf, Kidney Stairs and the Limestone Cut entrance. Individual wharves specialised in particular trades; for example, Hubbuck's Wharf in paints, Morton's Sufferance Wharf in preserved foods, chocolate and confectionery, and Millwall Dock in grain. Moreover, the manufacturing in and near Dockland, notably the processing industries, continued to be major employers. Thus, Chubb Round & Co.'s fibre works transformed coconuts into rope and matting.

Yet, London's industrial base was increasingly characterised by light industry using electrical power. This development of factory employment and factory districts meant the decline of workshops and thus of the working-class nature of the inner city. The new factory districts were linked to the development of LCC housing estates, each aspects of a form of development zoning that became more apparent over time.

Industry was generally kept at a distance from middle-class suburbia. The growth of suburbia reflected the desire for a life away from factory chimneys and inner-city crowding, a desire catered to in the posters advocating life in the new suburbs. Place and movement were particularly susceptible to change, as London altered and the motor car spread in a symbiotic development: cars encouraged housing of a lower density, while the new suburbs were associated with road systems constructed for cars. The tightly packed terraces characteristic of Victorian London, for the middle as well as the working class, were supplemented by miles of 'semis': semi-detached houses with mock-Tudor elevations, red-tiled roofs, and walls of red brick or pebbledash, with a small front and a larger back garden. Each house had a small drive and a separate garage, which was often structurally linked to the house. This was a suburbia representing the application of pre-First World War ideas of garden-suburbs, notably with an emphasis on space, calm and the separateness expressed in individual gardens.

Suburbia had spread in the late nineteenth century with the railways, but development then had generally not moved far from the stations. In contrast, car transport permitted less-intensive development, although, in practice, this often meant more extensive estates that were otherwise as densely packed as the basic housing model permitted. In advertisements, such as those that pushed the 'Metroland' linked to the expansion of the Metropolitan Line, cars were pictured against backdrops of mock-Tudor suburban houses. As with the car, the 'semi' expressed freedom: a freedom to escape the constraints of living in close proximity to others and, instead, to enjoy space. Semis were not the suburban villas of the wealthier members of the middle class, which continued to exist in what were now enclaves, but they captured the aspirations of millions, and offered them a decent living environment, including a garden. In *English Journey* (1934), J.B. Priestley wrote of the new England of suburbs and road houses: pubs built along trunk roads, many of which were found in outer London.

In part, suburbia was a response to the cult of the outdoors, one mediated through, and in, the suburban garden and the parks of new suburbs. Thus, suburbia was linked to a ruralist image of England. Names such as Wood Green expressed the aspirations for

LEFT

Butler's Wharf, on the south side of the river, opposite St Katharine Docks. When completed in the 1870s, this building was the largest wharf on the Thames, including what was reputedly the world's largest tea warehouse. It remains the biggest surviving range of what is known as a dockland 'canyon', in which overhead bridges link the warehouses on the river frontage with further buildings across the road of Shad Thames to the south. Over the last 25 years or so the buildings have been extensively restored and converted.

RIGHT

London's river wharves continued to be developed until remarkably late. The Metropolitan Wharf on Wapping Wall, close to the former eastern entrance to London Dock, was built and redeveloped from the 1860s to the 1890s. It now accommodates some 16,000 m² of office space.

PHOTOGRAPH: CARNEGIE, 2009

new neighbourhoods. This appeal was seen across the arts. In music, it was found in the positive response to Edward Elgar and Ralph Vaughan Williams, and, in painting, to the popularity of 'authentic' rather than modernist works. Indeed, there was an attempt to take this ruralism into the inner city. The most influential of the tour guides, *In Search of England* (1927), by the Birmingham-born H.V. [Henry Canova Vollam] Morton, a work whose twenty-fourth edition appeared in 1937, presented London as linked to the national life of the countryside:

> The squares of London, those sacred little patches of the country-side preserved, perhaps, by the Anglo-Saxon instinct for grass and trees, hold in their restricted glades some part

Despite the establishment of the Port of London Authority, the important river wharves, including Hay's Wharf seen here, were left in the ownership of private companies. The continuation of the Free Water Clause (see page 236) helping to maintain trade at river wharves such as this. The original caption for this atmospheric photograph refers to the fog clearing to reveal Tower Bridge in the distance. Possibly taken from London Bridge, this view shows the southern bank of the Upper Pool. Nicknamed 'London's Larder' on account of the huge quantities of dry produce that was unloaded here, Hay's Wharf is now Hay's Galleria, a riverside shopping arcade.

© HULTON-DEUTSCH COLLECTION/CORBIS

of the magic of spring. I suppose many a man has stood at his window above a London square in April hearing a message from the lanes of England.

More bluntly and harshly, the novelist D.H. Lawrence, criticising suburbia, referred to 'little red rat-traps'. More than any other, the poet John Betjeman captured the spirit and identity of the endless Middlesex estates, and the poignant loss of rural beauties which they represented. Writing in the late twentieth century, satirist Alan Coren was to quip, 'Were Edgware on a lake, would Venice stand a chance?'

Suburbia, which came into use as a pejorative noun in the 1890s, certainly reflected sameness and national standardisation. Indeed, a predictability of product helped in the marketing and selling of the new housing. The houses were mass-produced and had standardised parts. They also looked similar, as did their garages. A degree of individuality was provided by the gardens but they generally had similar plantings, for example cherry trees. These houses were not the villas of the Victorian period, but they reflected a similar aspiration for space and privacy, and were certainly far more a realisation of the suburban ideal than terraced housing.

In part, this similarity was because of the role of brick as the standard building material and the dominance of much brick-making by the Fletton process using the Jurassic clays of the East Midlands, whose high carbon content cut the cost of firing. Feeding the new suburbia, brick-making developed as a massive industry between Bedford and Bletchley and also near Whittlesey on the Cambridgeshire/Huntingdonshire border. Bricks, and other products for the housing market, such as prefabricated doors and windows, could be moved not only by rail, but also by the new expanding road system.

At the same time, there were significant variations, which were understood and extrapolated by the residents of the new areas. Growing up in Edgware, listening to my elders, and doing a paper round (that is, delivering newspapers door to door), I became well aware of differences not only in street layout and decoration (for instance, trees along roads or not), and house size, density, and decoration (for example tiling), but also in supposed characteristics of particular streets, whether exotic (such as alleged spouse-swapping; it was then called wife-swapping), or, far more commonly, the more mundane alignments and lineaments of class.

Much new building was by private enterprise, often by speculative builders such as John Laing and Richard Costain. They were largely responsible for the plentiful supply of inexpensive houses by the mid-1920s. The ability to borrow at low rates of interest from building societies was also important. In the mid-1920s, houses cost between £400 and £1,000. This new housing was crucial to the process by which suburban culture, especially that in London, became increasingly defined and important, politically and socially. The suburbs had fairly standard mock-Tudor high streets and also enormous and lavishly

Public baths and wash-houses were established in working-class urban areas as part of a more general movement to improve public hygiene and health. This is the former wash-house on Manor Place, just off the Walworth Road. On 27 June 1944 the building, two railway arches and around 300 houses were damaged by a German V-I flying bomb. It is now a Buddhist centre and is a listed building.
PHOTOGRAPH: CARNEGIE, 2009

decorated picture palaces – cinemas – for example in Gants Hill, Becontree Heath, Hendon and Uxbridge. These cinemas represented the move of leisure to the suburbs. There, film studies were founded at Ealing in 1931. By the end of the decade, the biggest studios were at Denham, while Elstree was a key centre of film production from the 1920s.

Council-house building was also important, as well as providing a crucial link between housing and local politics. Treasury loans for local authority building had been available from as early as 1866, but most local authorities had been reluctant to incur debts. From 1919, however, as a consequence of Addison's two Housing Acts, grants replaced loans, and council-house building expanded. This expansion was designed to give bricks and mortar to the Prime Minister David Lloyd George's promise of 'Homes fit for Heroes' for troops returning home at the end of the First World War.

Following many of the recommendations made in the Tudor Walters Report of 1918, the Housing and Town Planning Act of 1919 sought to provide lower density housing for the working class. Minimum room sizes were decreed, as was the inclusion of internal bathrooms. Indeed, the public housing of the period was generally of good quality, and much of it is regarded as more desirable than much 1960s public housing, not least because of the human scale of the former. The implementation of the Acts was hit by the financial crisis of 1921–22, but they still led to much construction, as did Neville Chamberlain's Housing Act of 1923 and the Wheatley Act of 1924, which was passed by the Labour government. As a prime instance of the scale of the building, the London County Council's Becontree estate, begun in 1921 and finished in 1932, occupied 277 acres and consisted of about 26,000 houses; it housed 120,000 people. The LCC also built estates at St Helier near Morden, at Downham and at Watling, which between them housed about 89,000 people. Such estates were a sign of the LCC's power and ambitions, since elsewhere county councils were not in normal circumstances house-building authorities. Moreover, some of the boroughs built houses.

Council houses were increasingly important because the private rental sector had declined, in part because private landlordship had become less profitable, and there was therefore less private investment in the building of new properties for rent. Following the 1915 Rent and Mortgage Interest Restrictions (War) Act, tenants' rights became more secure, private landlordship less profitable, and renting from local authorities more important. Party politics played a role in this, notably Labour's hostility to private landlordship. The 1957 Rent Act, passed by a Conservative government, was a (botched) attempt to free up the private rental market. In contrast, the Labour government's Rent Act of 1965 established rent control on a secure legislative footing, a measure which hit the private rented sector hard.

In the inter-war years, there was also a rebuilding of some existing housing. The Greenwood Housing Act of 1930 gave local authorities powers to clear or improve slum (crowded and sub-standard housing) areas, in part as a realisation of long-standing beliefs

British governments have always been uneasy with the idea of powerful city-wide authorities, to an extent not seen in most other European countries. Since London grew well beyond its ancient limits a succession of major bodies (as well as dozens of specific boards, authorities and quangos) has been created to try to deal with broader city-wide issues. First there was the Metropolitan Board of Works (in Spring Gardens, 1855–89). Then came the London County Council (LCC, 1889–1965), which had wider powers over such matters as education, housing and planning. The LCC embarked upon the construction (1911–22) of the grand 'Edwardian Baroque' County Hall seen here. Then these buildings were home to the Greater London Council (GLC, 1965–86), the new strategic authority for the capital. To some extent London politics had created the GLC; and politics were to destroy it. For County Hall lies just across the river from the palace of Westminster and, from 1981, building on Conservative concerns in the 1970s, County Hall and Westminster were locked in a bitter ideological conflict. Under the radical Ken Livingstone things came to a head, and the Tories abolished the GLC. In turn, Labour created a new Greater London Authority (2000–), with an elected Mayor for all London. Livingstone became the first incumbent. By this time, County Hall had been sold off, and a new City Hall had to be built to accommodate the GLA and the Mayor. Meanwhile the City of London Corporation remained virtually untouched by all of this local government turmoil, showing remarkable powers of historical resilience.

that improved housing would enhance social mores. Passed by the Labour government of 1929–31, this Act provided local authorities with subsidies related to the numbers rehoused and the cost of slum clearance, and obliged them to produce five-year housing plans. The terms of the subsidies were renewed with an Act passed by the Conservative-dominated National Government in 1933, although Labour boroughs built more public housing than their Conservative counterparts. Much building was achieved thanks to the ready availability of labour and materials and low interest rates.

Not all commentators were favourable. John Betjeman, speaking on the West of England radio programme on 2 January 1939, urged his listeners to put aside illusions about London. His bleak account of the debasing of the city included an attack on the LCC's slum-clearance schemes:

> Of course, a lot of these houses ought to have come down. They're often riddled with vermin ... But look what is going up in their place. Flats of the wrong height ... And the arid, sunless recreation grounds of asphalt round a flat-block are hardly a compensation for the street playground ... Londoners, like all English people, prefer to live in a house.

Urban renewal took many forms. For example, cinemas such as the Ilford Hippodrome and the Rex at Stratford were converted theatres, part of the assault on music-hall by film. Nevertheless, music-halls remained part of the equation, now largely in a form of variety dominated by musicals. Dance halls were also important, their music and style part of the Americanisation of British leisure.

Linked to housing, public health remained a serious problem, although far less so than in the Victorian age. There were still significant variations across London. In Kensington, for example, infant mortality was higher in the poor areas in the north of the borough than in the wealthier south. As well as poverty, the provision of medical services was also important: areas with comprehensive services, such as Stepney and Woolwich, had lower rates of infant mortality than Kensington, where there was no universal provision. In the 1930s improved care from midwives and in hospitals was an important factor in the fall

Slums at Millwall in 1932. Three small boys pose for the camera from slightly precarious vantage points, while a young women hangs out the washing. This view shows the back yards of Totnes Terrace (*left*) and Totnes Cottages (*right*), part of the small Barnfield estate to the south of Millwall Dock on the south-western coast of the Isle of Dogs. Typical of many small nineteenth-century housing developments, the houses were built in close proximity to industrial areas. Beyond the wall in the background is the Finnish three-masted barque *Penang* which in July 1932 lay in the tiny Britannia dry dock (originally Tyndal's dock) after unloading its cargo of grain from Adelaide, South Australia. The Thames, therefore, runs past beyond the ship's stern. Like many others, the Barnfield housing estate was developed by modestly financed private builders, in this case as part of a mixed scheme comprising housing and industry in the 1860s. On the river bank next to the dry dock was the curiously named Drunken Dock and its associated workshops, which was a late eighteenth-century mast pond (near modern Mast House Terrace), although this industrial site changed use several times, from gun works to ship-breakers. In the twentieth century planners strove to separate housing from industry to a much greater degree.

in infant mortality across London, while, in the national context, London was relatively over-provided with hospitals, and areas that had good access, such as Stepney, had low maternal mortality rates.

Under the Local Government Act of 1929, county borough health duties and powers greatly expanded, and it was possible to take over Poor Law institutions. In London the LCC took over both hospitals and schools and sought to establish effective healthcare and hospital provision without the stigma of the Poor Law.[1] Under Labour, in control of the LCC from 1934, when it won 51 per cent of the vote, London was seen as a demonstration of the value of municipal socialism, one intended to appeal to those casting their votes in national elections, both in London and further afield. Indeed, by 1939, the LCC had nearly 60 per cent of all the municipal hospital beds in England, while, in 1935, the LCC had ended the ban on married women teachers, a key measure of gender discrimination. In London, Morrison constructed a coalition of support encompassing not only manual workers in deprived industrial districts, but also voters who were more prosperous. Clerks and teachers were among Labour's LCC candidates. Thus, Labour's electoral position in London did not match its opponents' claims that it was a sectarian party thriving on social antagonism, although Labour was helped by the movement of Conservative voters to suburbia beyond the LCC boundaries. Labour retained control of the LCC until its dissolution in 1965.

Moreover, London's importance to the national Labour Party was indicated in 1931 when George Lansbury, MP for Bow and Bromley, was elected Labour leader, a post he held until 1935, when he was succeeded by another London Labour MP, Clement Attlee, although Attlee beat Morrison who had a genuine Labour base. Lansbury had won fame in 1921 when, as leader of Poplar Borough Council, he and other council members were imprisoned for six weeks for refusing to authorise payment of money to the LCC which they claimed that the borough, a centre of poverty, could not afford. Poplarism, however, was brought low by legislation by the Conservative government: the 1926 Board of Guardians (Default) Act, the 1928 Emergency Provisions Act, and the 1929 Local Government Act which transferred power over poor relief in London from local Guardians to the LCC.[2]

Meanwhile, concern – at least in the mind of planners – about the rate of the spread of suburbia and the threat to the environment, combined with a growing willingness to accept government control, led to the passage of relevant legislation. The Housing, Town Planning Act

The now disused coal-fired Battersea Power Station. The station was built in two phases in the 1930s and 1950s. At its height over 1 million tons of coal were delivered by ship to the station to produce up to 500 MW of power. Each week about 2 billion gallons of Thames water was used to create steam before helping to heat thousands of homes in Pimlico and being returned to the river.

PHOTOGRAPH: CARNEGIE, 2008

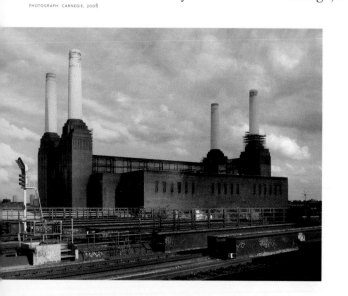

of 1909 was the first piece of British legislation to use the term 'town planning'. John Burns, the President of the Local Government Board, introduced the legislation in 1908 by telling Parliament that it set out to 'provide a domestic condition for the people in which their physical health, their morals, their character and their whole social condition can be improved … to secure the home healthy.' The Greater London Regional Planning Committee was established in 1927, and another Town and Country Planning Act followed in 1932. The Restriction of Ribbon Development Act of 1935, which attempted to prevent unsightly and uncontrolled development along new or improved roads, such as those leading from London, was an admission of a serious problem.

Interest in planning increased in the late 1930s, prior to the devastation wrought by German air attack. Morrison pressed for a Green Belt that would put a limit on the city's advance, yet at the same time he was engineering a change in its electoral composition by establishing big council estates in the suburbs, such as Watling in what is now Burnt Oak, as part of an attempt to 'build the Tories out of London', a policy similar to that adopted by the Socialists in Vienna. In creating a Green Belt, Labour also wished to preserve accessible open spaces for the city population, while the surrounding rural councils were supportive of attempts to stem the sprawl of the city. The Green Belt (London and Home Counties) Act of 1938 arose from a local government initiative, and was followed by the 1940 report of the Barlow Commission proposing more state control over development, especially in the London area.

Meanwhile, change in London's material world was wide ranging. In 1926, John Logie Baird gave the first public demonstration of television in London, and, six years later, the BBC moved to new offices in Portland Place. In 1920 Hounslow, the first civil aerodrome

Radically different styles of retailing: on the left is the figure above the central doorway of Selfridge's on Oxford Street (1909), an enormous, rigorously designed art deco temple of shopping, second only to Harrod's in size; on the right is Liberty's on Great Marlborough Street (1924), one of London's most important Tudor-revival arts and crafts buildings, with rambling design and re-used timber.

PHOTOGRAPHS: CARNEGIE, 2009

in England, closed as Croydon was made the London Customs Air Port. In 1928, in turn, Croydon was officially opened as the new Airport of London, and, by the end of the decade, about twenty aeroplanes daily were leaving. Weekly flights from London began to Cape Town (1932), Brisbane (1934), and Hong Kong (1936).

At the same time, there was also a reluctance to engage with the new. It was only in 1945 that the trustees of the Tate Gallery in London agreed to the opening of a small room devoted to abstract art. The gallery, founded in 1897, was way behind the Museum of Modern Art in New York, not least because it lacked funds. In the inter-war period, the Treasury was loath to increase support for the arts, but taste was also an issue. James Bolivar Manson, the Tate's director in the 1930s, was a painter of flowers and was opposed to Post-Impressionism, Cubism, Expressionism, Surrealism and to living British artists such as Sickert and Moore. This stance affected the acquisition policies of the Tate.

Similarly, the avant-garde Bloomsbury Group, centred in London, had only a limited impact on sales compared to many of the middle- and low-brow writers of the period. In

Higher education in what was to become the linked establishments of the University of London was created in two broad waves during the nineteenth century. First came the London Mechanics' Institute (the progenitor of Birkbeck College) in the early 1820s, first in Chancery Lane and later in Fetter Lane. Then in 1828 a pioneering experiment in secular education, inspired by the radical ideas of Jeremy Bentham, was set up as London University to educate 'the youth of our middling rich people'. Its non-denominational nature was not at all to the liking of more traditionally minded Englishmen, and Rev. George D'Oyly (a Lambeth rector), and the Duke of Wellington no less, helped organise the gaining of a royal charter in 1829 for the establishment of the rival King's College. Remarkably given their very different beginnings, the two amalgamated as the University of London in 1836, with the earlier institution taking the new name of University College London (UCL). The second wave of institutions began in 1879 with Royal Holloway, the gift of Devon medicine-salesman Thomas Holloway (though the idea for a women-only college was said to be his wife's). Goldsmith's College followed in 1891 for 'men and women of the industrial, working and artisan classes'. The final Victorian institutions were Queen Mary (and Westfield) College and the London School of Economics and Political Science (LSE) in 1895. In 1916 came the School of Oriental and African Studies and, finally, in 1964, the Franks report led to the establishment of business schools in Manchester and London.

The amalgamated University of London now has well over 130,000 students. In the 1920s, and already expanding, the university decided to buy a block of land in Bloomsbury from the Duke of Bedford. William Beveridge, the social reformer, pressed through a scheme for the construction of Senate House, his vision for the university being 'for the nation and the world' rather than just for London. In the pioneering spirit of the age, the building was no throw-back to comparable Victorian buildings elsewhere, still less a pastiche of Oxbridge colleges. Designed by Charles Holden, the 1930s' Art Deco monumentalism of Senate House was said to be the inspiration for Orwell's Ministry of Truth in *Nineteen Eighty-Four* (1949).

PHOTOGRAPH: CARNEGIE, 2009

An S-type bus of the London General Omnibus Company (LGOC) photographed with police escort on board on 18 May 1926: a volunteer driver keeps the service running during the General Strike. The open-topped S-type bus had 56 seats, but the smaller K-type was far more numerous on London's streets between the wars. This bus is bound for the newly developed Golders Green and the terminus was, appropriately, the Underground station. Everyone in the photograph wears a hat.

music, Rimsky-Korsakov, Schönberg, Hindemith and Prokofiev were influential, but Elgar and Vaughan Williams were performed far more frequently.

Modernism had relatively little impact in architecture, despite Giles Gilbert Scott's Battersea Power Station, and the designs of Berthold Lubetkin, who worked in part for Finsbury Council and was responsible for the Highpoint block of flats in Highgate (1935), as well as the Penguin Pool at the Zoo (1934). Charles Holden produced the design for the Senate House of the University of London, a vast Modernist lump begun in 1932. The university site in Bloomsbury had itself been acquired by the government from the estate of the Duke of Bedford in 1920. Liberty's, off Regent Street, built in 1924, using Elizabethan timber, better expressed the widespread desire for a style suggesting continuity, not the new, while there was controversy over the destruction of part of Nash's Regent Street. A poster for the British Empire Exhibition held at Wembley in 1924–25 showed Elizabeth I being rowed on the Thames towards a Tudor warship, with the caption 'Britain's Past and Present Beckon You to Wembley. British Empire Exhibition'.

There was also a political dimension to the tension between the challenge of the new and conservatism. In 1926 London was a centre both of the General Strike called by the TUC, and of opposition to it. Thus, volunteers, protected by police and troops, drove buses from depots, as well as Underground trains, and kept many power stations in operation. The 114,000 volunteers also worked in the docks and distributed food. In turn, strikers attacked buses and lorries breaking the strike, and battled the police in centres of the left, including Poplar and New Cross. Had the crisis lasted for longer, it might have become a traumatic moment in the city's industry.

London seemed a centre of new ideas and practices, and yet was also characterised by important continuities. For example, Virginia Woolf argued, in *Street Haunting: A London Adventure*, an essay of 1927, that London threatened the established order by offering liberation and delight to women who had formerly been marginalised. Yet, many of the new female voters supported the Conservatives.

A more fractured account was offered by the American-born poet T.S. Eliot (1888–1965), who lived in London from 1915, following a number of careers including teaching, working for the Colonial and Foreign Department of Lloyd's Bank, editing a quarterly review, and working as a publisher. He gave a prominent role to the city in his poem *The Waste Land* (1922), an account of post-war Europe as a sterile land awaiting revival. Commuters as spectral figures provided one image:

> Unreal City,
> Under the brown fog of a winter dawn,
> A crowd flowed over London Bridge, so many,
> I had not thought death had undone so many,
> Sighs, short and infrequent, were exhaled,
> And each man fixed his eyes before his feet.
> Flowed up the hill and down King William Street,
> To where Saint Mary Woolnoth kept the hours
> With a dead sound on the final stroke of nine.

The Thames is polluted by human detritus and sexual activity:

> ... empty bottles, sandwich papers,
> Silk handkerchiefs, cardboard boxes, cigarette ends
> ... The nymphs are departed.
> And their friends, the loitering heirs of City directors ...

Highbury bore me. Richmond and Kew
Undid me. By Richmond I raised my knees
Supine on the floor of a narrow canoe.

A sense of doom is captured with London the latest in a series of doomed world cities

What is the city over the mountains
Cracks and reforms and bursts in the violent air
Falling towers
Jerusalem Athens Alexandria
Vienna London
Unreal.

At the same time, London also offered intimations of a prospect of salvation, again with the theme centred on the Thames:

'This music crept by me upon the waters'
And along the Strand, up Queen Victoria Street.
O city city, I can sometimes hear
Besides a public bar in Lower Thames Street,
the pleasant whining of a mandoline
And a clatter and a chatter from within
Where fishmen lounge at noon: where the walls

The British Museum in Bloomsbury. The institution was founded as a 'universal museum' in 1753 and located at first in Montagu House, also in Bloomsbury. The enormous purpose-built neo-classical museum was built between 1825 and 1850. The vegetation in front of the Musuem, untypical of London, was planted as part of a temporary exhibition in early 2009.

PHOTOGRAPH: CARNEGIE, 2009

Of Magnus Martyr hold
Inexplicable splendour of Ionian white and gold
… Elizabeth and Leicester
Beating Oars
The Stern was formed
A gilded shell
… The peal of bells
White towers.

The possibility of redemption and rebirth is located with reference to the Indian Upanishads, not set in London, and indeed near the close the nursery rhyme line 'London Bridge is falling down falling down falling down' is the last reference to the city, and yet the passages already cited suggest that, alongside the squalor of modern life in London, Eliot could glimpse light of an ethereal quality.

Meanwhile, films were spreading images of London to new audiences. Silent films often included location shooting in London. *The Sign of Four* (1923) was an updated Sherlock Holmes adaptation concluding in a spectacular boat chase down the Thames. *Blackmail* (1929), directed by Alfred Hitchcock, the first British talkie, featured exteriors of the British Museum. There were also early documentaries, including *Scenes of London Life*. In contrast, there was less location shooting in 1930s films, as sound sent film-makers back into the studios.

Fictional accounts of the city included a number of novels dealing with the harsh realities of life, such as *London River* (1921) by the left-wing novelist and journalist Henry Major Tomlinson (1873–1958), who had been born in Poplar and had worked in a shipping office. Virginia Woolf wrote an essay on the docks, the first in *The London Scene: Six Essays on London Life*, essays originally published in *Good Housekeeping* in 1931, while George Orwell's *Down and Out in Paris and London* (1933) described the poorly paid life he had experienced in the late 1920s. Archibald Joseph Cronin (1896–1981), a Scottish doctor who practised in London from 1928 to 1930, before becoming a novelist, described in his novel *The Citadel* (1937), a practice in Paddington, 'a baddish locality' with 'all these moth-eaten boarding-houses' full of 'seedy, even doubtful characters', and afflicted by winter fogs.[3] In his autobiography, Cronin contrasted the opulent image of London in springtime with a reality of seediness, noting that he and his wife 'had never imagined that there were so many alcoholic or broken-down doctors in London, or so few houses that were not dingy and damp, with cavernous basements and attics like mousetraps'.[4]

A cultural preference for continuity was especially notable in the 1930s, the years of the National Government and of a pronounced conservatism. The rags-to-riches fantasy of the smash-hit musical *Me and My Girl* (1937), the source of the 'Lambeth Walk', celebrated the

'Cockney spirit', but was scarcely subversive. For the middle class, the cultural preferences of the 1930s were for an appearance of rural and natural life and values, both as part of an organic society. These preferences seemed to find their fulfilment in suburbia.

At the same time, contributing to a profound shift in material culture, there was much change in the circumstances of life for many Londoners. In particular, household electricity supplies expanded greatly, replacing coal, gas, candles and human effort. This replacement had an impact on the consumption of power and the sales of electric cookers, fridges, irons, water heaters and vacuum cleaners. Such expenditure reflected, and helped to define, class differences in London. Whereas radios, vacuum cleaners and electric irons were widely owned, in part thanks to the spread of hire purchase, electric fridges, cookers and washing machines were largely restricted to the middle class.

This difference in goods was linked to the major social divide between those who employed others and the employed, although as far as home-help was concerned the latter were increasingly the daily help rather than full-time domestic servants. Whether defined in terms of income, occupation or culture, the middle class was proportionately more important in London and the South East than in any other region, a situation that remains the case today. The new 'white goods' required space and this accentuated the relative deprivation of much inner-city housing as the kitchens there were too small for many of the new labour-saving devices.

The conservative attitudes of the 1930s also affected the response to immigration. Ethnic issues were less pronounced politically and socially than they had been in the 1840s–1850s, the period of mass Irish immigration, or than they were to become later in the 1960s. Russian Jews had entered Britain in large numbers from the 1880s until the Aliens Act of 1905. There were fresh restrictions on immigration in 1914 and 1919, testifying to a loss of confidence. As a result, immigration declined in the 1920s and 1930s, and was not a major social or political controversy in the mainstream, although the issue had some purchase from 1933. Moreover, there was a widespread low-level racism and anti-semitism. They could at times lead to violence, but were more commonly a matter of social assumptions and institutional practices, as in exclusion policies for golf clubs or private schools or housing. In comparison with the situation in London in the 2000s, there was also very little racial co-habitation or inter-marriage.

There was a widespread assumption, frequently reiterated in popular fiction, that foreigners were particularly associated with crime and drug-taking in London. Detective novels often contrasted rugged British heroes with foreign residents of London generally presented in terms of supposedly undesirable physical characteristics such as shifty looks and yellowish skin. The heroes relied on their fists, their opponents on knives. In practice London's key gangsters were the Sabinis, led by an Anglo-Italian, Charles 'Darby', and linked with the Italian criminal world and specialising in gambling rackets. Similarly, prostitution in London was largely seen as a problem with foreign origins, and this affected the perception of the Soho district where prostitution was dominated by the Italian Messina brothers. Alec Waugh, a London-based novelist, described Soho in 1926 in terms of 'a swarthy duskiness, and oriental flavour; a cringing savagery that waits its hour'.[5]

Politically, London was the centre for the right-wing extremism of Sir Oswald Mosley's British Union of Fascists (BUF). The national headquarters were in Chelsea, and the BUF's first rally was held in Trafalgar Square in 1932; but this movement was unacceptable to the bulk of London opinion. Mosley, a member of the social élite who had been successively a Conservative, Independent and Labour MP, saw himself as a second Benito Mussolini, the Fascist dictator in Italy, but it proved easier to borrow the latter's black shirts as a party uniform than to recreate the political circumstances that had permitted the Fascist seizure of power in Italy. The demagoguery of Mosley and the violence of his supporters helped discredit the BUF, while the government maintained firm opposition to public violence.

Mosley's move into more aggressive anti-semitism in 1934–35, as with his projected march through Stepney on 4 October 1936, brought him no benefit, and when, in 1937, the BUF contested east London seats in the LCC elections, it did badly, winning only 16 per cent of the vote. East London was the centre of Jewish life in the capital, but the majority of the local population was not Jewish. The Left and the trade unions were powerful there,

After the war Mosley returned to politics and to controversy in London. In 1948 a number of large meetings were held by his Union Movement, often in Jewish areas of east London, which were broken up by anti-Fascist protesters. His Movement had some electoral support in places such as Stepney and Bethnal Green, but not elsewhere. This photograph was taken on 1 May 1948 at one of his rallies. Policemen can be seen, as well as a number of bodyguards.

© HULTON-DEUTSCH COLLECTION/CORBIS

and provided most of the 100,000 demonstrators who opposed the projected march through Stepney in 1936; in the event, the greatly outnumbered Blackshirts followed police advice and marched west from near the Tower, and not east into Stepney.

While cosmopolitanism was contested in London, there was also a strong reiteration of the theme of the Greater Britain, a relationship between Britain and the outer world focused on the empire. Every year, on Empire Day, which had been launched on 24 May 1896, Queen Victoria's birthday, large parades were held in Hyde Park. Moreover, the British Empire Exhibition in 1924-25, for which the first Wembley Stadium was built in 1923, was a major public occasion, celebrated in the press and the newsreels, and commemorated by a set of stamps. The assertion of empire was also seen in architecture, with the new Dominions paying for large buildings in the centre of London. Thus, in the Aldwych, Australia House, built in 1912-18, was followed by India House, built from 1928 to 1930. The site was shared by Bush House, built in stages between 1923 and 1935.

Much of the grand building in inner London remained a matter of serving the interests of commerce. As during the Victorian period, this could involve the destruction of the former City. Thus, All Hallows, Lombard Street, a Great Fire victim rebuilt by Wren, was closed in 1937 and demolished in 1938-39 to clear the way for the new headquarters for Barclay's Bank. In contrast, no parks were established in inner London.

The Conservative Party was very strong in outer London, and the expansion of suburbia served its interests. Having sat for Dundee as a Liberal, Churchill moved to suburbia (first as a Conservative-backed Constitutionalist and then as a Conservative), sitting for Epping from 1924 to 1945 and then for Woodford until 1964. There were also safe Conservative seats in inner London, although inner London was a key centre of the Labour Party, which controlled municipalities such as East Ham.

Left-wing activity was more varied, with the Communists numerous in working-class east London. Nevertheless, the impact of the Communists was limited. The most violent episode occurred in late 1932 when the arrival of marchers organised by the Communist-run National Unemployed Workers Movement (NUWM) and backed by many Londoners, led to large-scale fighting with the police, notably on 1 November when the demonstrators sought to hand in a petition to Parliament. As at many such times, ranging from the Gordon Riots of 1780 to the G20 protests of 2009, this episode was a consequence of London's role as capital city, which ensured that it was the focus of public order issues. Thereafter, there was far less violence from the Left; the NUWM march of 1934 and the Jarrow Crusade were both peaceful. Public displays of radical activity included the invasion of the Highbury pitch at half-time during a match between Arsenal and Charlton Athletic in January 1939, with unemployed demonstrators holding up a placard 'Kick With Us For Work Or Bread'. In practice, the general prosperity of the London region lessened social tension.

While Association football had enjoyed its first flush of enthusiasm in the industrial North, the number of London clubs increased. In a nostalgic nod to the area's former noble landowners, Tottenham began life in 1882 as the Hotspur Football Club. Arsenal was founded in 1886, but Chelsea not until 1905. Of the London clubs, Arsenal enjoyed the greatest early success, becoming the first southern team to win the League, in 1931. During the 1930s, Arsenal drew large crowds, like the other major London clubs. Football facilities had been expanded with the building of the stadium at Wembley Park, on which work was completed only four days before it was used for the first Football Association Cup Final in 1923; the Rugby League Cup Final was played there from 1929.

Despite some economic recovery from 1933, the problems of that decade added to the long-term challenge to Britain's economic position, especially from the USA, a challenge that had become more potent as a consequence of the costs of the First World War. The liberal economic order that had been created by Britain in the nineteenth century, and which had underpinned her strength, had been severely damaged by the war, while Britain also sold much of its foreign investments in order to finance the cripplingly expensive war effort. The serious financial strains of war had led Britain in effect to come off the Gold Standard, the convertibility of sterling and gold (as she had done in the French Revolutionary and Napoleonic Wars), and in 1919 she formally did so to avoid deflation. This was a step taken against the wishes of the City as, prior to the war, the Gold Standard and fixed exchange rates had strengthened the City's international position.

After the war, the British sought to recreate a liberal economic order focused on free trade and a revived Gold Standard, which they re-joined in 1925. The City pressed firmly

for these steps, the latter in order to provide stable finances. However, in the face of the economic nationalism of rivals, particularly France and the USA, the major problems of servicing debts, and the limitations of conventional financial and monetary concepts, the British had only limited success, and this problem hit the City. Economic nationalism at the level of major powers interacted with an extensive opposition to market mechanisms and preference for protectionism. These trends were greatly accentuated in the 1930s' slump, further damaging the international economy. World trade collapsed during the Depression, hitting London's economic role.

The influence of the City, however, has also been regarded as detrimental as far as British industry was concerned. Rejoining the Gold Standard in 1925 led to an overvalued currency, which hit exports. In turn, the Gold Standard was abandoned in September 1931 as a result of pressure upon sterling and the pound was then allowed to 'float' to find its own value against other currencies. This step hit the influence of the City. Protectionism was introduced in 1932. Thus, the traditional liberal economic order was dead long before the Second World War broke out. Nevertheless, after the early 1930s, the financial community remained powerful in Britain, its viewpoint central to British economic strategy, and this position helped ensure that in the 1930s there was only limited economic planning based on government intervention.

However, the City's role had diminished markedly. The end of the Gold Standard and of free trade led to a reluctant focus by the City on domestic investment. The dollar was clearly dominant, and London's international financial importance did not really re-emerge until the 1960s. Moreover, the limited commitment of Labour to the City's traditional role was to be shown in the 1940s, when wartime controls were maintained by the post-war Labour government, while the Bank of England was nationalised.[6] The implications of this decline for London's more general fortunes were overlaid by other themes of the 1930s and 1940s, especially the Depression, the Second World War and the start of the Cold War, but there were few signs then of the City's expansion in the late twentieth century.

The Second World War brought much more disruption to London than had the First. A savage air assault was anticipated at the beginning of the war, when there was widespread preparation for airborne gas attacks and large numbers of cardboard coffins were prepared. Under the apparent threat of such attack, 690,000 Londoners were evacuated by rail from London in September 1939, while black-out regulations were implemented. In the event, the attacks did not come until the following autumn (by which time many of the evacuees had returned), and did not include gas attacks.

From 7 September 1940, the German air force (the *Luftwaffe*) bombed London heavily. The German word Blitzkrieg – lightning war – was shortened to give a name to this terrifying new form of conflict: the Blitz. On the night of 24–25 August, London had been bombed as a result of a German navigational error: at that stage the Battle of Britain was a struggle for air mastery over southern England that did not entail an attack on the city. The RAF responded by bombing Berlin, which led the *Luftwaffe* to switch to attacking London, rather than the bases of Fighter Command, possibly in the hope that this would cause British morale to collapse. On 7 September, 320 German bombers attacked; the inadequately prepared defences were taken by surprise and failed to respond adequately. There were only 92 anti-aircraft guns ready for action, and their fire-control system failed. The British fighter squadrons also proved inadequate. Some 430 people were killed in the East End, where the docks were hit hard. Another 412 were killed in a night raid on 8 September. It was only on 11 September that anti-aircraft fire was sufficiently active to force the Germans to bomb from a greater height.

From 7 September until mid-November 1940, the Germans bombed London every night bar one. There were also large-scale daylight attacks between 7 and 18 September, as well as hit-and-run attacks. The attack on the moonlit night of 15–16 October proved particularly serious, with 400 bombers active, of which only one was shot down by the

A policeman hands a victim a mug of tea amid V-2 bombing wreckage. Tea and cigarettes were palliatives for the fear and shock felt by many under bombardment and the fear of attack.

© CORBIS

RAF's 41 fighters. The railway stations were hard hit, while Battersea Power Station was struck, as was the BBC headquarters at Portland Place. By mid-November, when the attacks became less focused on London, over 13,000 tons of high explosive bombs had been dropped on London as well as nearly one million incendiaries.

At first German aircraft losses were modest, apparently less than 1 per cent, in large part because the anti-aircraft defences were inadequate, as were the British fighters. Without good aerial radar, it became difficult to hit German bombers once they had switched to night attacks in September 1940 because they were operating near the edge of their fighter escort range. By the late spring of 1941, however, the defence became more effective, thanks to the use of radar-directed Beaufighter planes and ground defences.[7]

From mid-November to the end of February 1941, eight major raids were mounted on London, and, thereafter, the focus was on the ports until May 1941 when, after a devastating raid by 550 planes, on the night of 10–11 May, the bomber forces were moved to prepare for the invasion of the Soviet Union launched the following month. Air attacks on London were still mounted subsequently, but the worst months of the Blitz were over.

In bombing London in 1940–41, the German high command had set out to destroy civilian morale; indeed, before the war such an outcome had been widely anticipated. In the event, though there were occasional episodes of panic, on the whole morale remained high, with an emphasis on 'taking it'. There was an emphasis on forbearance and making do, notably at the docks, which continued operating. This helped ensure that Londoners were well fed.

Attempts to shelter from the bombing led some Londoners to seek refuge in the Underground system. Although initially banned from doing so, as the system was still running, citizens crowded into Tube tunnels, providing images for artists such as Henry Moore. Most of their young children had already been evacuated, but many children were in these tunnels. By late September 1940, about 177,000 Londoners were sleeping in the Tube system.

There was a degree of social tension in the response to the bombing despite the government's theme of equality in suffering. Thus, Londoners from the much-bombed dockside district of Silvertown, where there was a lack of shelters, forced their way into the Savoy Hotel's impressive bomb shelter. The docks were particularly heavily bombed, being the main target on 7 September 1940 and on many other occasions. Even in the early 1960s, a river trip from Hungerford Bridge down to beyond Tower Bridge went past serried ranks of burnt-out warehouses. Much of the dockland townscape was destroyed, especially the inter-connection of places of work and tightly packed terraced housing.

Film ensured that the Blitz was the first major episode of London's history that was captured dramatically for a wide audience, far more so than previous traumatic episodes such as the Black Death, the Peasants' Revolt, the Plague or the Great Fire. Photographs

of St Paul's, surrounded by flames and devastation, as that by Herbert Mason of the raid on 29 December 1940, acquired totemic force. Documentaries included *London Can Take It* (1940), shot during the Blitz and featuring iconic shots of St Paul's; *Christmas Under Fire* (1941), which included a tracking shot down an escalator to people sheltering on an Underground platform; and *Fires Were Started* (1943), which featured location shooting in the docks.[8]

Moreover, the bombing had an impact on literature and poetry. Elizabeth Bowen's novel *The Heat of the Day* (1949), a tragic love-story, has evocative descriptions of the atmosphere in the city while the air raids were still in progress. The lasting impact of the air attacks on writers was indicated by the number of novels in which characters were killed as a result. Louis MacNeice, an Irish-born poet who worked in London for the BBC, wrote *Brother Fire* (1943). The poem began:

> When our brother Fire was having his dog's day
> Jumping the London streets with millions of tin cans
> Clanking at his tail …
> Night after night we watched him slaver and crunch away

The beams of human life, the tops of topless towers.
… Fire … looting shops in elemental joy
And singing as you warmed up city block and spire.

In turn, from 13 June 1944, ground-to-ground V-1 flying bombs were launched at London, followed from 8 September by V-2 rockets. No fewer than 2,419 V-1s hit Greater London, with the highest casualties on 18 June when a V-1 hit the Guards' Chapel while a service was in progress, killing 121 people. This bombardment led to renewed large-scale evacuation of children in Operation Rivulet.

The V-2 rockets, which travelled at up to 3,000 m.p.h., could be fired from a considerable distance, and could not be destroyed by anti-aircraft fire as the V-1s could be. Their explosive payload was small and they could not be aimed accurately, but that was scant consolation to those killed and maimed. Over 2,700 Londoners were killed, and many more injured, by the 517 V-2s that hit London between 8 September 1944 and 27 March 1945. People could readily differentiate between the V-1, whose buzzing engine could be heard overhead until it cut out, heralding the landing of the bomb, and the V-2, inaudible to those on the ground as it approached at supersonic speed. In a use of deception, the British gave false reports of where the V-1s and V-2s were landing, in order to persuade the Germans to redirect their targets to fall short of London.

The V-1 bombardment of London resumed on 3 March 1945 when long-range V-1s were fired from the Netherlands. That month, 275 missiles were fired, indicating the extent to which the threat to London lasted until the close of war with resulting casualties and disruption. Current German writing on the supposed iniquities of Allied bombing does not discuss these attacks. If throughout, the V-weapon assault was irrelevant to the course of the conflict, nevertheless, in total, during the war, 29,890 Londoners, including one of my uncles, a young fire-watcher, were killed by air and missile attack and 50,507 seriously injured. Particular calamities included accidents such as the Bethnal Green disaster of March 1943 when 178 people died from suffocation as they rushed in panic out of an Underground shelter. Within the LCC area 50,000 houses were destroyed, along with another 66,000 in Greater London, while 288,000 required major repairs. Aside from the savage devastation of residential areas, particularly in Docklands but also across much of the suburbia of south London, many of London's historic buildings were also severely damaged, including the Guildhall, the House of Commons, the Inner Temple and Gray's Inn. Livery company halls and their records were also hit, as was Buckingham Palace. Despite being hit several times, St Paul's suffered remarkably little damage. Cecil Brown's 1945 panorama of the blitzed City depicted St Paul's defended by guardian angels.

Bombing, evacuation, rationing, and single-parenting, all central conditions of London life during the war, brought much disruption and homelessness, as well as the heavy demands of voluntary work in the midst of war.[9] Evacuation was a formidable undertaking and strain; large numbers of children were evacuated, as well as some accompanying adults. There were problems with homesickness and with parents missing children, and 'drift back' had to be resisted by providing parents with inexpensive train tickets so that they could see their children. There was also concern about infectious diseases that would be spread by London's children. Evacuation certainly revealed the gap between the life experiences of the inner-city children and those of rural England. It also captured the tension between traditional social practices, such as the poor girls from London who were placed in domestic service elsewhere, and the hopes of regeneration through the evacuation of many children from urban squalor to rural health.[10] Some wealthy families sent women and children overseas, mostly to North America, but this was impossible for the majority.

Social mores were greatly affected by the war. There was more freedom for women, because far more were employed while there was a general absence of partners, as well as different attitudes. In June 1943, the Mass-Observation Survey, reporting on female behaviour in some London pubs, found 'a free and easy atmosphere in which it was very easy and usual to pick up with a member of the opposite sex'. Aside from changes resulting directly from the war, such as the presence of large numbers of the military, aspects of life as diverse as crime and religion, work and the arts, were all affected by the war. Religious observance declined markedly, but the cinema remained very popular, including during the air raids. The varied impact of the war included an attempt to disguise the city not

Military personnel are used to unload supplies during an unofficial strike by dockers in October 1945. By far the most important and successful dock strike in London had occurred in 1889, when peacefully demonstrating dock workers had campaigned for 'the docker's tanner', a rate of 6d. per hour. A powerful new dockers' union was another outcome of that stoppage. Later strikes were usually less successful.

only with the blackout but also, for example, with the security restrictions that affected the *A–Z Atlas and Guide*.[11]

The extent to which the war led to a consensual society in London is unclear. There was certainly a language of inclusiveness and sharing, and a stress on the 'Home Front', which made social distinctions seem unacceptable. Yet, there was also resistance to government policy, not least with the insistent 'black market', which proved a way to evade rationing. Nevertheless, overwhelming reality measured up to reputation: Londoners did display tremendous fortitude, and individual and collective self-reliance and mutual assistance, in the face of a sustained and deadly assault. It was a noble stance in a great cause.

The devastation of the Second World War pushed forward the planning process. In 1943 the Ministry of Housing and Local Government was created, providing a context for a national planning policy. A Town and Country Planning Act followed in 1944. Moreover, Professor Patrick Abercrombie, a leading town planner, was appointed to draw up plans for London, and in 1943 the *County of London Plan* by Abercrombie and J.H. Forshaw was published. The LCC area, however, was too small to provide an effective basis for planning. Already, in 1927, the Greater London Regional Planning Committee had been established, while, in *The Government and Misgovernment of London* (1939), William Robson had pressed for a single metropolitan authority for the whole of London. In 1944, Abercrombie's *Greater London Plan* looked at the wider regional situation as a key context for London, putting the LCC in a planner's framework. This plan suggested moving houses and jobs away from London to New Towns built beyond the Green Belt on greenfield sites. New industry was to be banned within inner London, and 415,000 people were to be moved from it to the New Towns. There was no sense of consultation being necessary or desirable, and, read today, the plan seems disturbingly naïve, not least in its assumptions about providing prosperity. The plan mirrored the Social Democrats' plans for Stockholm and took the zoning of urban space as an axiom of planning analysis and policy.

The overriding drive was for a reconstruction that would not entail a return to the pre-war situation. This conviction characterised the governance of London in the late 1940s, especially by the Labour governments of 1945–51, but also by the LCC and the boroughs. Labour did well in London in the general election of 1945, winning such seats as Wimbledon. The Labour leader and new Prime Minister, Clement Attlee, was an experienced London politician, in 1919 the first Labour Mayor of Stepney, and from 1922 MP for Limehouse, a seat he held until 1950 when he became MP for West Walthamstow. In many respects the 1940s in London were Labour years, as other prominent Labour leaders such as Ernest Bevin (Wandsworth Centre), Herbert Morrison (South Hackney) and Harold Laski (Chairman of the party) were also London figures, although Bevin's origins were in the South West. As with the reconstruction of the city, however, Labour in power was to prove better at short-term progress than at fundamental improvement.

CHAPTER

9

There were people and cars and big, red buses everywhere – it wasn't a bit like Darkest Peru.

MICHAEL BOND, A BEAR CALLED PADDINGTON (1958)

W E C O U L D B E G I N this chapter with the saga of the Millennium Dome, but it would be inappropriate to dignify the mindless rubbish that filled the edifice – the last shout of New Labour's vacuous 'Cool Britannia' – with such attention. Instead, it is a film, *The Long Good Friday* (1980), directed by John Mackenzie, that will get this chapter started. Voted by *Empire* in 1997 as the best British movie ever made, this film was controversial when it came out because it suggested that the Provisional Irish Republican Army (IRA) was well-nigh invincible. The resulting controversy helped delay the film's release, but also distracted attention from the film's depiction of a London in change. The protagonist, Harold Shand, played by Bob Hoskins, was a symbol of a transformed city. A self-made 'boy from Putney', Shand was a millionaire businessman with ambitions for Thames-side property development. He was also corrupt, and his 'Corporation' was an organisation spanning crime and business. Criminal London were presented as awash with new money, but also under pressure from stronger international forces. Wooing American investors, Shand was attacked by a shadowy group which used extreme violence and turn out to be the IRA, who have been inadvertently crossed by Shand's gang. The IRA were able not only to wreck his favourite pub – that, as a classic London image of locality and longevity, had long since replaced the parish church – but also to capture Hoskins at the close.

The *Long Good Friday* was more than a brilliant film. It recorded social change, not least with Shand's new money, seen in his clothes, flat and Rolls Royce (the victim of a car bomb), and his best friend, a homosexual stabbed to death when cruising at a swimming pool. Moreover, the film, much of which was shot on location, suggested that London

CONFRONTING A NEW AGE, 1945–2010

Building Westway, the elevated section of dual-carriageway that carries traffic on the A40 closer to central London from the west. This photograph was taken on 12 August 1969, not long before it was completed.

was changing physically under the influence of the property development and new money represented by Shand, and also that gangsterism and big business were at least similar. The film also implied that London had both been laid open, and had laid itself open, to foreign influence, if not control, in part by the American investors, themselves linked to the Mafia, and also by the IRA. Only a film of course, but Barrie Keefee's script captured a sense of profound uneasiness already at the outset of a decade that was to bring profound change, to the Docklands, to the City, and to much else of the physical and social fabric of the city.

Moving on to the Millennium Dome at Greenwich, the building and the contents arranged as a national celebration of the Millennium, were fancifully compared by some to the Great Exhibition, but, by then, the world and attitudes of 1851 were very distant. More therefore was at stake than the failure of this tacky celebration. Indeed, confidence in Western values had been assailed over the previous forty years, and a multi-cultural London found many nineteenth-century attitudes abhorrent. Moreover, London no longer takes the position it once did at the centre of the Western world. This change is due not so much to the fate of the city, or even of Britain as a whole, important as they have been, but rather due to the decline of global interest in Britain as a model. Alongside this, national self-confidence, and, with that, the confidence of London, had fallen dramatically, and this continues to be the case.

On 21 November 1947, this photograph was taken from Buckingham Palace as thousands of Londoners gathered around the Victoria Memorial at the entrance to Buckingham Palace to cheer the newly married Princess Elizabeth and Philip, Duke of Edinburgh, and members of the royal family when they appeared on the palace balcony following the wedding in Westminster Abbey.
© BETTMANN/CORBIS

In the period covered by this chapter, London was more greatly affected by the decisions of national government than it had been over the previous sixty-five years. Most obviously, due to government policy, the shape of the city changed less in the post-war years than in the earlier period, or, looked at differently, the city came to encompass much of the south-east of England as the Outer Metropolitan Area expanded and commuting to London spread. The key element in the shape of the more restricted (and conventional) understanding of London was the planning regime, and, in particular, the determination by planners to control the extent of contiguous suburbia.

Legislation took forward pre-war ideas about restricting London's development, and favouring, instead, a combination of a Green Belt with planning Garden Cities in the greater South East. Under the post-war Labour governments of 1945–51, the New Towns Act of 1946 was followed by a new Town and Country Planning Act in 1947. New Towns were designed to complement Green Belts: London was to be contained, with a Green Belt, and New Towns were to be built outside the Belt. The first, Stevenage, was chosen in November 1946. Within three years, another seven were designated for London overspill: Harlow, Hemel Hempstead, Crawley, Bracknell, Basildon, Hatfield and Welwyn Garden City. Similar policies of planned residential decentralisation were seen in urban policy elsewhere, and with similar results, leading to new towns outside Paris and to satellite suburbs near Stockholm.

The New Towns became major centres of employment in their own right, but the growth of dormitory settlements which were not planned in that way led to an increase in long-distance commuting into London. Moreover, the growth of both the New Towns and dormitory settlements contributed to the large-scale shift in population from London to other parts of the South East. Outside London, the population of the South East rose rapidly. That of Berkshire, for example, more than doubled between 1931 and 1971. Expansion there was concentrated in the east of the county, the part best suited for commuting to London. Thus, building of the New Town at Bracknell started in 1950, and, by 1981, the population there was 49,000. With time, especially from the 1970s, commuting from further afield became more common, notably from East Anglia, the Midlands and the West Country. Long-distance commuting was encouraged by the practice of the weekly commute, which entailed living in London during the week.

The London Green Belt was finally secured with an Act of 1959. Thanks to its Green Belt, which has remained reasonably firm, despite development pressures, especially those linked to the M25, London did not leap forward from Edgware to Elstree, and the Northern Line extension via Elstree to Watford, planned before the war, was not built, although preparatory work had been done. Nevertheless, as much urban development simply passed the Green Belt, it created new pressures further afield, for example around Ipswich and Reading. There was also a major expansion in the population of Peterborough and Northampton. Thus, if London is seen in terms of a wider commuter belt, rather than the area currently covered by the Greater London Authority (GLA), then the shape of the city has changed greatly, indeed more significantly than ever before, and its frontier of settlement is now out past Peterborough.

This issue raises the question of the scope of any study of London. In particular, if the City is seen as an inadequate basis for discussion of say London in the sixteenth century and, still more obviously, the nineteenth, or the LCC area for the 1930s, it is unclear why the recent or present situation should be defined in terms of the GLC and GLA. The basis for the study of London is therefore problematic, indeed inherently unstable, and this point challenges the attempt to discuss the long-term history of London in terms of the particular resonances of its centre or central area.

Expansion did not only take place outside London. Within the Greater London area, council-house building was halted by the Second World War. Thereafter, it revived, driven on by severe wartime damage to the housing stock which left many living in temporary accommodation or living with extended families, as well as by expectations of a better life after the war, and a post-war rise in the birth-rate. Under legislation of 1944, councils had the right to purchase bombed sites.

Labour, in power in Westminster from 1945, as well as still in the LCC, associated itself with the housing revival. The Temple Hill council estate in Dartford, opened by the Prime Minister, Clement Attlee, in July 1947, was an example of the council-funded housing designed both to force people from slum dwellings and to replace war-damaged stock. The houses on this estate were concrete with pre-fabricated parts. However, a severe shortage of resources in the post-war economy, as well as the priority given to industrial reconstruction after wartime disruption, ensured that the house-building that took place was insufficient. In the late 1940s, by necessity, many London families remained with their parents long after they wished to move.

Problems with the housing supply were an important aspect of a generally troubled city during the austerity years of the late 1940s. Rationing continued into the mid-1950s; there were serious shortages of coal, the basic source of energy and fuel; people were often cold; and much of inner London remained a wasteland of bomb sites, which was captured in the films of the period, such as *Passport to Pimlico* (1949). Other films carrying location shots from London included *Hue and Cry* (1947) and *The Blue Lamp* (1950). Both were produced by Ealing Studios and offer a real sense of place, using the bomb sites as locations, as well as White City Stadium in the latter. *The Lavender Hill Mob* (1951) continued this trend.

The political and trade union situation was unsettled. Troops were used to contain strikes, which were illegal until 1951. The government claimed that Communist conspiracies were behind the strikes, most prominently the London dock strike of 1949. The docks were particularly prone to unofficial strikes, in part because the dockers resented the discipline of the Dock Labour Scheme introduced in 1947. This scheme brought a measure of job security, but lessened the worker freedoms enjoyed under the earlier, casual system of employment. There were dock strikes during each year of the Labour government, although most labour relations was far less adversarial.

There was a massive extension of the power of the state with a series of nationalisations. These included the Bank of England (1946), the hospitals (1948), railways (1948), the electricity supply (1948), and gas (1949). Far more Londoners were brought into state employment, which underlined the possibilities for central planning, as did the shortage of resources in the private sector. The creation of the National Health Service in 1948 represented an opportunity to improve medical services in London. The NHS also marked a tremendous extension of state control and direction. Hospitals in the London region were in effect nationalised. In the long term, it is far from clear that health provision benefited greatly from the new system of control, but, at the time, there was a strong sense of new beginnings, and the provision of a universal 'free' (only at the point of delivery) health service was perceived as a reward for winning the war.

The Conservatives saw the shortage of houses as an electoral opportunity and, in the election of 1951, which they won under Churchill, made much of a promise to build

Chatting in a street of council housing in the new town of Hemel Hempstead, Hertfordshire, 27 March 1954.
GETTY IMAGES

more homes. Helped by a higher allocation of government resources, co-operation with the house-builders, and a cutting of the building standards for council houses, the Conservative government, which remained in power until 1964, achieved its target, and this success permitted extensive rehousing in the 1950s. Londoners from the East End were rehoused in new council-housing estates which included those at Debden, Hainault and Harold Hill. The key political figure, Harold Macmillan, Minister of Housing and Local Government from 1951 to 1954 (and Prime Minister 1957–63), was MP for Bromley from 1945 to 1964.

The effects of this rehousing are a matter of controversy as it is unclear how far problems readily apparent during the 1960s existed during the 1950s when there was a greater desire simply for new housing. The buildings of the 1950s, many of which were low-rise and fairly generous with space, for example the Lansbury Estate in Poplar, should be distinguished from the system-built tower blocks largely built in the 1960s. There is considerable evidence to suggest that the problems of poorly built estates were much more apparent in the 1960s, and that earlier developments were often better built and more popular.

The 1950s was also a decade of low recorded crime rates in London, certainly in comparison with what was to come. Furthermore, the experience of poor Londoners changed greatly as a result of the building. Many of the new houses provided people with

The infamous Kray twins, Ronnie (1933–95) and Reggie (1933–2000), with their mother Violet and their grandfather Jimmy. East London's most notorious criminal gangsters, the brothers became Cockney legends and well-known celebrities of a kind in the 1960s before their eventual arrest and life imprisonment.

© HULTON-DEUTSCH COLLECTION/CORBIS

Hyde Park Corner in May 1962. A traffic underpass was built below the new five-lane roundabout around the Wellington Arch. Park Lane became a major through-route. The Park Lane London Hilton is being built in the background.
© DAVID LEES/CORBIS

their first bathrooms and inside toilets. The dynamics of family space, and the nature of privacy, changed as a result.

Nevertheless, a critical view about slum clearance and re-housing dominated subsequent discussion. Aside from the social disruption of the move to new locations, a disruption particularly felt by those who had never previously moved, many of the new neighbourhoods were poorly planned and unpopular with their occupants. These new neighbourhoods tended to lack community amenities and means of identification, such as local shops and pubs. Moreover, the social fabric that had helped Londoners to cope with strain was sundered. Families were separated from relatives, hitting the support systems crucial for childcare and for looking after the elderly. On the new housing estates, there was a decline in the three-generation extended family and a move towards the nuclear family, which hit traditional communities and patterns of care. Grandparents were more socially and geographically isolated as a result of these changes, and many old people found the estates alien, if not frightening.

Furthermore, the inter-connection of work and tightly packed terraced housing seen in many pre-war neighbourhoods was not recreated in this rebuilding. In dockland areas, for example, instead of trying to preserve close communities, or implement utilitarian notions linked to harbour activities, generalised notions of supposedly progressive town-planning were applied, without reference to local experience or historical associations; the dire consequences of these policies can still be seen today. Whereas there had been a considerable degree of proximity between working-class and other housing in the Victorian period, there was now a more marked differentiation, which could be regarded almost as a segregation of the working class onto housing estates.

More generally, concern about urban sprawl and the pressures arising from the 'baby boom', as well as a critique of suburbia, not least in Tom Nairn's 1955 attack on 'subutopia', encouraged higher-density housing than in the inter-war years or indeed immediately after the Second World War. Alongside architectural and planning fashions, and land prices, themselves greatly increased by constraints resultant from Green Belt policies, all of which encouraged high-density housing, this concern about sprawl contributed to a high-rise development which matched that around many European cities. Pre-fabricated methods of construction ensured that multi-storey blocks of flats could be built rapidly and

Ranks of prefabs in Stoneyard Lane, Poplar, 1977. This method of construction allowed basic, temporary accommodation to be provided to communities devastated by bombing during the war. Many continued to be occupied a generation later. Beyond the houses to the right is the West India Dock Road, with the docks themselves further on.

© HULTON-DEUTSCH
COLLECTION/CORBIS

inexpensively, and the LCC and some borough councils in the 1960s took pride in their number, size and visibility.

Extolled at the time, and illustrated in guidebooks, municipal multi-storey flats were subsequently attacked as of poor quality, ugly, out of keeping with the existing urban fabric and street pattern, lacking in community feeling, and as breeding grounds of alienation and crime. Frequent heating and ventilation problems caused condensation; lifts often broke down; vandalism became a serious problem; and the morale of tenants, unsurprisingly, fell. Flat roofs let in water, while many public spaces, such as stairwells, were neglected and indeed sites of urination and crime. Moreover, in place of individual gardens, there were unfenced green spaces for which none of the residents had responsibility and which were apt to be desolate, sometimes becoming dumping grounds for rubbish.

For many Londoners, this – and not Carnaby Street and the new 'swinging London' of the 'pop scene' that attracted so much international attention – was the 1960s. Moreover, the mid-1960s saw increased concern about poverty in London, although, in practice, what were termed 'problem' families had already been an issue in the 1950s. Equally, the 1960s in London could be seen in terms of serious industrial decline, with consequences in terms of rising unemployment.

New estates were designed as entire communities, with elevated walkways dubbed 'streets in the sky'. Most estates, however, were failures, poorly built and not contributing to social cohesion, which was abundantly true, for example, of the LCC's Elgin Estate in Paddington. In 1968 four people were killed when part of the pre-fabricated Ronan Point tower block in Newham collapsed following a gas explosion, just two months after the building had been finished; this tragedy was reported widely, and seen as symptomatic of a more general failure of tower blocks and modern construction methods.

Disenchantment continued, so that the decision of English Heritage in 1998 to list five blocks on the Alton Estate in Roehampton as an architectural masterpiece was widely deplored by the tenants. Elsewhere, there were many demolitions by the 1990s, not only of high-rise estate buildings, but also of low-rise, deck-access blocks, such as the Chalkhill area in Brent, demolished in 1998–99.

This post-war rush of public building of what often turned out to be inadequate, short-lived housing, was followed by a steep decline in construction from the 1970s on. Many council dwellings were in need of fresh investment, a problem also true of sections of the private rental market, especially in poor areas where the quality of provision was anyway bad. A resultant lack of decent, affordable housing was correctly seen as a comment on the failure of public provision, and this lack became a particular issue for those termed essential workers, such as teachers and nurses. Too few new houses were being built, while the cost of rehabilitating existing housing stock was often seen as prohibitive. All of this contributed to a growing sense of a crisis in housing.

Affordable housing was a political issue, but one that neither of the major political parties could address successfully, in part because of the inherent clash between the governmental wish to control and allocate, and the exigencies of commercial value. These exigencies had played a role in the late 1950s and early 1960s in what was known as Rachmanism: the use of the 1957 Rent Act to push out low-paying tenants in order to raise rents or redevelop properties. The use of intimidation, which revealed an under-current of violence in much of London, made the practice a scandal, but the same tendency played a role more generally. On the other hand, rent controls, the response of the national Labour government elected in 1964, hit landlords' profits, led to the replacement of private landlords by owner-occupiers, and resulted in a decline in the amount of property available for rent. This decline reduced the flexibility of the housing market and exacerbated the consequences of the decline in new public housing from the 1970s. The private rental market was to revive in the 2000s in large part due to the ease of obtaining buy-to-let mortgages, but that revival contributed greatly to an unsustainable rise in London property prices.

Successive governments encouraged 'brown-field' building on derelict ground within existing urban areas in London, and pressed for greater housing density, but these wishes were at marked variance with public demands for space within and around their homes. In what has amounted to a rejection of what appeared to be the hostile nature of crime-ridden townscapes, as well as of government views of the desirability of high-density socially mixed populations, a small but growing number chose to move out into gated communities within London. A survey of British Social Attitudes in 1999 by the National Centre for Social Research showed that those who lived in big cities were the group keenest to move, and current polls indicate that many Londoners would prefer to move out. Anxieties about crime and about the quality of local schools were often cited by those dissatisfied with metropolitan life. These anxieties affected both those living in affluent owner-occupation and in neighbouring public housing estates where social deprivation and alienation were pronounced.

Alongside much unattractive and poor-quality municipal housing in the 1960s, there was also a brutal rebuilding of municipal centres within London, for example in Swiss Cottage, and also in outer London, such as the massive redevelopment of central Croydon as a major office centre. Professional planners played a major role in this process, which sought both to cope with traffic congestion and to provide modern images for the centres. Modernism was to the fore. And much was torn down. In the 1960s, the great Doric Arch, Great Hall and Shareholders' Room were needlessly destroyed when Euston station was rebuilt (see page 298). Social change was also registered, as aristocrats sold their town houses. One of the grandest, Londonderry House in Park Lane, the site of numerous fashionable inter-war parties, was sold in 1962 and demolished, to be replaced by the Londonderry House Hotel.

The progressive architectural style and planning ideas of the 1930s became an orthodoxy that was used for the widespread post-war rebuilding, for urban development, and for the new construction made possible by the investment in hospitals, schools and New Towns. A centrepiece was the first major post-war public building, the Royal Festival Hall (1951), designed for the Festival of Britain's South Bank Exhibition, by Sir Robert Hogg Matthew, the Chief Architect to the London County Council. The Thames-side site, previously largely factories and wharves, had been extensively bombed during the war. Offering a Labour vision of progress, the Festival, which was visited by close to 8½ million people, reflected confidence, or at least interest, in new solutions, but, in fact, most people were less confident than at the time of the Great Exhibition a century earlier. Moreover, whatever the success of the Royal Festival Hall, the ugliness of much subsequent Modernist building, such as the Chelsea Barracks of the 1960s, led to depressing, if not inhuman, vistas.

In 1968, when this photograph was taken, the riverbank of the Pool of London still bristled with cranes, although the volume of traffic was now tiny compared to the heyday of this, the original heartland of the port of London. This view shows a Routemaster bus crossing north on London Bridge, with several ships to be seen tied up near Tower Bridge.

Later in the twentieth century, new space was found for development on the riverbanks as a result of the closure of the docks. The closure of the East India Docks in 1967, the London Docks and Surrey Commercial Docks in 1970, and of the Royal docks in 1981, was matched by the failure of associated industries and a major rise in unemployment. Docklands had been thriving in the 1950s, but it declined rapidly thereafter, with the redrawing of global trade routes as imperial links ebbed. These challenges were exacerbated by the failure of the port to match competitors benefiting from post-war development, especially Rotterdam, such that there was a move of activity from London back to the Low Countries in at least one aspect of their long-standing rivalry and relationship. London's dockers did not respond well to the change in working practices required by containerisation, and this was a major reason for an industrial militancy that encouraged the shift in freight business to Rotterdam. The first British container ship sent to Australia, the *Encounter Bay*, sailed from Rotterdam in 1969 because of an industrial dispute at Tilbury. Moreover, within Britain, ports such as Felixstowe and Dover proved better able to respond to the challenges and opportunities of containerisation because they were less unionised, whereas the London docks faced serious and persistent labour problems. Militant trade unionism scarcely encouraged investment in London.

Aside from containerisation, there was a rise in roll-on roll-off trade, with lorries driving directly onto ferries, which benefited Dover, Felixstowe and Harwich. By 1975, Ipswich, Felixstowe and Harwich together ranked second only to London in both the value and tonnage of non-fuel exports, and, by 1994, Felixstowe handled nearly half the country's deep-sea container traffic. London, by then, had been hit by a vicious spiral of technological change, notably the acceleration of containerisation, and its impact on a labour-intensive workforce prone to union militancy and disruption.

With London's maritime trade focused 26 miles down-river at Tilbury, the derelict Docklands provided an unprecedented development opportunity near the centre of a major city. Already, in 1969, a plan to transform St Katharine Docks into a marina was launched. Never a great commercial success, the docks had been damaged during the Blitz and finally closed to commercial traffic in 1968 and sold to the GLC. The redevelopment plan entailed the demolition of many of Thomas Telford's original large warehouses: Warehouse A was replaced by the concrete lump that is now the 800-bedroom Tower Hotel.

Development was politicised with the Conservative government of Margaret Thatcher (1979–90) taking a close interest in directing the process. The creation of the London Docklands Development Corporation (LDDC) in 1981 led to the regeneration of much of east London, with the building of houses and offices and improvements to the transport system. Some dock basins were filled in, for example in the former Surrey Commercial Docks in Rotherhithe, and new roads and houses were constructed. New industries in Rotherhithe included the printing works of the *Daily Mail*.

The LDDC was a government body designed to circumvent the constraints of the Greater London Council and local boroughs, both of which were under Labour control and regarded as anti-entrepreneurial, while the Conservative government also abolished the South East Economic Planning Council because its planners were seen as antipathetic to growth. Indeed the government regarded the local authorities, workers and unions as conspiring together in a way that was destroying their communities and damaging the economy.

An enterprise zone was created on the Isle of Dogs in 1982, and the LDDC lasted until abolished by the Labour government in 1998. There was no comparable regional economic planning for London as a whole. The regeneration was heavily subsidised as the government bore all of the cost of clearing the site and of infrastructure, especially transport, a significant subsidy from a government that decried subsidies.

Brutalism of the 1970s on a grand scale: an 800-room concrete hotel next to St Katharine Docks.

PHOTOGRAPH: CARNEGIE, 2009

The financial centre of Canary Wharf on the site of one of the former West India Docks on the Isle of Dogs, upon which work started in 1988, proved an abrupt contrast to earlier patterns of work within Docklands. By 2003 Canary Wharf contained 13.1 million square feet of office space, and many City companies had moved their headquarters there, including newspapers from Fleet Street. The social context of employment in the Isle of Dogs, and London as a whole, was transformed, although, from a different perspective, the contrast between Canary Wharf and the continued poverty of the borough of Tower Hamlets suggested rather a reshaping of traditional patterns of social differentiation. Indeed, there was criticism of the LDDC on the grounds that it brought few benefits to local people, instead helping to create jobs and houses that were inappropriate to them: they were unable to afford the new houses, while the new jobs required skilled workers who came in from outside the region. Tower Hamlets had wanted to use the land for industrial development that would create blue-collar jobs. Conversely, there was an unfair comparison of the LDDC with the GLC's less-than-inspiring attempt to develop Thamesmead on the Erith and Plumstead Marshes as a new town within London itself: the GLC had fewer resources for the task and notably did not benefit from a comparable investment in infrastructure.

The office tower blocks of Canary Wharf were a symbol of the new economy, and were seen in that light. The bombing of the Canary Wharf tower by the IRA in 1996 was intended not only as a practical demonstration of the capacity to hit hard at Britain's

This former
spice warehouse
in St Katharine
Docks was
converted into a
mock balconied
timber-framed
public house
– the Dickens
Inn – in the
1960s, shortly
after the dock
was closed, but
well before the
more recent
redevelopment
of the rest of
Docklands.

PHOTOGRAPH: CARNEGIE 2009

economy, but also as a symbolic strike at the legacy of Thatcherism. This new economy was a system in which London and the South East were clearly the focus of economic power, not least as there was a serious decline in traditional manufacturing regions, such as the North East and South Wales, in the 1980s. The Conservatives, and the Establishment in general, became ever more focused on London, the South East, and the world of money and services there, largely to the detriment of traditional interests that they had also represented. This process continued under Tony Blair, Labour Prime Minister from 1997 to 2007, with the South East being responsible for a growing share of GDP. Yet, as far as London was concerned, the situation was more complex, with marked differences in prosperity between parts of the city. One indication was the nature of tenure. Owner-occupied households were more common in the outer boroughs, and rented households in inner London, a situation that remains the case to the present day.

Unlike in the inter-war years, the transport system in London changed not with the expansion of suburbia but with new capacity within the already built-up area. From the 1960s, the Underground expanded considerably. The Victoria Line, opened in 1968–69, the first automatic underground railway in the world, was followed by the Jubilee Line, completed in 1979, the Piccadilly extension to Heathrow, opened in 1977, and the Jubilee extension to Greenwich and Stratford in 1999. The Docklands Light Railway was opened in 1987, and its extension to London City airport in 2005 and to Lewisham in 2009. The expansion of the Underground from the 1960s helped, to a degree, to compensate for the earlier neglect of south London, although part of that neglect was due to the intractable sub-surface of south-east London. Although not part of the Underground, the Heathrow Express provided a rapid underground link to the airport, which assisted the growth of centralised national air travel from Heathrow. The role of public transport was shown, moreover, in the large Underground station at North Greenwich on the Jubilee Line built to serve the Millennium Dome. However, the expansion of the Underground also led to neglect of the smooth running of the rest of the system. Insufficient attention was given to making it efficient, user-friendly, reliable and comfortable, and lines like the Northern became notorious for poor service.

At the same time, the significant role of London as an international transport hub was enhanced and underlined in 1992 when the Channel Tunnel was opened to rail travel. Initially Waterloo, where the Eurostar terminal was completed in 1994, was the London terminus, but, from 2007, St Pancras, represented as a glitzy cross between Victorian engineering and modern consumerism, took this role. The move was designed to underline London's role as a domestic hub, as the move to St Pancras permitted through services from the north of England.

A fighter airfield in the war and the site of one of London's oldest prehistoric settlements, London (Heathrow) airport opened in 1946, and was followed by Gatwick in 1958, the year in which Croydon Airport closed. By 1999 Heathrow handled 62 million passengers,

Part of Terminal 5 at Heathrow, photographed in March 2008, just as it was opened. A military airfield since the First World War, the site was developed further for the RAF in the 1940s, the name coming from a small row of houses on Hounslow Heath. When Terminal 1 was opened in 1968, Heathrow was already handling almost 15 million passengers annually. It is now approaching 70 million.

© ANDY RAIN/EPA/CORBIS

making it the fourth busiest airport in the world and the busiest outside the USA. It was also a key centre of employment for west London, and doubly important because of the collapse in alternative employment, especially with the decline of the engineering and electrical industries in Ealing and Hounslow from the 1960s. Gatwick, Stansted, Luton and London City airports contribute to London's role as a plane hub. The last was opened in Docklands in 1987. By 2008, there were 480,000 flights over London a year, a formidable challenge to the city's environment, and, due to the noise imprint, part of the local pattern of London's politics.

On the roads, meanwhile, trams were finally totally replaced by diesel-engined motor buses. London's last tram ran in 1952, and the last trolleybus in 1962. The cost of electricity and the maintenance costs of the wires hit trolleybuses, while motor buses benefited from greater manoeuvrability. The rise and fall of the trams and the trolleybuses are a reminder of the rapidity of change in communications. From the 1990s, there was a small-scale revival of trams in Croydon, now seen as a viable alternative to buses. More Londoners, however, came to travel by car, while commuting, much of it by train, but, as the M25 shows every weekday, a lot by car, became more significant in the South East. In 1981–91 alone, there was a 7 per cent increase of commuting into London. Bus use in London has risen considerably in recent years, but production, while once a major London industry, followed most of London's manufacturing into decline, with the London bus works closing in 1976.

At the neighbourhood level, major road routes became obstacles, as their high street sections were turned into busy through-routes, for example at Hendon Central or along the South Circular. This problem encouraged the building of new through-routes unrelated to existing neighbourhoods, with the M4 being driven through the Osterley estate in 1965, and the GLC proposing, in the Greater London Development Plan, an inner London motorway box. The plan also encompassed orbital motorways in London's suburbia, as well as motorways designed to link London to the national motorway network. There was large-scale opposition, however, and most of the plan was discarded, although the western and eastern parts of the inner box were built. In turn, roads such as the Westway caused destruction as they were built, and left blight in their aftermath. In her novel *A Certain Justice* (1997), P.D. James observed:

Westway had, after all, been relatively prosperous, a comfortable enclave of the respective, reliable, law-abiding lower middle class who owned their houses and took a pride in clean lace curtains and carefully tended front gardens, each a small triumph of individuality over the drab conformity. But their world was crashing down with their houses, rising in great choking clouds of ochre dust. Only a few houses were now left standing as the work on the road-widening went inexorably ahead … Soon there would be nothing but tarmac and the ceaseless roar and screech of traffic thundering westward out of London. In time even memory would be powerless to conjure up what once had been.

The M25 around London, completed in 1986, became the busiest route in the country, as well as helping to define London's shape. The usage of the M25 indicated the need for an orbital route, not least due to the growing congestion caused by heavy traffic trundling through London, much of which was caused by the long-term switch of Britain's trade away from the Atlantic ports and towards the Continent. Yet the usage of the M25 also showed the extent to which new roads led to new demand. This demand contributed to the pollution in London, and also to a more general environmental degradation.

Those neighbourhoods that were not bisected by through-routes were still affected by the car. Side streets became 'rat runs', quick shortcuts linking busier roads, and the sides of all roads filled up with parked cars. Parking space came to take a greater percentage of London's space, and the problems of parking became a major topic of conversation. In response, the Congestion Charge was adopted in central London in 2003 as a way to try to limit the movement of cars into the city centre, and the Congestion Charge Zone was extended westward in 2007 in order to cover Kensington, Chelsea and part of Westminster.

While often deplored by planners, commentators and many Londoners, cars were widely used and a democratising mechanism, making work and leisure more accessible. Greater mobility for most, but not all, of London's population, however, both exacerbated contrasts between different parts of the city and also emphasised social segregation. Thus, car ownership brought a sense – albeit perhaps an illusion – of freedom, and an access to opportunities and options for many, but not all.

The division of the population into spatially distinct communities, defined by differing levels of wealth, expectations, opportunity and age, was scarcely new in London's history, but it did become more pronounced during the twentieth century, and an obvious aspect of what was termed the underclass was their relative lack of mobility. This was doubly important because of links between cars, status, independence and notions of virile masculinity. The theft of cars reflected their appeal. At the same time, buses, cycles and walking remained important as means of travel, the last mostly much underrated in accounts of London's transport system.

In addition to the built environment, there was a transformation in London's air. The problems of air quality in part reflected London's location in a bowl created by surrounding hills, as well as the particular difficulty created by warm air trying to rise, but being trapped by high-pressure skies above. The trapped air, if polluted by smoke, provided obstacles to vision and breathing. The nightmarish quality of a London smog was captured in Patricia Wentworth's novel *Ladies' Bane* (1954):

It was rather like a slow motion picture. That was the fog of course. Noting could really move in a fog like this. The buses would be stopped – and the cars – and the people who were abroad would crawl like beetles and wish to be at home again – and the watches and clocks would all slow down and time too.

The very bad London smog of 1952, which killed more than 4,000 people and even asphyxiated cattle at Smithfield Market, led to the designation of London as a smokeless zone in 1955 and to the Clean Air Act of 1956, which required the conversion of buildings from coal-use and made individual households responsible for the cost. This legislation was made possible by the fact that (as never before) the means for such conversions were now readily to hand. Gas became the principal source of heating. However, as with clean water and the end of cholera a century earlier, improvement was not instantaneous. London had a further smog in 1957 and then lost another 750 people to a serious smog in 1962, which led to another Clean Air Act in 1968.

The decline of London's industrial base, which was especially pronounced in the late 1960s and early 1970s, also contributed to the change in the character of the capital's pollution. The conversion to smokeless fuel led to an atmosphere that was no longer acidic nor heavy with sooty smuts, and helped ensure that London became cleaner and brighter. Yet, other particulates and chemicals became more significant in London's environment, in part as a consequence of more traffic. As a result, there has been far greater concern about, and mapping of, levels of gases such as carbon monoxide, ozone, sulphur dioxide, hydrocarbons and nitrogen dioxide.

The legacy of past pollution was also heavy. The Millennium Dome, built in Greenwich in 1997–99, is on the site of what had been Europe's largest gasworks producing coal gas in a process that produced toxic waste, including arsenic, asbestos and cyanide. To clear the site, much of the waste was buried in rural dumps, while the site was sealed with crushed concrete, plastic and clay, and each building had to have a gas-tight membrane underneath.

The improvement of the water quality of the river Thames led to the return of fish, with the first salmon for a century caught there in 1974. However, the water situation was a complex one. Under London, the water table rose as industrial extraction, for example by breweries, declined. The resulting flooding of cellars and underground carparks led to investment in pumping away water. An analysis of multiple satellite radar images acquired by the European Radar Satellites between 1992 and 2003 revealed an uplift in elevation in north-east London around Docklands as the factories that took water from boreholes closed. This rise in the water table led also to one in land elevation. In contrast, there were areas of subsidence, notably from St James's Park to London Bridge along the route of the Jubilee Line extension, and also south-west from Battersea Park, where there is a tunnel for electricity cables. Moreover, the water table fell in south-west London due to increased extraction.

Indeed, development in London and the South East, not least the greater number of appliances such as washing machines and dishwashers, strained water supplies and emphasised the problems stemming from the absence of a national water grid. As a result, the re-use of water is particularly high in London, with water being recycled at successive treatment plants and, on average, flowing through several people on its way to the sea.

Bazalgette's great achievement, which had been so important to the ability of London to overcome disease and create a safer living environment, was supplemented in the late twentieth century by improvements to the water supply designed to deal with the problems posed by the corrosion of the cast-iron pipes through which water was supplied. Like Bazalgette's system, this involved another major work of engineering. The Thames Water Ring Main, constructed at a depth of about 135 feet (roughly twice that of the Underground system) from 1988 to 1993, linked the treatment works at Coppermills, Hampton, Kempton, Walton and Ashford Common, to the pump-out supply shafts. The Ring Main is 51 miles long and by 2008 the system was supplying about 1,300 megalitres daily.

Fish might be a welcome sign of the improvement of the Thames, but most Londoners were affected more directly by a marked increase in the populations of rats and foxes; the growth in the volume of rubbish, much of it non-biodegradable, proved especially attractive to such scavengers. Moreover, assumptions about appropriate attitudes toward animals ensured that the repertoire of means hitherto available for action against vermin was markedly restricted, with limitations on the poisons that could be used. Shifts in attitudes were complex. Thus, as Mayor in the 2000s, Ken Livingstone judged unacceptable the pigeons fed by tourists in Trafalgar Square, seeing them as a health and environmental hazard. At the same time, alongside the increase in vermin, there were also more benign developments, such as the growth in the number of herons, encouraged not just by the return of

London's first historian, John Stow, is buried in the parish church of St Andrew Undershaft, seen here in front of 30 St Mary Axe – the 'Erotic Gherkin' – in the heart of the City. The 1992 IRA bomb which damaged the Baltic Exchange building, the site of 30 St Mary Axe, also destroyed St Andrew's large seventeenth-century stained-glass window. The present St Andrew's was built in Perpendicular style in the sixteenth century.

PHOTOGRAPH: CARNEGIE, 2009

fish to the Thames but also by the increased popularity of ponds. A marked rise in the number of parakeets is also notable.

Alongside changes in London's housing, there were others in demographic structure. First, there were important shifts in the location of ethnic groups. As a percentage of the local population, the largest Irish populations in Britain were in Liverpool, Glasgow, Manchester and Dundee, but during the twentieth century many drifted south to developing industrial areas such as the Midlands, Luton and north London. As well as following work, the Irish, like other migrant groups, were influenced by family and friendship networks, and went to places where they knew people. In this way, Kilburn became the capital of the Irish in England after 1945. Within the London economy, the Irish played a major role in construction work and the NHS. With time, Londoners of Irish origin moved out along the axis of Kilburn, so that the Irish population of Kingsbury increased from the 1950s.

Other, earlier immigrant groups also moved out of inner London and into suburbia. Jews moved from the East End into north-west London, and, in turn, from Golders Green to Edgware and then, in the 2000s, into Hertfordshire, notably Radlett. Their movement out of the East End created spaces for Bangladeshis and other immigrants. Alongside the movement within the region of Jews, there was a decline in the Jewish community, in large part due to 'marrying out' with non-Jews. As a result, Jewish community activity was increasingly that of a remnant.

New immigrant groups had varied trajectories. The Second World War led to large numbers of refugees as well as a shortage of labour in London. Poles, many former soldiers who did not welcome the prospect of Communist rule, were joined by Estonians, Latvians, Lithuanians and Ukrainians. Until Italian economic growth became more marked from the 1960s, the Italians were another important immigrant community.

Immigration from the Empire brought in Hong Kong Chinese and Cypriots, the latter focusing on Camden Town. There was also immigration from Malta, with criminals taking over prostitution and pornography in Soho, developing links with the Vice Squad that affected the reputation of the Metropolitan Police as a whole in the 1960s and 1970s. From the 1950s, there was large-scale immigration from the New Commonwealth, especially the West Indies and south Asia, although many of the immigrants intended only a limited stay. A temporary labour shortage in unattractive spheres of employment, such as transport (especially the buses) and nursing, led to an active sponsorship of immigration that accorded with the Commonwealth idealism of the period. The overwhelming majority of the West Indian immigrants who arrived in the 1950s and early 1960s planned to save money in order to buy land in the West Indies and return; but they only gained low-paid jobs and never earned enough.

Black people encountered severe discrimination in the housing market, as well as much personal hostility. Many immigrants found landlords unwilling to accept them as tenants. The cooking smells of West Indians and Indians were criticised, while the former were condemned for loud parties and alleged sexual immorality. Racism played a role in neighbourhoods and workplaces, and 'White flight' came to take a role in the housing pattern. Notting Hill in 1958 witnessed a race riot, with white thugs attacking recently settled blacks. In response, the Notting Hill Carnival was started the following year, while Oswald Mosley failed in his attempt to exploit the immigration issue during the 1959 electoral campaign. At the same time, the limited incorporation of West Indians into the community was shown in the 1959 election: of the 7,000 West Indians entitled to vote in North Kensington only 1,000 did so. The immigrants rapidly became a subject of literature; Colin MacInnes (1914–76), who was born in London but grew up in Australia, focused on the West Indian community and race relations in his novel *City of Spades* (1957), going on in *Absolute Beginners* (1959) not only to discuss youth culture but also the Notting Hill race riot of 1958.

Much of the initial New Commonwealth immigration was from the West Indies, but south Asia subsequently became more important. Areas such as Southall came to seem 'Little Indias' to other Londoners, and the railway station there is almost unique among English railway stations in having bilingual signs, in this case Punjabi. Due to immigration, there were significant variations in settlement patterns across London. For example, whereas over ten per cent of the population of six boroughs – Hounslow, Ealing, Brent, Harrow, Redbridge and Newham – were of Indian background in 1991, thirteen

By the sixteenth century, when John Stow was compiling his *Survey of London*, several streets lay beyond the city walls to the north in Cripplegate ward. Aldersgate Street ran northwards from the city gate, and east of this ran 'Le Barbycane', behind which was a house known various as Bas Court, Willoughby House or 'Barbican'. Stow attempted an etymology for the place-name: 'On the west side of the Red crosse, is a streete called the Barbican, because sometime there stoode on the North side thereof, a Burgh-Kening or Watch Tower of the Cittie called in some language a Barbican.' This whole area suffered terribly in the Blitz, and by the time of the 1951 census only a handful of families lived in Cripplegate. Such was the destruction that the whole area was redeveloped into the Barbican estate, whose Grade II-listed Shakespeare and Cromwell Towers can be seen here. Built in the decade after 1965 (and designed by the same firm responsible for the Golden Lane estate of maisonettes just to the north), the Barbican estate consists of terrace blocks as well as the three towers which, at over 400 feet, are among London's tallest.

PHOTOGRAPH: CARNEGIE, 2009

Well-tended
window
boxes soften
somewhat
the concrete
regularity of the
Barbican estate
terraces.
PHOTOGRAPH: CARNEGIE, 2009

boroughs had a percentage smaller than 2.5. The concentration in the case of Bangladeshis was more pronounced, with over 10 per cent in Tower Hamlets (replacing the Jews who had moved out), over five per cent in Newham and Camden, and fewer than one per cent in most of the boroughs. From the late 1990s, Tower Hamlets promoted the Brick Lane area as Banglatown, an idea originating in the late 1980s. Indeed, Brick Lane became the stereotypical cultural centre for successive waves of immigrants. Additional immigrant flows included Vietnamese to Hackney in the 1980s, and Iraqis to north-west London in the 1990s and 2000s.

London faced the major social burden of immigration: half of the net international immigration to the UK was to the city. Partly as a result of this, the city's population – which had risen to about 8.7 million by 1938, before falling to 8.193 million in 1951, 6.8 million in 1981 and 6.7 million in 1988, as large numbers moved to new housing in the Outer Metropolitan Area outside London – rose to 7.2 million in 2001. From mid-2007 to mid-2008 alone, London's population rose by 0.83%, compared with a UK average of 0.7%: only East Anglia, Northern Ireland and the South East had a higher percentage increase. The population is predicted to reach 8.1 million by 2016, although immigration into Britain is running far higher than predicted, which suggests that London's population will become even larger.

Whatever the overall figure, the contrasts in population density within London remain very pronounced. Despite the post-war redevelopment of the bombed-out Barbican area, the City remained an area devoted to commerce, not housing, and many of the flats in the Barbican were not, as originally intended, used by clerical workers, but instead town bases for workers with primary residences elsewhere. In 2008, the City had only one primary school, the Sir John Cass Foundation Primary School in Aldgate, where the City meets the East End. Many of the pupils are the children of first-generation immigrants. As a sign of continuity, the school's origins date to 1710, when it was founded by John Cass (1661–1718), a City alderman and sheriff. In the City in 2008 there were 350,000 commuters, but only 9,000 residents. Although medieval population figures are unreliable, it seems likely that the City of London was home to more people at the time of the Norman Conquest, and at every other intervening period, than it is today.

The rate and impact of immigration to London were contentious, not least because recent immigrants were especially prone to evade the census, which made it difficult to evaluate the extent of immigration, as well as affecting the linked central government financial support to the boroughs. Indeed, the worst responses to the 2001 census occurred in inner London. Prostitution was a particular issue, with many women brought illegally into the country, frequently against their will, often from eastern Europe countries such as Albania. The recession of 2008–09, however, led to the return of many foreign migrants, notably to Eastern Europe.

In response to changes in the ethnic composition in London, there were developments in religious provision. The first Hindu temple in London was opened as late as 1962, but at Neasden the largest Hindu temple outside India opened in 1997. For the latter, the many different woods and marbles were shipped from around the world to the region of Gujarat in India where specialised craftsmen carved the extraordinarily elaborate details and shipped the vast 'kit' to London for assembly. The process of change across the centuries can be seen in the Fournier Street Mosque, formerly a Huguenot church and then a Jewish synagogue before becoming a mosque. The rise in the Moslem population had already led to the opening in 1978 of the Central London Mosque in Regent's Park.

In turn, the Church of England was not only ministering to a smaller percentage of London's population, but also faced serious problems. In the widely read *Honest to God* (1963), John Robinson, Anglican Bishop of Woolwich, sought to address the inability of the Church to reach out to many, especially in run-down urban areas, by pressing the need for a determination to respond that would include a new liturgy. The Church of England was not alone in facing problems. Catholic churches in London suffered a decline in congregations between 1989 and 1998 of 19 per cent; although the Baptists reversed an earlier fall, instead seeing a 11 per cent increase. In turn, Polish immigration in the early and mid-2000s helped to increase the size of Catholic congregations.

Alongside an understanding of change from a thematic perspective, it is instructive to adopt a chronological one. The 1950s are a useful backdrop as this was a decade in which change was largely within established social, economic, political, cultural and religious patterns. The Conservatives, in power nationally from 1951 to 1964 (although Labour ran the LCC), did not support large-scale state intervention. The nationalisations of the 1945–51 Labour government were largely left in place, but there was no equivalent to the extension of state control seen with the National Health Service. Instead, the rebuilding of London in the 1950s was largely by private developers. The Conservative government overturned previous planning controls, ensuring that tall buildings were constructed despite the protests of the LCC. Thus, in 1956, a Regency terrace looking onto Hyde Park was purchased by Charles Clore who built the 28-storey London Hilton on the site. Much of the city was rebuilt, while large buildings further west included the Bowater Building in Knightsbridge.

Meanwhile, the culture of the period was essentially conformist. In the West End, audiences flocked to see plays by Noel Coward, both old (such as *Private Lives*, 1930) and new (for example *Look After Lulu*, 1959) alike, as well as plays by Terence Rattigan (*The Winslow Boy*, 1946) and William Douglas-Home (*The Chiltern Hundreds*, 1947; *The Manor of Northstead*, 1954). The audiences were also very large for the short stories Agatha Christie adapted for the stage: *The Mousetrap* (1952; and still showing today) and *Witness for the Prosecution* (1953). *Look Back in Anger* (1956), by the London-born John Osborne, set in London and staged at the Royal Court Theatre (it was turned into a film in 1959) was very different, however, in its angry attack on Establishment values and hypocrisies, as was the highly influential art exhibition 'This is Tomorrow' staged in 1956 at the Whitechapel Art Gallery.

Nevertheless, the 1950s, especially the early 1950s, was in many respects an attempt to return to 1930s' London. Physically, there were many similarities, not least with coal fires and smog, while the attempt to keep the city as the imperial metropole appeared valid in the 'New Elizabethan Age' proclaimed to mark the coronation of Elizabeth II in 1953. Clothes were more similar to those of the 1930s than those of the 1970s, and reflected hierarchies of class, gender and age. Sexual policing continued, with homosexual acts illegal, while erotic entertainment also fitted into these hierarchies.[1]

In the late 1940s and 1950s, there was a also shift toward the Conservatives in the general election results for seats in the LCC area. Having done very badly in 1945, the average Conservative gain and Labour loss by the 1950 election was 4.8%. Between the 1950 and 1951 elections, the percentage change was a Conservative loss of 0.1%, but then between the 1951 and 1955 elections, a gain of 1.7% and between those of 1955 and 1959 a gain of 2.1%. In the 1959 general election, Labour won 24 of the 42 seats in the LCC area and the Conservatives the other 18, but in Middlesex the results were 8 and 21 respectively, in the Kent and Surrey suburban constituencies 2 and 13, and in Essex 9 and 5; leading to a suburban total of 19 Labour and 39 Conservative seats and an aggregate LCC and suburban figure of 43 Labour and 57 Conservative. Leading Conservatives, including Churchill, Macmillan, Edward Heath (for Bexley), and Reginald Maudling, sat for suburban seats.

In turn, the 1960s destroyed a cultural continuity that had lasted from the Victorian period. This destruction reflected the impact of social and ideological trends, including the rise of new forms and a new agenda moulded by shifts in the understanding of gender, youth, class, place and race, as well as by secularisation. London was both a stage for change and a moulder of it: it was a stage in particular for the 'Swinging Sixties', the idea of new lifestyles and fashions that were presented to the world from a series of London settings, such as the clothes boutiques of Carnaby Street and the Abbey Road recording studios. Working-class talent provided a powerful infusion of energy in this world of show, a world in which pop stars, hairdressers and photographers were celebrities. The mid-1960s saw a cycle of 'Swinging London' films including *Darling* (1965) and *Blow-Up* (1965), both of which examined the morals and mores of the permissive society.[2]

This permissiveness was a matter not only of the activities of newly prominent, but also

This Henry Grant photograph shows Carnaby Street in 1967. The first of many 'boutiques' opened in the late 1950s, and the street became a favourite location for the trendy followers of popular music and culture.
MUSEUM OF LONDON

of the former social élite, many of those members became what would previously have been regarded as decadent. Gambling in the capital was scarcely new, but milieux such as John Aspinall's Clermont Club in Mayfair (which was linked to organised crime) were more public from the 1960s onwards. Moreover, there was an overlap between such milieux of the former social élite and those of the newly prominent and fashionable.

London was also a moulder of change, as was seen by the fate of the Liverpool beat. To become first national and then a world presence, it was necessary for the Beatles to be repackaged in and marketed via London. Other Merseysiders – Cilla Black, Gerry and the Pacemakers, and the Swinging Blue Jeans – made the same journey from Liverpool to London. Similarly, British youth culture was reconfigured toward metropolitan interests, notably with the hippies and drugs of the 1960s. In turn, to reach a wider audience, punk had to be taken up by London's record companies and television.

Consumerism meanwhile was reconfiguring the metropolitan world. For Alfie, played by Michael Caine in the 1966 film of that name, women, clothes and cars were commodities that proved one could get on in the world without the privileges of birth and education. Supermarkets provided new, anonymous shopping spaces.

Politically, there was change. Already, in March 1962, the ability of the Conservatives to take their suburban electoral strongholds for granted had been proved deeply flawed when they lost Orpington to the Liberals in a parliamentary by-election with a huge swing: a 14,760 Conservative majority became a 7,885 Liberal one. Two months later, there were major Conservative losses in the local elections. In the 1964 general election, the Conservatives won ten seats in the LCC area and 36 seats in the suburban boroughs, while Labour won 32 and 22 respectively. The Conservatives took 42.2% of the overall popular vote, Labour 45.3%. In the 1966 general election, Labour surged forward at the expense of the Conservatives, taking 36 seats in the LCC area, 30 in the surrounding boroughs, and 49.9% of the popular vote, compared to 6, 28 and 40.7%. The volatility of London politics was to become more apparent in the following decades of economic transformation and social challenge.

Institutionally, London itself was transformed. The Herbert Commission on Greater London Government, a royal commission which met from 1957 to 1960, proposed revisions in the two-tier system of the LCC, including 52 metropolitan boroughs and a separate City of London handling local government functions, and a Greater London Council (GLC) to handle large-scale issues. In the event, under the London Government Act of 1963, the Conservative government's decision to abolish the LCC and Middlesex and to establish a Greater London Council passed Parliament against much Labour opposition. However, helped by the government yielding to pressure from areas that wished to be excluded – Staines, Sunbury, Esher, Walton, Banstead, Epsom and Caterham – the Conservatives were weaker in the GLC area than had been anticipated, and in 1964 in the first GLC elections, Labour won 64 of the 100 seats including nearly every marginal borough. The other 36 seats were taken by the Conservatives.

The Greater London Council (GLC) formed in 1965, added most of Middlesex, and much of Essex, Hertfordshire, Kent and Surrey, to the LCC area. These changes reflected the extent to which the LCC had been outgrown. The LCC area, 117 square miles, contained 3,200,000 people in 1961, but the GLC covered 610 square miles with over 7,000,000 inhabitants. In turn, the GLC was not affected by the reorganisation of local government elsewhere in England in the early 1970s. Within the new GLC area, the boroughs were totally reorganised into 31 boroughs and the cities of London and Westminster.

One of the remarkable features, indeed, has been the survival of the ancient City of London Corporation as an independent body within the capital. Somehow, the quaintly named 'Mayor and Commonalty and Citizens of the City of London' has avoided every major reform of English local government, from the Municipal Corporations Act of 1835 to the Royal Commission on the Amalgamation of the City and County of London of 1894, and all of the twentieth-century reforms.

The City of London still has its own police force; with around 1,200 officers and just three police stations (Bishopsgate, Snow Hill and Wood Street), it is the smallest force in England, but is quite separate from the Metropolitan Police which patrols the rest of the capital. The Lord Mayor, meanwhile, serves just for the City, his post (there has only ever been one female Lord Mayor of London) being quite distinct from the capital-wide post of Mayor instituted in 2000. The 681st Lord Mayor was 'elected', in 2008, in time-honoured fashion: accountant Ian Luder (from the Worshipful Company of Coopers) was chosen by Common Hall, a congregation of the ancient Livery Companies of the City that once a year also still chooses the City's two sheriffs. The City is still run from the Guildhall, which still stand on its historic site at the heart of the City. And it still has its ancient ward structure, its aldermen, its Court of Common Council, and a unique – some would say uniquely undemocratic – voting system. For within the City of London non-resident business people can quality to vote; in 2009 the business vote – abolished everywhere else in the 1960s – still enfranchises some 24,000 business people, who therefore outnumber local residents by three to one. Reform proposals continue to be debated, but the problem is seemingly intractable – it is a local authority with a tiny population which nevertheless welcomes each day some 300,000 business commuters – and it continues to defy all such efforts. Meanwhile the City of London Corporation continues in its own way.

The ancient City of London authority can be viewed as a charming survivor of a former age, sitting comfortably alongside other much-loved features of London history such as ravens at the Tower, Beefeaters and jellied eels. But the authority has also frequently been criticised as hopelessy anachronistic, 'an unreconstructed old boys' network whose medievalist pageantry camouflages the very real power and wealth which it holds'.[3]

In the wider GLC of the 1960s many of the earlier boroughs had been in effect single-party monopolies of power, with relative social homogeneity diminishing the chance for effective political pluralism. The consolidation of boroughs in 1965 reduced this homogeneity by linking many disparate areas. St Pancras joined Holborn and Hampstead in the new borough of Camden, while Battersea joined Putney and Tooting in Wandsworth, and Westminster absorbed Marylebone and Paddington, and Chelsea merged with Kensington. The boroughs opposed amalgamation but they lacked the public support that had held up the process in the 1890s.

These amalgamations appeared to lessen the need for the over-arching authority of the GLC, not least because the independence of the boroughs meant that there was scant support for the idea of the GLC as a strategic metropolitan authority. Moreover, central government retained control of the police and took that over transport from the GLC. The central government rate support grant also lessened the role of the GLC as a redistributive agency between the boroughs. The new boroughs created in 1965 did not engage public loyalty, however, and residents were more likely to identify with parts of the borough, often related to former boundaries and communities. Partly as a result, with ties adversely affected by geographical and social mobility, rehousing, and a disengagement from a bureaucratic local authority, community localism were limited, certainly more so than in many other towns, and again usually well below the borough level. The boroughs indeed acquired a stronger administrative role, while partly losing their representative one.[4]

The political consequences of the formation of the GLC, bringing together the Labour LCC with Conservative suburbia, or inner with outer London, was initially unclear. Having overturned Labour control in 1967 thanks to the unpopularity of the national Labour government (with 82 seats to Labour's 18), the Conservatives, re-elected in 1970, lost power in the GLC in 1973, as a result of a vociferous and popular campaign against road-building plans that drew much from Abercrombie's 1944 scheme. Labour took charge, bringing to a rapid close plans for the Ringways and the Motorway Box and for a redevelopment of Covent Garden that would also put an emphasis on through-roads.

The City also changed as a system of financial and mercantile power. In the financial sector, the power of established practices and the City Establishment was challenged, leading to changes in the practice of corporate finance and also more effort to appeal to shareholders. A series of contentious takeovers registered the effort. In 1958, the successful contested takeover of British Aluminium saw S.G. Warburg, a banking house then outside the City Establishment, outmanoeuvre the latter, not least by writing to shareholders over the heads of their boards and by talking to the press. At the same time, takeovers extended London's influence. In 1969, Barclays and Martins merged. Martins was the last national English bank to have its headquarters outside London and, with the merger, Liverpool lost this status.

The confidence and optimistic energy of the 1960s swiftly gave way to concern and division, both of which had already been present during that decade as the Labour government of Harold Wilson (1964–70) manifestly failed to arrest national decline. This concern had cultural as well as political and social dimensions. The serious problems of the 1970s – economic crises, rampant inflation, serious labour disputes, and political instability, seen, for example in IRA bombs – led to a sense of cultural malaise. These problems also led to the anger seen in the violence of the punk aesthetic, such as *London Calling* by the Clash, or the Sex Pistols' *Never Mind the Bollocks Here's the Sex Pistols* (1977).

This sense of malaise affected the perception of London as well as the amount of effort that could be, and was, put into improving and preserving the urban environment. In his dyspepsic novel *Jake's Thing* (1978), Kingsley Amis described urban neglect in Mornington Crescent:

> weeds flourished in the crevices between the paving-stones, a number of which had evidently been ripped out; others, several of them smashed, stood in an irregular pile. Elsewhere there was a heap of waterlogged and collapsed cardboard boxes and some large black plastic sheets spread about by the wind … along with after-shave cartons, sweet-wrappers, dog-food labels and soft-drink tins.

Labour continued its dominance of London. In the 1970 general election, it took 33 seats in inner London to the Conservatives 9, and 22 to the Conservatives 39 in outer London,

The two-year-long dispute at the Grunwick photograph processing centre boiled over into tense and violent confrontation during June and July 1977. The mainly female and Asian workforce wanted to improve their working conditions, but the dispute centred upon union recognition. Some ministers of the Labour government supported the strikers' and union's cause, while the employer sought the help of the right-wing Freedom Association in attempting to deny the workers' claims. The dispute was seen as a test-case, a microcosm of the wider debate over union power that was paramount in the late 1970s.
GETTY IMAGES

while, in February 1974, Labour won 50 seats and 40.3% of the popular vote in Greater London and the Conservatives 42 and 37.7%. The Liberals won no seats. However, the inner London heartland of Labour was troubled by declining parliamentary weight. Under a redistribution authorised by Parliament in November 1970, Greater London lost eleven seats while sixteen new ones were created in South East England.

Tensions between the trade unions and the Labour government of 1974–79 also hit Labour's popularity in London. Indeed, in 1977, violent mass picketing in support of a union-recognition strike at the Grunwick film processing factory in north London (where the employees felt harshly exploited) raised serious issues about the possibility of maintaining public order. Moreover, in the winter of 1978–79, London was hit hard by the 'winter of discontent', with strikes by refuse collectors leading to mounds of uncollected rubbish in the streets. Ambulancemen and hospital ancillary workers were among those who went on strike, and this disruption led to a rallying of support to the Conservatives under Margaret Thatcher in the 1979 election. With a national swing that was especially strong in suburbia Thatcher won power as Britain's first female prime minister. Just two years earlier, meanwhile, as a reminder of older continuities, many by then of marginal significance, the Carpenters' Company had rejected the admission of women to the Livery.

Other pressures contributed to the political mix and added different levels of action and anxiety. In the 1980s, racial issues played a major role in disturbances in London. In 1981, crowds rioted, looted and fought with the police in Brixton and Southall, as they also did outside London, most prominently in the Toxteth area of Liverpool. Relations between black youth and the police were a specific issue, and became the focus of the report from the Scarman Inquiry that was set up after the Brixton riots. Lord Scarman blamed 'racial disadvantage' for the riots. The Broadwater Farm riots followed in Tottenham in 1985, with a policeman murdered during the rioting, while Bernie Grant, the prospective Labour MP, congratulated local youths on giving the police 'a bloody good hiding'. Broadwater Farm

This '100-odd metre long, turreted, metallic grey thing lying in its own sunken rectangle,' is the 1960s' Pimlico High School, which was designed in 1964 in the Architects' Department of the Greater London Council under the leadership of John Bancroft. Award-winning brutalist architecture, described at the time as 'a futuristic aircraft carrier, education factory and greenhouse,' the building presented challenges from several points of view, including heating and ventilation and security. Due to educational rather than architectural failings, however, the school was placed in 'special measures' in 2006; it is now an academy and is being completely rebuilt, in a slightly more traditional style, by Westminster City Council.

PHOTOGRAPH: CARNEGIE, 2008

itself was a supposedly model estate that rapidly became a classic instance of the social failure of these disastrous environments.

The role of the police continued to be contentious. In October 1994, the 28,000-strong Metropolitan Police Force contained only 679 ethnic-minority officers. In the 2000s, the failure to secure a conviction after the murder of Stephen Lawrence, a young black man, led to accusations of institutional racism on the part of the police, which was a finding of the official inquiry. Such accusations are far easier to make then to substantiate, but, as a related problem, there have appeared to be problems in the treatment of black officers.

Inner-city discontent was not simply a matter of racial issues, but, in part, a consequence of the economic transformation caused by the decline of manufacturing. The results included the loss of unskilled and semi-skilled work, and the development of an economy of shifts and expedients which led to an openness on the part of some to criminal behaviour such as drug-dealing.

London, meanwhile, proved a major centre of formal opposition to the Thatcher governments of 1979—90. This opposition focused on the GLC which was led by Ken Livingstone, 'Red Ken', a vocal Labour militant, who had displaced his moderate colleagues in 1981 and who deliberately challenged Thatcher. The 'Fare's Fair' Policy – public subsidies to cut bus and Tube fares – was a particular point of contention, as was Livingstone's highlighting of unemployment figures. 'Fare's Fair' angered outer London boroughs, such as Bromley, that did not benefit from the Underground, and was ruled to be illegal.

In turn, in fulfilment of a pledge during the 1983 general election campaign, the GLC was abolished by the Local Government Act in July 1986. This Act ended all the metropolitan authorities, and left London without an overarching authority, and with power exercised by the boroughs as well as residuary bodies and the national government. Thatcher, MP for Finchley, was in part driven by suburban dislike both of inner London and of the controlling tendencies of a centralising London authority. County Hall, the headquarters of the LCC (and then GLC) from 1922, was disposed of and much of it was converted into flats in 1995. In 1990, the abolition of the Inner London Education Authority fulfilled another of Thatcher's goals, as it was also seen as a centre for Socialist control.

The property developer who built Centre Point in the 1960s, Harry Hyams, was criticised for greedy speculation by some for refusing to let the building other than to a single tenant, which led to Centre Point remaining empty for years.

PHOTOGRAPH: CARNEGIE, 2009

Meanwhile, Livingstone's anger had been expressed in his *If Voting Changed Anything, They'd Abolish It* (1987), although, once the GLC had gone, support for it fell.

As with much of its political history, this episode found London reflecting, but also exemplifying, national trends. The Act was part of a wider process of centralisation that took place under Thatcher: some fifty Acts of Parliament were passed transferring power from local government to Westminster and Whitehall. For example, the Rate Act of 1984 allowed the government to put a ceiling on rates, and thereby to control local authority finances. There was a distant comparison with the pressure brought by Edwin Chadwick on the London authorities in the mid-nineteenth century (see pp. 278–9).

At the same time as centralisation at the national level, there was also a driving back of public powers at the local level. The extension of compulsory competitive tendering to a wide range of local government services in 1988 was designed to challenge the role of council workers, and the influence of their unions. It led to the entrance of private-sector contractors into public-service work, for example refuse collection. Certain Conservative London authorities, especially Wandsworth and Westminster, were flagships for this process, while Labour counterparts, such as Lambeth, were markedly opposed. Although taking part at the national scale, the privatisation of London's utilities, such as water and gas, also ensured a loss of public control and patronage.

The sale of council houses, a key Thatcherite policy, was also intended to help in shifting the electoral composition of London by lessening the vested interests behind Labour. The policy was defended as an assault on council fiefdoms and an empowerment of individuals, most of whom were expected to vote Conservative. The council houses were sold to their tenants at a heavy discount, and many of the former tenants rewarded Thatcher by supporting her in the 1983 and 1987 general elections. In Westminster, council house sales were encouraged as a means of gerrymandering: in its 'Building Stable Communities' the Conservative-controlled council sold houses in such a way as to help ensure continued electoral success. The policy was eventually declared illegal, and the district auditor ordered council leader Dame Shirley Porter and five others to pay back the staggering sum of £27 million.

Council-house sales contributed to growing spatial differentiation between socio-economic groups across London, a differentiation that has thwarted all efforts to prevent it. This process was not restricted to the exclusion of the poor, but, instead, operated all along the social scale, such that in boroughs such as Westminster, Kensington and Chelsea the middle classes have now been largely supplanted by the seriously affluent.

In social terms, the council house sales opened up a divide between skilled manual workers and welfare dependants who did not switch to the Conservatives but whose electoral turnout was low and falling. Whereas Britain swung to the Conservatives as a whole by only 0.3 per cent between 1979 and 1992, the swing in London was 1 per cent, although, in turn, this was less than the swing in the South East, which was 2.8 per cent.[5] Thus, the traditional relationship between inner and outer London had in part been transformed into one between London as a whole and outer suburbia. Indeed, in the local elections of 1994, the Tories lost Barnet and Croydon, and only held Bromley, Kensington, Wandsworth and Westminster.

Nonetheless, electoral differences between inner and outer London continued. In the 1983 general election, when Thatcher's position was greatly strengthened, the swing to the Conservatives was inversely related to unemployment, with an inner zone that was characterised by an unemployment level in the recession of 1981 of at least 8% delivering a swing lower than an outer zone where the unemployment rate had been lower. The Conservatives also benefited from division among the opposition in 1983, winning 56 seats on 43.9% of the vote in Greater London to 26 (29.8%) for Labour and 2 (24.9%) for the Liberal/Social Democrat Alliance.

In the 1987 general election, the Conservative advance was greatest in Greater London and the Outer Metropolitan Area, the combination of which provided nearly a quarter

Since 2002 the Mayor of London, the London Assembly and the GLA have occupied Foster and Partners' City Hall on the south bank of the Thames. Beyond can be seen Guy's Tower. At 43 storeys, this is thought to be the tallest hospital building in the world and dates from 1974.
PHOTOGRAPH: CARNEGIE, 2009

of the British electorate. That year, Labour lost Thurrock, its sole seat in the Outer Metropolitan area, while the two seats across the country in which the Conservatives had the biggest increase in their share of the vote were Newham South and Ealing North.

Alongside electoral developments and concerns about the nature of London's changing society, there was also an aesthetic anxiety about the nature and intention of developments. Modernist functionalism had driven the pace of development with buildings such as Eric Bedford's BT Tower (1964), Richard Seifert's uncompromising slab-like Centre Point (1967), Basil Spence's contemporaneous, but uglier, Home Office building at 50 Queen Anne's Gate, and Richard Rogers' Lloyd's (1986). However, Modernism was increasingly criticised by conservation movements and on aesthetic grounds. Indeed, buildings such as Denys Lasdun's National Theatre (1965–76) and the Institute of Education in Bedford Way, Camden (1970–78) were attacked as the 'New Brutalism', lacking a human scale and feel. This criticism was popularised by Prince Charles in the 1980s and 1990s, perhaps most memorably with his description of the initial plans for the extension to the National Gallery as a 'monstrous carbuncle'. He also condemned the plans for the new British Library as a 'dim collection of brick sheds and worse'. By the 1980s Modernism was being challenged by a neo-classical revival pioneered by Quinlan Terry.

Nevertheless, a determination to embrace modern shapes and materials, and to focus on functionalism, was seen in important works of the late 1990s and early 2000s, such as Nicholas Grimshaw's Eurostar rail terminal at Waterloo. Far from being seen as a redundant form, skyscrapers were built and also projected in the 2000s, including 30 St Mary Axe, the Swiss Reinsurance Tower (2002) – generally known as the gherkin or the erotic gherkin – which was designed by Norman Foster on the site of the Baltic Exchange

Until 1997 the Reading Room in the Great Court of the British Museum was the heart of the British Library, where any serious researcher could secure an admission ticket and pursue their enquiries. Among those to avail themselves of the facilities (and the freedom of expression that could be found in a capitalist empire) were the great anti-capitalists Karl Marx and V.I. Lenin as well as campaigners for home rule, M.K. ('Mahatma') Gandhi and M.A. Jinnah.

PHOTOGRAPH: CARNEGIE, 2009

The British Secret Intelligence Service (MI6) building, Vauxhall Cross, on Albert Embankment. The James Bond film *The World Is Not Enough* (1999) included a pre-title sequence in which these headquarters were attacked, followed by a powerboat pursuit down the Thames culminating in a climax at the Millennium Dome. The accompanying novel, by Raymond Benson, described the MI6 headquarters and the Dome as eyesores. Soon after the film's release, an IRA splinter group launched a mortar attack on the MI6 building, causing minor damage.

PHOTOGRAPH: CARNEGIE, 2009

wrecked by an IRA bomb in 1992. Indeed, as Mayor, Livingstone, in part under pressure from developers, supported the idea of clusters of high-quality skyscrapers in order to retain London's financial pre-eminence, to secure benefits from developers including affordable housing, to assert identity through impressive architecture, and to maintain the sustainability of the city in the face of development pressures.

Much other work was far removed from neo-classicism, including Richard Rogers' Millennium Dome (2000) and his Terminal 5 at Heathrow, Foster's Millennium Bridge, and his egg-shaped Greater London Authority building (2002), Rogers' Tate Modern (1999), and the award-winning Canary Wharf Tube station. Tate Modern, like the Millennium Dome and Bridge, the GLA building and the London Eye, provided a series of new vistas, notably to riverside scenes. Some were impressive, others slightly ridiculous. Rogers' unimaginative 2008 plans for the redevelopment of the Chelsea Barracks site to produce a new crowded barracks of high buildings providing expensive residential property indicated that, at least in this major case, little had been learnt about reconciling the profit motive to the needs of livable environments, let alone aesthetics. Pressure from Prince Charles helped lead to the abandonment of these plans in June 2009.

There was also the reworking and refurbishment of existing buildings. That of the Royal Festival Hall in 2007 by Rick Mather is part of a major programme of work designed to improve the whole waterfront site. The Great Court of the British Museum has been successfully reinstated, with a glass canopy designed by Foster, while Somerset House was transformed from 1997, as Inland Revenue offices were replaced by the Courtauld

Gallery and other activities geared to visitors, including ice-skating. Battersea Power Station, closed in 1980, is due for completion as a residential and services complex in 2010. More generally, brownfield sites have provided opportunities for new developments, for example on former railway land. The process of refurbishment was also seen in entire areas, including Covent Garden (from the 1970s), Notting Hill and Shoreditch. Gentrification was also seen in Islington.

The nature of patronage was also instructive, being largely for public or financial purposes. New buildings included the very expensive headquarters of the security services: Thames House for the Security Service MI5, and Vauxhall Cross for the Secret Intelligence Service, MI6. The varied role of public patronage was shown in Greenwich where the self-consciously new Millennium Dome was matched by the taking over of part of the Royal Naval College by the University of Greenwich.

There were also issues of practicality and purpose, as with the Millennium Dome or the wobbles of the Foster and Antony Caro Millennium Bridge in 2000, wobbles that indicated a failure to plan likely usage and that led to a more general concern about the engineering of public works in London. The length of time taken to bring projects, such as the new British Library, to fruition led also to worries about the planning process. Nevertheless, the attraction of London as a market was shown by the Millennium Dome which was purchased by an American company and, renamed the O2 Arena, became a popular venue for pop concerts.

While London extended its already-strong sway over the English regions in the second half of the twentieth century with the new media of radio and television, and 'Estuarine' became the pervasive accent of England, the cultural world of London was itself open to foreign influences. The USA proved particularly influential, most obviously through popular music and the ubiquitous television, but there were also important Continental influences. From the Second World War, French plays, especially by Sartre and Anouilh, were frequently performed in translation. From the mid-1950s, Brecht had a significant impact, and major productions were staged in the National Theatre in the 1960s. The 'theatre of the absurd', a term applied in 1961 to non-realistic modern drama, was centred in Paris, but was followed in London, where works by Samuel Beckett and Eugene Ionesco were produced frequently. Beckett influenced the London playwright Harold Pinter. In London concert halls, the works of the Russian composer Dmitri Shostakovitch were frequently performed in the 1950s and 1960s, and in the 1960s and 1970s those of Luciano Berio, Pierre Boulez and Witold Lutoslawski.

London was also the focus for competition over cultural values, specifically the tension, if not 'culture war' between the criteria and ranking set by the artistic Establishment that influenced and directed government funding, and those that made sense in the vernacular culture of popular taste. The use of government patronage on behalf of the artistic

Establishment was regarded as normal in the corporatist 1960s and 1970s and led to the establishment in 1976–77 of the publicly subsidised National Theatre in a new complex on the South Bank. Tate Modern followed. From the 1980s, however, this use of patronage caused growing anger, notably with the National Lottery grant of £78.5 million in 1997 to update the Royal Opera House, an amount widely criticised as disproportionate. Moreover, avant-garde works, such as some of those that won the annual Turner Prize, were regarded by some critics as ridiculous.

At the same time, London's cultural centrality continued despite, for example, the development of provincial museums. In the mid-1990s, 50 per cent of the Scottish sales of tabloid newspapers were of London titles and 75 per cent of those of the 'quality' press. James Kelman's novel *How Late It Was, How Late* (1994), an account of a drunken former convict stumbling along the streets of Glasgow and also a prominent Scottish literary declaration of cultural self-determination, was published in London by an English publisher and won the Booker Prize, a national award presented in London.

The impact of global pressures on established practices, whether traditional or recent, was disconcerting. In his novel *Money* (1984), Martin Amis described his part of London 'going up in the world. There used to be a third-generation Italian restaurant across the road … It's now a Burger Den. There is a Burger Shack too, and a Burger Bower.' American pressure occurred across London life and activity. In many respects, London became a branch of New York, a key aspect of the shift of emphasis from Britain to the USA. Thus, on 21 December 1965, the world premier of *Thunderball*, the fourth James Bond film, was held in New York, the first time that a Bond premier was held there rather than in London; the first London showing followed eight days later.

This shift was instructive because the first James Bond film, *Dr No* (1962) began with a view of imperial Westminster: a night shot of Big Ben and the Thames, as a prelude to the casino scene also set in London. Big Ben and Whitehall were to be employed in many other films, for example *Octopussy* and the re-make of *The Thirty-Nine Steps*. They were symbols not only of Englishness, but also of the timelessness and power of a strong Britain. Big Ben and Whitehall were also used in episodes of *The Saint*, a popular television programme of the period starring a stylish agent. In the 1965 Bond adventure *Thunderball* the villainous SPECTRE forces the government as a signal to order Big Ben to strike seven times at 6 p.m., a sign of a fundamental disjuncture.

Alongside the cultural challenge from the USA, great variety was offered by the ethnic diversity of London's population. An acceptance of different cultural traditions was seen in June 2002 when the celebration of the Queen's Golden Jubilee brought carnival dancers and gospel singers into The Mall. More edgy transitions were seen in popular music, with Asian influences playing a role in the musical forms known as Grime and Dubstep, and also in the development of Asian-British films, which became a highly successful genre.

Changes in restaurant provision reflected not only the globalisation of product and corrosion of standards noted by Amis (my father's comment on McDonalds was that at least they provided convenient lavatory facilities, a major plus), but also a long-term shift in cuisine. In P.G. Wodehouse's *Ukridge* (1924), the 'ordinary' Price family of Clapham Common are imagined having 'cold beef, baked potatoes, pickles, salad, blanc-mange, and some sort of cheese every Sunday night after Divine service'. Over eighty years later, the menu is very different, both in content and in variety. Londoners now face a range of products heavily mediated by the dominant supermarkets, but also enlivened by the choices available as a result of new fashions and of ethnic diversity. The gastronomic geography of the capital is richly varied. There has been a marked rise in vegetarianism, while, as far as meat is concerned, chicken has become more popular, beef less so, and mutton has largely disappeared, let alone eel pies. Chinese and Indian restaurants have become very prominent, not just in areas with concentrations of immigrants, while their cuisines are also extensively stocked in supermarkets. The National Catering Inquiry published in 1966 indicated that 11 per cent of Londoners had visited an Indian restaurant at some point. The percentage subsequently increased sharply in the late 1960s, 1970s and 1980s, with newly affluent young males playing a key role, while the cuisine was altered to suit British tastes. Brick Lane was promoted by Tower Hamlets council as 'London's Curry Capital'.

In contrast, Afro-Caribbean cuisine and restaurants have had scant impact either on the white British diet or that of other ethnic groups, in marked contrast to the strong Afro-Caribbean impact on popular music. Other ethnic groups that have also failed to make a wider impact include Somalis. The contrasts in part reflect the availability of investment capital and of entrepreneurial networks in the restaurant trade.

London and the South East are in the forefront of changes in British cuisine, moving furthest towards fruit, vegetables, fish and pasta, and also to a world of foreign restaurants and Continental-style coffee-houses, such as Caffè Nero. At the same time, there was a process of differentiation within London. Thus, the largely uniform Indian and Chinese restaurants of the capital were counterpointed by very different establishments catering for a more affluent clientele, notably after the Bombay Brasserie was opened in 1982. This differentiation was linked to one among the restaurants and staff, as most Indian restaurants were run by Bangladeshis and Pakistanis, while their more expensive rivals were generally run by Indians.

Fiction provided a marked sense of transition in London, with the city offering an unsettling backdrop for Martin Amis's novels *Money* (1984), *London Fields* (1989) and *The Information* (1995). His was a depiction of a cityscape and society under strain, and buckling under the pressure of change, a theme also seen in Margaret Drabble's *The Radiant Way* (1987). A troubled view of London, specifically the Docklands, could also be noted in Iain Sinclair's novel *Downriver; Or, The Vessels of Wraths* (1991), while the often-sinister ambiguities of the city's past emerged from the novels of Peter Ackroyd, for example *Hawksmoor* (1985), *The House of Doctor Dee* (1993) and *The Clerkenwell Tales* (2003), or, for the more recent past, Jake Arnott's *The Long Firm* (2000).

Ethnic identities and issues of assimilation and difference emerged as key themes in a series of novels including Hanif Kureishi's *The Buddha of Suburbia* (1991), Zadie Smith's *White Teeth* (2000), Monica Ali's *Brick Lane* (2003), and Gautam Malkani's *Londonstani* (2006). British-born descendants of immigrants have contributed much to an understanding of the creation of new, multiple identities. Kureishi and Smith have been particularly successful in doing so for the benefit of readers who lack their background.

Some of the films of the period, such as *Mona Lisa* (1986), showed London as patterned by crime, with class, sex and race suffused by themes of individualism that some critics linked to Thatcherism. Even in *Sliding Doors* (1997), a romantic film set in London, an attack by a mugger plays an important role in the plot. In Hanif Kureishi's films *Sammy and Rosie Get Laid* (1988) and *London Kills Me* (1992), London emerges in an ambivalent fashion, reflecting the absence of cohesion.[6]

The continuing social reality in London was of geographic differentiation. Local contrasts deepened in the 1980s, in part owing to shifts in housing, especially the skewed pattern of council-house sales. The better housing in the wealthier areas sold, while the public sector increasingly became 'sink housing', rented by those who suffered relative deprivation.

At the same time, a sense of lack of fixity, of a flux in perception, was captured by Julian Barnes in his witty novel *Metroland* (1981): 'the value of Kilburn depended on not knowing particularities, because it changed to the eye and the brain according to yourself, your mood and the day.' The book's title was a conscious reference to John Betjeman's eulogy to suburbia. Another testimony to change was *House of Ghostly Memory*, the concrete cast of an East End terraced house that won Rachel Whiteread the Turner Prize in 1993, only for the council to demolish the house soon after.

The art-world in London in the 1990s was particularly vibrant, to its supporters, and disorientating and self-indulgent, to its critics. 'Freeze', an exhibition master-minded by Damien Hirst and held in 1988 in a warehouse in Docklands, was the origins of the Britart movement, which took much of its anger from the determination by artists living on the breadline to reveal the harshness they saw; in short this art was a savage product of the harshness of much of 1980s' London. The success of the movement owed a lot to the financial and entrepreneurial backing of Charles Saatchi, a collector who had made a fortune in advertising, and who from 1992 organised exhibitions named Young British Artists.

Drawing on punk and pop culture, the works of Hirst, Chris Ofili, Marcus Harvey, Tracey Emin, and others, set out to shock, as did their lifestyle. The controversy reached a height with the 'Sensation' show at the Royal Academy in 1997, which led to unprecedented media attention on British art. Although Hirst's animals were on display, much of the controversy related to Harvey's large portrait of the sadistic murderess of children, Myra Hindley, a portrait painted in 1995 with the template of a child's hand. The painting led to controversy within the Academy, with the resignation of four Academicians, while two artists threw ink and eggs respectively at the painting.

The range of printed opinion over 'Sensation' indicated the ability of the arts in London to focus attention. On the one hand, there was the clash between social convention and individualism, but other critics saw the show as part of the rhythm of cultural change, with the former rebels having stormed the London bastions of the artistic Establishment. This was an aspect of a long-term process in which genres that would not have been considered art became lauded classics.

The opening of the Tate Modern (1999), built in the disused Bankside Power Station originally designed by Giles Gilbert Scott, provided a showcase for modern art, but the debate over fashion was given an annual outing in the popular media with the award of prizes to works that did not strike most Londoners as art. This was particularly so with the Turner Prize, which was won in 2001 by a light installation. Emin, an artist not obviously talented in a conventional artistic sense, even exhibited her unmade bed. In 2002 Ivan Massow, the Chairman of the Institute of Contemporary Arts, was forced to resign after he described most conceptual art as 'pretentious, self-indulgent, craftless tat'; he was particularly unimpressed by Emin's work. Fashionable attention focused on some of the areas in which the artists lived, such as Shoreditch, Hoxton and Whitechapel.

Rebellion had entered the mainstream. Thus, to reach a wider audience, punk had had to be taken up by record companies and television. Tamed in the interests of commercial viability, punk ultimately entered the cultural mainstream, giving birth to new and positive music, such as 'two tone' bands, and affecting style in fashion and design. Vivienne Westwood, who first came to prominence because of her links with the Sex Pistols, was, by the 1990s, one of the country's leading fashion designers. The 1990s were also the decade of Britpop in which the London band Blur took the leading role.

Britart was readily purchased because London in the mid- to late 1990s and early to mid-2000s was largely prosperous, in large part due to the strength of the service sector. A high rate of female participation in the workforce was also important to the general prosperity, both to middle-class London and also to the economy of the working class. Margaret Calvert celebrated this in her roadsign-style exhibit *Woman at Work* displayed at the Royal Academy in 2008.

However, the high rate of de-industrialisation in the 1970s had led to a major rise in unemployment, while there was also what, in the 1990s, was increasingly termed the underclass. Large numbers of beggars appeared on the streets of London. The closure of mental hospitals created serious problems, as the alternative policy of 'care in the community' proved inadequate. Cases of tuberculosis among the homeless rose. Parts of London, especially on the South Bank, became a 'cardboard city', as the number who slept rough, usually teenagers who had left home to look for work, or to escape parental pressure, increased. The so-called underclass challenged confidence in urban living, but was not a new problem. There are parallels between late twentieth-century ideas of the underclass and the late nineteenth-century notions of the residuum.

More generally, contrasting health indices in London were dramatic, with the death rate for social class 5 males far higher than for social class 1 males. Rates of obesity among children, a clear indicator of future health difficulties, and often the product of limited choices in food, are particularly high among the poor of east London. The majority of the city's population was more fortunate. In place of a mid-twentieth-century stress on a (then) sexy form of consumption – alcohol, cigarettes and gambling, all made glamorous in films such as *Alfie* – came healthy eating and an emphasis on firm stomachs, gyms and personal trainers. This shift reflected a change from enjoying things that were supposed to be bad for one towards the vanities of trying to look good. In London, smoking (and not going to the gym), as a result, became very much part of a dwindling working-class culture.

Fads, however, operated in different ways. For example, opposition from 2002 to the MMR vaccine given to children to protect them from measles, mumps and rubella led, in parts of south London, to a fall in the vaccination rate and thus to increased risks of the diseases striking. This episode demonstrated that the precariousness of the earlier defeat of infectious illnesses was not apparent to those foolishly motivated by a faddish anti-authoritarianism.

The underclass proved an ironic counterpoint to the claims made on behalf of the Millennium Dome at Greenwich. Although its subsequent failure led the Labour government to seek to distance itself from the Dome, the project was earlier seen as an affirmation of the government's determination to modernise Britain. Indeed, in December 1999, Tony Blair rounded on critics of the project whom, he claimed, 'despise anything modern', and stated, instead, that the Dome was a 'triumph of confidence over cynicism, boldness over blandness, excellence over mediocrity'. The opening ceremony was similarly used to affirm an image of modernity, although, in the event, the entire project revealed the folly of the government's claims.

A sense of rising crime was also an issue in the late twentieth century. An increase in criminality, notably in contrast to the 1950s, was related to a widespread breakdown in the socialisation of the young, particularly of young males. The percentage with criminal records rose. Crime hit most in run-down neighbourhoods, further de-socialising life there, and encouraging outward movement by those who could afford it. Although blamed by many commentators on Conservative government between 1979 and 1997, crime had, in fact, increased from the 1950s and, for much of this period, unemployment rates were low and the standard of living of the poor rose. Indeed, robberies in London rose by 105 per cent between 1991 and 2002, a period of falling unemployment.

Thus, an economic explanation of rising crime in London appears less pertinent than one that focuses on social dislocation, especially family breakdown, while detailed variations chronologically owed much to changing age profiles, in the shape of the number of adolescent males. Knife crime became more prominent in London in the 2000s, in part because large numbers of young men began to carry knives in order to give themselves a sense of protection. The resulting killings led to a change in the age profile of violent death among males. The extent to which this crime was connected to particular ethnic groups, notably Somalis, was highly controversial. In defeating Ken Livingstone in the mayoral election of 2008, Boris Johnson made considerable play of the need to reduce youth crime and to deal with disorder on public transport.

Despite the rise in crime, life in London was more regulated, for poor and wealthy alike, and, with the massive spread of CCTV, life was literally under supervision. In Timothy Mo's novel *Sour Sweet* (1983), the tax inspector upbraids the Chinese restaurateur in London: 'Do you realise you have a legal obligation to keep a record for Sales Tax and Purchase Tax? You do? Where is your till roll then? A cash book, a day book, your invoices in order? Would it be impertinent of me to enquire why you bother with a cash till at all when you have no record of your business?' Such an approach left less space for autonomy or independence, unless permitted by government or, indeed, criminous, and this was a situation that impoverished the range and dynamism of activity that are

Once again, London was at the centre of the politics of protest on 31 March 1990, with an estimated 200,000 demonstrating against the Poll Tax, although only a small number rioted in Trafalgar Square. The furore over the tax was most acute in Scotland, where it had been introduced a year earlier, and this opposition encouraged restless Tory MPs to move against Thatcher, feeling that she had lost the ability to respond to the popular mood.

© HOWARD DAVIES/CORBIS

One Canada Square (1991) is the tallest building in Britain, at 235m, with 50 floors, and around 115,000m² of office space. Alongside this now stand twin 199.5m office buildings which were built in 2002. This is one of the most ambitious dockland redevelopments in the western world, standing among what for two hundred years had once been the great West India Docks in the Isle of Dogs. The whole scheme has been named Canary Wharf, derived from the name of one of the berths of the old North (Import) Dock which handled fruit from the Canary Islands.

PHOTOGRAPH: CARNEGIE, 2009

so important to the vitality of society. *Only Fools and Horses*, a long-running and popular television series set in Peckham, depicted a world of semi-legal expedients as a residue of the entrepreneurial spirit. *Minder*, another popular series, did the same.

There was also more overt opposition to government. Although most Londoners paid the Community Charge or Poll Tax introduced by the Thatcher government, there was also a mass demonstration in Trafalgar Square on 31 March 1990. Some 200,000 supporters took part, and the demonstration culminated in a riot involving a small number of demonstrators. The resulting scenes suggested the precariousness of public order.

Similarly, economic change did not generally lead to a violent response, but the move of newspaper production from Fleet Street was resisted in the case of News International: in 1986, Rupert Murdoch broke the restrictive practices of the print unions by moving to a new plant at Wapping, located in the newly filled-in western part of the London Docks of 1805. There was violent picketing, but it was thwarted by the police. At the same time, Murdoch was successful in part because he could turn to the Electricians Union to provide an alternative labour force.

The move in newspaper production was part of a process in which manufacturing continued to move out of central London. There was also an important decline in manufacturing jobs in Greater London, bringing to an end a period of growth in the 1950s and 1960s, one in which London's manufacturing assets had also become more important thanks to the decline of manufacturing in the traditional heavy industrial areas such as the North East. Small firms in inner London proved especially vulnerable as they lacked liquidity and space. Moreover, it was difficult for these firms to compete with larger concerns built on greenfield sites. By the 2000s, much of London had de-industrialised or, rather – in a crucial difference in phrasing and implication – been de-industrialised. Indeed, industrial estates were frequently sites for warehouses and large retail units.

The decline of manufacturing industry ensured that service activities became proportionately more important. Retail was the most significant in employment, although financial services brought in more money. Moreover, tourism was seen as a job creator, a source of income and a possible tool in urban regeneration. Other service activities included what was now termed the sex industry, one that involved the exploitation of many young women brought in from eastern Europe. The sex industry also had an impact on the arts, as in Allen Jones' painting *London Derrière*, a view of a dominatrice exhibited at the London Academy in 2008.

Some health provision also moved out of the centre and into outer London, notably the large hospital at Northwick Park, as well as into the South East as a whole. In some cases, entire hospitals moved, St George's from Hyde Park Corner to Tooting, while other inner London hospitals merged: St Bartholomew's with the London Hospital and Queen Mary and Westfield College in 1995, and St Mary's with Imperial College. There were also mergers in university institutions, notably of Bedford and Royal Holloway colleges and of Westfield and Queen Mary Colleges; in each case with related changes in land-use.

Meanwhile, the financial services industry was transformed. In 1986, the City was deregulated in the 'Big Bang', a key element in the 'bonfire of the regulations' under the Conservative governments of 1979–97 and one designed to retain British financial competitiveness, especially with Frankfurt. Restrictions on the activities of financial concerns were removed or relaxed, with, for example, the end of minimum commissions on the stock market. The hyper-active open trading floor became an important image of the new London, and the bonus culture a matter of public report.

At the same time, the profits and bonuses reflected a high level of activity, as well as an ability to respond to opportunities. Thus, the City proved effective at developing trading in new financial instruments such as euro-bonds. Partly as a result, the City became more prominent in the British economy and also more closely linked into a world network of financial centres, the other key-points in which were New York, Tokyo and Hong Kong. London benefited from its time zone position which enabled it to do business while New York, Tokyo and Hong Kong were open. At the same time, the City's financial place within Europe was challenged by Frankfurt, although, as part of this challenge, German and Swiss banks established themselves in London notably by purchasing British merchant banks. Indeed, the effectiveness of the City, despite the relative decline of the British economy and the loss of sterling's role as a stable international reserve currency, owed much to the liberal attitude of the government to the growing role of overseas banks in the City.

Substantial fortunes were made, helping fuel the property market in London, while a speculative building boom changed the face of the City, not least with large Modernist buildings. The functionalism of large, open trading floors prevailed in skyscrapers such as the NatWest Tower. The Lloyd's Building, opened in 1986, was followed by the Broadgate Centre, on the site of the former Broad Street station, in 1991.

The growth in the City's international role led to a large-scale arrival of overseas financiers, which helped fuel the service sector, while the 24-hour nature of City trading as a result of its role in global money markets led to pressure to live close to work. This pressure accentuated the drive to develop areas near the City, such as Spitalfields, for housing. Clerkenwell and Hoxton followed in the 1990s. Moreover, the practice of weekly commuting increased, with a lifestyle of City flats and rural houses replacing the pull of suburbia for many workers in financial services. Rising property values encouraged the movement of markets out of central London. Covent Garden Market moved to Nine Elms in 1974, Billingsgate Market to the Isle of Dogs in 1982 (where most of the fish now arrives by road), and Spitalfields Market to Stratford in 1991.

More generally, Conservative policies were linked to a major change in the experience of work, one that London shared with the wider South East. Economic activity was

There has been a wholesale market at Spitalfields since the seventeenth century, although the present buildings of what is now known as Old Spitalfields Market on Commercial Street date from 1887. The market was moved to the New Spitalfields Market in Waltham Forest in 1991. The western portion of the old market has been rebuilt as modern offices, but the eastern end, seen here, remains a popular general market for local people. This photograph was taken from the steps of Hawksmoor's Christ Church, Spitalfields, which was completed in 1729.

PHOTOGRAPH: CARNEGIE, 2009

transformed: management, research and development jobs were increasingly separate from production tasks. The former concentrated not in traditional manufacturing regions, but in parts of the South East. This was a key aspect of the degree to which the Establishment in general became more focused on London and the South East, with the world of money and services more important than traditional industrial interests. No other part of the country saw office development to compare with that in London's Docklands in the 1980s. As London and the South East had higher average earnings than those elsewhere in the country these regions also paid a disproportionately high percentage of taxation, As a result, Londoners benefited from the major cuts in taxation under the Conservatives. Income tax, capital-gains tax, and corporate taxation were all cut: the standard rate of income tax fell from 33 per cent in 1979 to 25 per cent in 1988, while the higher rate was reduced to 40 per cent, where it stayed until increased in 2009.

In turn, the greater purchasing power that resulted, as well as rising real earnings and easier credit, fed through into consumer demand that helped the service sector. Spending became a major expression of identity, and indeed a significant leisure activity. The move to 24-hour shopping and the abolition of restrictions on Sunday trading were symptomatic of this shift. Yet, as a reminder of the variety concealed within aggregate regional indices, there was also much poverty in London and the South East, exacerbated by the recession of the early 1990s. Furthermore, support for the Conservatives ebbed markedly in London, where, in the 1992 election, the swing to Labour was particularly strong. In the following election, 1997, Labour won national power as well as affluent London seats such as Putney.

The economic growth that had followed the recovery from the recession of the early 1990s and the abandonment of the European Exchange Rate Mechanism, benefited both

Re-invention, redevelopment and layers of history. This photograph shows Nicholas Hawskmoor's 1730 church of St Anne, Limehouse, beyond the redeveloped Limehouse Basin where the Regent's Canal joins the Thames.

PHOTOGRAPH: CARNEGIE, 2009

London and the new Labour government. Skyscraper office-blocks that had seemed unviable filled up, and rents and profits rose, to the benefit both of the City and of a government that used its tax revenues to support its social programmes across the country. Indeed, the City served as an equivalent to North Sea oil, and with a similar lightness of regulation and favourable tax regime. Financiers and the architects they sponsored referred to London as Manhattan-on-Thames. This city provided the key setting for Labour's pursuit, at once nervy and complacent, of an image of Cool Britannia.

The governmental structure of London changed as a result of Labour's victory. The Blair government which won power in 1997 set out to recreate an overall authority for London, and, under the Greater London Authority Act of 1999, the GLC was in large part restored, although in a different form. The Greater London Authority is responsible for the same area as the GLC. The new governmental system includes an elected Mayor as the head of the executive and the Mayor and assembly together constitute the Greater London Authority. The Mayor's responsibilities include transport, police, fire and preparing a strategic plan for the city, although not education or social welfare, while mayoral powers are also affected by those of both central government and boroughs, for example in the area of transport. Thus, the boroughs are responsible for most of the roads.

Ken Livingstone, who, in May 2000, became the first elected Mayor, had been the head of the Greater London Council until it was abolished in 1986. Tony Blair had not wanted the radical Livingstone, a marked critic of Blair's New Labour, returned to power and, instead, devised an electoral college to choose Labour's candidate. This college was used to deliver the choice to Frank Dobson, a loyalist London MP, in February 2000, but, in the election held three months later, Livingstone, who had resigned from the Labour Party, stood as an independent and won.

By then Cool Britannia was ebbing, and the al-Qaeda attacks on the USA in 2001 led to new concern about the nature of London's multi-culturalism. A failure to control Islamic extremists had already resulted in French anti-terrorist police describing London as Londonistan, and this term became more common, not least because of the inability of the government to prevent radical preaching that stirred up hatred against the host society. Deadly suicide bomb attacks on the London Tube and bus system on 7 July 2005 lent fresh point to these concerns, which were exacerbated by the hunt for other would-be bombers. The febrile atmosphere of July 2005 highlighted worries that Britain's traditional tolerance, and especially the openness of its capital to immigrants and multi-culturalism, might be sowing the seeds for mass destruction or at least large-scale murder.

While this issue remained acute, London was also named Londongrad as a result of an influx of wealthy Russians who invested in property and, even more conspicuously, with Roman Abramovich in ownership of Chelsea Football Club. This influx was simply the most obvious strand of an inflow of wealthy foreigners that, in part, reflected the strength of the financial services industry, as well as a favourable tax regime for 'non-doms', non-domiciled foreigners, that lasted until national tax changes in the late 2000s. The sense of London as providing a relatively safe haven was also important to the 300,000 or so Russians who lived there by 2008.[7]

Having been re-elected as Mayor in 2004, beating the Conservative candidate Stephen Norris, Livingstone was defeated in 2008 by the Conservative, Boris Johnson. The bitterly fought election revealed the major divides of the city, with inner London largely supporting Livingstone, only to be outweighed by outer London. Livingstone increased the number of first preference votes, but Johnson won after the redistribution of second preferences. There was major and justified concern about corruption and favouritism in Livingstone's circle, as well as suspicion of his fiscal policies. Furthermore, Livingstone's maverick stance on foreign policy, especially his support for Arab radicals, offended some, offering an echo of the earlier impact of immigration on political alignments. Livingstone sought to combine modish political concerns with a wooing of recent immigrant groups, as with his criticism of the Victorian heroes commemorated on statues in Trafalgar Square, such as Sir Henry Havelock, an opponent of the Indian Mutiny, and his suggestion, in 2007, that a statue of Gandhi be erected there.

Partly because of the limited extent of the Mayor's authority, transport proved a key issue for mayoral plans and politics, especially in response to the increased demand caused by a rising population. Although the question of mayoral authority played a major role, not least in 2000–03 in a bitter struggle over the financing and control of London Underground, Livingstone also pushed a modernisation of London in terms of an attempt to shift the emphasis from private to public transport. This policy had environmental, social and political aspects, including an unsuccessful opposition to the part-privatisation of the Underground, a measure which was backed by the Labour government. The Congestion Charge introduced in 2003 was seen by Livingstone as a way to reduce car traffic, improve journey times and cut pollution. Indeed, key traffic routes such as Park Lane, Grosvenor Place and Hyde Park Corner, are major producers of pollutants such as nitrogen dioxide. At the same time, there was a socio-political dimension, with car use associated with class-selfishness in the form of petrol-guzzling 'Chelsea tractors', and public transport presented as more benign. In 2008, Johnson was to scrap Livingstone's recent western extension of the charge zone. Traffic was a theme or occasion in novels set in London such as Ian McEwan's *Saturday* (2005).

Aside from introducing new-style, low-entry, 'bendy' buses, which were intended to overcome the problem of disabled access more successfully than the Routemasters they replaced, but whose unpopularity Johnson exploited in the election campaign, Livingstone aimed to improve public transport capacity by large-scale construction projects designed to provide an enhanced rail system comparable to the RER in Paris. The key project,

Crossrail, was intended to link Paddington to the West End and the City, while Crossrail 2 is planned to link Dalston to Victoria.

The viability of these projects, requiring large-scale public and private investment, was always unclear, and the financial crisis and recession of 2008–09 made this even more the case, both by hitting public finances and by making it harder to raise private capital. The same point could be made about the 2012 Olympic Games, which are designed to ensure the regeneration of Stratford and the Lea valley. As with the attempt, from 2003, to regenerate the economically depressed and often derelict Thames Gateway area to the east of London, such schemes are easier to plan than to fulfil. Indeed it has been argued that Blair ignored and suppressed evidence suggesting that the Olympic Games would not bring the projected regeneration. Given the widespread currency of his reputation for deceit, it is not surprising that such claims have surfaced.

The Gateway, covering more than forty miles of Thames riverbank, and extending into Kent and Essex, is an £9.6 billion project including more than 160,000 new homes by the end of the 2010s. In 2008, as part of the regeneration, plans were announced to create the largest man-made national park in Europe. This would entail the decontamination of industrial and polluted areas as part of the creation of 22 parklands. Tensions remain, however, between development and environmental protection, notably of the shoreline.

At the same time, the failure to achieve large-scale improvement in the transport infrastructure ensures that the travelling circumstances of Londoners were similar to those of the Tudor period: dark and crowded. This situation, moreover, appeared less bearable than in the past because of higher living standards and expectations, as well as comparisons with other cities, notably Paris. Such comparisons seemed more pertinent to Londoners as more of them travelled for pleasure than ever before, in part thanks to the availability of cheap flights from Gatwick, Luton and Stansted in the 2000s, as well as the establishment of Eurostar services through the Channel Tunnel.

The political dimension of transport was seen in November 2008, when the new Mayor, Johnson, announced the abolition of the western extension to the Congestion Charge Zone. Critics claimed that Transport for London would lose £70 million annually as a result, and that the consequence would be an increase in fares. There was contention over the consultation process, indicating the range of pressures at play. On one hand, it was suggested that air pollution and congestion would rise in the area if the charge was abolished, while there was also concern about the consequence of the charge for commercial activities within the zone. Johnson also opposed the plans approved by the government in January 2009 for a third runway and sixth terminal at Heathrow, a scheme the government sees as a major creator of jobs.

Concern over the Congestion Charge Zone highlighted a classic issue in the history of London, that of the difference between the city and the area outside, notably with contrasting economic circumstances. Thus, in 2008, agitation against the westward expansion of the zone was in part coordinated by the Friends of Portobello, a group that argued that the charge affected commerce there adversely and would benefit the Westfield shopping centre, opened in Shepherd's Bush in 2008 and located just outside the zone. By March 2009, this £1.7 billion development was in serious difficulties as a result of the recession, with nearly 10 per cent of the 280 stores vacant.

Policing was another key issue for mayoral plans and politics. In part, this situation reflected concern about law and order and the effectiveness of policing, but other aspects also played a role. One was the relationship, real and alleged, between policing and race relations. There was also the political question of control. The Metropolitan Police falls under the authority of the Home Secretary and the Commissioner is appointed by the Home Secretary. This situation involved tension with the Greater London Authority, and, in October 2008, the new Mayor, Johnson, indicated that he had lost confidence in the leadership of the Commissioner, Sir Ian Blair. Although Blair claimed that he had the full backing of Jacqui Smith, the Labour Home Secretary, he felt himself obliged to resign the following month. In part, this episode was an echo of old struggles between national and metropolitan government, alongside that between representatives of two rival political parties. Blair complained that Johnson's stance was a highly political step that could destabilise the police service, but, in practice, all the major political parties intend to increase political control of the police.

St George Wharf, a major riverside development, in Lambeth, with Vauxhall Bridge in front. There are plans for a large residential tower to the south of these buildings, which at almost 600 feet high would be the tallest residential building in the UK.

PHOTOGRAPH: CARNEGIE, 2009

Concluding themes are necessarily personal and very much affected by the present. The financial crisis of 2008–09 threw into doubt the idea that, thanks to its financial importance, London could thrive as a world city while the rest of Britain suffered relative decline. The impact of the weakening of this financial motor will probably be dire for city and country alike. Indeed, London was referred to as Reykjavik-on-Thames by some commentators, including the *New York Times*. This description, a linkage to the parlous financial plight of Iceland, captured the impact of the failure both of sound finances and of Labour's regulation of the financial sector. This failure led to excessive and risky liabilities on the part of the banks which, in turn, produced a banking crisis, a drying-up of credit, and the triggering of a recession that owed much to a failure not only of the fiscal system, but also of both government and people to live within their means.

Over a longer time-scale, the post-war fall and then revival of London's population numbers have been crucial to its post-war history. Each of these developments reflected expectations about living conditions, notably the move into New Towns beyond the Green Belt after the Second World War as people sought more space, for themselves as well as their cars. In turn, the pressures of immigration over the last decade have led to an increase in the city's population. So also has the desire among the affluent and the young to live in London, notably inner London, and this desire has been fed by the conversion of premises, especially the warehouses of Docklands.

Although the latter has indicated an imaginative use of premises, in general it has not proved easy to plan in response to changing and competing demands for housing, and this difficulty has affected both private house-builders and public policy. Indeed, there has been a marked contrast between the major increase in provision in the inter-war years, and the limited building of the last decade. In part, this contrast reflects differences in the planning regime, especially given Green Belt legislation and problems with gaining approval for developments, although the planning regime was already a factor in the inter-war years, notably at the borough level. The availability of mortgages was also an issue, as the building societies that provided inter-war loans were demutualised as a consequence of the Big Bang, becoming like banks. Thus, the specialised provision of mortgage capital was lost. In the long term, there will be a contrast between the lasting imprint of inter-war suburbia in large parts of London, and the more patchy legacy of more recent years.

There is a ragged end to the account of recent decades, as it is necessarily incomplete. By the time these pages are read, London might have experienced terrorist atrocities comparable to that in New York in 2001. There might have been an environmental disaster. Alternatively, the city, hit hard by the recession, may muddle on, at once frustrating and invigorating.

10

W HILE the last chapter began with a film, this one starts with a play, Richard Bean's *England People Very Nice* which began a run at the National Theatre in February 2009. The play, set in Bethnal Green, deals with the waves of immigration to this cockpit of the East End: Huguenots, Irish, Jews, Bangladeshis and Somalis. At one level, the play is about assimilation, with immigrants becoming Cockneys, so that the barmaid ends up as a woman of Irish-French extraction married to a Jew and with grandchildren who are half-Bangladeshi. At the same time, there are darker currents which are far from hidden. First, there is the backdrop of a xenophobic mob angry at the Huguenots for taking jobs, the Irish for being Catholics, and the Jews for producing Jack the Ripper (for which there is no evidence), and also accusing the Bangladeshis of being 'curried monkeys'. The British National Party, a far-right organisation that has become more active in London in the 2000s, is an element in the story.

Even darker are the young Bangladeshis in the last act who lack their elders' willingness to accept British values. The youngsters, in contrast, hate the other British as infidels, admire Osama bin Laden, and seek a British caliphate, with the intolerance and bloodshed this entails. An imam with two hooks for hands is an obvious reference to a radical preacher who violently denounced the host society in the 2000s. Bean's play captured central questions about the ability of London to cope with its diversity, or, more specifically, with one of the current iterations of a long-standing issue. The prospect of the Thames running 'with blood' is frequently mentioned in the play. Whether this prospect is a likely one or not is unclear.

A different challenge is posed by climate change, which accentuates the long-standing risk of the drowning of some or much of London, and of its hinterland. While global warming is a key factor, there are also issues specific to a smaller region, notably long-term and continuing structural adjustments, from the removal of ice cover during the latter stages of the Ice Age. As a consequence of these adjustments, at the same time that Scotland and northern England experience uplift, a downwarping is especially apparent in

INTO THE FUTURE

East Anglia and the South East. The resulting risk of flooding led to the construction of the Thames Flood Barrier at Woolwich (1982), a major feat of civil engineering celebrated in the Engineering Achievements set of stamps in 1983, which bears comparison with Bazalgette's work in the nineteenth century on the sewerage system and the Thames. Once seen as a white elephant, the Barrier has turned out to be rather useful and also a tourist site that is well worth the journey.

Now, however, it appears that this barrier and the other flood defences offer insufficient protection. Climate change thus is a major challenge to London, as indeed it is to all coastal cities. There will probably be a need for a new barrage, as well as raised banks for the Thames and its tributaries in order to cope with the risk that a higher North Sea will prevent the movement of river water downstream. Thus, alongside the general issue of rising sea level and its consequences for river levels, these levels will also be related to tidal patterns in the North Sea, not least seasonal high tides and tides linked to winds in the shape of storm surges. Such flooding would be a major challenge, both to particular areas, such as Richmond, and also to the operation of the entire Tube system.

It is also unclear how far the prospect both of higher sea levels and of storm surges make plans for developments in the estuary unviable. In particular, these threats pose issues for the Thames Gateway plans and also for the idea, advanced most recently by Boris Johnson as Mayor, that a new airport should be built to the east of London in place of the proposed growth of Heathrow, notably the projected but controversial third runway. Such a location had already been pursued in the plan for an airport at Foulness. Airport expansion is a specifically London issue.

More generally, the rise of sea levels indicates the instability of the environment and the dependence of human history on physical factors over which human control is limited. Yet, the very ability of cities to create viable living environments also suggests that such control is possible and, moreover, that the end-result may be prosperous, safe and even pleasant. For example, the capacity to insure commercial property is an important limitation of risk, while the creation of the wide-ranging Underground system reflects human capability to mould the environment.

In many respects, the challenge from climate change is far more serious than previous emergencies, such as the Great Fire or the Blitz, as they were time-limited and did not prevent a rapid process of recovery. The difficulty with raised water levels, by contrast, is that of an environment that has changed, and to an unprecedented extent in the history of the city. In competitive terms, moreover, London's position near the sea makes its future situation more serious than Frankfurt, Paris and Manchester. The investment requirements of new flood defences are considerable, and it is unclear that the planning regime is capable of mounting a swift response. This point is equally pertinent at the national and regional level. Any new flood defence system will have to be handled at a level above, and more extensive than, that of the Greater London Authority.

Other changes that may arise from global warming will not necessarily be specifically so serious for London and other coastal cities. For example, warming may lead to summer droughts, winter storms, and the onset of diseases such as malaria. Each of these problems

Installed between 1974 and 1982, the Thames Barrier's cylindrical hollow gates revolve and fill with water when submerged to prevent excessively high water levels reaching central London. Four of the gates are wide enough to allow ships to pass between. The barrier was designed and operated by the Greater London Council, but when that body was abolished in 1986 a succession of government bodies – Thames Water, the National Rivers Authority and now the Environment Agency – has operated it. Flooding is nothing new to London: John Stow recounts a tale that in 1236 'a great number of inhabitants … were drowned, and in the great Palace of Westminster men did row with wherries in the midst of the Hall,' while on 7 December 1663 Pepys wrote, 'There was last night the greatest tide that ever was remembered in England to have been in this river, all Whitehall having been drowned.' But Britain is tilting, and the South East sinking, and this will only be exacerbated by the seemingly inevitable rise in sea levels caused by global warming. Might a second Thames Barrier be required?

PHOTOGRAPH: GEOFFREY HAMMOND, 2005, ISTOCKPHOTO.COM

will pose a threat to living conditions, with malaria possibly leading to pressure for the drainage of surface water, as in the Lea valley (and also garden ponds), but these problems are unlikely to make a distinctive impact on London's future.

Nevertheless, water availability will probably be a key issue for Londoners. It is unclear that rationing by price will solve the problem. Combined with continuing demands on land for housing, and a resulting commitment to smaller units, the issue of water availability will probably affect planning regulations, with, for example, a move from baths to showers, which use less water. Harsher summers will also take the green sheen off London's parks and, in the face of hose-pipe bans, will lead to pressure for different plantings in gardens. The impact of climate change on immigration is unclear, but likely to be important as desertification in, for example, north Africa and Spain will greatly encourage the northward movement of people. There may also be a large-scale return of expatriates.

In May 2009, the impact of urban heat islands was noted in a report which suggested that the city would become much hotter. Yet the consequences of climate change do not generally enter into discussions of London's future. Instead, the emphasis is usually on demography, housing, transport, economic fortunes and the challenges to social cohesion. Alongside these topics, energy availability is another key issue, one that faces Britain as a whole, not least with the obsolescence of much of its generating plant. In the late 2000s, the London Array Project, a plan to build 341 wind turbines in the Thames estuary with the capacity to generate 1,000 megawatts of electricity, was supported by the Brown government, but, in 2009, hit major problems, from its backers because it was highly uneconomic.

As far as demographic trends are concerned, predictions about London's future are closely intertwined with those for the country as a whole. Within the latter, the absence of population controls, for example on the destination of immigrants, is such that London's appeal as the prime destination is unlikely to be countered. Yet, there are differences between particular migrant flows, and it is unclear whether economic problems and the costs of living in the city will lessen London's appeal. These problems are held responsible for the return home of many young Poles and Australians in 2008. Yet, serious economic problems in other areas, such as much of eastern Europe, may well encourage migrants to remain in Britain. This factor appears particularly pertinent for the Irish, some of whom returned to Ireland during the Celtic Tiger years of the early 2000s, but have since been hit by the severe downturn in the Irish economy.

The availability of jobs seems more important to immigrants than that of housing, as employment permits entry into the housing market, while existing immigrant communities also offer a degree of shelter. This situation is as much the case with young Australians and French workers seeking a few years' employment, as for Bangladeshis planning to settle in Tower Hamlets. The movement of Australians from Earls Court, where they settled in large numbers from the 1960s, may well encourage a new generation of immigrants, with a related change in the character of the district.

For, even if the economy is under strain, opportunities in London may be better, and certainly may appear better, than those elsewhere, notably for those from impoverished areas with fewer opportunities. The net effect may be a diminution in the 'European' character of London and an increase in the relative number of immigrants from the Third World. The problems this entails are frequently emphasised, but there are also positive comments. The multiplication of the variety of restaurants may be the most cited by tourists, but this trend is an aspect of the key contribution of immigrants to the service sector, notably in providing many of the workers who keep the NHS going, as well as providing key cleaning and maintenance services. The willingness of many immigrants to work unsocial hours is important in sustaining shift work as well as unsocial hours services, such as late-night shopping, much of which was pioneered by Indian corner shops.

Another consequence of persistent economic problems would be a difficulty in sustaining London's building stock, especially the large projects brought to completion in recent decades, let alone those that are unfinished. There are other issues involved in the ability to sustain resistance to hostile creatures such as cockroaches, rats and mice. A sense of challenge increased in the 2000s with the problems of speed of infection and hospital cleanliness involved in 'super bugs', especially MRSA. Economic difficulties may well ensure that the resistance to these and related challenges diminish, both because of a crisis for public finances and due to the reduced profitability of private concerns, such as the water companies. Indeed, the failure of the latter to maintain the sewers to earlier standards has been blamed not only for the leakage of water but also for the marked recent increase in the population of rats.

This issue of hospital infections also raises a classic problem about the viability of cities, namely whether the concentration of people (and other life) they represent causes a particularly acute race between possibilities for human life and the threats to it. The popularity of fictional disaster scenarios, such as the the 2002 film *28 Days Later* or the BBC series *Survivors* (2008), is notable as it indicates the degree to which such concerns, especially about vulnerability to epidemics, enjoy a powerful purchase in the public imagination.

At the same time, such scenarios are not new, while cities also present the greatest opportunities for addressing major problems, not least due to the availability of finance and human talent, as well as the most significant pressure for doing so. While London's past may serve as a reminder of the persistence of some problems, it is also a testament to adaptability and change. The considerable number of industrial estates, factories, power stations and transport depots that were found in much of London in the 1970s have gone, but the resulting spatial pattern has still varied. Whereas the decay of the inner city has been replaced by prosperity and change, it has been to a certain extent at the expense of the inner suburbs. As another instance of adaptability, the Millennium Dome eventually found a solution in the O2 Arena. Similarly, for every fiasco, such as the rebuilding of Wembley Stadium – which cost far too much and was delayed, there is a success, in this case the Emirates Stadium, and Wembley now is judged a great success. Time heals many wounds, especially financial ones and delays, if the outcome works.

The situation with population movements is also unclear. To take fictional disaster scenarios, their relationship with short-term demographic pressures is unclear, but this lack of clarity underlines the degree of unpredictability involved in discussion about future trends. This point can be taken further by considering uncertainties about political trends elsewhere and the degree to which they may affect population pressures in London. In particular, the stability of the Maghreb (North Africa) is an issue. There are political consequences, as with the extent of Islamic terrorism among Algerian immigrants, a point demonstrated in the lethal bombing campaign of 2005 on the Underground.

Economic trends are not the sole issue. Population movements also reflect political instability elsewhere, and that instability shows scant sign of easing. Thus, London's cosmopolitan character may become both more pronounced and more diverse, a situation that, in turn, will attract renewed immigration even as it creates problems, notably in housing provision and in education. The extent to which this trend is seen as positive or negative rests in part on the reader's perception of national identity and interests, but there are also questions specific to London or particularly apparent there. From mid-2009, 55 per cent of all births in London were to mothers who had been born outside the country, rising to 75 per cent in Newham and 73 per cent in Brent.

The balance between an exuberant welcoming of expansion, diversity and the future, and an anxious questioning of implications, is often a very fine one. These divisions play a role in London politics, for example in the mayoral election of 2008, and are also linked to the detailed patterning of the city in social, ethnic and cultural terms.

In some respects, the diversity of the city is part of the global identity it shares with other such cities. In contrast, once major commercial and imperial cities that lost these roles also became less diverse, for example Alexandria and Constantinople. Indeed, the monoglot city is often, although not invariably, failing or a second-rate/rank city. Shanghai and Tokyo, however, are relatively monoglot.

Yet, there are also rises and falls among global cities, and room for querying aspects of contemporary London's situation, not least with reference to other cities. This process is not new. A laudatory tone characterised William Mildmay's *The Police of France: or, an Account of the Laws and Regulations Established in the Kingdom for the Preservation of Police and the Preventing of Robberies* (1763), and he had earlier praised the French system of grain provision to their major cities. London, in comparison, appeared disorganised, or rather dependent on private enterprise. The contrast reflected London's position in a very different public culture. Thus, the Tory MP William Shippen warned the House of Commons in 1722, in a debate over quarantine regulations touched off by the outbreak of plague in Marseille the previous year, of the danger of 'citadels and Bastilles round and round the City'.[1] Such an option for London appeared unacceptable.

Today, there is room for questioning whether London can remain in its current position relative to other global cities. 'The Road to Wealth: How to Know London', the title of an early nineteenth-century board game, no longer appears so pertinent. In part, London will be affected by the continuing relative decline of Britain, which accelerated markedly during the financial and economic crisis of the late 2000s. The extent to which Britain became a debtor nation followed on from an earlier openness to foreign investment that led to the movement abroad of control over assets, as when the British Airports Authority was sold to a Spanish company, complicating the issue of the future of Heathrow and Gatwick.

The dramatic fall of asset values in 2008–09, and the scale of borrowing from abroad made necessary by limited domestic savings, put real strain on the financial architecture of the City of London and the more general prosperity of the metropolis and the wider South East, with large-scale job losses in early 2009. The resulting capacity of city, region and, indeed, central government faced with falling tax revenues and rising indebtedness, as a result, to meet the expenditure necessary for fundamental improvements in infrastructure is unclear. The spending preferences displayed by the Labour government in 2008 were scarcely encouraging, as there was a marked preference for encouraging consumer spending rather than investing in infrastructure.

Recent financial and economic events are potentially extremely adverse for London, and certainly for its self-image. An average price fall of 11.95% in Greater London between January 2008 and January 2009 scarcely encourages a sense of well-being. Moreover, the rate of unemployment rose, to 4.2 per cent of the working population, by June 2009, although that compared with a national rate of 7.2 per cent. Within London, long-standing differences in prosperity and opportunity were underlined, with rates lowest in Chelsea and Wimbledon (1.8 per cent), and highest in east London, notably in Hackney South and Shoreditch (7.4 per cent). At the same time, in London there has been quite a long run of a feeling of resurgence since the mid-1980s, bolstered in recent years not only by the financial services (and cultural) boom, but also by the establishment of the mayoralty for London and by the magnet London has become for many of the ambitious from around the world, as well as for the dispossessed.

That is a longer trend than the last year of uncertainty and now gloom. Will London re-balance itself and, after adjustment, take it in its stride, or will the banking contraction show that basing London's future on financial services was an illusion, a 'dead cat bounce' in the long run of decline? The forthcoming Olympics are also a huge short-term risk factor because if, as is still very possible, it is seen by the world as a relative failure, it is unclear how easy it will be to shrug off this failure.

The lack of investment is serious because much of the often-Victorian infrastructure, in particular of sewers, Tube services, and buildings, is in parlous condition, while post-Victorian investment has frequently been inadequate. In some cases, particularly the Underground, the issue is as much poor management and unhelpful union attitudes as a lack of investment. More generally, aside from the problems of maintenance and refurbishment, there are the issues posed by new requirements and challenges, and, again, it is unclear that there is sufficient investment to cope with the demands. The Thames Tideway project, for example, is intended to provide an overflow system to cope with the impact of heavy rainfall on the sewage system. Such projects are necessary if London is to continue as a safe and attractive living environment.

London here faces problems that are both particular to a city of its scale and also general to Britain as a whole. For example, the woeful failure, at the national level, to invest in the power supply poses issues for London, which has always imported energy, and, more particularly, for buildings dependent on electricity for air conditioning and lifts. There are also problems common to major cities but most pronounced in the case of London, for example the competing demands of the inner city and the wealthy suburbs.

Whatever the situation, London will be in the forefront of national attention, even though the views of the city no longer have the prominence in national politics or identity that they did in the eighteenth and nineteenth centuries. Then, the views of London were commonly presented by populists as indicative of the voice of the incorruptible part of the nation, as well as being important in their own right.

At the same time, there was also critical concern about the role that London took as the

River barges being towed upstream under Blackfriars Bridge, July 2009. When it was was first set up in 1896 the firm of William Cory & Son Ltd carried coal into London. Now, from its depot at Walbrook Wharf among other locations, the company's principal business is removing waste from the city for recycling or disposal, at least for now, in the enormous landfill site at the former gravel quarry of Mucking Marshes just east of Tilbury.

PHOTOGRAPH: CARNEGIE, 2009

cutting-edge of public politics. In April 1757, George, 2nd Earl of Halifax complained about the support voiced by the Common Council of London for William Pitt the Elder, then in opposition, writing of 'the violent and indecent proceedings of the City ... The Crown ought and must name its servants without such intervention'. Later that year, returned to power, Pitt set up an inquiry into the failure of a military expedition against Rochefort in order to assuage public discontent. He showed his concern about opinion in London and the danger of hostile address from the City, by sending a message to the Mayor to inform the City that an inquiry had been set up. Horace Walpole, conservative on social and constitutional matters, like his colleagues in the Commons, complained, arguing that 'confusion may follow from incorporating the mob of London with the other parts of the legislature'.[2] There are no equivalents politically today, and, during the government of Gordon Brown, London no longer played the part in Labour politics it had done in the 1940s. The City's opinion, however, remains crucial in fiscal policy.

Yet, there is still an equivalent today to the role of London as show, a function captured by the young Samuel Johnson in 1775. Going to see a regatta on the Thames:

> I thought I should run the risk of being crushed to death or thrown into the water. One might almost have walked over the Thames and through every part of it on the boats, which could scarcely pass by each other; the streets were paved with heads, the houses were all ... covered with faces, on the shore all along on each side of the Thames was a moving quay which seemed to hem in the water, and Westminster Bridge was exactly like a rich fringe formed by the people who sat across the ballustrades sideways over the heads of those who were peeping through them ... When a number of people are brought together, there is always some end proposed by their assembling, I mean something to draw them together, something to be seen, but in this case they all appeared to me to be assembled for no other purpose than to see each other, which without doubt is a secondary consideration in most conventions, and in this a sight well worth going to see, but it is a new way of entertaining the public, who indeed may console themselves with the thoughts of adding to the entertainment, and of looking on themselves to be as well the entertainers as the entertained.

The following year, Johnson went to spectate at the trial for bigamy of the Duchess of Kingston. He reported seeing about 120 peeresses, some with amazingly contrived hair.[3] As another dramatic show, the cast for the performance of Handel's *Messiah* at Westminster Abbey in 1784 was over 500 and the £7,000 profit went to charity. This already was a world of public occasion and celebrity laid out in an almost voyeuristic fashion, and one that made Londoners appear to be participating in the pageant of the age. The present-day is no different.

At the same time, this world of public show and the consumption of spectacle could have a harder edge, not least an openness to exploitation and fraud. In 1749, the New Theatre in the Haymarket was hired, probably by John, 2nd Duke of Montagu, a noted prankster, for the performance of 'Harlequin's Escape into the Battle'. The large crowd, tricked by their gullibility into attending the advertised show of a singer getting into a quart bottle, was not mollified by the offer of the return of their admission money and, in the resulting riot, the theatre was badly burned.

London's past serves as a remainder of the persistence of issues and problems that might otherwise seem of the moment. Crime and public order and decency are obvious instances. It is salutary to read 'Paddler', writing in Kingston's local paper on 3 July 1880, that he sought 'relief from the noise and turmoil of the City in the enjoyment of a leisurely paddle on the river in these long twilight evenings' only to face 'the noisy and immodest proceedings of the evening bathers' and their 'foul and disgusting language which assaults one's ears and serves to call attention to the immodesty which might otherwise pass unnoticed'.[4] Similar comments can be found in other papers across the country, as correspondents called for moral improvement.

What is striking about London is that the city is particularly a focus for concern (and fascination) about crime, especially violent crime, and also for moral panics linked to sexual and other activity and anxieties. Television sustains the impressions created by nineteenth-century newspapers, especially the Sundays. Thus, as I write in February 2009, BBC2 offers a series *Moses Jones*, a supposedly sophisticated crime drama set in London, in which Ugandans provide plot and villains, while the impressive detective is of African origin, while ITV1 provides *Whitechapel*, in which a copycat Jack the Ripper is the villain. Lest London be seen as insufficiently deadly, ITV also offered *In the Line of Fire*, a two-part documentary about CO19, the Metropolitan Police firearms division, and its often violent confrontations with armed criminals. The impact of such reiterated images, as well as of reports of what is (by national standards) a particularly high level of gun and knife crime, is important for creating an overly violent impression among Londoners about the city, and, especially the inner city, thus fortifying spatial divisions. Outsiders are more inclined to see London as a whole as violent, or at least threatening, and indeed as a second New York.

The extent to which the future may involve a return to past problems is also unclear. A mass epidemic like the cholera attacks of the nineteenth century, let alone the Plague of 1665 or the Black Death, is a possibility. Alongside such apocalyptic possibilities, there are the prospects of a mismatch between pretensions and possibilities. The potential represented by the people of London may not be matched by a capacity for successful collective action. That is the current challenge, and upon its success hinges the future of the city.

POSTSCRIPT: THE
BIOGRAPHY OF A CITY

A dream Victorian London, where Sherlock Holmes rides in a hansom cab through the fog and housemaids behind shuttered bedroom windows allow their lecherous employers to unribbon their stays.

A.N. Wilson went on to pull no punches in his vigorously written history of London:

in arches under the embankment barefoot children starved to death. In the capital of the richest empire the world had ever seen was poverty which would compare with the most deprived parts of Africa and South America in the twenty-first century.[1]

L ET US LEAVE ASIDe for a brief moment the question as to how many (very few), and what percentage (very low) of the city's children actually starved to death in Victorian London, and how these figures compared with rates in Constantinople, Beijing or Addis Ababa in that period (very favourably). The point here is that London's history has often served as an opportunity to express both present discontents and particular angers on the part of the author. Wilson, for example, was very hostile to the character and results of Victorian and twentieth-century property development in London, while Roy Porter was also very scathing about the latter.

Such a writing of the past in terms of the priorities of the present is scarcely new. There are, however, particular fault-lines in writing the history of a city. One relates to the emphasis to be placed on the city as an organic entity – what the brilliant Porter termed 'the deep pulse of the city',[2] an approach also seen in the works of Peter Ackroyd and in Iain Sinclair's recent time-bending book on Hackney[3] – as opposed to the less popular argument that such an organic character is less real than apparent, and also that the city is in large part a palimpsest recording new pressures, most of them external in origin. The emphasis on an organic entity also matches the commercial (publishing) need for a more lyrical, personal or emotional style, one that focuses on the 'feel' of London, conveys the feeling that the author is engaged with the subject, and also adds to the sense of engagement between the reader and the book.

This tension can be seen in Porter's foreword to Stephen Inwood's first-rate *History of London*. Porter closed with the sort of triumphant affirmation expected in such works: 'Stephen Inwood shows how the history of London is truly the history of Londoners,' but, earlier, he noted that 'London's future, perhaps more than ever, nowadays depends upon a balance of forces which is global, not merely national'; while Inwood wrote, 'it is often difficult to avoid crossing the line between London's history and England's'.[4]

Just so, as for London such a distinction is not particularly helpful. Indeed, a history of the city that underplays that of England, and of London's intertwining with world history, misses the point. London was founded by conquerors, the Romans, served their purposes, and fell soon after they left. So total a relationship between city and outside forces was not to be repeated but, nevertheless, it is important not only in the account of London's politics, a politics that was particularly driven home when it was under the control of foreign troops or overawed by fortifications, but also to its economy.

A city that relied heavily on trade could not but be greatly affected by these external links. To foreign eyes, London trade used to be regarded as a cornerstone of the burgeoning success of the British economy and nation. Whereas, in the seventeenth century, few tourists ventured into the business end of London and those who did were often critical, in contrast, by the late eighteenth century a trip into the city was a must, including for foreign aristocrats. The Royal Exchange was believed to symbolise positive features of British society; the Bank of England was a tourist site; and particular awe was reserved for the new West India docks opened in 1802, a key facility for the Atlantic world.[5]

Communications have been a crucial element in the city's history, one that helped explain why it was able to take on a global role. Conversely, the decline of London's relative position in recent years has in part been matched by that of the city's docks, as well as of the country's merchant fleet and ship-building. London's financial position now relies, instead, upon electronic communications with which London is well provided. However, the current controversy over the future of Heathrow indeed takes on part of its weight from the question of London's future as a world city in the sense of a key nodal point in the world's web of communications and transport. Supporters of the scheme highlight the alleged risk of failing to implement it. Indeed, failure to sustain London's position as a world city might well leave it to a fate similar to that of once-mighty Constantinople in the nineteenth century: a decayed imperial city, its past splendours a counterpoint to present poverty. The contrast pointed out by A.N. Wilson for the age of Victorian majesty would then be all the more brutal.

How far looking back is itself a sign of decline is unclear. There was a long tradition of writing urban history in London, and England as a whole, including in the eighteenth and nineteenth centuries, periods of unprecedented growth.[6] Indeed, such history was an aspect of the assertion of status, and notably so in societies reverential of the past and referential to it. Thus, claiming noble origins and an exalted past, as was the case during the Middle Ages and the early modern period, was as a piece with the pursuit of status. Moreover, when freedoms were seen as privileges rather than as liberties, it was especially important to claim such a past, not least because it implied a particular relationship with the Crown, the fount and source of such privileges.

At the same time, there was a pride in the new and the distinctive, and in structures and buildings such as London Bridge or the Royal Exchange. This pride in the new became especially strong in the eighteenth and nineteenth centuries, periods in which much of the past was rejected unless utilitarian purposes could be found. Such a process was especially apparent after the Glorious Revolution of 1688–89. A culture of 'improvement' was linked to the rejection of the Stuarts, and there was a fascination for new institutions and buildings: the Bank of England, Greenwich Hospital, Westminster Bridge, Somerset House, and so on. Guide books focused on these and other new buildings, and not on old Gothic works, although it was in Westminster Abbey that London's sculptors presented some of the most potent images of modern imperial activity and identity.[7] A similar pattern can be seen in the depiction of Paris, with a concern with the Invalides, the Madeleine, the Place de la Concorde, and not with the Marais. In the event, London won the struggle between the cities, first in the Seven Years' War (1756–63), and then with the Napoleonic Wars, and its triumphs were celebrated very publicly in place-names such as Trafalgar Square and Waterloo Station, as well as in prominent memorials and public statues.

The key point is that, as with New York in the twentieth century and Shanghai more recently, it was the London of the new that was of interest, and that was pursued by a society that was also investing heavily in the future, most notably in the docks, but also in industrial plant such as the Albion Mill. In turn, the Victorians disliked much of the Georgian town-building, but also built for new, a process dramatised with the destruction that accompanied the building of railway stations and lines, as well as with their department stores, hotels and neo-Gothic churches.

The damage done by such work can be appreciated better as a result of our ability to see and understand the devastation wrought by 1960s' planners and buildings; and possibly A.N. Wilson should have focused on the entire communities disrupted by Victorian builders, rather than (or as much as) the poor children who attracted the attention of contemporary philanthropists.

Various themes can be noted when considering the last sixty years. On the one hand, there is the continued search for change and the new, a search that brings together the entrepreneurial quest for profit with the desire of authority to plan and build. Yet, the legacy of the new in the last sixty years is a mixed one. This is the London of Westway and Centre Point, of the slab-like towers of housing estates, of concrete hotels and the Home Office building, and of the Millennium Dome. The question that emerges – one already seen in the 1970s with its strong sense of malaise – is whether London, and indeed Britain, is no longer capable of solving its problems, and that the recent history of the city is a record of this failure. Such an analysis can be sharpened up by pointing out that, alongside progress, for instance in the water supply system, there are also difficulties in ensuring infrastructure improvements such as Crossrail.

Looked at from a national perspective, however, investment in projects such as Crossrail could be seen as highly disproportionate. The benefits that London receives over the rest of the country are highlighted by considering what such sums could achieve if spent on the rest of England. Another perspective is offered by the possibility that a future government might decide to move the capital to Loughborough or Rugby, each of which is geographically more central. A Eurosceptic might argue that the capital has already moved to Brussels, while a less partisan observer could observe that the overweighting of the parliamentary representation of Scotland, Wales and some English areas ensures that the South East, especially Greater London, is in fact relatively under-represented.

Yet, frequent reference to London as a whole is only partially correct, for although the city as a unit has an impact on the outside world, it is experienced by Londoners (and indeed by many visitors) as a complex assemblage of districts and communities, each and all affected by the shifting substrata of class and ethnicity. This point has been true from the city's very beginnings, and underlines the extent to which its history is different to outsiders and inhabitants. This point also affects the coverage of the city's history. Inhabitants might anticipate due attention to that of their suburbs, but, to an Argentinean interested in London's role as an exporter of capital in the nineteenth century or a Newcastle reader aware of the city's role as the major market for North East coal, the history of Hendon or Clerkenwell as distinct areas is of scant relevance.

As the current proposals for expanding Heathrow indicate, many schemes for change are not without serious costs in terms of disruption and the deterioration in living conditions. A crude equation of change with progress is now scarcely acceptable, as is indicated by the more enduring architectural disasters of what in the 1960s was referred to as urban 'renewal'. Whatever the hopes of the time, these were scarcely progress, and there are also doubts about the long-term consequences of the educational changes of the period, notably the end of the grammar schools and the creation of very large comprehensives.

The same point about the ambiguous value of change can be made about Britart and other self-consciously new developments in the arts. By 2009 critics were increasingly very disillusioned with Britart, while Altermodern, the Tate Triennial 2009 exhibition that claimed to offer an alternative to postmodernism, was widely criticised as lacking cohesion or aesthetic content.

Complex themes of change and continuity can be seen very clearly in the visual images that are produced of the city, such as commemorative stamps, which essentially date from the 1950s. Two stamps were issued earlier, in 1924, for the British Empire Exhibition in London, and another five in 1929 for the Postal Union Congress, also held in London; but none of these stamps had any visual reference to London. The two stamps issued for the Festival of Britain in 1951 did not include any reference to the Great Exhibition a century earlier, although alongside the Festival, a large exhibition was held at the Victoria and Albert Museum to celebrate the Great Exhibition. Moreover, in 1950, His Majesty's Stationery Office issued an official commemorative album about the Great Exhibition.

The London of new buildings was celebrated in stamps from the 1960s. The International Geographical Congress in London in 1964 was marked with a set including 'Flats near Richmond Park. Urban Development'. Another emphasis on novelty was the set produced for the opening of the Post Office Tower in 1965. This featured two stamps, the first with the Tower and Georgian Buildings, and the second with the Nash Terraces fringing Regent's Park. In each case, the emphasis was directly upon the Post Office Tower, and the other buildings were in the shade, both visually and in terms of the colour. In 1975, the National Theatre was commemorated in the set for European Architectural Heritage Year, and in 1983 the Thames Barrier in that for engineering achievements. A Datapost motorcyclist against a London backdrop including new tower blocks appeared in the 1985 set for the 350th anniversary of the Royal Mail public postal service.

Yet, the overwhelming majority of images of London focused on its past, and the dominant impression was very different to that just given. The 700th anniversary of Simon de Montfort's Parliament led to a stamp showing Hollar's 1647 engraving of Parliament's buildings (1965); an air-battle over St Paul's appeared in the set for the 25th anniversary of the Battle of Britain (1965); there were two stamps for the 900th anniversary of Westminster Abbey (1966); and St Paul's appeared in the 1969 set of cathedrals. St Paul's, Covent Garden, followed as part of the Inigo Jones series (1973), and then two stamps of the Houses of Parliament for the Commonwealth Parliamentary Conference in 1973, and another for the Inter-Parliamentary Union Conference in 1975, four stamps linked to William Caxton for the 500th anniversary of British printing (1976), and the Tower and Hampton Court for the historic building series in 1978. 'London 1980', the montage of buildings presented on a stamp for the International Stamp Exhibition, was largely an account of traditional scenes – the Tower, Tower Bridge, St Paul's, Big Ben, Nelson's Column, Westminster Abbey and Eros, with only the Post Office Tower to mark the new.

Similarly, the series London Landmarks, designed by Sir Hugh Casson in 1980, provided stamps of Buckingham Palace, the Albert Memorial, the Royal Opera House, Hampton

Court and Kensington Palace, with nothing more modern. Greenwich Observatory was featured in the 1984 set for the centenary of the Greenwich Meridian, the mails leaving London in 1828 for a 1984 series on mail coach runs, and the Crystal Palace and the Albert Memorial for a 1987 series on Queen Victoria. Kew Gardens were celebrated with a series in 1990, Greenwich appeared anew that year, and St Paul's with searchlights in a Europa Peace and Freedom series in 1995. The role of the past was also demonstrated in the five-stamp 1989 series on the Lord Mayor's Show, a period of fundamental transformation in the City, and in the five-stamp series on Shakespearean theatres that appeared in 1995, which was a period of great activity on the modern London stage.

The weight of the past was not only very strong in stamps. In the powerful visual images offered on the screen, there was a continuing tension between historical London, as in *Shakespeare in Love* (1998) a quaint London, as in *Four Weddings and a Funeral* (1994) or *Love Actually* (2003), and more edgy accounts, such as *Mona Lisa* (1986), *Sliding Doors* (1998) and *Lock, Stock and Two Smoking Barrels* (1998). Moreover, there is a retro London on film, created in *Absolute Beginners* (1985), based on the Colin MacInnes novel of 1959 and set in the 1950s, and the Victorian Gothic London of films such as *From Hell* (2001) and various Sherlock Holmes adaptations.[8] The past could also be used for didactic purposes, as in a 2007 visit by Dr Who to Shakespeare's London in which the Doctor informs his black companion that Africans then lived in London, thus helping to ground an idea of identity that is of relevance today.

London's history has in fact been covered unevenly on the screen. Medieval London has been largely ignored, as has much of the Tudor century. Films tend to be set at court (such as *Elizabeth: The Golden Age* (2007); the series *Blackadder II* (1986)) and rarely deal with the streets. Olivier's *Henry V* (1944) opens with a panorama of London in c.1600, but it is a model shot and, thereafter, the first act takes place within the theatre. Perhaps the most authentic images of street life appear in *Shakespeare in Love*, and the *Doctor Who* episode 'The Shakespeare Code' (2007), although even these scenes are quite limited.

By contrast, there is a vast range of sources for the Victorian period, with the film image drawing upon visual culture, including magazine illustrations, paintings and photography. Fog, gaslight and hansom cabs were the dominant images of the later Victorian period.[9] There were some excellent city scenes in 20th Century-Fox's *The Hound of the Baskervilles* and *The Adventures of Sherlock Holmes* (both 1939), the latter with a wonderful climax at the Tower of London. The Hammer horror films also had some London references, particularly their 1959 remake of *The Hound of the Baskervilles* mystery. *Murder by Decree* (1979) was a fascinating Holmes-meets-The Ripper film with some effective London sequences. The various Jack the Ripper films have provided extensive coverage of the dark side of the Victorian East End. The Herbert Wilcox/Anna Neagle biopics *Victoria the Great* (1937) and *Sixty Glorious Years* (1938) included London scenes from earlier in the reign, not least an assassination attempt on Constitution Hill, and, more recently, the London crowd played a role in *Young Victoria* (2009). The film *The First Great Train Robbery* (1979), directed by Michael Crichton and starring Sean Connery as a gentleman-thief in 1850s' London, who plots to steal Crimean War gold from the London to Brighton express, has both a nice contrast and a significant linkage between high-society and low-life locations. *Royal Flash* (1975) has a dramatic scene set in a London brothel.

A similar range in coverage can be seen in television treatments. In a popular satire on the age, Johnny Speight created the memorable character of bigoted working-class Conservative Alf Garnett in *Till Death Us Do Part* (1965–75), while the police dramas *The Sweeney* (1975–78) *and The Bill* (1984–) brought to an abrupt end the cosy image of the kind-hearted London bobby which had been built up carefully over twenty years in *Dixon of Dock Green* (1955–76). Television portrayals of modern British life still focus heavily upon London, and a disproportionate number have been set in the East End. As in the art and literature of previous generations, these more recent images often concentrate on the real or imagined badness – or at least the 'earthy reality' – of the area. Such portrayals can easily be regarded as part of a long sequence stretching from the work of Hogarth and Dickens to that of Doré and Jack London.

One of the most widely seen and therefore most important programmes has been *Eastenders*. This gritty and sometimes bleak soap opera, which centres upon the improbably eventful lives of the residents of the fictional borough of Walford, was first broadcast in 1985, and has been screened around the English-speaking world ever since. At Christmas 1986 more than 30.1 million people were estimated to have tuned in to watch 'Dirty' Den Watts (Leslie Grantham) hand over divorce papers to Angie (Anita Dobson). The editorial aim had been to portray 'London, today …', and the series has regularly depicted topics such as rape, homosexuality, child abuse, violence and murder.

Perhaps there is nothing new here. People have been migrating to London, marvelling at London, writing about London, castigating, praising or condemning London, for hundreds of years. In this sense the city, though self-absorbed, could hardly be self-contained. It has never been able to get on with its business unobtrusively, out of the public gaze. It is constantly picked out by the spotlight of publicity, or refracted by the prism of reputation. London is central to the national experience, familiar to all, if only dimly or from afar.

In these ways, London's history does belong to the whole country. As the first truly 'world city' in the nineteenth century, indeed, it belonged to the whole world. Past glories might now be dimmer; other cities might have risen to positions of greatness or rivalry; the International Cricket Council might recently have moved its headquarters to Dubai after a century in St John's Wood; but, despite this, London does still remain very much at centre-stage. The vibrancy, the life and the buzz are all still there.

NOTES AND REFERENCES

Abbreviations

Add.   Additional Manuscripts
AE. CP. Ang.   Paris, Ministère des Relations Extérieures, Correspondence Politique, Angleterre
BL   British Library
HMC   Historical Manuscripts Commission
NA   The National Archives, London
SP   State Papers

Note to Preface

1. Montagu to George Lyttelton, 23 Sept. 1762, Huntington, Library, Montagu papers 1420.

Note to Chapter 1: Roman capital (pages 10–23)

1. R. Merrifield, *The Roman City of London* (1965), p. 44.

Notes to Chapter 2: Anglo-Saxon centuries, 410–1066 (pages 24–43)

1. A terminology made famous by Bede in the eighth century.
2. S. Bassett (ed.), *The Origins of Anglo-Saxon Kingdoms* (1989).
3. A.R. Rumble, *Property and Piety in Early Medieval Winchester* (2002).
4. B. Arnold, 'England and Germany, 1050–1350', in M. Jones and M. Vale (eds), *England and Her Neighbours, 1066–1453* (1989), p. 43.

Notes to Chapter 3: Medieval developments, 1066–1485 (pages 44–81)

1. A. Vince, *Anglo-Saxon London: an archaeological investigation* (1990), pp. 40–1.
2. Ex. Inf. Bob Higham.
3. V. Harding and L. Wright (eds), *London Bridge: Selected Accounts and Rentals, 1382–1538* (1995).
4. C. Davidson-Cragoe, 'Fabric, Tombs and Precinct, 1087–1540', in D. Keene, A Burns and A. Saint (eds), *St Paul's. The Cathedral Church of London* (2004), pp. 127–42.
5. A term borrowed from French usage.
6. J.C. Holt, *Magna Carta* (2nd edn, 1992), pp. 56–7.
7. D. Keene, 'Text, Visualisation and Politics: London, 1150–1250', *Transactions of the Royal Historical Society*, 18 (2008), pp. 89–90.
8. Keene, 'Text, Visualisation and Politics', p. 80.
9. O. Creighton and R. Higham, *Medieval Town Walls: an archaeology and social history of urban defence* (2005), p. 210.
10. P. Coss and M. Keen (eds), *Heraldry, Pageantry and Social Display in Medieval England* (2002).
11. T.F. Tout, 'A Medieval Burglary', in his *Collected Papers*, III (1934), pp. 93–115; P. Doherty, *The Great Crown Jewels Robbery of 1303* (2005).
12. C. Barron, *London in the Later Middle Ages: Government and People, 1200–1500* (2004), pp. 255–61.

13. G. Milne, *The Port of Medieval London* (2003).
14. H.S. Cobb (ed.), *The Overseas Trade of London. Exchequer Customs Accounts, 1480–81* (1990).
15. B.M.S. Campbell, J.A. Galloway, D. Keene and M. Murphy, *A Medieval Capital and its Food Supply*

(1993).
16. P. Nightingale, *A Medieval Mercantile Community: The Grocers' Company and the Politics and Trade of London, 1000–1485* (1995).

Notes to Chapter 4: London under the Tudors, 1485–1603 (pages 82–113)

1. D.E. Harkness, *The Jewel House: Elizabethan London and the Scientific Revolution* (2007).
2. J. Oldland, 'The Wealth of the Trades in Early Tudor London', *London Journal*, 31 (2006), p. 143.
3. P. Clark, *European Cities and Towns, 400–2000* (2009), p. 37.
4. L.B. Luu, *Immigrants and the Industries of London, 1500–1700* (2005).
5. For a perceptive overview, see A.L. Beier, 'Londra, 1500–1700', *Storia Urbana*, 67–8 (1994), pp. 151–76.
6. J.F. Merritt, *The Social World of Early Modern Westminster-Abbey, Court and Community, 1525–1640* (2005).
7. I.W. Archer, 'Government in Early Modern London: The Challenge of the Suburbs', *Proceedings of the British Academy*, 107 (2001), p. 139.
8. I.W. Archer, 'Conspicuous Consumption Revisited: City and Court in the Reign of Elisabeth I', in M. Davies and A. Prescott (eds), *London and the Kingdom* (2008), p. 57 and 'City and Court Connected: The Material Dimensions of Royal Ceremonial, c.1480–1625', *Huntington Library*

Quarterly, 71 (2008), p. 179.
9. N. Younger, 'If the Armada Had Landed: A Reappraisal of England's Defences in 1588', *History*, 93 (2008), pp. 328–54.
10. C.E. Challis, 'Apprentices, Goldsmiths and the North in Sixteenth- and Seventeenth-Century England', *Northern History*, 37 (2000).
11. P. Griffiths, *Lost Londons. Change, Crime and Control in the Capital City, 1550–1660* (2008).
12. I.W. Archer, 'Hospitals in Sixteenth- and Seventeenth-Century England', in M. Scheutz *et al.* (eds), *Hospitals and Institutional Care in Medieval and Early Modern Europe* (2008), p. 59.
13. T. Hitchcock and J. Black (eds), *Chelsea Settlement and Bastardy Examinations, 1733–1766* (1999), p.91.
14. J. Gurney, *Brave Community: The Digger Movement in the English Revolution* (2007).
15. John Stow's *A Survey of London: Written in the Year 1598* has recently been republished in several editions; a transcription of the text is also available online at www.british-history.ac.uk

Notes to Chapter 5: Confronting the Stuarts, 1603–1714 (pages 114–165)

1. E. McKellar, *The Birth of Modern London: The Development and Design of the City, 1660–1720* (Manchester, 1999); P. Griffiths and M.S.R. Jenner (eds), *Londinopolis: Essays in the Cultural and Social History of Early Modern London* (2000).
2. J. Peacey, 'To Every Individual Member: The Palace of Westminster and Participatory Politics in the Seventeenth Century', *Court Historian*, 13 (2008), pp. 132–3.
3. See L. Hollis, *The Phoenix, St Paul's Cathedral and the Men who made Modern London* (2008).
4. T.F. Reddaway, *The Rebuilding of London after the Great Fire* (1940), pp. 306–8.
5. H. Berry, *Gender, Society and Print Culture in Late-Stuart England: The Cultural World of the 'Athenian Mercury'* (2003).
6. Farmington, Connecticut, Lewis Walpole Library, Hanbury Williams papers, vol. 67.
7. W.H. Quarrell and M. Mare (eds), *London in 1710. From the Travels of Zacharias Conrad von Uffenbach*

(1934), p. 12.
8. Gage to Charles Hotham, 19 Aug. 1749, Hull, University Library, Hotham papers DDHo 4/3.
9. Harris to Sir Charles Hanbury Williams, 6 July, 16 Oct. 1750, Farmington, Connecticut, Lewis Walpole Library, Hanbury Williams papers, vol. 68, fols 146, 151.
10. G.S. De Krey, *London and the Restoration, 1659–1683* (2005).
11. B. Cottret, *The Huguenots in England. Immigration and Settlement, c.1550–1700* (1992).
12. W. Gibson, *James II and the Trial of the Seven Bishops* (2009), p. 71.
13. D. Gerhold, *Carriers and Coachmasters* (2005).
14. BL. Evelyn papers 49, fol. 36. This was not the famous diarist.
15. AE. CP. Ang. 288, fol. 23.
16. D. Manley, *Secret History*, pp. 2–3.
17. P. Borsay, 'Geoffrey Holmes and the Urban World of Augustan England', in C. Jones (ed.), *British Politics*

in the Age of Holmes (Chichester, 2009), p. 132.

18. M. Davis and A. Saunders, *The History of the Merchant Taylors' Company* (2004).

19. J. Childs, *The British Army of William III* (1987), pp. 171–2.

20. R. Wodrow, *Analecta* (4 vols, 1842–43), III, 156.

21. K. Verdery, *Transylvanian Villagers* (1983), p. 157.

22. R. Norton, 'Recovering Gay History from the Old Bailey', *London Journal*, 30 (2005), p. 49.

Notes to Chapter 6: The centre of all, 1714–1815 (pages 166–223)

1. BL. Loan 721/1, fol. 135.

2. Ryder Diary, Sandford; Royal Archives, Cumberland Papers 7/287.

3. Weston to Robert Trevor, 1 Oct. 1745, Aylesbury, County Record Office, Trevor Manuscripts, vol. 51.

4. BL. Add. 58213, fol.216.

5. BL. Add. 63469, fol.137.

6. H. R. French, *The Middle Sort of People in Provincial England, 1600–1750* (2007).

7. C. Williams (ed.), *Sophie in London, 1786* (1933), pp. 94–5.

8. H.W. Lawrence, 'The Greening of the Squares of London: transformation of urban landscapes and ideals', *Annals of the Association of American Geographers*, 83 (1993), pp. 90–118.

9. HMC. *Hastings Mss.* p.37.

10. V. Barrie-Currien, *Clergé et Pastorale en Angleterre au XVIII Siècle: le Diocese de Londres* (1992).

11. NA. SP. 100/3.

12. *Gentleman's Magazine*, 7 (1738).

13. H. Hoock, *The King's Artists: The Royal Academy of Arts and the Politics of British Culture, 1760–1840* (2003).

14. AE., Mémoires et Documents Ang. 1, fols 25–6.

15. George Villiers, 4th Earl of Jersey, to Lady Spencer, 2 Dec. 1763, BL. Althorp Mss. fol. 101.

16. T. Evans, *'Unfortunate Objects': Lone Mothers in Eighteenth-Century London* (2005); A. Levene, *Childcare, health and mortality at the London Foundling Hospital, 1741–1800. 'Left to the mercy of the world'* (2007).

17. A. Neale, *St Marylebone Workhouse and Institution, 1730–1965* (2003).

18. Le Coq, Saxon Envoy in London, to Augustus II, 13 Oct. 1727, Dresden Staatsarchiv, 2676, fol. 300; AE.CP Aug. 565, fol. 161.

19. B. Marsden and C. Smith, *Engineering Empires* (2005), pp. 58–60; Hume to James Oswald, 1 Nov. 1750, Hockworthy Papers, folder 2.

20. AE. CP. Ang. 265, fols 18, 24.

21. *Annual Register for 1776* (4th edn, 1788), 2nd section, pp. 119–22.

22. Pulteney to Swift, 2 Dec. 1736, BL. Add. 4806, fol. 178.

23. See Preface, page vii. Montagu to George Lyttleton, 23 Sept. 1762, San Marino, California, Huntington Library, Montagu Papers no. 1422.

24. Sheffield Archives, Watson Wentworth collection R1–327.

25. Townshend to Walpole, 16 July 1723, NA. SP. 43/4, fol. 88.

26. BL. Add. 35412, fols 209, 184.

27. BL. Egerton Mss. 1711, fol.184.

28. BL. Add. 64939, fol.81.

29. BL. Add. 63749A, fols 249, 256, 262.

30. Elizabeth to George Grenville, 12 May 1768, San Marino, California, Huntington Library, Stowe papers Box 22(13).

31. George Villiers to Lady Spencer, 6 Dec. 1763, BL. Althorp F 101.

32. BL. Add. 70990, 37833, fol.4.

33. NA. SP. 78/277, fols 67, 116.

34. *Hyp Doctor*, 28 Aug. 1733; *Daily Gazetteer*, 23 Nov. 1736.

35. These trial reports are used in T. Hitchcock and R. Shoemaker, *Tales from the Hanging Court* (2006).

36. Winchester, Hampshire County Record Office 9H73 G309/31.

37. Connell (ed.), *Portrait of a Whig Peer*, p. 197.

38. Hatsell to John Ley, 28 Nov. 1792, Exeter, Devon Record Office, 63/2/11/1/53.

39. H. Twiss (ed.), *The Public and Private Life of Lord Chancellor Eldon* (3 vols, 1844), I, 398.

40. R.C. Allen, *The British Industrial Revolution in Global Perspective* (Cambridge, 2009).

41. J. Burke (ed.), *William Hogarth, The Analysis of Beauty, with the Rejected. Passages from the Manuscript Drafts and Autobiographical Notes* (Oxford, 1955), pp. 226–7.

42. R. Paley (ed.), *Justice in Eighteenth-Century Hackney: The Justicing Notebook of Henry Norris and the Hackney Petty Sessions Book* (1991).

43. *Considerations*, p. 12.

44. *Applebee's Original Weekly Journal* 12 Dec. 1724.

45. George to Pitt, 26 Ap. 1805, NA. PRO. 30/8/104, fol. 435.

Notes to Chapter 7: The world city, 1815–1914 (pages 224–309)

1. E.W. Marrs Jr (ed.), *The Letters of Charles and Mary Anne Lamb III* (1978), p.96.

2. S.J. Braidwood, *Black Poor and White Philanthropists. London's Blacks and the Foundation of the Sierra Leone Settlement 1786–1791* (1994).

3. A.L. Beier, '"Takin' It to the Streets": Henry Mayhew and the Language of the Underclass in Mid-Nineteenth-Century London', in Beier and P. Ocobock (eds), *Cast Out: Vagrancy and Homelessness in Global and Historical Perspective* (2008).

4. J.R. Walkowitz, *City of Dreadful Delight. Narratives of Sexual Danger in Late-Victorian London* (1992).

5. J. White, *London in the Nineteenth Century: 'A Human Awful Wonder of God'* (2009), pp. 148–51.

6. *Svedenstierna's Tour of Great Britain 1802–3* (1973), p.7. For another visitor see K. Lach-Szyrma, *London Observed: A Polish Philosopher at Large, 1822–24*, edited by M.K. McLeod (2009).

7. K. Bailey, *House Building and Builders in Wandsworth, c.1850–1915* (Wandsworth, 2005).

8. J. Conlin, 'Vauxhall on the boulevard: pleasure gardens in London and Paris, 1764–1784', *Urban History*, 35 (2008), p. 29.

9. I. McCalman, *Radical Underworld: Prophets, Revolutionaries and Pornographers in London, 1795–1840* (1988).

10. Addington Papers, Exeter, Devon Record Office 152 M/C.

11. C. Fox (ed.), *London: World City, 1800–1840* (1992).

12. R.E. Swift, 'Policing Chartism, 1839–1848: The Role of the "Specials" Reconsidered', *English Historical Review*, 122 (2007), p.695.

13. D. Goodway, *London Chartism, 1838–1848* (1982).

14. J.A. Auerbach, *The Great Exhibition of 1851: A Nation on Display* (1999); J.R. Davis, *The Great Exhibition* (1999).

15. J. Hall-Witt, *Fashionable Acts: Opera and Elite Culture in London, 1780–1880* (2006).

16. P.T. Smith, *Policing Victorian London. Political Policing, Public Order, and the Metropolitan Police* (1984).

17. G. Tyack, *Sir James Pennethorne and the Making of Victorian London* (1992).

18. S. Koven, *Slumming: Sexual and Social Politics in Victorian London* (2004).

19. A.D. Harvey, 'Parish boundary markers and perambulations in London', *Local Historian*, 38 (2008), pp. 180–93.

20. A. Tanner, 'The Casual Poor and the City of London Poor Law Union, 1837–1869', *Historical Journal*, 42 (1999), p. 204.

21. P.J. Corfield, *Vauxhall and the Invention of the Urban Pleasure Garden* (2008).

22. A. Windscheffel, *Popular Conservatism in Victorian London, 1868–1906* (2007).

23. H. Pelling, *Social Geography of British Elections, 1885–1910* (1967), pp. 56–8.

24. N. Draper, '"Across the Bridges": Representations of Victorian South London', *London Journal*, 29 (2004), p. 36.

25. M. Squires, '"Mobilising the Masses": Town's Meetings in the London Borough of Battersea, 1900–1945', *The Local Historian*, 27 (1997), pp. 163–82.

26. P.E. Malcolmson, 'Getting a living in the slums of Victorian Kensington', *London Journal*, 1 (1975), pp. 28–55.

27. *Julian Browning Autographs and Manuscripts*, catalogue 24 (2001), p. 7, item 55.

28. J.S. Bratton *et al.*, *Acts of Supremacy: The British Empire and the Stage, 1790–1903* (1991); P.H. Hoffenberg, *An Empire on Display: English, Indian, and Australian Exhibitions from the Crystal Palace to the Great War* (2001).

29. T. Hunt, *Building Jerusalem: The Rise and Fall of the Victorian City* (2005).

30. J.W. Barry, 'The Streets and Traffic of London', *Journal of the Royal Society of Arts*, 47 (1898–99), p. 9.

31. C. French, '"Death in Kingston Upon Thames": Analysis of the Bonner Hill Cemetery Burial Ground Records, 1855–1911', *Archives*, 28 (2003), pp. 43–4.

32. A. Tanner, 'Dust-O! Rubbish in Victorian London, 1860–1900', *London Journal*, 31 (2006), pp. 157–78.

Notes to Chapter 8: Troubled glories, 1914–1945 (pages 310–347)

1. J. Stewart, '"For a Healthy London": The Socialist Medical Association and the London County Council in the 1930s', *Medical History*, 32 (1997), pp. 417–36.

2. J. Shepherd, *George Lansbury: At the Heart of Old Labour* (2002).

3. A.J. Cronin, *The Citadel* (1983 edn), pp. 220, 225.

4. Cronin, *Adventures in Two Worlds* (1952; 1977 edn), pp. 161–2.

5. S. Slater, 'Pimps, police and filles de joie: foreign prostitution in interwar London', *London Journal*, 32 (2007), pp. 53–74.

6. D. Kynaston, *The City of London: III, Illusions*

of Gold, 1944–1945 (1999); R. Michie and
P. Williamson (eds), *The British Government and the
City of London in the Twentieth Century* (2004).

7. R.J. Overy, *The Battle* (2000); P. Addison and J.A.
Crang (eds), *The Burning Blue: A New History of the
Battle of Britain* (2000).

8. J. Chapman, *The British at War: Cinema, State and
Propaganda, 1939–1945* (1998).

9. P. and R. Malcolmson (eds), *A Woman in Wartime
London: the Diary of Kathleen Tipper, 1941–1945*
(2006).

10. R. Samways (ed.), *We Think You Ought To Go; An
Account of the Evacuation of Children from London
during the Second World War* (1995).

11. H. Creaton, *Sources for the History of London,
1939–45* (1998).

Notes to Chapter 9: Confronting a new age, 1945–2010 (pages 348–399)

1. F. Mort, 'Striptease: the erotic female body and
live sexual entertainment in mid-twentieth-century
London', *Social History*, 32 (2007), pp. 27–53.

2. R. Murphy, *Sixties British Cinema* (1992).

3. R. Andrews *et al.*, *The Rough Guide to England*
(2006).

4. J. Davis, *Reforming London. The London Government
Problem, 1855–1900* (1988), pp. 256–7.

5. A. Seldon (ed.), *How Tory Governments Fall* (1996),
p. 413.

6. S. Broke and L. Cameron, 'Anarchy in the
U.K.? Ideas of the City and the *Fin de Siècle* in
Contemporary English Film and Literature', *Albion*,
28 (1996), p. 655.

7. M. Hollinsworth and S. Lansley, *Londongrad: From
Russia with Cash: The Inside Story of the Oligarchs*
(2009).

Notes to Chapter 10: Into the future (pages 400–409)

1. Windsor Castle, Royal Archives, Stuart Papers
57/125.

2. Halifax to James Ostwald, 15 Ap. 1757, Hockworthy,
Ostwald corresp., folder 2; Horace Walpole, *Memoirs
… George II*, II, 291.

3. Samuel Johnson to Elizabeth Johnson, 24 June 1775,
to his mother, 22 Apr. 1776, Exeter, Devon CRO.
552/M/F4/1.

4. D. Robinson, 'Local Newspapers and the Local
Historian: The *Surrey Comet* and Victorian Kingston',
Archives, 31 (2006), p. 39.

Notes to Postscript: the biography of a city (pages 410–416)

1. A.N. Wilson, *London. A Short History* (2004), p. 86.

2. R. Porter, *London. A Social History* (1994), p. xv.

3. I. Sinclair, *Hackney, That Rose-Red Empire. A
Confidential Report* (2009).

4. S. Inwood, *A History of London* (1998), pp. xxii, xxi,
7.

5. P. Gauci, *Emporium of the World. The Merchants of
London, 1600–1800* (2007).

6. R. Sweet, *The Writing of Urban Histories in
Eighteenth-Century England* (1997).

7. D. Fordham, 'Scalping: Social Rites in Westminster
Abbey', in T. Barringer, G. Quiley and D. Fordham
(eds), *Art and the British Empire* (2007), p. 99.

8. C. Brunsdon, *London in Cinema: The Cinematic City
Since 1945*.

9. G. Barefoot, *Gaslight Melodrama* (2002).

SELECTED
FURTHER READING

General

Ackroyd, P., *London: the biography* (2000)

Barker, Felix, and Jackson, Peter, *The History of London in Maps* (1990)

Barton, N.J.V., *The Lost Rivers of London* (1962)

Brimblecombe, P., *The Big Smoke: a history of air pollution in London* (1987)

Clark, P. (ed.), *The Cambridge Urban History of Britain*

Clout, H., *The Times History of London* (5th edn, 2007)

Doolittle, I., *The City of London and its Livery Companies* (1982)

Inwood, S., *A History of London* (1998)

Kerrigan, C., *A History of Tower Hamlets* (1982)

Leapman, M. (ed), *The Book of London* (1989)

Pevsner, N., *London* (1952–7)

Porter, R., *London. A Social History* (1994)

Ross, C. and Clark, J., *London: the illustrated history* (2008)

Rubinstein, S., *Historians of London* (1968)

Saunders, A., *The Art and Architecture of London* (1988)

Smith, A., *Dictionary of City of London Street Names* (1970)

Tames, R., *London. A Cultural and Literary History* (2006)

Thom, C., *Researching London's Houses* (2005)

Thompson, F.M.L., *Hampstead* (1974)

Walford, Edward, *London Recollected* (1987)

Chapter 1: Roman capital

Lobel, M. (ed.), *The British Atlas of Historic Towns III, The City of London: From Prehistoric Times to c. 1520* (1989)

Merriman, N., *Prehistoric London* (1990)

Merrifield, R., *London – City of the Romans* (1983)

Milne, G. *The Port of Roman London* (1985)

Milne, G., *Roman London* (1995)

Morris, J., *Londinium: London in the Roman Empire* (1982)

Chapter 2: Anglo-Saxon centuries, 410–1066

Brooke, C.N.L. and Keir, G., *London 800–1216: The Shaping of a City* (1975)

Clark, J., *Saxon and Norman London* (1989)

Keene, Derek, 'London from the Post-Roman Period to 1300', in *The Cambridge Urban History of Britain, I: 600–1540* (2000)

Vince, A., *Saxon London* (1990)

Chapter 3: Medieval developments, 1066–1485

Barron, C., *London in the Later Middle Ages: Government and People, 1200–1500* (2004)

Bird, R., *The Turbulent London of Richard II* (1951)

Bolton, J.L. *The Medieval English Economy* (1990)

Brechin, D., *The Conqueror's London* (1968)

Milne, G., *The Port of Medieval London* (2003)

Minney, R.J., *The Tower of London* (1970)

Myers, A.R., *London in the Age of Chaucer* (1972)

Rosser, A.G., *Medieval Westminster* (1989)

Schofield, J., *Medieval London Houses* (1995)

Sutton, A.F., *The Mercery of London Trade, Goods and People, 1130–1578* (2005)

Thrupp, S.L., *The Merchant Class of Medieval London 1300–1500* (1962)

Williams, G., *Medieval London: From Commune to Capital* (1963)

Chapter 4: London under the Tudors, 1485–1603

Archer, I.W., *The Pursuit of Stability: Social Relations in Elizabethan London* (1991)

Beier, A.L. and Finlay, R. (eds), *London 1500–1700: The Making of the Metropolis* (1986)

Berry, H., *Shakespeare's Playhouses* (1987)

Brigden, S., *London and the Reformation* (1989)

Clark, P. and Gillespie, R. (eds, *Two Capitals: London and Dublin in the Early Modern Period* (2001)

Finlay, R., *Population and Metropolis: The Demography of London, 1580–1650* (1981)

Fisher, F.J., *London and the English Economy, 1500–1700* (1990)

Foster, F., *The Politics of Stability: A Portrait of the Rulers of Elizabethan London* (1977)

Griffiths, P. and Jenner, M. (eds), *Londinopolis: Essays in the Social and Cultural History of Early Modern London* (2000)

Manley, L. (ed.), *London in the Age of Shakespeare* (1986)

Merritt, J.F., *The Social World of Early Modern Westminster* (2005)

Pettegree, A., *Foreign Protestant Communities in Sixteenth-Century London* (1986)

Rappaport, S., *Worlds within Worlds: Structures of Life in Sixteenth-Century London* (1989)

Ward, J.P., *Metropolitan Communities: trade guilds, identity, and change in early modern London* (1997)

Weinstein, S., *Tudor London* (1994)

Chapter 5: Confronting the Stuarts, 1603–1714

Ashton, R., *The City and the Court, 1603–1643* (1979)

Boulton, J. *Neighbourhood and Society: A London Suburb in the Seventeenth Century* (1987)

Brenner, R., *Merchants and Revolution: Commercial Change, Political Conflict and London's Overseas Traders, 1550–1653* (1993)

De Krey, G.S., *London and the Restoration, 1659–1683* (2005)

De Krey, G.S., *A Fractured Society: The Politics of London in the First Age of Party, 1688–1715* (1985)

Earle, P., *A City Full of People: Men and Women of London 1650–1750* (1994)

Ellis, M., *The Coffee House: A Cultural History* (2004)

Gauci, P., *Emporium of the World. The Merchants of London, 1660–1800* (2007)

Glaisyer, N., *The Culture of Commerce in England, 1660–1720* (2006)

Hanson, N., *The Dreadful Judgement: the true story of the Great Fire* (2001)

Harris, T., *London Crowds in the Reign of Charles II: Propaganda and Politics from the Restoration until the Exclusion Crisis* (1987)

Hearsey, J.E.N., *London and the Great Fire* (1965)

Hollis, L. *The Phoenix, St Paul's Cathedral and the Men who made Modern London* (2008)

McKellar, E., *The Birth of Modern London: the development and design of the city, 1660–1720* (1999)

Pearl, V., *London and the Outbreak of the Puritan Revolution: City Government and National Politics, 1625–43* (1961)

Seaver, P., *Wallington's World: A Puritan Artisan in Seventeenth-Century London* (1985)

Shoemaker, R.B., *Prosecution and Punishment. Petty Crime and the law in London and rural Middlesex, c. 1660–1723* (1991)

Slack, P., *The Impact of Plague in Tudor and Stuart England* (1985)

Summerson, J., *Inigo Jones* (1966)

Summerson, J., *Sir Christopher Wren* (1953)

Chapter 6: The centre of all, 1714–1815

Andrrew, D.T., *Philanthropy and Police: London Charity in the Eighteenth Century* (1990)

Arnold, D. (ed.), *The Metropolis and its Image: Constructing identities for London, c. 1750–1950* (1999)

Burford, E.J., *Wits, Wenches and Wantons: London's Low Life: Covent Garden in the Eighteenth Century* (1992)

Byrd, M., *London Transformed: Images of the City in the Eighteenth Century* (1978)

George, M.D., *London Life in the Eighteenth Century* (1966)

Landers, J., *Death and the Metropolis: Studies in the Demographic History of London 1670–1830* (1993)

Linebaugh, P., *The London Hanged: Crime and Civil Society in the Eighteenth Century* (1991)

McClure, R.K., *Coram's Children: The London Foundling Hospital in the Eighteenth Century* (1981)

Ogborn, M., *Spaces of Modernity. London's Geographies 1680–1780* (1999)

Rendell, J., *The Pursuit of Pleasure: gender, space and architecture in Regency London* (2001)

Schwarz, L., *London in the Age of Industrialisation: Entrepreneurs, Labour Force and Living Conditions, 1700–1850* (1992)

Summerson, J., *Georgian London* (1970)

Chapter 7: The world city, 1815–1914

Ackroyd, P., *Dickens' London: an imaginative Vision* (1987)

Alexander, S., *Women's Work in Nineteenth-Century London* (1983)

Barker, F., *Edwardian London* (1995)

Barker, T., *Moving millions: a pictorial history of London Transport* (1990)

Bell, A.D., *London in the Age of Dickens* (1967)

Brodie, M., *The Politics of the Poor: the East End of London 1885–1914* (2004)

Davis, J., *Reforming London: The London Government Problem, 1855–1900* (1988)

Day, J.R., *The Story of the London Bus* (1973)

Dyos, H.J., *Victorian Suburb: a study of the growth of Camberwell* (1961)

Feldman, D. and Jones, G.J. (eds), *Metropolis London: Histories and Representations since 1800* (1989)

Fishman, W.J., *East End, 1888* (1988)

Fox, C. (ed.), *London – World City, 1800–1840* (1992)

Fried, A. and Elman, R. (eds), *Charles Booth's London* (1969)

Greeves, I.S., *London Docks, 1800–1980* (1980)

Halliday, S., *The Great Stink of London* (1999)

Hardy, A., *The Epidemic Streets* (1993)

Horrall, A., *Popular Culture in London c. 1890–1918: the transformation of entertainment* (2001)

Kynaston, D., *The City of London [from 1815]* (1994–2001)

Lees, L.H., *Exiles of Erin: Irish Migrants in Victorian London* (1979)

Luckin, B., *Pollution and Control: A Social History of the Thames in the Nineteenth Century* (1986)

Mace, R., *Trafalgar Square: Emblem of Empire* (1976)

Neal, I., *Victorian Babylon: people, streets and images in nineteenth-century London* (2000)

Olsen, D.J., *The Growth of Victorian London* (1983)

Schmiechen, J.A., *Sweated Industries and Sweated Labour: The London Clothing Trades, 1860–1914* (1984)

Schneer, J., *London 1900. The Imperial Metropolis* (1999)

Smith, P.T., *Policing Victorian London* (1985)

Stevenson, J. (ed.), *London in the Age of Reform* (1977)

Summerson, J., *The Life and Work of John Nash Architect* (1980)

Summerson, J., *The Architecture of Victorian London* (1976)

Weightman, G. and Humphries, S., *The Making of Modern London, 1815–1914* (1983)

Werner, A. (ed.), *Jack the Ripper and the East End* (2008)

White, J., *London in the Nineteenth Century: 'A Human Awful Wonder of God'* (2009)

Wise, S., *The Blackest Streets. The Life and Death of a Victorian Slum* (2008)

Young, K. and Garside, P., *Metropolitan London: Politics and Urban Change, 1837–1981* (1982)

Chapter 8: Troubled glories, 1914–1945

Abercrombie, P., *Greater London Plan, 1944* (1945)

Abercrombie, P. and Forshaw, J.H., *County of London Plan* (1943)

Donoughue, B. and Jones, G.W., *Herbert Morrison* (1973)

Goss, S., *Local Labour and Local Government: A Study of Changing Interests, Politics and Policy in Southwark, 1919–1982* (1988)

Hall, P.G., *The Industries of London since 1861* (1962)

Howson, H.F., *London's Underground* (1981)

Jackson, A.A., *Semi-Detached London: Suburban Development, Life and Transport, 1900–1939* (1973)

Johnson, D., *V–1, V–2: Hitler's Vengeance on London* (1982)

Marriott, J., *The Culture of Labourism: the East End Between the Wars* (1991)

Saint, A. (ed.), *Politics and the People of London: The London County Council, 1889–1965* (1989)

Stewart, J.D., *Bermondsey in War 1939–45* (1981)

Trench, R., *London Before the Blitz* (1989)

White, J., *The Worst Street in North London: Campbell Bunk, Islington, Between the Wars* (1986)

Ziegler, P., *London at War, 1939–1945* (1995)

Chapter 9: Confronting a new age, 1945–2010

Benyon J. (ed.), *Scarman and After* (1984)

Brownhill, S., *Developing London's Docklands* (1990)

Clout, H. and Wood, P. (eds), *London: Problems of Change* (1986)

Dench, G., Gavron, K. and Young, M., *The New East End: Kinship, Race and Conflict* (2006)

Eade, J. *The Politics of Community: Bangladeshi Community in East London* (1989)

Esher, L., *A Broken Wave: the Rebuilding of Britain, 1940–1980* (1983)

Foley, D., *Controlling London's Growth, 1940–60* (1963)

Glass, R., *Newcomers: the West Indians in London* (1960)

Glass, R. (ed.), *London: Aspects of Change* (1964)

Glendinning, M. and Muthesius, S., *Tower Block* (1994)

Hall, P., *London 2000* (1963)

Hall, J.M., *Metropolis Now: London and its Region* (1990)

Harrison, P., *Inside the Inner City: Life Under the Cutting Edge* (1992)

Humphries, S., and Taylor, J., *The Making of Modern London, 1945–1985* (1986)

Jenkins, S., *Landlords to London: The Story of a Capital and its Growth* (1975)

Keith, M. *Race, Riots and Policing: Lore and Disorder in a Multi-racist Society* (1993)

Munton, R., *London's Green Belt: Containment in Practice* (1983)

Pilkington, E., *Beyond the Mother Country: West Indians and the Notting Hill White Riots* (1988)

Scarman, Lord, *The Brixton Disorders* (1981)

Simmie, J. (ed.), *Planning London* (1994)

Thomas, D., *London's Green Belt* (1970)

ILLUSTRATIONS

The picture research for this book has been a fascinating exercise for all those involved. It has revealed a deep knowledge and affection for the place among most of those who lived in London.

Of the many institutions and picture libraries consulted, I would like to single out the following for their help and advice: Sean Waterman at the Museum of London was unfailingly helpful and knowledgeable about that important museum's holdings; Gemma Perrett at the Guildhall was immensely patient and helpful; Anna Smith at the Wellcome Library; Susan Palmer at Sir John Soane's Museum; Gudrun Muller, Julie Cochrane and Sarah Beighton at the National Maritime Museum, Greenwich; Christine Reynolds at Westminster Abbey; David Payne at Southwark Cathedral; Felicity Premru at the London Museum of Transport; Silka Quintero of the Granger Collection, New York; Judy Aitken of the Cumming Museum; Sam Kadeen at the picture library Corbis; Victoria Hogarth at the Bridgeman Art Library; Martina Oliver at Getty Images; the helpful staff at British Museum Images and those at the Bibliothèque Nationale de France, Paris; Lynda Clark at Tate Images; Glasgow University Library Special Collections for the image of the Aldgate Cartulary; the many churches who kindly allowed internal photography; The Euston Arch Trust; The National Archives; Neil Robinson at Lord's; and Annie Heron at Historic Royal Palaces; David Hale at Mapco; the Ironbridge Gorge Museum; Séamus McKenna at the Guildhall Art Library. Thank you, too, to the many people who allowed or helped in the taking of the modern photographs.

Illustrating the history of London comprehensively would take many volumes. I am very conscious that aspects of the city's history are very poorly represented here. The suburbs, domestic housing and people's workplaces in the capital are hardly covered at all. In the main we have concentrated attention on the ancient City rather than more distant, outlying parts which became integrated with the capital at a later date. With a great deal more time, we would have been able to take many more illustrations of the many interesting historical items that can be found in the city and particularly inside London buildings: the grand staircase at Home House, perhaps; or the inside of Middle Temple Hall; or some of the Livery Halls. But, then, the aim was not to produce a comprehensive or primarily pictorial history, and the exigencies of modern publishing – and the inflated reproduction fees now being charged by some of our illustrious national institutions – have resulted in the sometimes lop-sided and perhaps inadequate selection of illustrations. I hope that, in aggregate, however, those that are reproduced here give a decent flavour of the city and its past, as well as showing that, despite the Great Fire, the Blitz and constant rebuilding, there is still a great deal of historical interest to be seen during a walk on the streets of London.

Alistair Hodge, publisher

INDEX

Index entries in *italic* type refer to illustrations or, more usually, to the text of their accompanying captions.